THE COLLEGE CLASSROOM:
Conflict, Change, and Learning

THE COLLEGE CLASSROOM:

Conflict, Change, and Learning

RICHARD D. MANN

Stephen M. Arnold

Jeffrey L. Binder

Solomon Cytrynbaum

Barbara M. Newman

Barbara E. Ringwald

John W. Ringwald

Robert Rosenwein

JOHN WILEY & SONS, INC.

New York   London   Sydney   Toronto

Library of Congress Catalogue Card Number: 77-130431

ISBN 0-471-56712-4

Printed in the United States of America

10 9 8 7 6 5 4 3 2 1

PREFACE

If you were to interrupt a college teacher and ask him what is going on in his class, his answer would probably focus on the material being covered at that moment. The content of the lecture or discussion would be central to his awareness of what was happening. But if you pressed him a bit and asked if that were really all that was going on, he would probably be able to identify other events: two students whispering, one looking especially pleased at the political implications of the teacher's last comments, some misgivings on the teacher's part about whether he had represented the facts correctly, and so on. What are these events? What happens in college classrooms beyond the appointed tasks of "covering" and "mastering" the material of the course?

This book presents a study of some of these events, especially the interpersonal and emotional events that occur in the classroom. It is by no means an assault on the importance of the content of education. It merely expands the focus to include aspects of the teacher-student interchange that are often ignored. The fact that as teachers we so often ignore the noncontent issues of the classroom can be traced partly to our ignorance and partly to our pessimism. Our ignorance is revealed when we find out how little we understand about what caused a particularly sluggish class or a confusing, violent interchange over a minor issue. Our ignorance is revealed when we find that for unknown reasons things which "worked" one term flop terribly the next. And our pessimism is revealed when upon wondering what to do about our failures, we are forced to conclude that we had better not even bother to find out why things happened as they did. The "other" part of teaching and learning, the world of emotional and interpersonal realities, is usually seen as a hopeless quagmire. Better to push ahead, we say, than to veer off the beaten (content) path into the murky world of emotion. Our pessimism is revealed by our fear that it might take all term to figure out why one session was so fruitless. Obviously, it is better to avoid the whole business.

We are as subject as anyone else to the confusion and pessimism just described, but we have tried to call on our other identities as researchers and psychologists to prevent such situations from becoming chronic. We have tried to band together to study the process of teaching and learning with the hope that we can comprehend the interpersonal reality of the classroom more accurately than before and then do what needs to be done. This is a tall order for any research undertaking, especially given the nonrepetitive nature of the teacher's world.

Our exploration took us in several directions: toward understanding the teacher's role from a new and broader perspective, toward understanding the diversity of students more sensitively, and especially toward understanding how things develop in the classroom. The intellectual and the interpersonal life of the college classroom is in a constant state of flux. Crises, partial adaptations, new challenges, some failures, and some genuinely creative solutions: the interpersonal world is a kaleidoscope of shifting realities. But can we understand these changes and can we use this understanding to formulate a new sense of the goal of college teaching?

The search for a new conception of both the process and the goal of education is central to this effort. The notion we find most useful is essentially a generalization of Bion's concept of work. By the time we are done with our presentation we hope to have put substance into the abstract notion which can now only be stated baldly: the proper goal of the college classroom is "work," and only by understanding the obstacles to work that flow from the complexity of the teacher's task, the students' diversity, and the nature of group development can the teacher make his optimal contribution to this goal.

The challenge of coming to understand this process better will not be met by one study. This effort is more in the form of a proposed model than a definitive statement. It chooses the path of the intensive case study rather than the survey of many classrooms. Its research style is a mixture of quantitative, observational techniques and qualitative analysis of transcript and interview material. We arrive, in the end, with some generalizations across our limited data and with the beginnings of a theory about how the college classroom develops.

These products should be seen as a challenge to all college teachers to begin collaborating with one another, to begin sharing their observations, quantitative or otherwise, so that the regularities and variety of our classroom may be better understood. The challenge is implicit in the choice of this exploratory, case approach. It says, "Well, this is what happened, as best we can understand it, in these few cases. Now, is it like that in your field, in your college, in this decade? If not, what is it like? What other types of students, what other developmental phases, and what other dynamic processes have you observed and do you feel should be added to this new body of knowledge?"

Implicit in this study and in the challenge that we hope it will present to others is a notion that it is still important to understand the internal workings of the college classroom. Simply by avoiding other issues so explosively manifest in today's colleges, we might seem to be implying that the only (or even the most important) changes in college education are those having to do with the classroom. We really do not think that at all. As two of us have tried to show in another volume (Cytrynbaum and Mann, 1969), many of the ideas presented here suggest and clarify the kinds of off-campus or field courses in which all of us have been involved. The old patterns of education are breaking down, and new and legitimate criticisms of the university's role in society suggest that further changes are likely. It seems to us, however, that the need for clarity about what happens in the process of college teaching is going to become greater rather than less. As open enrollment programs and their approximations come into effect, as the politics of the academy are more and more forced into public debate, and even as the classroom's locus and content changes, the teacher's task becomes all the more complex. The importance of knowing what the teacher is feeling about his subject matter and about the students will increase. The importance of developing new and sharper images of the students and their diverse reactions to their education will increase. The need to develop a humane enough and a complex enough sense of the educational relationship is acute, and to this end we offer this exploratory venture.

The authors of this volume were fortunate enough in being part of a larger and wonderfully vital group of teachers. Our main assignment was introductory psychology, but we branched out in various directions. As we recall with appreciation those whose contributions made these research efforts doubly exciting, we would mention first our colleagues in this teaching culture, especially Jim Ledvinka, Jeff Paige, Stan Samenow, Phil Newman, Dan Perlman, Rory O'Day, Kalen Hammann, and Graham Gibbard. Dana Silverberg Bennett and Myrna Wolfson Wolosin spanned this teaching world and our research project, and we owe them a special debt of gratitude. Dana's work on the follow-up study was a crucial part of the data collection, and both of them played important roles in the evolving definition of what we wanted to study. Three other members of the research team were our colleagues in teaching as well. John Hartman not only scored one group but he carried out with great skill the heavy responsibility of training the other three scorers. Doug McClennen was another of the four scorers and stayed with the project during its early days. Martha Cohen Arnold also combined the role of teacher-colleague with an important place in the chaotic days of finding our sense of direction amidst all the quantitative data we had created.

We would surely have drowned in our own data had it not been for Dick Cabot and Honor McClellan. Dick wrote a whole family of programs which restored order, and Honor inherited the often thankless job of keeping the research efforts from flying off in a million directions. Subject to cross-currents of requests, pleas, and their own good sense, Honor and Dick somehow managed; and we are terribly aware of how many times they helped us move through the jumble to the simple truths we have tried to present in this study. Liz Silverberg's part in our long journey was also an important one: she helped us develop and apply the teacher-as scoring system developed during the latter phases of our research.

Marg Koski has earned our special respect and appreciation. She has typed more versions and drafts of this report than any of us can recall, and both by her work and her encouragement she kept alive our often flagging sense that we would ever manage and complete our task. We owe much of the success of this complex and often precarious venture to Marg and to the steady, competent work of Audrey Warren in our early days.

We wish to express our appreciation to our colleagues who have advised us along the way and as the manuscript neared completion. Jim Donovan and Roddy Wares were particularly helpful critics of our writing. Ted Mills deserves our special appreciation for his criticisms and suggestions which helped us to make some much needed revisions of the first draft. Bill McKeachie was generous with both his consultation and his support throughout the project. It was he, together with Drs. Isaacson and Milholland, who made it possible for this study to be supported by their long-term grant from the Office of Education. In addition to Bill McKeachie's role in the project, we were particularly fortunate to have his support in the department where, as chairman, he had for years helped to create the kind of environment in which research and innovation in teaching were likely to occur and to receive the necessary support.

Richard D. Mann   *Barbara M. Newman*
Stephen M. Arnold   *Barbara E. Ringwald*
Jeffrey L. Binder   *John W. Ringwald*
Solomon Cytrynbaum   *Robert Rosenwein*

CONTENTS

CHAPTER 1

THE MEANING OF WORK

IF college teachers were to discuss their teaching with one another, which at present they hardly ever do, it would soon be apparent that controversy and confusion abound beneath the polite and self-assured facade so chacteristic of an educational institution. There is controversy over the proper goals of a college education, over the best techniques for reaching even the goals that can be agreed on, and over how to determine the relative success of the different techniques. Beyond this, there is widespread confusion within the minds of educators about the legitimacy and effectiveness of various procedures. The teacher is under pressure from students, colleagues, and administrators, and from his own ideals and convictions. These forces often imply or demand that he move as quickly as possible in apparently incompatible directions, and his world becomes a pressure cooker of seemingly irresolvable alternatives.

Our hope in this volume is not to provide definitive answers to the "Should I do A or B?" questions which flood the teacher's mind during periods of stress. Neither is it our intention to argue that one goal or one technique should be chosen over another. Our hope is to broaden the conception of what is happening between teachers and students and to suggest larger goals within which at least some of the alternatives can be transformed into challenging and even soluble problems for the teacher and the students to work on together.

Toward this end we first address ourselves to the definition of the teacher's task as an educator. Surely the familiar pedagogic argument ("The teacher's job is to get across information." No, it's to motivate students." "No, it's to certify a certain level of proficiency." And so on.) needs to be replaced by a broader conception of the several distinct aspects of teaching, each of which is legitimate and even crucial under certain to-be-specified conditions.

There are many ways to analyze the components of the educational task, but we have chosen to focus on the teacher and his role relationships to the students. We have tried to unravel the strands of the teacher's total role by answering in six different ways the questions: Who is the teacher? In what capacity does he stand before his class?

As we observed teachers in action, talked with them after class, and reflected on our own experiences, a set of six different identities emerged. Each element of what we have called *the "teacher-as"* *typology* represents a distinguishable aspect of the teacher's total relationship with the class. The teacher-as typology is but one possible way of carving up the diverse intentions, behaviors, and perceptions that constitute the teacher-student relationship, but it will provide a basis for going further into the analysis of the educational process.

The Teacher as Expert

The most obvious answer to the question "In what capacity does the teacher stand before the class?" is captured by the teacher as expert. This aspect of the teacher role conjures up the disparity between teacher and student with respect to the knowledge, experience, and wisdom they can apply to the subject matter of the course. The teacher is the expert, at least within a certain defined area of knowledge. His presumed expertise underlies both his right to be there and the students' interest in taking the course. They imagine they will learn something from him: from his lectures, his comments in class, or in the margins of the graded papers—somehow the initial imbalance of expertise will be altered if the educational contract has been fulfilled.

Whether the channel of communication is the assigned reading or the nonstop lectures or the give-and-take of classroom discussion, the essential issue here is the role relationship between the teacher as expert and the students. The student may be the passive note-taker, but this is not the only possibility. The student who best fulfills the hopes of the teacher as expert might be better described as diffusely curious, motivated to satisfy intellectual drives of his own, and genuinely interested in the material presented or assigned by the teacher.

We need not belabor this aspect of the teacher's role. With only slight variations the teacher as expert plays a major role in nearly every college classroom in the country. If anything, our difficulty is less one of describing the teacher as expert than of broadening the conception of teacher beyond the confines of this traditional view.

The Teacher as Formal Authority

In what other capacity does the teacher stand before the class? Who else is he? Consider the teacher as he presents his proposals regarding when the final paper will be due and how much it will count. Clearly, at that moment, he is not the teacher as expert. The students are not raising their hands to challenge his command of his field but to challenge, or at least to engage, the teacher as formal authority. The whole process of education in an institutional setting raises so many issues of authority (for example, grades, credits, and requirements) that the teacher as expert may sometimes wonder whether knowledge or a smoothly functioning bureaucracy is more important to the college. The students may wonder, too.

The pressures on the teacher to function as a formal authority arise from several sources. Viewed from the perspective of the larger social structure within which the college classroom is located, the teacher is an agent not only of instruction but also of control and evaluation. He is responsible to a group of administrators and external agents who expect him to insure uniformity of standards and a justifiable evaluation system based on merit when he presents his set of grades at the end of the course. Future employers, draft boards, graduate schools, scholarship committees, and Deans' offices may all indicate their need for a meaningful and averageable estimate of a student's performance. The chaos which is anticipated if a pass-fail or nongraded system were instituted reflects the amount of commitment the formal system has to a merit-oriented grading system. In addition, teachers are expected to cooperate with university officials in seeking student compliance with the university's rules, regulations, and standards of decorum, so that neither the administration nor the university is publicly embarrassed. Teachers enter the classroom with their power clearly established and institutionalized, whether they like it or not.

Functioning as a formal authority may involve the teacher in setting clearly defined standards of excellence, goals, and deadlines for assignments, as well as those instances of moment-to-moment control over classroom procedure and decorum. The teacher's influence in this area is derived ultimately from his power to banish the student from the classroom in the interest of maintaining an environment in which other students can learn and, more commonly, from the teacher's capacity to be punitive in his examining and grading practices. Although this ultimate power might never be invoked, the fact remains that in most classrooms it is typically within the teacher's domain to define what is relevant for class discussion, when an issue should be raised privately after class, who will speak in class, and what kinds of behavior are unacceptable or disruptive.

It follows, then, that we would include within the set of activities initiated by students not only the familiar requests for clarity regarding assignments and grades but also those which address the issue of the teacher's control over the classroom interaction. Thus the basic aims of the formal authority strategy are the integration of the student into the norms of the larger formal system, the enforcement of these norms, and the provision of a classroom structure and clearly defined expectations designed to insure a minimum of disruptive activities (see Jackson, 1963; and Trow, 1960a, 1960b). Some teachers mistrust students, are convinced of their irresponsibility, and are fearful that they will get out of control and turn the classroom into a "blackboard jungle." They are convinced that their authority is all that prevents a state of anarchy in the classroom. Other teachers seem more concerned about student passivity and complacency. For them the usefulness of assignments and grades lies partly in their capacity to curb student laziness, but grades are also seen as curbing the students' tendencies to be mistaken about their ability and their accomplishments. The grade can say "You don't know this material as well as you think you do," but it also can say "You may not know it all, but relative to your classmates you have a right to feel some pride in your performance." The entire process of examining and grading involves the teacher as expert as well as the teacher as formal authority. Clearly, one aspect of the teacher's power is his capacity to define success and failure in terms of the kind of exam, the content of the exam, and the standards applied to the students' work.

In addition to serving as a representative of the formal structure, the teacher is also a member of a particular field or discipline in which he has a great deal invested and into which he is interested in recruiting new members. This brings us to the teacher as socializing agent.

The Teacher as Socializing Agent

An understanding of the teacher as socializing agent requires a consideration of the context in which higher education exists. First, the teacher is in possession of certain information and is responsible for providing a structure within which he can share his knowledge; he is also a member of various overlapping groups of which the students are either marginal members or outsiders. Futhermore, the students' goals typically reach far beyond a particular classroom or course. The teacher is usually a member of the community of scholars, accredited by a professional and academic discipline, and he is also a member of an institution that may be highly relevant to a student's occupational aspirations. The teacher resembles in some sense a gatekeeper to a vocational world. He serves as a representative of his field, and especially of the values, assumptions, and style of intellectual life that characterize his discipline. Frequently, it is he who does or does not pass a student to the next plateau or screening process, or he may do so with varying degrees of support and pleasure. It is soon apparent to students that acceptability within the standards of the intellectual community involves more than the ability to master the intellectual material. In a very real sense the college teacher can serve as a recruitment officer for his field, and his functions tend to include the identification of a bright and exciting prospect, the selection of the most likely candidates via a continuous process of selective encouragement and discouragement, and the provision of a form of training and experience that equips the student apprentice so that he can tackle the next set of hurdles or initiation rites (Adelson, 1962).

When undergraduate programs are adapted to this aspect of higher education, they tend to become highly "preprofessional." The student is encouraged to take courses that would be useful to him in graduate school. He is engaged in discussions of the underlying commitment to science or humanism or financial success which seems to the teacher to be a necessary condition for acceptance into training programs at a higher level. But we should not overlook the socializing activities of the teacher whose relevant reference group is the more broadly defined community of scholars. Although teacher may shun the more explicit forms of creating "little graduate students," he may feel very strongly about the extent to which the university is an appropriate place only for those who share his political or social values or his notions about what the process of education is all about.

Students also make their contribution to the establishment of this aspect of the total task. For many, there are features of the intellectual community or of the activities of a particular specialty per se which are attractive. For some students, to begin to imagine their future in terms of a particular occupational goal is to crystallize their still developing interests and passions; for others, it makes concrete and reachable a future that assures them of the necessities and pleasures of life as they see them. There are students who are motivated primarily by their alienation from or rejection of the life style associated with their parents, their community, or their peers; many of these students are inclined to approach other socializing agents in order to test out the possibilities for a meaningful future commitment (see Keniston, 1967; and Peterson, 1968).

Thus a teacher and his students may be bound together in many ways within the socializing relationship. In trying out the discipline or profession that the teacher represents, the student may acquire sacred artifacts or the awkward mimicry of an accepted intellectual pose or pretentious vocabulary. Fortunately for him, most teachers overlook these ungainly beginnings. A faculty member may remark to a colleague that such and such a bright undergraduate seems to be "coming into the field," although he may feel constrained to conceal his sense of pleasure at the implication that his field has proved capable of attracting yet another valuable recruit.

How does the teacher as socializing agent or gatekeeper typically function in the classroom? Keeping in mind that we have been describing a process of acculturation in which new norms, values, and ideas are synthesized with the old, let us focus on the classroom process. Here we would include brief lectures or anecdotes which convey to the student the positions members of his field take on different issues, why they line up the way they do, some sense of his own position, and the process by which he arrived there, as well as some statements which convey his research interests and intellectual style.

A teacher is often drawn into or initiates discussions of how one goes about entering the "inner circle"; that is, how one applies, which advanced degree programs are good, what admission requirements are like, what future courses would be relevant, and so forth. In these instances, the teacher may be providing his students with a fair amount of factual information, leading one to believe that he is functioning as an expert. However, the main thrust of the teacher's effort is still in the direction of socialization.

The goals of information transmission, evaluation, control, and socialization or recruitment are a legitimate and rather traditional part of the dominant academic culture which heavily influences classroom functioning and the values of higher education. In introducing the teacher as a facilitator, an ego ideal, and a person, the goals and prototypic behaviors we shall describe tend not to have the same aura of legitimacy in academic circles. We shall argue that they should. Let us begin by considering the teacher as facilitator.

The Teacher as Facilitator

There are times in the teacher-student relationship when the teacher seems much less absorbed with his own expertise, his power, and his field than with the aspirations of the students. The teacher as facilitator seems to conceive of his role differently mainly because he conceives of the students differently. By not assuming that he can specify what skills or goals they bring with them, he creates for himself the complex task of determining what individual students have come to do, what they seem able to do already, and what they might need help in doing better. Thus the student-centered teacher is usually opposed to what he might call "imposing" his goals or agenda on a group of strangers. In this view the major task facing the teacher is to construct goals for the class that express the students' sense of what should come next in their intellectual development.

From this it follows that the typical activities of the teacher as facilitator may entail far more listening and questioning than lecturing and assigning. To involve the students in formulating the goals, questions, and content of a course may prove to be a difficult process if the students are reticent or disbelieving. Furthermore, the teacher as facilitator may find that much of his energy goes to working on student discouragement, frustration, and paralysis if the goals and especially the means to those goals prove to be more difficult than they were initially thought to be.

In practice, the teacher as facilitator may address himself to two general sources of student learning impediments. On the one hand, he may sense that students are capable of productive intellectual effort only to the extent that impediments such as fear of failure, self-abasement in the face of authority, or depression resulting from excessively high standards are removed, reduced, or at least confronted (Adelson, 1962). This may lead him to invest a considerable amount of concern and energy in reducing emotional and interpersonal blocks to learning in a variety of fairly direct ways. On the other hand, the teacher as facilitator may operate more like an administrator than a counsellor, as he addresses himself to a variety of situationally determined impediments. Students may not be familiar with how the library system works or where to find relevant reference material. The teacher as facilitator may guide the students through the library or prepare a handout on reference materials and where to find them. Many students would find it difficult, without assistance, to gain access to the field experiences which would make their intellectual work more relevant; a facilitator might enter here. The teacher as facilitator might aid students in their own battle for ungraded or more socially relevant courses. He could structure his class in such a way that it was entirely student centered so that it was based on individual student programs of study, or he could leave the decision about class structure up to his students. He might not hand out a list of assigned readings but instead might prepare an extensive, annotated bibliography from which students made their own decisions about what they were to read.

In whatever form he chooses, it is clear that the teacher as facilitator tries to respond primarily to the student's own definition of his goals and his unique sense of himself as a learner. The student's goals may be quite divergent from those of the teacher but, then, facilitating someone's learning and development often involves a recognition of the substantial differences between individuals in terms of what they value and what they are seeking.

The Teacher as Ego Ideal

The function of the teacher is broader than that of providing information, control, and entry into the elite. It also extends beyond that of helping the student realize his own goals and potentialities. It is with some embarrassment that most teachers begin to sense the possibility that some of their students use them as models of what a good historian, or a well-educated man, or a fine person might be. They use their teacher in the continuous process of formulating and approaching their ideals. It may be only some of the students some of the time, and the idealization may be limited to certain aspects of the teacher's total performance, but this process is an important part of the college classroom.

When a student stands back in awe of the teacher's ability to rattle off a string of dates or equations, he may be saying that this teacher's knowledge and memory power are both impressive and desirable. When student is drawn to one course after another given by the teacher whose intellectual passion and drive help define his model of a good person, he may be using the teacher as an ego ideal. He may walk out of the lecture thinking not about its content but about how he can find something which fires him up as much as the professor is inspired by his chosen field. Whether the quality of the teacher being admired is his self-discipline, his encyclopedic memory, or his patience, it is clear that at least some students respond to their teachers as potential or actual models.

Viewed from a general perspective, it would seem that one very important cue to which students respond when they accept their teacher as an ego ideal is any indication that the teacher enjoys what he is doing. Not only does he evidently enjoy teaching, but he seems to find something in that situation which is personally liberating and exciting. He seems to have more than enough energy for the task at hand, more than enough self-confidence, and a belief that the activity or the ideas involved are sufficiently worthwhile to care deeply about them. Why do some students report that the enthusiasm of a particular teacher was contagious and caused them to work unusually hard in that course? One answer might be that students and teachers alike are striving to make their lives and the activities in which they engage congruent with their developing sense of what is important and what is satisfying. The presence of a person who can so unconflictedly involve himself in a body of ideas or a kind of teaching or a practical or personal philosophy sets in motion various responses. Some students may become alienated by the teacher's exuberance, some are envious and resentful, but some find in that teacher at that moment someone with whom they can identify and who can serve for them as an ego ideal.

Another reason why a particular teacher's performance may be so attractive for others is that the performance also satisfies the teacher's own standards of excellence, and thus one part of his entire performance involves the communication of his pleasure with himself. He acts as if he feels brilliant, more fully alive, more patient and sensitive; that is, he is capable of satisfying whatever standards of self-judgment are applicable at that moment.

The Teacher as Person

The sixth and last aspect of the teacher-student task relationship is the teacher as a person. The teacher as person aims at engaging students in a mutually validating relationship. Ideally, both the student and the teacher feel sufficient trust and freedom to share their ideas and personal reactions, not only to the course material, but also to matters that may fall outside the usual definition of what is relevant in a classroom.

In thinking about the teacher as person, our focus is a little different in that we shall attempt to describe some of the functions served by more personal, out-of-role behaviors on the part of teachers and students. A teacher may use himself, his personal feelings, or his experiences to facilitate a transition to another task strategy or additional movement within a current strategy. Thus he may share with the students his own sense of discouragement about the movement of the class in order to encourage them to share their feelings and work together on the problem. In this instance the adoption of a person strategy is in the interest of facilitation. Or a teacher may relate a dream in order to make a concept more concrete and real; that is, personal material may be used to pursue expert goals.

We also observe that both the teacher and the students are vitally interested in having themselves, and not simply their task-related selves, validated within the relationship that is developing in the classroom (see Sunderland, 1967; Bugental, 1967; Bennis, et al., 1964; Shutz, 1967; and Leonard, 1968). Basic human and interpersonal themes, including trust, desire for respect, concerns about intimacy and affection—in short, the full range of human needs, are very much a part of the teaching-learning interaction.

Consider the efforts by teachers and students to indicate that they continue to exist beyond the classroom. The implication may be that each is telling the other that if he continues to be seen solely in terms of his activities within the classroom, then the relationship cannot help but remain a highly limited and less than ideal situation. Teachers sneak in little anecdotes about their own days as students, about their families, or their political activities. Students allude to their summer vacations, their problems with parents, their weekends, their religion, their sexual encounters, and their skirmishes with the law. Each is involved in a process of asserting that he would like more of himself to be validated than simply the limited part that joins with the others in the pursuit of narrowly defined course goals.

The other parts of oneself, for both the teacher and the students, are not simply the aspects that exist outside the classroom. Equally important are those feelings and reactions which, while not explicitly part of the agenda for class discussion, press on one's consciousness. Thus an individual in the classroom may be impelled to break through the task-oriented discussion to comment on an absurdity that has just occurred to him or to express irritation or a sudden burst of pleasure. A teacher may acknowledge that he looks forward to coming to class and really enjoys the contact with his students. Although it tends not to be discussed as an official part of the teacher-student relationship, all the participants in the classroom drama bring with them needs for affiliation, needs for pleasurable interaction with increasingly familiar associates.

For both teachers and students the gradual and sometimes agonizing growth of mutual trust, respect, and affection can be a liberating and extremely rewarding aspect of the teaching-learning experience (Gibb, 1964). The sense of being more than a product, more than just another name on a class list, can be of great importance, especially for students who have strong affiliative needs or who are committed to confirming different parts of themselves. The development of some awareness of the teacher as a person and an appreciation of the conflicts with which he is struggling can reduce much of the mistrust and alienation of the classroom situation. An equally useful outcome may be associated with a growing tolerance for mutual ambivalence in the student-teacher relationship.

We would not want to leave the impression that these communications of personal experiences, feelings, and out-of-role identity are irrelevant to the manifest task of teaching and learning. If one of the latent goals of the teacher as an ego ideal is to convey the relevance of the course material to what is worthwhile and exciting in life, then the latent function of the teacher as a person is to convey that the intellectual matters under discussion are not irrelevant to the conduct of a life that is within the range of the students in the class. To the extent that the teacher can convey how he came to be interested in these matters or how his interests are sustained by their application to issues of concern to him in his "everyday life," the student can come to understand the relevance of the teacher's career and knowledge to his own interests and personal needs. Although one can imagine that a passionate and thoroughly admirable teacher may inspire some students to join the quest for his version of the Holy Grail, one can also imagine that other students are more affected by hearing of the haphazard routes by which some academics found their way into the fields. Some of the reasons why a career is chosen or an interest sustained are far from the stylized versions selected for inclusion in the "Lives of Great Men" mythologies. Thus the teacher as person is not only addressing his own need to be recognized. He is also performing the vital task of puncturing the various mythic constructions that students may have developed. The net effect of this is both to decrease the awe in which he is held and to increase the extent to which his interests reveal him to be an ordinary mortal in pursuit of a recognizable and manageable set of goals. Futhermore, as the teacher begins to make available this kind of information about himself, he is also enabling the student to be "all there" and to work on the integration of his disparate elements in an accepting and trust-inducing interpersonal environment.

If we can settle for the six-part typology of teaching functions presented above, we can attempt to clarify two of the most important processes affecting the college classroom: (1) the teacher's efforts to define and act on his priorities and (2) the coming together of the teacher's priorities with those of the students.

The teacher-as typology suggests six ways in which the teacher may define his task. But each teacher must work out for himself the relative importance of each aspect. Thus we can easily imagine the teacher who is caught between "getting lots of material across" and "getting the students to explore their own reactions to even a small amount of material," and we would describe this dilemma as one that opposes being the expert with being the facilitator.

We can imagine without much difficulty the teacher who enjoys giving well-prepared and dramatic lectures but who also feels that these performances make it more difficult for him to get to know the students; he is experiencing a conflict between the teacher as expert and/or ego ideal and the teacher as person. Much of the teacher's uncertainty, as he designs a new course or responds to a specific event, drives from irresolution over how much to emphasize the various aspects of his role.

Even if we ignore for the moment the students and their pressures on the teacher, it is not difficult to understand some of the reasons for this irresolution. In some educational environments the teacher as expert is by far the most legitimate part of the teacher role. The internal struggle over how much to leave room for the teacher as facilitator, for example, may reflect real pressures from one's colleagues not to depart from the usual model of the college teacher. Or the teacher himself may sense that although he would like to emphasize a specific role, he would not be likely to do a good job or to feel comfortable. Thus the teacher may concede the importance of expanding his role to include other aspects of teaching but, in fact, be unwilling to depart from the teaching style that has in the past provided security and self-esteem.

The process of deciding who one shall be or shall try to be as a teacher, who one must regretfully give up trying to be, and who one will energetically try not to be—this process is a complex and often difficult one. Some teachers adopt a strategy of settling for one or two aspects; others seem to dash from one to the other in rapid succession. Why they choose or change strategies, and with what effect, are questions our empirical study explores. For now it is sufficient simply to note that the teacher is often in a quandry even before the students arrive on the first day. The students' presence complicates the whole process enormously and to this we now turn our attention.

Our investigation of how the students wish to define the educational relationship led us to try to develop a typology of students' conceptions of themselves. We thought to construct a "student-as typology" out of their answers to the question "Who am I in the classroom?" However, as we began this process it became clear that we were closely approximating the already developed teacher-as typology and, rather than overload our analytic model with an excess of terms and labels, we have chosen to look at the students in terms of who they want the teacher to be. For a student to say he wants the teacher to be the facilitator, the expert, or whatever is, of course, also a statement about who he wants to be in the classroom setting. Therefore we shall continue to use the six teacher-as labels, but now we are seeking to clarify the impact of students on the evolving definition of the educational contrast.

Much of what we shall need to say about "the students" must wait until we have presented our empirical data for the simple reason that the students have quite varied ideas about who they want the teacher to be and about how they wish to define their own role as students. One important question, then, to which our study will address itself concerns just how students do vary. At this point we can do no more than suggest that some students might prefer the teacher as expert, others demand that the teacher be the formal authority, and so forth through the six teacher-as functions. Only with our data behind us can we say in a convincing fashion what the major kinds of student pressures seem to be and how they may influence the teacher.

What we can say now is that the educational relationship involves the coming together of a teacher with his set of priorities and sense of the task and a classroom full of students each with his or her own sense of the best possible teacher-student relationship. Imagine a teacher who wants to be mostly the expert, would secretly like to be seen as a model of brilliance and intellectual passion, has decided he must abandon any efforts to be the facilitator, and cannot stand being the formal authority. Imagine next that he walks into class only to find a clear and repetitive demand that he clarify his role as formal authority. The students' priorities, in this class at least, begin with issues of the work load, evaluation, and fairness. We do not mean to imply that this impasse is permanent, but at this one moment the most important fact about the classroom is the divergence between the teacher's and the students' priorities.

If we turn from this hypothetical situation back to the reality of the college classroom, we notice one thing immediately: it is seldom possible to sense a coherent pressure from "the students." Rather, the pressures come from every direction. Not only do five students want the teacher to clarify his version of the formal authority function; two others want him to repeat his definition of the course objectives; three more want to argue a point made in the first lecture; and still others are acting uninvolved, frustrated, or in ways which the teacher cannot even decipher. Thus the teacher-student interaction involves not simply the convergence or divergence of two sets of priorities, but a whole array of divergences, with some students being more vocal or insistent than others.

In its general form we can see two sources of stress in the task area: first, that the teacher and each student enter the situation with different goals and conceptions of what the classroom should be like and, second, that even the goals on which there is agreement are difficult to reach. It takes more than simply stating the desired role relationship. The teacher may want to be the expert, and he may find at least some support for that definition of his role. But then he must try to be the expert. Very shortly the question arises: "How is the teacher as expert doing?" And the teacher as expert has a partner in this process, the student who is supposed to be learning the material generated by the expert. How is the student doing?

Before long the question of how the teacher-student relationship will be defined is joined by questions about the actual process and its relationship to the stated goals. Fantasy meets reality; intentions are tested against performance.

It is precisely at this point that the classroom process multiplies in complexity, and we must broaden our conception of the educational relationship. People have feelings about the way things work out in groups. They have hopes and expectations, they see how things are going, and they react. Even if we stick to the hopes and priorities expressed in the teacher-as typology, the classroom is very quickly a place where one's hopes and priorities are put to the test. The teacher is disappointed by the sluggish response of the students to his questions. The students are overwhelmed by the erudition of their teacher. The teacher is pleased by the ease with which the paper assignment was accepted. Two students are quietly disgusted at the lack of freedom in the course structure. And so on. Each of these statements makes reference to one or more aspects of the teacher-student task relationship *and* to the affective state stemming from how the task relationship is proceeding. We have gone beyond the world of plans, priorities, and educational philosophies to the classroom itself, and what we find is a world of feelings and emotions.

Some of these feelings are reactions to oneself in action. The teacher is getting upset that he seems to himself to be so halting and confused. He seems to resemble not at all his own image of the exciting lecturer or the gracious and rewarding discussion leader. And he has feelings about that discrepancy between reality and his ideals. Or perhaps at another moment he is delighted with himself for a point well made or a menacing challenge skillfully handled.

The student may be reacting to his own performance as well. He may be sitting there wondering why he ever thought he was college material or why he did not try to answer the last question raised by the teacher. He, too, has feelings about his performance, and these feelings are all bound up with his image of how things should go. He may be feeling proud of himself that he was quick to come up with the right answer, or he may be proud that he had the courage to challenge the teacher when he proposed a particularly rigid formula for grading the course. He is watching himself, seeing how things are working out.

In addition to these self-absorbed musings of teachers and students, we find the whole range of feelings each stirs up in the other. The rise and fall of fear, scorn, admiration, anger, shame, and so on is as much a part of the classroom reality as the task activities we discussed earlier.

Probably all teachers will agree that the teacher-student relationship has its emotional aspects. They can recall the times when they have felt elated or upset and times when the students expressed feelings of unmistakable intensity. But the question remains: What is the role of emotions in one's conception of the educational process? Are emotions something to recognize but ignore as much as possible? Are these emotional messages simply the exhaust of a system at work, noticeable but not worth one's attention for long? We think not.

Our operating hypothesis is that the emotional or affective aspect of the classroom interaction is an integral part of the total teacher-student relationship. The affective states experienced by both teacher and students, whether expressed directly or not, are inevitably part of this developing relationship. To ignore this aspect of what is happening in the classroom is to ignore the very evidence one so desperately needs in order to figure out both how the class is going and what, if anything, needs to be done in the way of change.

Things do not always work out as one intends. The ever-changing affective state of the classroom participants stands as both an effect and a cause of the extent to which things approximate the various intended outcomes. That disappointment and frustration follow on one's own failure in the task area is clear, and it is equally clear that how teachers and students feel about one another stems from the way each has approached the various aspects of the task. What is often easy to overlook, however, is that these feelings have effects on later task interactions. If the teacher has given a brilliant lecture in the first class which caused some students to feel hopelessly stupid, then the way these students will act subsequently and their set toward the teacher's next lecture is at least partly a result of this affective consequence. The feeling of being stupid, the feeling that the teacher is over one's head, and the growing suspicion that he enjoys lording it over poor little freshmen—these affective realities are both a result and a cause of the student's involvement in the task area. Maybe the student will give up hope. Maybe he will begin to press the teacher to be less the expert and more the facilitator or the person. Any number of things might happen.

The point is that we need to develop a conception of the teaching-learning process that recognizes the importance of the affective states. In our view, it is only by reminding oneself constantly of the back-and-forth, mutual cause-and-effect interplay between the task domain and the affective domain that one can understand the educational process.

Perhaps the problem is that we need some new way to talk about how the task and affective processes should be related to one another.

We need a new way of stating the desired outcome of college teaching. If we believe that both task and affective issues must be considered simultaneously, then we imply that the goal of the classroom is not simply the task goal. The goal of the classroom is larger than the expert's goal of transmitting knowledge. It is larger than all six task goals put together. Our notion of the goal for the classroom would entail some optimum interplay between the task goals and the goals of people with feelings. What do people with feelings want? It must depend on the feelings.

The teacher who is overcome with scorn for his students wants some relief. Maybe he wants to leave the class. Maybe he wants to blast them and startle them into new ways of thinking. However he does it, he wants to change the inner and/or the outer reality which creates in him a sense of being trapped into a classroom with people he cannot respect. People who are anxious or discouraged want to stop feeling that way. People who are confused want to stop feeling confused. At first glance, then, it would seem quite simple to conclude that the goal of the classroom is to reduce the level of unpleasant and uncomfortable affect to a minimum. However, this would be a real mistake, since ignoring the task goals of the class is as wrong as ignoring the affective goals.

The solution would seem to lie in the construction of a goal that expresses the importance of both processes, and for us that goal is best expressed by the concept of *work*. Bion (1960) first developed this notion in discussing the complex goals of self-analytic groups, but his sense of the interconnections between the group's task and its interpersonal-affective process is very useful in this setting as well. Work is the process of doing what needs to be done. It is the process of addressing, in the proper balance for the moment, the demands of the group's formal task and the demands of the individual group members that stem from their developing relationships with one another. The concept of work expresses our conviction that neither the task goals nor the interpersonal goals should be the sole focus of the classroom as a system.

If it is useful to define the proper goal of the college classroom as work, we may begin to explore more precisely two very important questions. (1) What is the role of emotion in the teaching-learning process? (2) What is the role of the teacher? Our entire empirical study is addressed to these two questions, and we shall come back to them in our concluding chapters. What we can say now must therefore remain on an abstract level.

Our analysis of the role of affect in the classroom proceeds on several assumptions. First, we assume that in the classroom, as in any social interaction, the participants will experience many emotional and personal reactions to the task events that are taking place. They may or may not wish to express these feelings. They may or may not be aware of these feelings. But with varying degrees of intensity the affective states of teachers and students are a constant accompaniment of the task activity of the group.

How are these states related to the task? It is tempting to conjure up two stereotyped scenes. In one the class is filled with anxious and resentful students whose affective state is clearly a detriment to their ability even to concentrate on the teacher's lecture. In the other, the class is filled with attentive and respectful students whose affective state is clearly contributing to their ability to learn from the teacher. From these stereotyped images of the bad class and the good class it would be only a short step to the conclusion that some affective states are detrimental to the task and others aid in reaching the task goals. In this frame of mind we might then list the negative, disruptive affects. We might include anger, terror, discouragement, rebelliousness, indifference, and so on. We might list the useful, facilitating affects. And when we were done, we would have a most unhelpful statement about the reality of the college classroom.

It is easy to forget the times when each of the so-called negative, disruptive affects proved to be very useful indeed in the pursuit of intellectual goals. It is easy to forget the times when one learned just to spite the teacher at whom one was angry, learned precisely because one was anxious about failing, or learned in an effort to overcome one's growing sense of incompetence and stupidity. And some of the times when one felt only awe and respect for the teacher turn out, in retrospect, to be times when one's own critical faculties were not growing at all but were instead melting in the warm glow of affection and deference.

The role of emotion turns out to be very complicated indeed, and we can return to the concept of work in order to make sure that some of this complexity is built into our view of teaching and learning. If work is doing what needs to be done, it follows that for the class to be spending time trying to reduce the level of student anxiety might be called work under some conditions and not under others. It would depend on one's assessment of whether the affective state, be it anxiety or any other potentially disruptive affect, was standing in the way of task activity. If the students (or the teacher, for that matter) are excessively anxious, if they need to be reassured before they can move on in the task area, then work involves the effort to provide that needed reassurance. But if anxiety is not a serious problem, and if the class is eager to get on with things, then to spend time trying to reassure the class would lead the class away from its task goal and not toward it. The process of moving toward both task and affective-interpersonal goals at once cannot be described independently of an assessment of where the class is with respect to each goal, where it has been, and what, if anything, is blocking its progress toward both goals.

Sometimes affect is clearly disruptive. At other times the affect is potentially disruptive but is used in the service of the task goals. This is where the teacher comes in. If the proper goal of the classroom is work, then the proper role of the teacher is as the formally designated leader of the work group. That is, his role entails not only leadership in the task domain, however broadly and complexly defined this task may be. The teacher is also the appointed leader of the informal, interpersonal situation in which these task goals are to be pursued. His task therefore involves (1) trying to keep to a minimum the affect which actually interferes with the pursuit of the task goals; (2) trying to direct the energy of whatever affect is aroused into the service of the task; and (3) trying to insure that the task activities of the class remain in the service of the affective-interpersonal goals of the participants. Sometimes the interconnected domains of task and affect combine to produce an upward spiral of effectiveness and pleasure, both intellectual and personal. At other times the spiral goes down and down.

To understand better the ways in which the teacher can serve as leader of the work group and the ways in which he can thwart or destroy work are the major goals of this study. In order to accomplish these goals we need a way to observe and describe the affective interchange in college classrooms. We have been terribly vague thus far about what we think are the major affective states which teachers and students experience. Our first assignment is to be more precise about this by presenting our observational methodology for the study of classroom interaction. Second, we must begin to come to grips with the diversity of the students as they arrive with their array of priorities, perceptions, and interpersonal styles. Third, we must begin to appreciate how the classroom develops as a system.

We proceed now to the description and analysis of four classrooms. If we can understand the partial successes and failures of these classes and these teachers, we may thereby make a contribution toward understanding the meaning of work in other settings. We may also demonstrate the usefulness of developing a broader conception of the nature and proper goal of college education.

CHAPTER 2

VARIETIES OF AFFECTIVE EXPERIENCE

However teachers and students may feel about being explicit about their emotional responses to the events which take place in the classroom, there is ample evidence that from kindergarten through graduate seminars the affective component of classroom interaction is ubiquitous. Teachers meeting other teachers or students meeting other students after class act at times as if the cork had been pulled from a bottle within which the pressure had been mounting to the explosion point. "My God, what a class!" or "What a bunch of idiots!" or "You wouldn't believe what he pulled today." If these cathartic postclass samples were all that we had to go on, our effort to describe how the college classroom develops would be difficult indeed. It is for precisely this reason that we have studied not the lecture hall but the small discussion section because here we find a second sort of evidence regarding the feelings of the participants.

With the aid of a tape recorder one is able to create a record of the transactions within a classroom which differs rather strikingly from the typical postsession recollections of any of the participants, especially those of the teacher. Whereas most members of a task group tend to recall the task-relevant events (what was covered or how far the group progressed), the tape recorder picks up events which few of the participants would be likely to consider "significant": periods of irrelevant joking and laughing, long pauses after a question from the teacher, a certain edge to the way some students ask for clarification, and so forth. We are suggesting here that what to some of the participants may seem like mere "background noise" can and should be seen as material of significance. These seeming irrelevancies are the portals through which we may enter the affective experiences that invariably accompany task activity in human groups.

Of what form are these affective experiences? Different observers, in this still primitive stage of our knowledge, would undoubtedly prefer different formulations, but we can at least make a start by saying that one part of the affective experience is that of liking or not liking what is going on. Some people are relatively unaware of how they feel when they are involved and pleased with their surroundings; others are relatively unaware of their angers and their dissatisfactions. Whatever their conscious awareness may be, many of their actions betoken an underlying evaluation of the events around (and within) them. Closer inspection of the emotional aspects of what goes on in the college classroom reveals more than the sense of liking or disliking what is going on. We hear unmistakable signals of personal distress, or anger that shades into defiance and rebellion, or the excited and self-satisfied pursuit of knowledge. A list of the various affectively toned or almost exclusively emotional comments would seem to be endless. How, then, shall we proceed to bring order out of these data?

Our assignment in this chapter is twofold. First, we shall describe a scoring system designed to capture at least some of the major affective messages heard in the classroom. The member-leader scoring system contains the 16 categories that are the building blocks for all our subsequent analyses of student differences, teacher behavior, and changes over time. However, between the categories and these major data analyses we have interposed an intermediate level of data analysis: the search for dimensions or factors that underlie the affective experience of teachers and students. We shall ask, in the second part of this chapter, how the 16 categories go together for teachers, and later for students, in an effort to create dimensions even more general and appropriate than the single categories. Thus we start with the categories but move quickly to the search for teacher factors and student factors. Throughout, our goal is to create empirical measuring rods for assessing the most important aspects of how the classroom participants are feeling and acting. Before we present the categories and factors, we need to discuss the particular set of classrooms, teachers, and students to which we plan to apply our empirical measures.

The empirical study which forms the core of this effort to understand the college classroom is more in the nature of a case study than it is the result of a well-drawn sample of college classrooms in general. We studied four classes in depth, and all were lecture-discussion sections of an introductory psychology course. Although we shall try in numerous ways to generalize across the four classrooms, our major purpose in spending so much time in analyzing so few classes is simply that we were and still remain convinced that the case study approach is a useful way to begin a new avenue of exploration. Given the relative paucity of material on what teachers and students are feeling, on how these feelings change and influence each other, and so forth, there seemed to be ample justification for detailing just how complex and intertwined are the causes and effects of emotional interactions in the classroom.

Four teachers and slightly over 100 students—this is the cast of characters. Perhaps a few brief introductions are in order. We have labeled the classes A, B, C, and D and have given the teachers the corresponding pseudonyms.

All four teachers had had but one term of teaching when they took on the classes we observed and analyzed in this study. Naturally they were tense. Mr. A, however, was the most manifestly ill at ease of the four teachers. A casual observer, asked to select those affective states which most characterized Mr. A's class, would undoubtedly point first to the anxiety expressed by the teacher and to something like apathy or uneasiness on the part of most students. The casual observer might note how frequently the teacher's open-ended questions to the class would go unanswered. It might be more difficult to determine whether this reflected mainly the students' stubbornness, guardedness, or their resentment of all the times their tentative answers had been dismissed as incomplete or irrelevant. Although it might well take careful analysis to understand the causes of this impasse, at least one phenomenon, then, that would be immediately obvious would be the teacher's inability to get a good discussion going.

How did the students feel about all this? We tried a number of techniques to find out: students rated the teacher, themselves, and the other students every three weeks; we interviewed them near the end of the term; we obtained some of their impressions and memories two years later, and above all else—we listened to what they had to say in class. How did the students feel about their class and about Mr. A in particular? They were not pleased with the class. Mr. A elicited a considerable amount of respect for his intellectual prowess, but his tension and his "embarrassed," "unsure of himself" stance within the class disappointed many students. The weeks of classes which failed to "get off the ground" expressed equally well the low energy of the students.

If the casual observer had dropped in on a few of Mr. A's classes and had sensed some of these things, he would have had a useful first approximation to the emotional underworld of Class A. But then there was the day Mr. A failed to show up for class and sent in his stead someone to explain that he had gone on the march to Selma. Mr. A returned full of energy and even fervor and, for at least some students, the whole term was redeemed by their first sight of a teacher who cared about things of genuine social relevance. But other students felt that his sudden trip was illegitimate, and the exam loomed larger in their minds than any civil rights march hundreds of miles away.

Mr. B and his class would strike the casual observer quite differently. Although it is not obvious who was, "deep down," the more tense, Mr. B's style was far more effusive, energetic, and reassuring. In fact, Mr. B was selected for the study to serve as Mr. A's counterpart. It seemed at that early juncture that Mr. B's style was essentially "counterphobic," involving a kind of rushing toward that which threatened him most. If anxiety was to some extent an issue for both Mr. A and Mr. B, one seemed to express what the other tried hard to deny.

Class B is the subject of a case analysis in Chapter 5, and we need here only sketch a few of the important emotional states which would seem especially obvious to anyone visiting this class. Early in the class' history one would have observed the teacher trying to present material he himself did not particularly enjoy or value. He made many mistakes, the students were rather quick to spot these, and before long he was on the defensive, flustered and off guard. Were the visitor to come half a dozen sessions later, he would find the group sitting around in a circle, with one student struggling to "present" some material. Mr. B was now a "resource person." Before long the visitor might sense the growing tension with this arrangement. The students' hostility had shifted from quarreling to complaining about the new structure, and the teacher's distress had shifted from intellectual defensiveness to doubt over whether he was providing the group with the leadership it needed and deserved.

This is probably as good a point as any to note that Mr. B had complete autonomy in running his own class. He and all the other teachers in Psychology 101 (Psychology as a Social Science) were essentially on their own. There was one central, mass lecture, but the other three hours in class, the choice of readings, the exams, and the grading were all up to the teacher. Therefore we can ask why this independently functioning teacher chose to alter the structure of his class, but this might soon lead to a realization that Mr. B was part of a larger group of about 20 teaching fellows. This larger group and its faculty coordinator had some part in Mr. B's decision, in that "getting a lot of discussion" was generally thought to be desirable. Just why it was desirable was never spelled out, but this and other pressures would need to enter into one's analysis of any teachers' feelings, perceptions, and actions.

As with class A, it would make a big difference at what point one visited class B. By the end of the term probably the most notable emotional state would be the high level of mutual support flowing back and forth between teacher and students. Much of this support from Mr. B to his class was responsive to a fairly dependent orientation, especially on the part of the females, but this was often mixed with periods of considerable independence.

Mr. B was pleased with the intellectual gains made by most students, and the students for their part were full of praise for Mr. B and the class. Although a few students remembered him as a bit "young" and "insecure," the consensus, even two years later, was that he had been an effective, warm, and intelligent teacher. How did this come about?

Mr. C resembled Mr. B in some ways. They were both students in clinical psychology. They were both expansive and high tempo individuals with an obvious desire to do well by their classes. Although we have not returned much to our original design for selecting "different" teachers, it may convey something to say that Mr. C seemed unique in his tendency to resolve dilemmas or impasses by generating an extraordinary amount of energy. The "hypomanic" or whirlwind style, as it came to be known, seemed to entail far more heroic challenge and preoccupation with the battle among the males than did Mr. B's more rewarding style. The verbatim transcript of one session in class C, found in Chapter 3, provides a dramatic illustration of Mr. C's style.

The casual observer in class C might sense how contagious Mr. C's enthusiasm or drive was for at least some students. Rapid-fire questions, each building toward some point to be made, were interspersed with student performances. As part of his open-throttle style, Mr. C gave the students a far more explicit sense of his approval and disapproval than most teachers provide. Some students, especially during the midpassage of the group, were very angry at Mr. C; some were enthralled. In short, the group seemed to have an emotional intensity not found in the other classes.

Mr. D was probably the most formal and distant of the teachers. His intellectual style was somewhat overwhelming for many students, and his class fought a losing battle against depression and resignation. Even two years later the students used such adjectives as cold, superior, and impersonal to describe Mr. D, and one student noted: "The instructor seemed to be bored teaching undergraduates. He impressed me as having a desire to teach grads, or something of a seminar class."

It is not surprising that the students, given their perceptions of the teacher, would also evaluate him negatively. They were able to recall and describe quite vividly the additional fact that he seemed both attractive and brilliant. Their sense of Mr. D as "sexy" and "good-looking" was thus mixed in with their bitter and angry recollections of Mr. D's interpersonal style. Self-report questionnaire data might tend to underestimate the rather widespread sense on the students' part of having failed, of being just as dull and ordinary as Mr. D seemed to be telling them they were. The depressive, self-critical tone to the class would only emerge from interviews, if skillfully conducted, or from listening to the ongoing classroom dialogue.

As we reflect on the variety found even among four classrooms, we can find certain intriguing phenomena. We have seen that both the teacher and the students are capable of hostility of diverse sorts, from the anger of the students being accused of bigotry by Mr. C to the sullen withdrawal of Mr. A's class when asked a vague and complex "discussion question." We can sense the distress of the students or the teacher as they enter perilous territory, or as they recoil, frightened, discouraged, or disgusted at their own failings. Clearly, much of the affect derives from the authority relationship which binds them together (and which leads so directly to the grade sheet). From Mr. B's retreat into the role of resource person to Mr. D's overwhelming first lecture, the teacher's feelings and actions revolve around the issue of dominance just as the issue of dependency shows through in both the syncophant and the rebel. We shall return to discuss additional ways we developed for assessing these and other feelings, but it is time now to present our major empirical method for making systematic observations of the emotional-interpersonal aspects of the college classroom.

The Member-Leader Scoring System

How does one go about capturing the kinds of emotional expressions or messages which people communicate to or about one another or themselves? Our principal research tool here is the 16-category member-leader scoring system (Mann, 1967). Before discussing in some detail the categories themselves, it may be helpful for the reader to have some idea of the orientations which a scorer brings to the task of using the scoring system. We begin with two central propositions, which are probably common to any attempt to make sense out of what people say. The first is that feelings may be expressed directly or they may be expressed indirectly or symbolically. The second is that any statement derives its meaning in part from the timing and context of the act. Perhaps the most pertinent analogy is that of the clinician faced with making decisions about the import of statements made by a patient in therapy. For example, if a patient suddenly begins to complain that people in his environment are not responsive enough to him, that they ignore or reject him, the therapist, given his previous history with the patient and the nature of their current relationship, might be led to infer that, among other things, the patient was feeling reproachful toward him and wished to change the therapist's behavior in the direction of greater responsiveness and warmth.

Take another example from one of the classes in our study (see Chapter 3). A group of students is engaged in an animated conversation about the overthrow of a repressive government in Southeast Asia, and this conversation occurs at a moment in the group's history when the teacher has just handed back a test which many people thought was not graded fairly. One might be justified in inferring that the "repressive government" is a symbolic equivalent of the teacher and that the feelings expressed toward it may be displaced or indirect expressions of feelings toward him. This is not to say anything about whether such symbolic expression is consciously intended; there may be some conscious screening of remarks by individuals or it may be something of which they are not aware, even preconsciously. Furthermore, any inference that the students might also be referring to their teacher should not be construed as discounting the integrity of their feelings toward the repressive government in question. The important point here is that, as most people are well aware, feelings may be displaced from their original object and directed toward substitutes. In the scoring system, a primary convention is that, although the content of a remark or statement (say, on the part of a student) may not make any *direct* reference to the teacher, the scorer listens very carefully for any implications for the teacher of those remarks or statements and uses the scoring categories accordingly. That is, he asks about each act whether at some level the act may indicate either the students' feelings toward his teacher or the teacher's feelings toward one or more of his students. In contrast to the more group-centered discussions examined in our previous studies (Mann, 1967), the four classrooms studied here departed only rarely from the traditional back-and-forth interchange between teacher and student. For this reason, although the scorers did distinguish between various levels of symbolic expression, these distinctions were not preserved in any of the data analyses to be presented, and the relatively rare symbolic acts were simply combined with the more direct and manifest indications of the participants' feelings.

Returning to the central propositions that a scorer brings to his task, we must now explain what is meant by saying that the scorer makes inferences about acts in a context of simultaneous and previously occurring acts. As the scorer listens to group interactions, he begins to build a picture of their pattern or structure. For instance, he may note that one person consistently makes disparaging remarks about the efforts of other students to find solutions to group problems. Remembering the other times when the member has spoken, listening carefully to the linguistic structure of the sentences, and paying attention to tone of voice and other extralinguistic cues, the scorer may conclude that the other students are not only serving as substitutes for the teacher, but that the student is in a subtle way expressing his own sense of inadequacy, powerlessness, and dependency relative to the teacher. Of course, as the person speaks further, the scorer may find that the equivalence he thought was there between teacher and other students is not all that precise, and he may be forced to reconsider his scoring.

The context must be closely attended to by the scorer when it is necessary to decide whether a symbolic referent is equivalent to the teacher or is perceived by the student to be the teacher's antithesis. To use an example from Mann (1967, p. 41): When a group member says, "Freud would never have badgered a patient with his interpretations; he would have waited until it made sense to the patient himself," it may be clear from the context that Freud is a symbolic equivalent for the leader. But it may not be the case that the member is indirectly attacking the leader for being too aggressive or manipulative. Instead, he may be supporting the leader's passive, nondirective style by equating him with the Great Man himself. Again, the scorer's acquaintance with the member's past history in the group, his feeling for what is going on at this moment, and the linguistic and extralinguistic cues can be helpful. This is clearly a complicated task; however, we found the degree of interscorer reliability satisfactory and, of necessity, scorers were chosen whose

---

IMPULSE AREAS

Hostility

1. Moving Against
2. Resisting
3. Withdrawing
4. Guilt Inducing

Affection

5. Making Reparation
6. Identifying
7. Accepting
8. Moving Toward

AUTHORITY RELATIONS AREA

9. Students: Showing Dependency
   Teachers: Showing Counterdominance
10. Showing Independence
11. Students: Showing Counterdependency
    Teachers: Showing Dominance

EGO STATE AREAS

Anxiety

12. Expressing Anxiety
13. Denying Anxiety

Self-esteem

14. Showing Self-esteem

Depression

15. Expressing Depression
16. Denying Depression

FIGURE 1-1   Member-Leader scoring system.

introspective, self-critical, and intuitive abilities were high and who had had prior experience with groups.

This brings us to the categories themselves. Figure 1-1 shows the category system. It should be noted that the categories map onto the expression of feelings in groups in some ways that correspond to dimensions of personal interaction already delineated in the literature. Thus the recurrent two-dimensional model of interaction with one axis representing hostility and attraction and the other axis representing degrees of power, influence, or status is captured by the Impulse Expression areas and the Authority Relations area (see, for example, Leary, 1957; Lorr and McNair, 1963; and Becker, 1964). We might also note here the contributions of Bennis and Shepard (1956) and Thelan and his co-workers (1954) with their quantification of Bion's concept of "basic assumption" and "work" groups, Schutz's analysis of interpersonal behavior (1957) in terms of needs for inclusion, affection, and control, and Couch's extension (1960) of Leary's work into a system for observing leaderless groups. The Ego State areas might be thought of as a cross-cutting dimension reflecting the student's feelings about his own vulnerability, competence, or his sense of personal worth in relation to the teacher. The most influential source of insight here has been the work of Bibring (1963).

The partitioning of the categories into six subareas arises from an important convention regarding the scoring of single acts. Acts may be scored once in each of the subareas, but the scorer is not allowed to score a single act within a single area more than once. This forces him to choose between *kinds* of hostility, affection, authority relations, or ego-states being expressed.

We shall present each category by defining its unique characteristics, attempting to delineate clearly its boundaries, and we shall give examples of relevant acts, most of which will be taken from the transcript of a class session reproduced and scored in its entirety in Chapter 3. The interested reader may refer to the quoted example in order to get a feeling for the context in which the example occurs.

Hostility

1. MOVING AGAINST

This category is scored when the expression of hostility seems directed by a student against the teacher (or vice versa when the teacher is scored) as a person, rather than as a response to him in his role as teacher or representative of the system. Expressions scored as Moving Against may take the form of scorn, sarcasm, mistrust, belittling, suspicion, and the like, but without a moralistic invoking of values or standards of judgment as weapons (see Guilt Inducing below). For example, in the transcript reproduced in Chapter 3, Mr. C, the teacher, is trying to deal with his most contentious and troublesome student who is attempting to defend an answer he gave to a question on a test about the determinants of Negro-white differ-ences in antisocial behavior. Mr. C, for reasons explored in that chapter, is very interested in having his students become more sensi-tive to the effects of environment on behavior. In the segment from which we quote, he is engaged in a real tug-of-war with Mr. Wicker, the troublesome student, a tug-of-war which culminates in the latter responding to Mr. C's questions about Negroes' being made to feel uncomfortable with whites by saying in a loud and angry tone, "Well, you just don't feel comfortable talking to him, so you don't associate with him" (Act 77).

In context, it is clear that Mr. Wicker is expressing his anger at Mr. C in a thinly disguised way, saying in some sense: "Get off my back!" Note that there seems to be a real desire at that moment on Mr. Wicker's part to hurt, offend, or retaliate against Mr. C, and this is the threat that runs through all acts scored as Moving Against. Thus this category closely resembles Bales' (1950) negative social-emotional category Shows Antagonism.

2. RESISTING

Resisting is scored when the student expresses hostility toward the role or role performance of the teacher. Unlike Moving Against, the hostility tends to be primarily reactive or responsive to teacher behavior, where in the former the hostility is more self-initiated or active rather than passive. In the classroom, Resisting may be seen when students disagree with points or suggestions a teacher makes (which in our study is probably its most typical form) or, more subtly, by impatience with continued discussion of a topic (e.g., "We've rehashed this argument enough times; I want to move on to something else"). A good example of Resisting occurs earlier in the same segment of the transcript already quoted. It is very clear that Mr. C is trying to get Mr. Wicker to perceive or at least agree with the idea that white people's derogation of Negroes is often a potent cause of decrements in Negro performance in many differ-ent dimensions. Mr. Wicker's response to Mr. C's repeated questions about a Negro's feeling of uncomfortableness around white persons is met by Mr. Wicker's statement (which he keeps repeating in some form or other), "Because his intelligence is not up to their level" (Act 68). It is interesting that under Mr. C's persistent pressure, Mr. Wicker's resistance turns into the more personal Moving Against (Act 77) which abruptly terminates the interaction (Act 78). Again, the critical attribute is that the hostility is relatively impersonal and directed at the other as a reciprocal role player, and thus this category is closer to Bales' (1950) category called Shows Disagreement than any other category in previously developed scoring systems.

3. WITHDRAWING

Unlike Moving Against and Resisting, Withdrawing represents a pulling away from the interaction, an attempt to decrease intensity and loosen previously existing bonds. At the extreme, this may take the form of statements about leaving the group entirely or ignoring the teacher. More frequently it takes the form of boredom, disinterest, or attempts to firmly exclude the teacher from the student's world. Withdrawal was often scored when a teacher asked a student specifically for a response, and the student responded by declining to enter into interaction (see Acts 99 and 100 in the transcript). Similarly, when a class responds to a teacher's questions by silence, this is typically a manifestation of Withdrawal, although this is again a matter of context. For instance, depending on the questions asked or the emotions the teacher is expressing, silence might be scored as Resisting or Expressing Anxiety (see below).

4. GUILT INDUCING

A common interpersonal tactic through which people express hostility is invoking standards of judgment or values that are claimed to have a superordinate claim on the behavior of the other individual. One of the major clues that lead one to score an act in this category is the use of evaluative terms (should, must, have a right to). It is the quality of legitimacy, of invoking the sense that a thing *must* be done, that characterizes this act, among other things, as Guilt Inducing. The tone that people use when trying to induce guilt often brings to mind words such as accuse, blame, and complain. (See Mr. C's implicit accusation that Mr. Wicker is a "prejudiced bastard" in Acts 307–311.) In a classroom setting, this often centers around formal demands that the teacher makes. Students complain directly or indirectly about the fairness of grading and grading policies, blame the teacher for overloading them with work, and accuse him of unwarranted rigidity or resistance to accepting their arguments. Perhaps central here is both the evocation of the legitimacy of demands or behavior and the expectation that the teacher should at all times be a fair, kind, thoughtful, strong, considerate, and generous authority figure. It is interesting to note that Guilt Inducing is scored as much for teacher behavior as for student behavior, which suggests that being the representative and setter of standards for what is good and proper behavior is a source of power which teachers can scarcely refrain from using.

Affection

5. MAKING REPARATION

Unlike the other forms of affection to be discussed, Making Reparation is scored when the person appears to be responding to some earlier expression of hostility (whether this expression actually occurred or not), or as a prior response to some form of hostility which is about to occur. The main element here is that the statement represents an attempt to undo or neutralize the effects of a hostile remark. For example, statements of the form, "I don't mean this personally, because I really like you, but. . . ," and then the person goes on to make a statement which is scored in an hostility category, represent one kind of Making Reparation. In another form, it is seen clearly when Mr. C apologizes to a female student for repeatedly mispronouncing her name (Acts 241 and 242). This example illustrates the point that while the scorer may not interpret an act as hostility (in this case, the mispronunciation of a name), the person being scored acts as if he has in fact done something to hurt or injure another person, and is trying to "make it up."

Still another form which Making Reparation takes is the denial of previous hostility, not only that which the person himself has expressed but which others have expressed. For instance, after a particularly hostile act on the leader by several members, one member who did not participate in this attack said, "I think all of you people are wrong for being so angry at him; I thing he's a nice guy." (For further discussion of the phenomena of making reparation and its function in personality, see Melanie Klein and Joan Riviere, 1937.)

6. IDENTIFYING

Identifying encompasses all those acts in which a student gives evidence of having taken on some aspect or quality of the teacher.

This may include mannerisms of speech, peculiarities of style, or personal values, general attitudes, and philosophy. For instance, in a group not studied here, several students began to use the words, "it seems to me that . . ." to preface their remarks shortly after the teacher had first used this (to him) common expression. Similarly, in a course which was quite unstructured and student centered, a student early in the group repeatedly defended unstructuredness and student autonomy as invaluable learning devices. Both of these would be scored Identifying.

What we are trying to capture in this category are the often indirect but highly significant forms of affection whereby one person communicates to a second person his unity or partnership in some enterprise simply by pursuing the activity without conflict. The student who picks up a point of the teacher's and elaborates on it at such length that one could not even detect that the teacher was the crucial audience for his remarks is not expressing affection directly, but we feel that, where relevant, we want to have a category to record those indirect modes of building solidarity with the teacher while not directly addressing him. By the same token, when the teacher conveys during a lecture or in a comment that the students are seen as a valued audience for his thoughts, he can be seen as expressing affection of a most important kind. Identifying in this sense means simply the process of using the other as part of the significant "we" who are undertaking the various intellectual and interpersonal tasks confronting the classroom. At times this process may be expressed through imitation of the other, at times merely through that implicit side-long glance which says, "We're in this together." (For some other problems that arise when scoring Identifying with Groups other than classroom groups, see Mann, 1967, pp. 49–51.)

7. ACCEPTING

Accepting is the counterpart of Resisting in the Hostility area. Just as the latter describes a primarily reactive response to role-behavior, so Accepting expresses the student's agreement with or approval of some aspect of the teacher's behavior *qua* teacher. For instance, after his futile attempts to change Mr. Wicker's mind, Mr. C turns to several students who very clearly accept the importance to environmental determinants of behavior. In Acts 107 through 127, Mr. Brewer, Mr. Monk, and Miss Jewel not only respond "correctly" but seem eager to offer further examples or explanations. But all of this remains very much on the level of the "good student" responding to the "good teacher." Similarly, Mr. C. compliments

Mr. Reed for bringing in some additional cognitive material by say-ing, "Well, you're bringing in the information we have been trying to read—that's good. . ." (Act 126), which in this context can be seen as an Accepting response to Mr. Reed's student role behavior (although note, in the transcript, the other scorings of this act).

Often, Accepting is quite hard to distinguish from Making Reparation, and again the scorer must pay attention to the context, especially the extent to which the person is ambivalent about his feelings; that is, the scorer listens for evidence that suggests whether this behavior sounds as if it is countering some other act. Accepting principally suggests support, and in this sense is distinguished from Identifying which suggests similarity.

8. MOVING TOWARD

Moving Toward is the counterpart of Moving Against in the Hostility area. Again, we make a similar distinction between behavior oriented toward the person and behavior oriented toward the role. Moving Toward acts express a feeling of personal liking, a desire to become more intimate or close. Occasionally it is difficult to dis-tinguish Moving Toward and Making Reparation, and again the scorer must be sensitive to the context in which the act is embedded. For example, when Mr. C says to Mr. Wicker, "so I'm not singling you out" (Act 142), in a context when Mr. C has in fact done just that, Making Reparation seems an appropriate scoring. But when a few moments earlier he turns to Mr. Wicker and says, "how does this sit with you, Mr. Wicker" (Act 139), the very personal quality of this remark prompts us to score it (among other things) as Moving Toward. Many of these acts by students are quite elliptical and guarded, perhaps because students do not want to be perceived by their peers as "buttering up" the teacher but, no matter how it is expressed, Moving Toward suggests some desire to establish, strengthen, or exhibit positive and personal bonds with the person and, in this way, contrasts with the more role-oriented, impersonal affection expressed in Accepting.

Authority Relations

9. STUDENTS: SHOWING DEPENDENCY; TEACHERS: SHOWING COUNTERDOMINANCE

The Authority Relations area attempts to capture, on the one hand, expressions of student concern with the power and influence of the teacher and, on the other hand, expressions of teacher concern with both his own and the students' power within the classroom. The category of Showing Dependency is designed for acts in which the student is perceiving himself as somehow inferior to the teacher in terms of power or resource control or when the student wishes the leader to exercise power or control and is trying to put him in this position by expressing his own inferiority. The kinds of power to which he is responding may be many, but in classrooms it typically is the power which a formal authority or representative of a system has invested in him, including both the power to determine who will or will not receive system rewards and also the power of superior knowledge and understanding which he has, or is accorded, as an expert in a particular field. The power to dispense crucial rewards and punishments seems particularly relevant to classrooms. One is often aware of times when students ask the teacher questions designed to ascertain the "rules of the game," to discover the exact behaviors that will lead the teacher to dispense rewards rather than punishments. A good example of this is contained in the following exchange (quoted in Mann, 1967, p. 53):

Female Student:	What is it we're supposed to do with the cases?
Leader:	Well, we discuss them. There are many ways to discuss them.
Male:	With what reference though? Are you looking for anything in particular?

Another good example of Showing Dependency when the issue is the role of the teacher as a formal authority occurs when Mr. Motley responds to Mr. C's question about the difficulties students might have had in criticizing the tests Mr. C gave, by saying, "Well, it's sort of hard to fight City Hall" (Act 183). Of the many feelings compressed into this remark, one clearly senses a concern with what is perceived to be a mighty Establishment whose ability to exercise influence and power far surpasses one's own.

Finally, a subtle form of Showing Dependency appears when the student seems to be implicitly assuming that the group is weak and the teacher is strong and that the teacher is the one who should do something about this sad state of affairs. Often these acts take the form of angry or impatient clamoring for the leader to be more helpful and supportive or, perhaps, to magically infuse the group with "life" so that it can "go." The implied passivity and weakness on the part of the student also seems to be a way of disowning responsibility for his own fate or destiny, in some sense giving it over to the teacher.

When the leader is scored, the category is called Showing Counterdominance. This captures those moments when the teacher moves against his real or perceived power by denying or disowning it. Very often this takes the form of a role-reversal, in which the teacher "plays dumb" by asking questions and deferring to the students' judgment. This category reflects the teacher's desire to push aside the barriers he may feel separate him from his students, barriers built into the power differential which, in fact, is an integral part of the traditional teaching situation.

10. SHOWING INDEPENDENCE

Students' acts scored in this category carry a sense of autonomy or real freedom from the effects of the teacher's power. This may take the form of working on developing one's own set of values or principles in an autonomous way, accepting responsibility for one's own behavior, or expressing a sense of equality or colleagueship with the other participant. For example, in response to Mr. C's suggestion that he is too rigid an authority, Miss Jewel says, "Well, I don't get that impression at all. I think that it's completely open—on the exam, especially—just drawn from your own past knowledge almost entirely, I thought." She then goes on, "and anyway, in our class discussion it was pretty open. I mean you weren't saying, 'This is it.' I didn't get that impression at all" (Acts 206–207). Although there seems to be a lot of Affection being expressed by Miss Jewel, it is also clear in Act 207 especially, that Miss Jewel is detailing her independent assessment of the situation in a fairly unconflicted way. That is, one doesn't have a sense that this student is responding to being dependent on Mr. C, or is denying her own incompetence. In fact, it has a flavor of wanting to act as an equal in the task of understanding and appreciating the material. Similarly, for the teacher's acts to be scored the scorer would need to sense that the teacher was here neither asserting nor denying his dominant role but simply staking out a relationship which transcended the power relations between him and the students. This is especially likely during the period of collaboration over intellectual and procedural matters where the teachers and students are genuinely involved, although with different capacities, in the mutual enterprise of the classroom process.

11. STUDENTS: SHOWING COUNTERDEPENDENCY;
TEACHERS: SHOWING DOMINANCE

This category points up the efforts that people who experience or who fear experiencing dependency sometimes make to rid themselves of such feelings. Included here are denials that one is, in fact, at all dependent on the teacher and also expressions of desires to destroy or do away with the power structure. Acts scored here, as distinguished from Showing Independence, typically have a more conflicted and defensive quality to them. For instance, in an interesting segment of the transcript in Chapter 3 (Acts 29–35), Mr. Wicker is at great pains not only to contradict and resist Mr. C, but also to demonstrate that Mr. C's power or influence over others in the class certainly does not hold for him! He expresses this neatly by cutting Mr. C off in midsentence several times, and then, as Mr. C turns to another student, says, "At least, that's the way *I* thought about it" (Act 35). It is as if Mr. Wicker is saying to Mr. C, "Don't imagine that you can bully me with your power; I've got my own mind, see?" Again, the intent of acts scored as Showing Counterdependency expresses some need to move to break away from a sense of dependency, rather than a clear expression of autonomy or freedom. In formulating this as well as the other two Authority Relations categories, we have been guided by the useful discussion found in Bennis and Shepard (1956).

For the teacher, this category is renamed Showing Dominance, and it is in this category that a tremendous number of teacher acts fall. This makes sense, since the category captures the times when the teacher is playing out the traditional role proscriptions—lecturing, calling on people, giving assignments or tests, making decisions for the group, and the like—but without necessarily invoking any moral standards or value stances in order to justify this. Showing Dominance is seen clearly when the teacher simply takes over, for instance, by interrupting an ongoing discussion among students to begin the lecture. Perhaps of most significance for the future of the relationship of student and teacher are the moments when dominance and Guilt Inducing or other hostility categories are paired.

Ego States

12. EXPRESSING ANXIETY

The definition of the Ego State categories owes much to Bibring (1963). He suggests that anxiety is a reaction a person has when he comes close to some threat that makes him feel vulnerable. The expressions may be direct expressions of anxiety (for example, "I feel very nervous in here today"), or they may be inferred from tone and quality of voice, as when we say that a person's anxiety was "betrayed" by the shakiness in his voice. Occasionally one finds anxiety expressed without an object being specified, but more often this is not the case. In the classroom, however, it is typical to find anxiety expressed through somewhat more indirect statements about vulnerability. For instance, right after the example cited above for Showing Counterdependency, Miss Jewel, who is not only sympathetic to Mr. C's position, but is also involved in a sexualized flirtatious relationship with him, says, "Well, I don't know—I don't know if I should argue this point now (over which Mr. C and Mr. Wicker had been quarreling) because I don't know if it's a matter of disagreeing with him or not" (Act 36). This is a complex act, since Miss Jewel is not only Making Reparation for Mr. Wicker's hostile remarks, and Showing Dependency where Mr. Wicker is Showing Counterdependency, but also Expressing Anxiety as Bibring defines it; that is, she expresses some sense that she might be hurt in some way if she were to get involved in the argument between Mr. C and Mr. Wicker at this point.

Anxiety may be inferred, as we have noted, from voice tone and quality. For instance, when Mr. C tries to make some kind of "peace treaty" with Mr. Wicker, Making Reparation and explaining his own involvement in the angry exchange, Mr. Wicker, rather than accepting the overture, denies that any anger existed. His "innocent" protestations (Acts 156–162) are greeted by other class members with general laughter, and this laughter, because of the nervous edge to it, is scored for Expressing Anxiety.

13. DENYING ANXIETY

Statements made by students or teachers that express a feeling of goodness, comfort, or relaxation can have one of two meanings. They can be expressions of self-esteem or they can be defensive denials of feeling scared, uncomfortable, or vulnerable. The critical attribute for scoring denial is the focus on negation. Thus, if a person says, "I am not feeling uncomfortable," the scorer might record this as Denying Anxiety. Of course, as always, the context of the act is critical in the ultimate scoring decision. Other, more or less subtle moments when this category becomes relevant revolve around strong protests against feeling inner distress or belittling the possible cause of anxiety. For instance, in the transcript already quoted from, Mr.

C asks Mr. Stall if he has anything to add to the argument in progress about the test. Mr. Stall replies, "I just thought it was a good argument. I like to sit back and listen to it" (Act 173). The slightly sarcastic or belittling tone here, coupled with the fact that Mr. Stall was not only a very quiet person but tended to speak with a nervous tone in his voice, seemed to justify scoring this act as Denying Anxiety. (See also the discussion of low participators in Chapter 4).

14. EXPRESSING SELF-ESTEEM

As noted above, acts scored here seem to be motivated by a need to express a feeling of positive satisfaction and comfort which does not seem to contain, or be a reaction to, feelings of distress. Often this takes the form of feeling competent or strong: "I really feel we have been able to work successfully together this semester"; other times it may come out as an expression of relief or reassurance: "Well, I'm finally feeling comfortable in this class." Interestingly, Expressing Self-esteem was scored very infrequently in our study, suggesting that either it is expressed in indirect ways which we have not yet been able to specify or that students (and teachers) rarely feel very good about themselves in college classrooms (at least, these college classrooms). We are tempted to suspect the latter possibility.

15. EXPRESSING DEPRESSION

Following Bibring, depression is viewed as affective reaction to a person's felt inability to cope with or overcome internal or external obstacles blocking the way to desired goals. Typically it is expressed in terms of incompetence. For instance, Mr. C, in response to a charge from a student that he was somewhat less than flexible in grading the exam, says, "So there's a little bit of rigidity coming through. Uhm—said very nicely, but a little bit of rigidity coming through on my part." (Act 195) In effect, Mr. C is admitting that he has not fulfilled his teaching duties or obligations in an important way and, in fact, has let a personal idiosyncrasy get in the way of effective teaching.

Mr. C not only expresses a sense of incompetence here but, we suggest, also some guilt over behaving in an irresponsible, possibly uncontrolled way. Often implied in Expressing Depression acts is a realization of the instability of internal controls and that the person may be helpless in the face of impulse arousal. Typically in these classrooms, however, the issue is competence and centers around the inability of the person to surmount obstacles because of some personal defect.

16. DENYING DEPRESSION

Denying Depression is similar to Denying Anxiety, except that here the defense is against feeling incompetent, powerless, or guilty. One thinks not only of simple negations but also of the more complex manic defenses discussed by Lewin (1950), as well as the guilt-deflecting defenses of self-justification and other forms of blame-avoidance. For instance, the arguments which many of the students in the transcript in Chapter 3 make in defending their answers to the exam questions are, as one might expect, full of acts scored as Denying Depression. Given students' personal investment in exams and grades, we could hardly expect them not to feel depressed if their answers are considered wrong or if their grades are low and, given the opportunity, we could also hardly expect them not to respond with attempts to counter these unpleasant feelings.

We have now completed our review of the 16 scoring categories, and we must add one brief note here concerning the definition of the unit of analysis. An act is defined as a burst of activity by a person which is internally homogeneous with respect to the feelings being expressed. As soon as the speaker alters significantly the feelings being expressed, so that the scorer finds that the categories indicated for the previous comments will no longer describe the speaker's feelings, one scored act ends and another begins. Thus, even a very long speech which conveys essentially the same feelings would be described as one act whereas a complex and unstable communication which oscillated back and forth between various feelings might be subdivided into many acts. In effect, the scoring convention resulted in a unit of analysis which was typically one or two sentences long, although the reader of Chapter 3 will note that a single act may be as long as one or two paragraphs of the transcript. A further consideration for defining acts is that when a member is interrupted, his next statement is considered to be the start of a new act, even if the scoring has not changed. Typically the number of acts per session using this system is about 200, although in the transcript in Chapter 3 there are over 400 acts to be scored, accurately reflecting the intensity and complexity of emotion being expressed in that session.

Although it would seem at first glance like a sensible question, there are serious difficulties in asking "What is the reliability of the member-leader scoring system?" The "reliability" of the scoring system depends on how many people and how long a time period is covered by the descriptive account which uses the categories. At the lower end, at the level of the single act, we can estimate the system's reliability by determining the extent of which two scorers agree on the placement of that act in a given category. The interscorer agreement varies somewhat from category to category, but in seven separate studies of interscorer agreement and the agreement of a scorer with his own scoring done at least six months previously, the percentage of agreement varies from a lower bound near 60% upward to a median close to 70% and, in some cases, reaches as high as 82% agreement. The reliability of scoring a single act is, however, not a very relevant issue, since throughout this study we shall combine acts to form portraits of larger time spans and of more than one individual student over the entire term. Our studies reveal, at least when one uses interscorer agreement as a minimum estimate of reliability, that the agreement between protraits formed over longer time spans or over a number of persons is above .75 (using rank-order correlations) for each category, and the median is above .80. From our various studies of interscorer agreement and the rescoring of previously scored material, we conclude that the amount of error variance that creeps into any description of the teacher or students which summarizes at least 20 acts is sufficiently low to warrant our confidence in such a description.

We have now finished our exposition of the categories we used to content analyze the interactions that occurred in our four classrooms. A word needs to be said about the multiple scoring of acts. We have already pointed out above that acts which contain the expression of a single emotion are rare and, indeed, one is often astonished at the richness of emotion expressed in single, sometimes linguistically short, acts. It would certainly be reasonable of the reader to wonder if this complexity is simply too overwhelming and whether by scoring many expressions of emotion in a concentrated act, one eventually ends up with an unmanageable, Jackson Pollack-like canvas, beautiful from a distance, but impossibly distracting close up. In part, this study is an attempt to answer that criticism in the negative. Even at the level of a single act, we feel that, rather than being intolerably confusing, multiple scoring provides the clearest account possible of the complex and shifting interaction.

Let one example suffice for now; the reader may want to raise this question again as he proceeds through our analysis of the data. We turn once more to the transcript in Chapter 3, and to Mr. Wicker's statement in Act 157. If the reader follows the transcript from the beginning to this point, he will note that Mr. Wicker has strongly and antagonistically resisted Mr. C's explanations about the answers to the exam questions. This open hostility seems to trigger off a wave of students to come to Mr. C's support, which he welcomes. By Act 157, Mr. Wicker has, in effect, been isolated from the main "camp," and has been placed in the awkward and embarrassing position of not only being the "odd man out," the person clearly in the wrong, but also of having to deal with Mr. C's attempts to resolve the conflict and make reparation to him. After Mr. C gets through telling the class how involved personally he had been getting in the argument, which elicited a laugh from the class, he says, attempting to get others to talk about their personal involvement, "Did that feeling sort of—um—was this part of what some of you people felt as well—or—?" at which point Mr. Wicker says, "I was just trying to pick up a few extra points" (Act 157). This act is scored for Withdrawal, Making Reparation, Showing Dependence, Denying Anxiety, and Denying Depression. In context, all seem appropriate; one senses Mr. Wicker opting out of the conflict, trying to minimize or neutralize the hostility. At the same time, he suddenly adopts a dependent stance ("I'm only a lowly student, trying to do what little I can to make it in a system where I control very few resources") and denies, as Mr. C seemed to suggest, that he felt in any way vulnerable or guilty about letting his emotions "run away" with him. This act, then, not only has the effect of chastising Mr. C for implying that Mr. Wicker was at all responsible for the disruptive affects generated in the discussion, but also catches Mr. C when he has made himself vulnerable by admitting that he, in fact, got somewhat defensive and overemotional. In effect, Mr. Wicker, through that combination of emotional expressions, has fairly effectively thrown the burden of blame and responsibility for what happened to Mr. C, with the further implication that there is no need to examine his own motives in defending his intellectual position. In this sense, Mr. Wicker seems to be saying, "If you raise this issue again, I'm going to come right back at you the same way as before, and since I know that I'm not as conflicted as you are, there is no need to examine whether or not my motives for holding the position I took in the argument were mixed in any way." In fact, when the issue comes up again, Mr. Wicker comes right back to the attack; however, this time, Mr. C clearly overwhelms him by his arguments.

We certainly grant that this is complicated but in a way that allows us to raise important questions. Why does Mr. Wicker need to conceptualize his relationship to Mr. C as if they were on a battle-field? Where does his anti-introceptive, externalizing style come from? What kind of work in the classroom is possible for such a person? How does his behavior affect the relationships Mr. C has with other students? How does it interfere with or facilitate their ability to work? This study is hopefully a start along the path to answering these questions.

Our major intent was to capture in a systematic way the emotional interaction of the classroom. Each session of each group was tape recorded. Each of the four sections met three times a week for an hour over the course of the semester for a total of approximately 41 sessions each. The tape recorder was attended to by an observer[1] assigned to each class who set up the recorder and the microphone for each session and who also took notes on the events occurring in each session, focusing particularly on the things that were of significance for the student-teacher relationships. Both observer and recorder were visible to members of the class, who were informed during the first session that they would be participating in a study carried out by members of the Psychology Department. They were assured of the confidentiality of the material and given an opportunity to switch to another section if they so desired (although no student did). Each student was paid ten dollars for his participation. The observer remained entirely within his role—non-reactive and nonparticipating—throughout the semester.

During the summer and fall of 1965, each observer (who had previously been trained for the task) scored each session of the class he had been observing, using the content-analysis system described above. The scored protocols for each group, as they were punched onto IBM cards for later analysis, comprise the core data generated in this study.

Since this study was exploratory, it did not seem appropriate to preselect students into the sections; indeed, prior to defining typologies or significant interpersonal vectors in the classroom, one would be hard pressed to decide on the most valid or interesting criteria on which to select students so as to maximize variability of behavior in the classroom. Moreover, students had some 33 sections to choose from in taking the course, and since all the teachers were relatively new, word of their teaching ability or attractiveness had not yet penetrated the student subculture; therefore it is highly likely that the students in our sample were representative of the population

[1] We gratefully acknowledge the assistance of Messrs. Jeffrey Binder, John Hartman, Douglas McClennen, and Mrs. Barbara Newman in this task.

of students taking the course. And, since Psychology 101 is elected by an overwhelming majority of freshmen and sophomores in the University, these students were probably representative of the student population at Michigan during the time of the study (Spring, 1965).

Beyond the scoring of the member-leader interaction, we collected and analyzed other data from the teacher and students. Each observer interviewed the teacher of the class he was watching, usually at one-week intervals, and interviewed nearly all of the students in that class toward the end of the term. In addition, the students were asked to complete four sets of paper-and-pencil questionnaires. Data were collected once before the term began and then every three weeks for a total of five administrations; other instruments were used at the end of the term; and, finally, four-fifths of the students filled out forms two years after the end of the course.

The various instruments are presented in Appendix A. They include: (1) a number of rating scales used prior to, during, and after the term which describe the students' perceptions of his teacher, the course, himself, other students, etc.; (2) The Interpersonal Outcome Inventory (IOI); (3) the course evaluation form, including a metaphor checklist; (4) the Follow-up Questionnaire used two years later; and (5) the standardized questions used in interviewing the students.

The Search for Underlying Factors

The member-leader scoring system does an adequate job of defining and scanning the affective domain, but we would be less than satisfied with the descriptive job it would permit us to do if we had to use all 16 categories to form our estimate of how the teacher or the student was feeling on a given day. Keeping track of 16 different dimensions at once is a difficult task, and in any case we would soon find that (a) we were "forgetting about" several categories as if to say that some categories seemed redundant and (b) some of our most interesting descriptions were based not on single categories but on pairs or patterns of many categories. Thus we would soon be keeping track of dozens of such composite attributes as ambivalence, the expression *and* denial of anxiety, acceptance *without* dependency, etc. The human mind is marvelously equipped for apprehending patterns, but we can do better than let these patterns multiply without limit and without objective justification for their prolif- eration. We can and should change our descriptive level from the 16 categories to the patterns of categories or dimensions we shall present as factors, the output of a statistical technique known as factor analysis. Perhaps a few words are in order about what, in our view, factor analysis can and cannot accomplish.

The basic idea underlying factor analysis is that any measure, no matter how descriptive and interesting in its own right, may be viewed as reflecting some pattern of presumably more basic or funda- mental attributes. Cattell (1946) has distinguished between *surface* traits, for which the categories would be the relevant analogue, and *source* traits, to which the factors sought in these analyses would be analogous. We shall use the terms phenotypic and genotypic in a similar manner to describe the categories and factors, respectively. The argument here would be that two feelings that are shown to go together may be viewed as phenotypic manifestations of some common, underlying affective process.

If Expressing Anxiety were found to be positively related to Ex- pressing Depression, as in a previous study (Mann, 1967), we might then conclude that both categories are, at least in part, reflections of a more basic or genotypic dimension called distress. Before pur- suing the actual data on the feelings of teachers or students, however, it is important to specify the two kinds of genotypic processes in terms of which we shall attempt to understand our factors: the situa- tional and the historical determinants of the observed feelings.

The situation may be such that given, for example, the particular task and structural realities, certain feelings have positive or negative associations with one another. To take one such case, we have found in this study that for the teachers to be dominant is inversely related to their tendency to be scored as Resisting and Accepting, two feel- ings that are, in turn, positively related to one another. On close examination it turned out that Showing Dominance (and talking a great deal of the time) are characteristic of the lecture style em- ployed on some days, whereas both Accepting and Resisting are characteristic of a more reactive discussion style employed on other days. The covariation of agreeing and disagreeing observed in the classroom might not be found elsewhere, but in this situation the genotypic dimension of lecturing versus discussing turns out to be of considerable importance.

The second class of genotypes that we must consider in trying to explain the observed covariation of two or more categories has to do with previously learned associations between feelings and between the several modes by which feelings may be expressed. For example, we find in this classroom study, as we did in an earlier study of more intense and volatile classroom groups (Mann, 1967), that for the students, Guilt Inducing and Showing Dependency are positively related to one another. Might this fact reflect some underlying genotypic process deriving from each student's prior contact with authority figures? There are indications that one antecedent of this pattern of dependency and complaining is a sense that authorities can be disappointingly weak. From these and other data we are led, then, to think about the personal histories of the group members out of which come interpersonal styles and predispositions that affect their perceptions and feelings in the classroom. This conviction is strengthened by additional evidence which indicates that Guilt Inducing in the very same set of classrooms is also, in the context of another factor, positively related to Showing Counterdependency. Evidently the classroom situation, while it produced disappointment in some, produced another genotypic process, which might be called rebellion or challenge, that is particularly active in other students or on other occasions.

The two genotypic processes, situational and historical, are hopelessly intertwined in most cases, but our effort in this discussion has been simply to alert the reader that neither explanatory set will do all the necessary work. A reasonable expectation about what factor analyses can yield, given the data in terms of 16 categories, is that we may learn from the covariation among the categories how individuals, influenced and constrained as they are by the major interpersonal styles available to members of this society, manage to organize the feelings that they are experiencing within the additional constraint of a particular task situation.

It must be evident that we are not likely in this study to emerge, as might those using factor analysis to study the dimensions of human abilities, with "invariant" dimensions applicable to any social situation. Our hopes are more modest. After appropriate statistical operations on the "going-togetherness" of the 16 categories, we can hope for three kinds of gains over the situation that obtains when we use simply the original set of categories. First, we shall have some greater sense of how the 16 categories go together. For example, we have found in this study that Expressing Anxiety and Expressing Depression do not, in fact, go together in any way that would cause us to invoke, for these data, any such genotypic process as distress; however, Expressing Anxiety does turn out to be positively related to Showing Dependency and negatively related to Identifying, which makes us wonder what kind of genotypic process could exist such that indentifying with the teacher turns out to define one end of a dimension while anxiety and dependency define the other end. More of that later; for now it is sufficient to indicate that factor analysis raises a whole series of questions as to why certain categories go together in a positive or a negative fashion.

If that were our only interest, however, the zero order correlation matrix would answer such questions in a perfectly satisfactory fashion. The second yield of factor analysis, not available from an inspection of the correlation matrix, involves an appreciation of the several meanings of a single category depending on the context in which it occurs. Each factor or dimension specifies several categories that go together to define the positive end of a dimension and, if bipolar, another set of categories defines the negative end of the dimension.

To take an example from the teacher's behavior, Showing Dominance turns out in this study to suggest three underlying processes, each of which is statistically independent of the others. One variant of the teacher's dominance occurs when the teacher talks a great deal, seems quite preoccupied with the content material, and scores relatively low on the categories indicative of a responsive, close teaching style. Variation one amounts essentially to a lecturing style within which dominance has its first meaning. The second context within which Showing Dominance occurs provides no evidence about what else is present, only evidence about what is absent. Dominance, in this factor, is the opposite of a somewhat hostile and depressed performance, and our task becomes one of understanding dominance in this sense, as an alternative to or escape from a certain bitterness and discouragement. The third factor or gestalt of feelings within which we find Showing Dominance suggests that dominance, in the context now of Resistance, is the opposite of two categories (Identifying and Showing Independence) which convey a kind of collegial and informal relationship. In the later sections of this chapter we shall discuss each of these factors. Our point here is that one value of factor analysis lies precisely in this kind of unraveling process wherein one can sense the several functions and meanings of a single category by learning about the several contexts within which it is likely, or unlikely, to occur. Showing Dominance turns out to indicate (a) a highly active or lecturing style, (b) a lifting of the depressive and discouraged feelings to which teachers are prone, and (c) a kind of distance or formality vis-à-vis the students. It all depends on whether one, two, or all of the three contexts are operative at the time.

The third advantage of factor analysis is that one is able to make the number of variables more manageable, to reduce the dimensionality of one's total set of measures. In questionnaire construction, where one might reduce several hundred items to five or ten factors, this is of enormous importance, but in our data this advantage is of less relevance. It is true that graphing or otherwise manipulating 16 categories could become burdensome, but our analyses yielded seven factors for both the teacher and the students. The savings are not enormous, and we feel that the gains derivable from the two sets of seven factors flow primarily from our ability to capture and estimate in quantitative terms at least some of the important underlying patterns of feelings.

Factor analysis of the 16 categories, whether for teachers or students, begins with the intercorrelations of the categories. What must be determined before one can calculate the intercorrelations is what constitutes a data-point, a segment of observed behavior which is the basic unit of the total population of data points. The time segment

Table 2-1

Dimensions of Teacher Behavior

			Factors				
Categories	I	II	III	IV	V	VI	VII
1 Moving Against		− −					
2 Resisting	++		−				
3 Withdrawing				−	++		
4 Guilt Inducing				++			
5 Making Reparation		−		++			
6 Identifying	−		++	−			
7 Accepting	++			−			
8 Moving Toward							++
9 Dominance	−	++	− −				
10 Independence			++				
11 Counterdominance						++	++
12 Expressing Anxiety				+	++		
13 Denying Anxiety					++	+	
14 Self-esteem					++		
15 Expressing Depression		− −					−
16 Denying Depression		− −					
17 Percent Teacher	− −						

chosen as the basis for these factor analyses was that period of time within which both the teacher and the group, taken as a whole, initiated 20 scorable acts. The 20-20 segment was chosen as the smallest unit of time for which stable enough data were available on both the teachers and the students, and the preference for the smallest possible time span reflected our sense that as the time span increased, dynamically disparate elements would be thrown together and thus obscure the underlying interpersonal processes.

Each factor analysis was based on a total, after pooling the data from all four groups,[1]* of 582 20-20 segments. For the factor analysis of the teacher's behavior, a 17th variable was added: the percentage of the acts in the segment initiated by the teacher relative to the total acts of the teacher plus the students. It is labeled $\%T$. Seven factors were extracted and rotated from each set of data.[2]

Tables 2-1 and 2-2 show in schematic form the major and minor loadings of each variable on the seven factors. In these cryptic sum-

Table 2-2

Dimensions of Student Behavior

	Factors						
Categories	I	II	III	IV	V	VI	VII
1 Moving Against					++		
2 Resisting		— —					
3 Withdrawing			+			— —	
4 Guilt Inducing	—				++		
5 Making Reparation				++			
6 Identifying	++	+					
7 Accepting						++	
8 Moving Toward				—		+	++
9 Dependence	— —						—
10 Independence	++						
11 Counterdependency		++			+		
12 Expressing Anxiety	— —						
13 Denying Anxiety			++				
14 Self-esteem							++
15 Expressing Depression				++			
16 Denying Depression			++				

* Here and below numbered footnotes refer to the Methodological Footnotes in Appendix A where a more technical description of methodological procedures can be found.

maries we have in effect reduced the complexity of the full factor matrix to an indication of (a) the direction of the relationship (+ or −) and (b) the magnitude of the loading (where ++ or −− indicate loadings beyond +.40 or −40, + or − indicates loadings from +.30 to +.39 or −.30 to −.39, and no entry indicates loadings from +.29 to −.29). The first factor for the teachers, for example, has major positive loadings from two categories, Resisting and Accepting, and has a major negative loading from %T and a minor negative loading from Showing Dominance and Identifying. The question now is how, other than through the not entirely unknown procedure of "free associating" to the array of titles of variables with major positive and negative loadings, we can come to understand the genotypic process.

After extracting the seven teacher and the seven student factors, what we did was to attempt to retrace our steps and identify the segments that best exemplified the positive and negative ends of each dimension. In order to accomplish this we needed to estimate how each segment would "score" on each of the 14 factors. Factor estimates were calculated,[3] and we then located from eight to 12 segments which were very high and a similar number which were very low on a given factor and were at the same time in the medium range on all other factors. We then returned to the tape recordings of these segments in order to determine the content, tone, and interpersonal dynamics of the particular segments. Our analysis of each factor will begin with a resumé of the particular categories with positive and negative loadings on the factor in question, but we shall then indicate in more qualitative terms what characterizes the most representative segments at each end of the pole. Finally, we shall summarize our impression of the major genotypic processes reflected in the factors that emerged from these analyses.

Teacher Factor I

I+	I−
Reaction	*Proaction*
Major positive loadings	*Major negative loading*
Resisting	Percent Teacher
Accepting	
	Minor negative loadings
	Showing Dominance
	Identifying

The most salient aspect of Reaction, the positive pole of Teacher Factor I, is that the teacher accounts for fewer of the acts than is usual; that is, the students do a higher proportion of the talking. Many of the teacher's comments are direct responses to student acts, a fact indicated by the importance of his Accepting-Resisting style in the segments that scored highest on this factor. The distinguishing quality of Reaction is a high degree of interplay among the participants in the classroom.

In Proaction, the other pole of this factor, most of the talking is done by the teacher. We find fewer Accepting and Resisting responses to the students, a reduction accompanied by an emphasis on dominance and identification. The dominance in Proaction is primarily that which we associate with an expert's lecture. Similarly adapted to a lecture model is the Identifying found here, represented, for instance, by the "we" in "where we seemed to be going in the last session leads me to say some things about. . . ." By acting in this way the teacher presumes, often without checking the degree to which it corresponds to reality, that he and the students are striding off into the unknown with roughly equal amounts of curiosity and task orientation. More often than not, the scoring sheets from segments that had extreme scores on Proaction include page after page of lecturing. The teacher carries on a monologue, proceeding by reacting to his own statements.

While the Proaction end of this factor denotes processes that are quite similar from one classroom to the next, Reaction denotes processes that differ somewhat across the four classrooms. In some classrooms there were long student-led discussions with no more than an occasional addition or suggestion from the teacher. In others, the highest degree of interplay consisted in the teacher's questioning the students or vice versa with little interaction among the students themselves. In studying the developmental history of the classroom, however, we can ask the same key question in all four cases. Why does the teacher during some specific periods of time switch to a style that allows more interplay than does the extreme of Proaction?

As one can imagine, there are innumerable considerations that may combine to nudge a teacher in one direction or the other along the Reaction-Proaction continuum. A proactive style, for example, may reflect a teacher's fears that were the students to get the floor, they would attack his methods and ideas or subvert progress via naïve comments or inane detours. At other times, however, we find the teacher lecturing because, for one reason or another, he had been unable to involve students in the reactive discussion he would have preferred. Or, still again, Proaction may indicate that the teacher feels he has something especially valuable to impart which he can best put across in a monologue.

The considerations that make the teacher move toward a reactive style as more comfortable or effective are similarly variegated. The teacher may, for example, feel a need to discover where the students stand either in regard to their depth of understanding of the material or their feeling about what has been happening in the classroom. He may also want to involve the students in the subject by getting them to think and speak actively about it or to foster their feelings of competence and excitement in reaching conclusions under their own steam.

Although there are inevitably some students who are anxious to talk more and others who would rather have the teacher lecture, the formal authority vested in the teacher gives him the final power to decide between reactive and proactive classroom styles. Usually he will alternate easily between them as the need strikes him. But this same decision can be responsible for major structural changes which propose to give one style long-term supremacy. For example, the teacher of Class B spent the 11th session presenting a plan whereby everyone would sit in a circle and students would be appointed to lead discussions. This plan was adopted and the next nine sessions score as highly reactive. By the end of this period, there was a general feeling that more structure was needed, and the teacher formally announced the beginning of a proactive lecture phase.

SOME REACTION SEGMENTS

1. A discussion among the students regarding child rearing continues for several minutes. When some confusion arises, Mr. B breaks in to pull a few of the threads together and to criticize some of the comments the students have made.

2. In the midst of a lecture on genetics, a number of students besiege the teacher with questions and criticisms. Mr. C replies to each of them, amending and broadening some of his previous statements in the process. He then proceeds with the lecture, but in the process asks questions and obtains answers more frequently to assure himself that the class is following his presentation.

SOME PROACTION SEGMENTS

1. It is late in the first session. Mr. B is explaining procedural and formal details and responding to infrequent requests for clarifica-

tion from the students. He then launches into a 20-minute explication of his plans for the class.

2. Mr. D is giving a long lecture about the use of scientific method in the social science. Just before the hour ends, the students ask some questions about the details of the assignment.

Teacher Factor II

II+	II—
Role Satisfaction	*Role Dissatisfaction*
Major positive loading	*Major negative loadings*
Showing Dominance	Denying Depression
	Expressing Depression
	Moving Against
	Minor negative loading
	Making Reparation

The hallmark of the segments that scored low on Factor II is the teacher's dissatisfaction with the state of affairs in the classroom. The two high loadings on depression reflect not only the teacher's frustration but also his inclination to blame himself for either causing or being unable to alter the discouraging state of affairs. An additional tendency to shift the blame to the students shows up in the large loading on Moving Against and the concomitant reparation for hostility expressed or felt.

Many things depress teachers and shake their confidence. Often, a whole set of antecedent conditions may be found together, signifying a pervasive failure of communication or lack of any consensus about goals. One such antecedent is the apparent inability of students to grasp and apply concepts and viewpoints which seem quite natural to their instructors. This can raise grave doubts in teachers about their ability to put ideas across and to judge accurately the needs of their students. It forces instructors to review hopes and schedules in midstream. On the other hand, the instructor may be tempted to suspect the students of laziness, passive aggression, or even crippling stupidity.

Other problems that arise frequently are more directly traceable to conflicting aims of the parties in the classroom. One is a tendency for the students' concerns about grades and tests to overshadow other elements of classroom life. The teacher feels himself cast as a distant ogre and may see the students as timeservers totally uninterested in what he has to offer. Another is that students in these classes are seldom as independent as instructors might have desired; they often favor passive intake of knowledge over any more active role in their own educations. At the other extreme, too much student independence leads, on occasion, to fears on the teacher's part that he is losing control of the class and that time is being wasted in fruitless discussion.

In classroom situations where the teacher experiences frustration and communication breaks down, he may be led into fantasies and actions which are self-contradictory and harmful to his chances of improving the situation. Rather than attempting to discover the true level of student understanding, he may imagine at one and the same time that his students do not understand him at all *and* that they are waiting to demolish every argument he makes. He may become so defensive toward criticism that he is unable to use the information it conveys in his attempts to resolve the problems which impede progress. He may inspire distrust by soliciting student suggestions as to how to improve the class only to treat these same suggestions as attacks which must be strongly countered.

During periods of Role Dissatisfaction, the teacher appears to doubt his ability to play the many roles that are part of his job. As an expert in his field, he feels he has nothing to say or is unable to communicate what he does have to say. He may feel he uses his authority too harshly or too weakly, or both, but at different moments. Filled with self doubts and facing an unresponsive or contentious class, he is especially unable to present himself as a model for emulation or to transmit his enthusiasm and involvement in his field.

It would be incorrect, incidentally, to think that the teacher's dissatisfaction is always completely evident either to himself or to the students. The importance of the category of Denying Depression is one indicator of the teacher's frequent attempts to suppress or ignore disruptive feelings when Role Dissatisfaction is present. Many of these segments roll by with no more indication that things are amiss than a dull note in the teacher's voice or an infrequent sarcastic remark. In other segments dissatisfaction may be hidden by forced joking or a feverish involvement with strictly intellectual material.

The segments drawn from the Role Satisfaction pole of this factor contrast with the bleakness of the picture just drawn. Depression, hostility, and reparation are low, and in their place one finds a high concentration of self-confidence and effective teaching. The positive loading on Showing Dominance indicates that the teacher is able to impart his knowledge or use his position to regulate the flow of the class without arousing his own fears of being sadistic, demanding, overpersonal, etc. His confidence high and his negative feelings toward the class eased, the teacher is free to stimulate vicarious excitement and involvement by letting students identify with his own experiences. The teachers seem generally relaxed in these segments and show a great deal more warmth toward the classes. They seem to enjoy the activity of teaching and to be genuinely concerned about what the students learn.

SOME ROLE SATISFACTION SEGMENTS

1. Mr. C is lecturing about psychological factors in the selection of marriage partners. He sounds relaxed and unhurried. One gets the impression that he is a married man helpfully explaining some of the phenomena of marriage to some friends who have not encountered them yet.

2. Under the leadership of one of the students, the class is discussing the psychosexual development of children. One student asks for clarification of a point and Mr. B explains it in detail, using the blackboard. The discussion is taken up again after he has finished. There is a smooth flow of interaction throughout the segment.

SOME ROLE DISSATISFACTION SEGMENTS

1. Mr. D is reviewing and summarizing an assignment on learning theory. His style in this segment involves asking questions as he goes along, but the students consistently fail to come up with the correct answers. As this process continues, his behavior shows increasing signs of weariness and depression. At one point, he is discussing a study done with problem solving in monkeys and asks how a problem was solved. There is a long uneasy silence. Finally, he says, "Come on, people. The monkeys were able to solve it."

2. There is to be an hour exam the next session, and both the teacher and the students are nervous. Mr. C is lecturing quickly, laughing, and joking a good deal. The students do not seem to understand the material very well. Mr. C appears bothered by this and unhappy about the emphasis the students place on the exam. At one point, after making an elaborate joke to illustrate a concept, he says, "If you don't get this you're in trouble. Any dramatic effect will do." He makes a number of comments to the effect of "Don't make a big deal out of this test." Then, to illustrate the conception of interaction effect, he remarks that an authoritarian personality would dislike a democratic teacher like himself.

Teacher Factor III

III+	III−
Colleague	*Formality*
Major positive loadings	*Major negative loadings*
Identifying	Showing Dominance
Showing Independence	*Minor negative loading*
	Resisting

The issue here is one of relative status and contrasting types of leadership. In the Colleague factor pattern, the teacher treats the students as equals and identifies with them. His classroom style in this situation casts him as a *primus inter pares* or even a co-explorer of the uncharted realms of psychology. There are other times, however, when the teacher acts somewhat distant and superior; in the segments with high scores on Formality, he tends to play more the part of the experienced guide than the role of co-explorer. We are left with the impression of a great difference in status between the teacher and the class. At the extreme, he resembles the boss or overseer.

Embedded in the polarity of this factor is the issue of ownership or responsibility in the classroom. A class in which the students are considered colleagues is to some extent "owned" by the students. They are apt to have more say in the directions and the content taken up. They will feel that they deserve some credit for a good class and that they bear some of the responsibility for improving a bad one. In an arrangement where the teacher functions as a formal supervisor, however, he will "own" the classroom and determine what the proper goals should be.

As with the Reaction factor pattern, the Colleague factor pattern differs in content from teacher to teacher. There are teachers who often treat students as academic equals and leave many of the decisions affecting the classroom situation in students' hands. For other teachers, acting as a colleague is no more than a slight unbending from a consistently formal style. Nonetheless, the teacher is always more informal and egalitarian on the Colleague end of the factor than on the Formality end.

At the extreme of the Colleague factor, we find the teacher who is willing to accept whatever the students happen to bring up as defining the subject matter for that day. The primary functions of this teacher center on facilitating the students' journey along paths of their own choosing, although this may occasionally expand to include presenting relevant vignettes from his own experience for the students to ponder as they consider the subject at hand. At the extreme of Formality, on the other hand, is the teacher who chooses the paths for initiating the class into the mysteries of a subject that he knows best. The issue of authority is especially pivotal for this factor pattern. A teacher trying to work his way into a Colleague relationship tends to play down the authority aspect of his role, while a teacher moving toward Formality stresses it in various ways.

The existence of Factor III helps us to distinguish two polarities which seem to be easily confused by new teachers. These are Formality-Colleague and Proaction-Reaction. At first thought one might think that discussions are bound to be less formal than lectures. Our data reveal that there is no anomaly in having a discussion presided over by a teacher whose stance is distant or superior or in having a lecture presented to people who are viewed by the teacher as colleagues. As we shall see later, teachers sometimes become considerably less proactive without effecting any changes in their underlying formality and distance from the students.

SOME COLLEAGUE SEGMENTS

1. Some students are attempting to figure out what pair of them will prepare some material for a future class. After they hit a few snags, Mr. B attempts to facilitate a resolution, for example "Libby, do you think it would be at all possible to work things out over the telephone?" They reject his solution and work out one they like better.

2. Mr. C is eagerly questioning Ken who has returned from a civil rights march in Alabama. After Ken makes some remarks about police brutality, the teacher launches into a story about his experience with some incredibly authoritarian state troopers. It is a long funny story which he tells in a quite informal manner.

3. A student is giving a lecture on infancy. At one point, Mr. B breaks in, apologizing, "Gee, I hate to interrupt, but I've just got to tell you about this thing that happened the other day." He relates a story about a baby he had observed over a period of time.

SOME FORMALITY SEGMENTS

1. Mr. C is handing back a test. He compliments the class liberally on their performance and then explains some of his grading. The students raise some objections, which he attempts to meet.

2. Mr. D is lecturing on perception and asking occasional questions as he goes. The students grope for the right answers. He tells

them if they are correct or not. He is the only person in the class who can claim to know the subject at all well.

Teacher Factor IV

IV+	IV−
Punitiveness	*Low Punitiveness*
Major positive loadings Guilt Inducing Making Reparation	
Minor positive loading Expressing Anxiety	*Minor negative loadings* Identifying Accepting Withdrawing

Punitiveness is an example of a unipolar factor. Rather than providing us with two distinct, opposed patterns, it allows us to speak only of the presence or absence of a particular aspect of the teacher's total repertoire. Thus the score of a segment on Factor IV is simply a measure of the extent to which the teacher acts punitively in that segment.

Guilt Inducing has by far the highest loading on this factor and is the most evident aspect of the high scoring segments. In these interchanges, the teacher berates the students for doing something wrong. He occasionally apologizes for doing this, insisting that he is generally pleased with the students despite his criticism. The teacher's discomfort in Guilt Inducing finds expression in his anxiety and in the relative brevity of such bursts. The tension aroused in the teacher during these segments is apparently hard to sustain, and an outburst of Punitiveness tends to be followed rather quickly by a switch into Role Dissatisfaction or some other factor pattern.

The tension involved is not too hard to understand. A number of students have failed to meet some goal that the teacher has set; for example, they may be espousing their prejudices rather than dealing with material on a scientific basis or may have failed to complete reading assignments. The teacher is attracted to using the powerful manipulating force of guilt to pull and push them toward attaining the unfulfilled goals but is restrained by other considerations from giving full reign to this tendency. One such consideration is the drop in his own self-esteem when he realizes that he is actually making the students feel badly. This is accompanied by fears that Guilt Inducing will destroy all possibility for future rapport. Another factor in his restraint is the knowledge that the students might not accept his assessment and might, instead, attempt to pass the blame for classroom deficiencies back to him.

Although it is reasonable to surmise that classroom conditions are far from optimal during periods of high in Punitiveness, it is perhaps less obvious that Guilt-Inducing occasionally represents an advance for the teacher. It is a fact, however, that many new teachers shoulder a disproportionate amount of blame for a lack of work in the classroom. They have themselves spent long years as students and have a lingering empathy for the common student strategy of avoiding work whenever possible. Besides, lack of experience and uncertainty as to professional skill make it very easy for the new teacher to feel that he himself is responsible for the students' failings. If students seem apathetic, he may feel he has driven them off with uninspired teaching or a poor performance in the matter of setting requirements.

In such an atmosphere, it may indicate a real gain in self-confidence for the teacher to remind the students that they, too, have some obligations to meet. Teachers in our sample chose varying times to do this. Some punitive segments occur at the beginning of sessions, indicating, perhaps, that the teacher had spent some time thinking about the issue of student responsibilities in the period between classes. At other times, internal constraints against being punitive were overcome by the teacher's need to defend himself against attack. For example, Mr. B's most punitive segment came after a student told him that a book he had assigned was "really horrible."

Since Punitiveness is accompanied by a tendency on the teacher's part to emphasize his standards of excellence, it is not surprising to find a diminished tendency here for the teacher to encourage student independence. The teacher is likely to place more stress on the students' acquiring familiarity with established norms and methodology than on their attempts to make progress on their own initiative.

We have noted that the low pole of Factor IV is defined primarily by an absence of this punitive syndrome. The largest of the negative factor loadings suggest that when teachers act less punitively, they may be more likely to identify with the students, accept what they say, and withdraw from confrontations.

SOME PUNITIVE SEGMENTS

1. In the session after an hour exam, students are arguing about the teacher's grading of a multiple-choice question.

> *Toby:* "It's a distinct possibility that the Negro has these genes."
>
> *Mr. C:* "Did you state that it's a distinct possibility? Because the vast majority of people stated very simply that Negroes are inferior to whites in I.Q."

Later, when one student refers to the fact that the teacher earlier had stated that their opinions were welcome, Mr. C replies, "What is the purpose of my giving you information if you don't use it? If I wanted your opinions, I would say, OK class, now we're going to do nothing for the next six weeks but sit around and listen to your opinions."

2. Mr. D is expressing his irritation over the giggling reaction of the audience to a lecture on Freudian elements in the story of Cinderella. He says, "What is it that bothers you people so much about hearing these things about childhood? I think you should ask yourself that question." And later, "I think one goal of psychology is facing these things in yourself."

Teacher Factor V

V+

Apprehension

Major positive loadings
Withdrawing
Denying Anxiety
Expressing Anxiety

Here we have another factor with significant loadings on only one pole. Withdrawing, an infrequently scored category, shows up far more often in high pole segments of Factor V than in the low ones. Anxiety either denied or expressed adds the remaining flavoring.

One gets the impression in listening to those segments high in Apprehension that there is some subsurface friction which may or may not break into open confrontation at any moment. The fact that the teacher resorts to occasional acts of Withdrawing does not necessarily mean that he is fleeing this encounter. Not flight but ambivalence about which way to move is characteristic of this mode. Perhaps the confrontation is necessary in that the underlying tension can be borne no longer. On the other hand, it is seen as potentially painful and apt to get out of control. The withdrawing illustrates only one side of the tension and may be more of a passing gesture than a real moving away.

When and why do some potential confrontations cause such anxiety and avoidance? One of the most common situations occurs when there have been ambiguous indications of student apathy or discontent. The teacher may want to ask the students precisely what they dislike or want changed, but he is afraid that their criticism might be unanimously harsh and personally painful or that it may lead to frustrating impasses. This is particularly true early in the term when the expressions on the faces of the new students represent unknown qualities and there has been no chance to build up bonds of mutual respect and trust within which criticism can be more easily tolerated.

Another potentially explosive issue in psychology classes arises in dealing with sexual or other emotion-arousing material. It seems that too personal or explicit a discussion arouses fear of the class' becoming hopelessly bogged down, frightened, or entangled, while failing to deal fully with such issues might take the emotional impact out of education and leave unresolved tensions. Again, we find an implicit threat to the teacher's control and the possibility that the classroom will become too personal for comfort. Therefore, instead of meeting the underlying problems head on, the teacher skirts their edges, first approaching a bit closer, then withdrawing for awhile on some convenient tangent. His performance presents the listener at times with an almost teasing quality as he builds toward confrontation and then subsides again. He may eventually precipitate consideration of the issue, or perhaps some student will, or else the class will somehow lead in a different direction and the issue will lose its immediacy. But for the time being, the teacher remains anxiously on the periphery, unable to take firm steps in either direction.

One point to note is that while potentially devastating issues present themselves more or less sharply in nearly every class session, the teacher only rarely falls into the cycles of anxious approach and avoidance which characterize this factor pattern. On some days he will straightforwardly either put off or deal with problems which create the greatest apprehension in others. As we have noted, one simple determinant of such behavior is how well he knows the students. This is only one of many factors contributing to the crucial issue of how strong and confident the teacher feels on the day in question.

SOME APPREHENSION SEGMENTS

1. Mr. A has been covering the educational theories of Bruner and Skinner. It is obvious that he is mentally comparing his own

teaching to their standards as he lectures, and after some hesitation he asks the class how one could improve the teaching of psychology according to the ideas of these men. The class seems more than willing to avoid the immediate implications of this question, as the first two or three students talk about teaching mathematics. Finally, Norma suggests that the class should be given more initiative and that he should allow them to hold discussions without interference. He very quickly and anxiously replies by asking the class, "What do you think?" When Dale affirms that he finds the teacher's guidance necessary, Mr. A becomes less anxious and begins supporting Norma's ideas, though on a rather abstract level.

2. A discussion of myths has led to a discussion of sexual intercourse as an example of how one activity illustrates a number of themes. Mr. C seems nervous and keeps making statements like, "We're way ahead of ourselves in terms of material covered, but keep these things in mind for the future." At one point after the discussion has turned to childhood fantasies, Roger asks if the mind doesn't have some means of blocking all this material. He replies with alacrity, "Yes, certainly, you're quite right. If we had all this stuff on our minds all the time, that would be just horrible. So somehow the idea of a blocking mechanism has to come in." He then postpones answering some other questions and begins lecturing on another topic.

Teacher Factor VI

VI+

Display

Major positive loadings
Expressing Self-esteem
Showing Counterdominance

Minor positive loading
Denying Anxiety

Teacher Factor VI is another unipolar factor pattern. The most relevant category for Display is Expressing Self-esteem, a very infrequently scored category accounting for less than 0.5% of all scores in three of the four classes. When teachers do openly express self-esteem, however, it can color a whole segment. Here we find it linked with counterdominance, indicating the teacher's refusal to play his traditional dominant role, and, less importantly, with the denial of anxiety.

If we could paraphrase what the teacher is saying in these segments, it might sound this way. "I'm willing to let you in on the secret of how great I am." The counterdominance displayed here is often by way of introducing the students to the teacher's inner thought processes, a presentation of the yet-to-be-revealed deftness and competence. The teacher steps outside his role just far enough to reveal that he enjoys being the all-powerful authority, the all-knowing expert, the superperceptive facilitator, or the all-around "cool guy." This seldom occurs with great openness or for any great duration, but it is impressive when found.

As before, we find a variety of situations in which this factor pattern appears. One of these is most commonly found late in the term and carries a note of self-congratulation on the process of the class. The students are working well, things are running smoothly, and the teacher is complimenting both the class and himself for this state of affairs.

When the Display pattern arises earlier in the term, the teacher's motives tend to be somewhat different. One purpose seems to involve an attempt to counter, by means of a public assertion of strength and confidence, the anxiety created by performing in front of a group of indifferent students. Another goal is to avoid the feeling that the students perceive the teacher as a cold, distant, formal authority with no life outside the limitations of his professional role. Besides being uncomfortable about having such a constricted and unaccustomed identity, he may feel that the students would exhibit far more effort and enthusiasm if they could get over seeing him only as a distant teacher figure. To students who are unresponsive, contentious or anxious, or who seem to be full of disabling transferences toward him, the teacher is saying, "Hey, look, I'm not that cardboard figure you think I am. I'm an interesting, three-dimensional person with a life outside this classroom."

Unfortunately, this early strategy can seldom meet the demands the teacher makes on it. The students' problems and concerns have foundations that are too sturdy and complex to be so easily put aside. The students are just as likely to react with suspicion and dislike to the teacher's boasting and his protestation of counterdominance as they are to be reassured by them. And perhaps they are not totally without justification in their suspicion; Display can mask both the teacher's hostility toward the students whose behavior causes him so much distress and his unwillingness to get to know the students well enough to deal more directly with the sources of their distance and their distrust.

Display can also appear simply because the teacher is taking advantage of the centrality of his classroom role to soak up a bit of the limelight. This can be quite enjoyable when the whole class is caught up by a spirit of triumph over some success, but it can leave the teacher feeling foolish if the class fails to respond to his stage-center pirouettes. This, coupled with the lack of success of Display in moving the students toward more work and greater friendliness, may well account for its diminution after the early sessions. When it appears later in the term, it has a more benign appearance; the students share in the teacher's exultation rather than having it thrust at them.

Despite the fact that students may be overwhelmed or angered by Display performances, in the right setting these gestures by the teacher act as a spur to student attempts to imitate the teacher along various dimensions. By acting on his latent narcissism, the teacher presents himself as a person worthy of emulation. Meanwhile, with his counterdominance, he communicates the message that he is not a distant god, but rather a person whom the students can emulate if they wish. While the Display factor includes some of the teachers' less effective efforts, such performances can be important in making the teacher's field and his work exciting and relevant to the students.

SOME DISPLAY SEGMENTS

1. Mr. C is talking about the links between early childhood experiences and adult character. He illustrates his points with a number of stories, most of which bring laughter, for example "Haven't you ever heard one of these guys say, 'I'm going to defecate all over you.' I don't know. Use your own terms." Ray, who appears rather worried about the damage parents can do to their children's personalities, asks, "Well, how do you handle something like toilet training?" The teacher replies that he does not think it is too hard and that "I think in all these cases that flexibility is a key issue. I think you have to be a pretty healthy person yourself." He continues his storytelling and falls behind his lecture plan, but affirms that, "As long as you keep asking questions, which I place as the highest form of teaching, it's all right if we don't cover everything."

2. Mr. B had passed a student on the street and said only the word "bang" to her. Giggling, she confronts him at the start of class to ask "What does 'bang' mean?" He explains to the class, "See, I was walking down South University Saturday afternoon with a bottle of wine in a paper bag and thinking about this class. You know, teachers don't always think one hundred percent benign

thoughts about their classes. And I looked up to see Peggy walking by and. . . ."

3. Mr. D had done an experiment using his class as naive subjects by presenting them with a problem designed to appear as a test question. The question could have been answered by following either of two paths. Now, he has revealed that he never intended to grade the question and tells the students why he thinks so many chose the option they did. He bases his argument on the idea that there was a high degree of fear of failure in the class. Lisa asks why he assumed that this was true, and he replies, "I don't know. It was just my intuitive perception when I handed people this piece of paper and noticed them suddenly go pale."

Teacher Factor VII

VII+	VII−
Warmth	*Low Warmth*
Major positive loadings	*Minor negative loading*
Moving Toward	Expressing Depression
Showing Counterdominance	

Here is a factor pattern dominated by the Moving Toward category. Quite simply, the teacher plays down his dominance and acts in a warm and friendly manner. In addition, we find a tendency for him to express depression less often than usual. The relaxed joking and the warm concern expressed in this pattern may reveal a more personal side to the teacher than is displayed in other classroom interactions.

As with Display, we find some difference in the quality of the Warmth factor depending on the time of its occurrence. In late sessions, it can express accumulated friendliness for people with whom the teacher has been working closely throughout a whole term. In early sessions, it is more an attempt to establish this friendly atmosphere.

Aside from the usual benefits accruing from warmth and friendship, there are special reasons for attempting to create such a climate early in the term. For one thing, the teacher may use Warmth to allay the anxiety and insecurity that many of the students experience when faced with a new classroom situation that is full of unknowns. Another motive can be the teacher's hope of getting the students on his side, so to speak, with a view to their working hard in his class later in the term so as not to let him down. Obviously, warmth will not provide a magical solution to all the concerns which keep a class from optimal functioning. It may, however, provide a start in the right direction if it is followed through by effective teaching which continues to take the students' concerns into account.

SOME WARMTH SEGMENTS

1. Mr. A is using the example of learning the names of the students to illustrate classical conditioning. He suggests that it would help if girls would reward him by smiling when he remembers their names correctly. In trying to lead the class to an independent formulation of conditioning, he says "There are two rules here, and psychologists have worked on them for many years, but I think you'll be able to tell me what they are right off."

2. At the start of a session, there is some mechanical trouble with the tape recorder. "We could turn that monster off," Mr. C tells the class. Then he gives back an assignment, remarking, "You've done a terrific job and should pat yourselves on the back tremendously. I think something like 60 or 70 percent were A's." After he finishes handing them back, he says, "What about that assignment, now that I've buttered you up. I dare you to say it was a lousy assignment."

3. The teacher is drawing X's and O's on the board to illustrate gestaltist theories of perception. When he asks the students to place these symbols into groups, they keep doing it in ways that surprise him. His standard responses to this is "My word, isn't that a surprise?" In answer to a student question as to whether their responses hadn't disproven Wetheimer's theories, the teacher answered, "Yes, and you can just see Wertheimer sitting down and drawing these things on a piece of paper and saying: 'Aha! I've discovered a new perceptual principle. Let's name it.'"

This concludes our account of the factor pattern for the teachers. Before we leave this area and proceed to a consideration of the patterning of student behavior, let us pause for a moment to put our findings into some kind of framework.

The teachers enter a classroom at the start of the term with professional goals of fostering student work and learning and with a variety of personal needs including a desire to be liked and respected and a need to establish an effective professional style. They have some ideas, in advance, of how to achieve these things, but they must be ready to respond to the nature of their particular classes and to learn, as time passes, to develop and refine their methods for reaching these goals. Their conceptions of the goals themselves are also bound, with time, to grow more complex and explicit.

It comes as no surprise, then, that five of our seven teacher factors describe activities that bear directly on the teacher's efforts to insure the kind of relationship and environment in which work can flourish. The two most important of these are the widest and most general, the factors named Reaction-Proaction and Colleague-Formality. Changing scores on either of these factors indicates that the whole framework of process and relationship in the classroom is being re-adjusted to accommodate any of a wide range of perceptions and strategies. The other three factors, Punitiveness, Display, and Warmth, may also be attempts to regulate the flow of interaction, but usually on a less all-encompassing basis than the first two.

Finally, we have two factors that lie more in the direction of the teacher's expression of ego-state. The first of them, Role Satisfaction-Role Dissatisfaction, is particularly useful in that it affords us a quick indication of the teacher's perception of how well the class is progressing toward the goals he holds. The other, Apprehension, picks out for us the pattern of teacher response which implies some lack of confidence and fear of encounter.

These seven factors give us a multidimensional picture of the teacher's apperception of and response to the developing classroom. Now we may move ahead by delineating the seven student factors which round out our descriptive equipment.

Student Factor I

I+	I—
Enactment	*Anxious Dependence*
Major positive loadings	*Major negative loadings*
Showing Independence	Showing Dependency
Identifying	Expressing Anxiety
	Minor negative loading
	Guilt Inducing

The Anxious Dependence pole of the first student factor reveals a fundamentally dependent orientation on the part of the students vis-à-vis the teacher. Experience first with their parents and then with a succession of elementary and secondary school teachers has led most students to various expectations of what a teacher should be: a person existing on a higher plane, doing the leading, taking the responsibility, making the rules, setting the assignments, evaluating, rewarding, punishing, and knowing at least most of the answers. Some of the students' responses to this figure have their origins in the very early family situation; others are adaptations to previous classroom experiences. The students' status as undergraduates at a good university confirms the relative appropriateness of both responses in the past.

The strategy of depending on the knowledge and authority of the teacher can foster a sense of security, but it can also lead to anxiety. The man who is assigned responsibility for the progress of the class is also assuming a great deal of power over the lives of the individuals in it. His assignments set the students running off to the library on evenings and weekends; his tests and grades may have overwhelming practical and symbolic significance. Nominally, the teacher has absolute control over such matters, but actually students are not without weapons in this arena. One that they can use to soften the hand of an authority who seems too strong to attack directly is to induce guilt in him, to imply that he is a heartless ogre if he persists in demanding assignments and harsh judgments. Both Anxiety Expression and Guilt Inducing go hand in hand with Showing Dependency in this factor pattern.

The teacher's capacity to arouse anxiety is not limited to his functions as judge and grader. Let us consider what happens when the teacher seems to be unwilling to take the dominant role which is the complement to the students' dependency. The students have learned to operate successfully by responding dependently to a dominant teacher, but they may well have had scant practice operating in some student-centered modes. The possibility of losing the teacher's protective leadership may be unsettling, as may be the possibility of attaining a new equality and even intimacy with a person in a position of authority. When students feel anxious over these issues, they may again respond by attempting to induce guilt in the instructor. The message may have changed from "You're a cruel and threatening judge" to "You're not teaching us the way you're supposed to," but the pattern of Showing Dependency, Expressing Anxiety, and Guilt Inducing remains intact.

As we shall see with all the student factor patterns, some students are much more likely than others to display a given pattern, and a segment with an extreme score on a factor might be caused as much by a sudden burst of activity from people high on a factor as by a change in the mood of the entire class. These interindividual differences partly depend on previous experience and will vary with such factors as sex of the student and manner of upbringing. With respect to Anxious Dependence, for example, there is little doubt that dependence on a male authority has different meanings for male and female undergraduates. We shall deal with some of these differences in more detail later on.

In some instances, however, the same students display extreme behavior on both poles of a factor. Such was the case in one session in which the teacher was previewing the types of questions to be expected on the final exam. This activity on the teacher's part led to one of the most dependent and anxious performances of the whole term, characterized by a long string of questions starting with the phrase "Will we have to know . . . ?" After answering a number of them, the teacher said, "Let's go back to the discussion about Walden II that we were having last time," and the class responded with a segment that was extreme on the opposite pole of the factor, with the same cast of characters leading the way. It appears that they had learned two distinctly different role relationships, either of which they could assume or discard at will.

One way of moving beyond anxious dependence on an authority is to start acting like him, a mode which we find in evidence at the opposite pole of this factor. This is most clearly seen in a loading on Identifying, and a parallel loading on Showing Independence implies a feeling of equality on the part of the students. Identifying is scored most frequently when the students' style approaches that of the teacher; they may attempt to make their arguments scientifically sound in the manner of the teacher's preferred style, volunteer their own knowledge of relevant material, or even utilize the teacher's peculiarities of phrasing.

We have given this combination of Independence and Identifying the name Enactment, since the students appear to be trying to enact the teacher's role. The concerns that led to Anxious Dependence have been resolved, at least for the moment, and this frees student energy for productive, task-related activities. During periods of high Enactment, the students make progress primarily through the effective use of their own faculties. The teacher's knowledge and experience are no longer the sole source of all enlightenment but, instead, are merely one of the many resources that are available.

SOME ENACTMENT SEGMENTS

1. A discussion concerning the social determinants of perception is in progress among the students. The issue has arisen of why the members of a certain African tribe perceive a rotating trapezoid in a way that is different from civilized Westerners, and students have split into two different positions on the point and are making arguments for one side or the other. Mr. B eventually breaks in, indicating

that he feels he has the correct explanation, but the students treat him as just one more party to the debate. Dave remarks, "Well, if that's the point you're trying to make, I can use the same argument against it as I used against Ned."

2. Mr. C is lecturing on the topic of identification with aggressors and is at first having trouble getting the students to recount any experience of their own as illustrations. Finally, Ken gives an example of Negroes on the Selma march wearing helmets like those of the state troopers. The other students are intrigued by this and start asking him questions about the behavior of the various groups in the march. The discussion runs on without the teacher's participation for some time and is finally cut off by the striking of the clock.

SOME ANXIOUS DEPENDENCE SEGMENTS

1. Mr. B begins a class by complimenting the students on their high level of understanding so far and by saying, "Since you have been assimilating the material so well, I think we can go beyond what we've been doing and try a new format." He then details a plan for future sessions which includes having everyone sit in a circle and having students give short lectures and lead discussions on assigned topics. When he finally asks how the students would feel about such a class, he is greeted with a long, tense silence. Then students begin anxiously questioning him about details, for example, "I don't quite understand the role of the discussant. What exactly do you have in mind?" A typical reaction is that such a class might not prepare the students sufficiently for tests, and Perry asks that the teacher summarize what has been learned at the end of each class.

2. Mr. B is explaining the format that he is planning to use for the final exam. He receives questions and complaints such as the following. "I don't think we'll have enough time." "Are we going to be tested on psychosexual theory?" "If it's going to be multiple choice, don't we have to reread all the articles? I mean, gee, we only have a week left before the exam."

Student Factor II

II+	II−
Consent	*Contention*
Minor positive loading	*Major negative loadings*
Identifying	Resisting
	Showing Counterdependency

The two poles of Factor I do not complete the story of student reaction to the dependency issue. Student Factor II, Consent versus Contention, pivots about the same issue. Students acting in the mode of Contention appear to be made uneasy by dependency, but their reaction is markedly different than that characterized by Anxious Dependency. When students acting in the latter mode were dissatisfied with their relationship to the teacher, they tended to resort to Guilt Inducing. That is, they attempted to force the teacher to be a bit more compassionate within his dominant role. In Contention, however, the students' aim is more in the direction of denying the teacher's right to play this role in the first place.

Students acting in this way exhibit, first, a resistance to much of what the teacher says and, second, a great deal of counterdependence, that is a rejection of the dependent role they feel they are being called on to play. One gets the impressions that much of their discomfort at the thought of being in this role has to do with dissatisfaction at having to submit to a more powerful figure. The road to emulating the teacher's power and prestige is blocked for the moment, perhaps by his hostility or by some clear demonstration of his superiority such as giving a test, perhaps by the students' inability to picture any other stable relationship with him. For these reasons, the students feel they can counter their powerlessness only by contentious self-assertiveness. Many of the segments which have high scores on Contention come in response to some action of the teacher which particularly stresses his dominance. Grading tests, settling assignments, or flouting his superior knowledge of the field are some of the teacher's activities which often trigger contentious responses. While it is no great surprise to find a student reacting this way to having his ideas treated as naive and silly, we often find contention appearing quite in the absence of any such provocation. The explanation for this may well be that the student transfers a generalized resentment of authority onto the particular classroom situation. A relevant example is the experience of Summerhill School in England (Neill, 1960) where it is found that new arrivals often spend their first months rebelling against the democratic staff members as if they were no different from the authoritarian overseers the students had encountered previously.

One thing worth mentioning about the high segment of this factor is that the student actors involved are primarily males. Assertion of strength, denial of weakness, and competitition for dominance are salient issues for males, particularly those at the age level of the students. Various reasons for this might be adduced: that competing for positions in a pecking order is part of man's animal heritage, that males replay Oedipal dramas in relation to male authority figures, and so on. At any rate, many male students seem unwilling to accept much domination by a male teacher, especially one only a few years older than they are. The teacher may be himself attracted by the challenge of competitive play in which he holds a favored position. The teacher's enjoyment of his dominant position seems occasionally threatened by the possibility that all the students will unite against him in a powerful alliance, and he may sometimes be seen testing out his strength to convince all parties of the sturdiness of his power.

It should not be thought that females never engage in Contention, but they do seem more often to play the part of a relevant audience in the jockeying for position among the males. One interesting case that we noted occurred when a female student who had acquiesced to the teacher's argument on a certain point suddenly found several males defending the cause that she had given up.

Another point to note is that the students do not seem to envisage a total victory in their battle. They may force the teacher into displaying a new respect or changing some exam scoring, but they do not really expect to break his authority over them. Strong denial of dependence may be used to cover some hidden desire for it, and some students appear to depend on having an authority there to contend with. A true expectation of independence and responsibility seldom has such a protesting ring to it.

The classroom situation at the consent pole of this factor is considerably more peaceful, with Resisting and Showing Counterdependency being at a low ebb. The only category association with this pole is a minor loading on Identifying and, in this respect, it somewhat resembles Enactment. However, the positive loading on Showing Independence and the negative loading on Showing Dependence that were associated with Enactment are both missing. Students here are more willing to allow some degree of dominance to a teacher with whom they identify. We detect more harmony as to goals between teacher and class and more student consent for the teacher's leadership.

SOME CONTENTION SEGMENTS

1. Mr. D has been asking questions to assure that the class is familiar with Riesman's three models for insuring social conformity. He asks, "Can someone give me an example of an other-directed university?" After Morton suggests that a school with many fraternities would fit the bill, he asks, "How about the University of Michigan?"

"Not all of it," he protests.

"Yes, why not? It bears a great similarity to Reisman's description."

Several students defend their school by averring that there are, after all, several real individuals on the campus. "How can you make a generalization about as many people as there are here?" asks Floyd.

"You were perfectly willing to make a generalization about 700 million people in contemporary India," he reminds them.

"Well, I think it is probably easier to make that generalization about India."

"Well, I think that is probably true because you don't know quite as much about India as you do about the University."

2. Mr. B is lecturing about conditioning and being rather condescending about the students' inability to grasp it easily. He takes as an example his own power to condition the class, for example, "I can reward you every time you talk and the result will be that we'll have a great deal of class response." Two boys argue about terms for awhile, but he manages to convince them that he is right. Then Eve confesses that she still doesn't understand. He tries to explain classical conditioning by using the example of teaching her to read: "First, I reward you every time you pick up the book, like 'Yes, Miss Hayes, you're holding it upside down. Very good!'" Lou breaks in angrily to say "That's not classical conditioning at all. That's operant." When the teacher hems and haws, Tom continues to press his argument that Mr. B's entire presentation has been wrong.

3. After a test, Mr. C is reviewing multiple choice answers. He comes to an example about a boy who, raised apart from his siblings, tested 210 in I.Q. "Twelve of you missed this one. What threw people off?" Ross begins to argue that an alternative choice also explains the phenomenon very well. For every sentence of his, the teacher has five in his own defense. Finally he admits that Peter's explanation is possible although rather more roundabout than his own. "Look," he says, "I'm going to write bad items. Let's not kid ourselves. But I think you're making the kind of inferences that require stretching when you can answer it by making minimal inferences." When Peter continues adamantly claiming that he has been wronged, the teacher argues, "OK, how many people have 210 I.Q.'s? How many of you have 210 I.Q.'s? Raise your hands." The discussion is finally cut off by the end of the period, but its consequences may be found in the session that has been reproduced in Chapter 3.

A CONSENT SEGMENT

1. Mr. B begins a session by saying that he has just a few details to cover before he turns the class over to a student panel. Among them is his preview of the material to be covered on an approaching test. Students ask a couple of questions about details, but seem neither anxious nor argumentative. Then the teacher declares himself finished, and the members of the student panel introduce their presentation.

Student Factor III

III+

Concealment

Major positive loadings
Denying Anxiety
Denying Depression

Minor positive loading
Withdrawing

The factor pattern of Concealment arises from the combination of two common defense mechanisms, denial and withdrawing. Apparently, whatever is responsible for underlying tensions in the students at times when Concealment occurs would cause even more discomfort were the tension to be admitted into full consciousness. Instead, the students laugh off their anxiety, deny that there is any reason for depression, shift the topic of conversation, or ignore the implications of disturbing lines of thought.

What causes the tensions that lead to denial for the student? One factor seems to be the study of human behaviors that shows our species up in a gloomier light than we might choose. Prejudice, wars, grotesque hidden impulses from the strange long-ago, intrusions into daylight of the irrationalities of the dream world; all of these are more or less impressed on the student in a first psychology class. It is understandable that students often seek ways to ignore such knowledge, or at least to avoid its personal relevance. The chroniclers of man's ways, they maintain, are looking only on one side; the analysts who find sex in everything are a little strange themselves, or "There's a guy in our dorm who fits that description almost perfectly."

The issue, then, seems to be one of the students' being driven toward admitting impulses and feelings which they usually suppress.

As we know from discussions of shame and guilt, this suppression can occur in two ways. One is the necessity to hide impulses from oneself as they would otherwise disrupt normal functioning or upset positive self-evaluations. The other is the urge to conceal "bad" or "strange" parts of the self from the social consciousness of the classroom because of the fear that either the teacher or the other students would disapprove or snicker. Naturally these two suppressive techniques serve each other, and in Concealment we find both in operation.

The material being studied is not the only aspect of the course that stirs up ego-alien feelings and a corresponding need to suppress them. Every social grouping has implicit rules about what may and may not be brought into the communal consciousness, and the classroom is no exception. Among the realities the student customarily hides, we find laziness, avoidance of work, boredom, disinterest, and strong negative feelings toward the teacher. Although the students may conceal some of these feelings even from themselves, the most salient need is to avoid displaying them in front of the teacher. This is particularly true if the teacher is intrusively probing into the students' feelings or acting punitive. Many of the segments with high scores on Concealment occur during confrontations in which teacher and students discuss with each other how they feel about the progress of the class. Even the strongest student criticism at these times filters through disclaimers such as, "I think that what we've been doing here is really valuable and that we're learning a lot of interesting stuff, but maybe it would be a little better if. . . . "

SOME CONCEALMENT SEGMENTS

1. Mr. A has presented alternative plans for how he will count the grades on assigned papers. Dave points out that under the system being discussed straight A students will have no incentive to do a good job. Two of the better students in the class disagree sharply, claiming that A students will work anyway because they are perfectionists and because they have more intrinsic interest in the material. They make it clear that they do not welcome the idea that getting good grades is their chief motivation for working.

2. On the previous evening the film "Night and Fog," a documentary about a Nazi concentration camp, has been shown. The class seems reluctant to begin work; there is a lot of laughter and talk until long after the hour has begun. When Mr. C says, "I just want to speak to some of you concerning a last paper for a few 'secs,' " class members make the association 'secs' = sex and laugh about it. Finally the class gets underway with the teacher's asking

the students how they felt about the film. Pat replies, "Maybe it hit so hard because it was a documentary, not just a movie with actors. Yet, you know, it was almost as if the people didn't look human, so the effect—I mean, I knew that they were, but they just looked so different." Another student, Arthur: "It was difficult for me to realize they were people because you see so much of this on TV and in the movies."

Jean asks, "Those nurses outside the ovens, did they know what was going on, do you think?"

"Well, they were knocking off 80,000 people a day at the peak," Mr. C replies. "They must have known somewhere."

Three segments in a row continue on the high extreme of this actor.

3. After a lecture on Freudian symbolism in the Cinderella legend, the class is quite skeptical. "Don't you think that was driving a little hard to say losing her shoe was losing her virginity? I mean, that was scraping the bottom of the barrel," Gloria asserts. And Lisa says, "After all, you can read something psychological into absolutely anything. They just read *so much* into it."

4. In the previous session a discussion of whether mothers should work aroused quite a bit of strong feeling. Now Mr. B asks whether the class felt the discussion was useful. Ned replies, "I certainly don't think it was a complete waste of time. Of course, the girls were beaten pretty badly. They were all confused and driven by emotion." Libby's answer is, "I thought it was very interesting, but it shouldn't have come up in class because it's too personal. It wasn't reasonable; it was just a fight. It's the kind of thing that should go on in extra time."

Student Factor IV

IV+	IV−
Discouragement	*Low Discouragement*
Major positive loadings	*Minor negative loading*
Expressing Depression	Moving Toward
Making Reparation	

The depression that has the highest loading on Discouragement has many causes. The most important of them has to do with the students' inability to perform effectively within the classroom. Realities such as uncomprehended lectures, poor grades on tests, and halting class discussions often spur students toward this factor pattern, but so may a cold, dissatisfied, or punitive performance by the teacher. There are times when this depression, compounded of self-percepts of sloth and stupidity and, possibly, the premonition of a low grade for the course, is countered by the insinuation that the subject is being inadequately taught, but this happens less than usual in segments high on Discouragement. Instead, we find Expressing Depression mated to the category of Making Reparation.

What appears to be happening here is that the students are accepting some of the blame for the failure of the class to perform as well as it might. We would not imagine that hostile acts directed toward the teacher suddenly cease, but the frequent reparation interspersed through them is important. The reparation expressed here also has two distinct sources. One is the students' direct apology for their poor performances; the other may be reparation for the real or suppressed attack on the teacher's adequacy in leading the class.

At first thought, the motive behind reparation would appear to be a desire to avoid the powerful teacher's wrath toward the students for their slowness, their laziness, or the decreasing number of questions. This motive is undoubtedly present, but there is another aspect that should not be overlooked. Melanie Klein (1936) has pointed out that the infant, after an episode of rage and anger, fears it has injured or destroyed the nurturing mother. The result is both depression and an attempt to restore or repair the damaged object. This same process can be distinguished in student discouragement. In their state of depression over the inability to learn, the students are more aware than ever of the need to have someone to provide both information and support. This creates a concomitant need to preserve the nurturant teacher, to avoid injuring or, less symbolically, alienating him. Klein's formulation includes the idea that adult work often derives a part of its motive force from the need to make reparation, an idea we might keep in mind in understanding the genesis of work phases in the classroom's developmental history. We have already noted that in many instances reparation occurs alongside of, or just after, an attack on the teacher. The question arises, then, as to whether the attack and the reparation come from the same quarter or are carried on by different groups. The answer is that both patterns occur. Sometimes we find attacking students hedging their arguments with various disclaimers. At other times, different students address the teacher with a more apologetic or supportive tone, as if to remind their classmates of the deference due him. Whichever way it happens, somebody sees to it that the message of reparation is aired.

Another major source of depression in the classroom is nothing more than the discouraging nature of some of the material presented. Examples include Nazi atrocities, schizophrenic behavior, and films on autistic children. The teacher may feel as depressed and helpless as the students in the face of such facts as the poor prognosis for the pathetic children in the film, but at least he has some greater familiarity with the problem than do the students who look to him for some way out of their distress. Again we find the need for a nurturant leader, again a tendency to deference and reparation on the students' part.

The only significant loading on the Low Discouragement pole of the factor is a minor one on the Moving Toward variable. We have a much friendlier picture here, with more play and laughter. These performances are addressed more to the personal characteristics of the teacher than to his superiority as a hard-to-please expert and authority.

SOME DISCOURAGEMENT SEGMENTS

1. Discussion of a multiple-choice test is in progress. Arthur is arguing over the correct answer to one problem, on which he was marked down. "It seems plausible to me," he begins, "I'm not saying I agree with it, but it seems plausible to me that it's all genetic. Maybe Negroes have different genes. I'm not saying I believe this, but it is possible." The teacher cuts off this argument prematurely because he wants to review the rest of the test before the end of the period. "The answer to number 12 was part C, Minus 93," he says. "Nineteen people missed it. Anyone want to tell me why?" Henry answers, "I don't understand this. The numbers seem to come in varying intervals." When Mr. C explains that this is irrelevant, Henry says "Oh, I see." Another boy says he had assumed the correlations had to be positive. "I just wasn't thinking," he admits.

2. Mr. D is lecturing about experimental methods and the concept of operationalism. He asks the class how they would test a phrenological assertion that the presence and size of a certain bump on the head indicated acquisitiveness. One student after another attempts an answer, all of which are rejected as impractical or inexplicit. Eugene finally hypothesizes that you could measure acquisitiveness by telling someone a story and seeing how many questions they asked about it. When the teacher points out that Ralph has confused acquisitiveness with inquisitiveness, he becomes quite dejected and says, "Gee, I'm sorry."

3. After a film about autistic children, there is a general depres-

sion about the state of human knowledge concerning this area. Students ask, "Excuse me, but could you define schizophrenic?" "Don't they know a cure?"

Student Factor V

V+

Challenge

Major positive loadings
Moving Against
Showing Counterdependency

Minor positive loading
Guilt Inducing

In that it includes large loadings on negative impulse categories and a smaller loading on counterdependence, Challenge bears some resemblance to our Contention factor (Student Factor II+). Here, also, the students launch an attack on the teacher; here, also, they vigorously deny any need for his help or protection. There are, however, important differences in the two factors which we would do well to explore.

The main clue to these differences lies in the differing natures of the negative impulse categories involved. The resisters of the Contention pole of Factor II are first, careful to maintain some appearance of equality with the teacher. The argument is presented as a serious debate in which both parties have rights and obligations and which can be settled by recourse to reason or additional data. The attack focuses on some kind of content, the correct answer to a test question, for instance, and fits fairly comfortably into the normal classroom procedure. Episodes of Contention may be of substantial duration, involve many students, and avoid the appearance of being personal attacks. The rebellious and power-testing aspects of these performances are typically played down or concealed.

The largest loading on Challenge belongs not to Resisting but to the category of Moving Against. This is the most direct and least subtle form of attack of the teacher. Moving Against is seldom as content-oriented as Resisting and cannot sustain the illusion of containing nothing more than an intellectual disagreement. It is intended to be more personally felt by the teacher and thus raises the possibility that he might retaliate. For these reasons, it most often occurs in very short bursts. It is most frequent at the beginning of the term before people know each other well enough to assure themselves that subtler messages can be sent and received. Occurrences do exist later in the term, but tend to become increasingly indirect or to attack symbolic equivalents of the teacher (fathers or psychologists or old men) rather than the teacher himself.

The other negative impulse category with a significant loading on Challenge is Guilt Inducing. As we noted when Guilt Inducing made an earlier appearance as part of Anxious Dependence, it is usually an attempt to sway a figure who is perceived as vastly more powerful. We do not find the students stressing their equality here as they do in Contention. Instead, we can see an internal strain between the Guilt Inducing, which implies a feeling of inferiority, and the Counterdependency that denies it. This inconsistency is another reason that Challenge is never sustained over a long period. Rather, it takes the form of a fleeting, often spontaneous side act with even less readiness than we found in Contention to follow through to any program for change. If Contention suggests an opposition speech in parliament by a member of a minority party, Challenge presents us with a picture of a solitary anarchist sneaking into the galleries, firing a wild shot, and dashing out the door.

Since Challenge is so little oriented to specific details, the teacher is likely to be hard put to find an appropriate response. Criticism may seem witheringly strong, and it is often difficult to pinpoint what, exactly, the students object to. The teachers' responses to such global threats vary in nature. When they are aimed at symbolic equivalents for the teacher, for example, fathers, he has the alternative of bypassing the hostile message and blandly agreeing with the negative assessment of the person or group in question. But when the attack is more directly personal, this is impossible. Our sample of four teachers showed some degree of interindividual variation in responses to direct challenges. One common response is retaliation in kind, an attempt to squelch revolt then and there before it can really get off the ground. A second is an attempt to question the attacking student further, to draw out both his true objections and their inconsistencies, and then deal with them openly. A third and not uncommon response, one prominent in the Apprehension factor, is simply withdrawing, turning to some other student only after minimally acknowledging what has been said. A fourth response is to attempt to vitiate the strength of the hostility by laughing it off or treating it as a friendly kidding.

This, then, is the picture of Challenge. A student is feeling wronged unhappy, and powerless. He nurses these feelings, perhaps until he perceives an intellectual slip or an obvious abuse of power. He then attacks suddenly and quickly subsides, after which the teacher usually attempts to continue the class with as little disruption as possible. Typically, we find no substantial confrontation, only a lingering hint of dissatisfaction and threat.

SOME CHALLENGE SEGMENTS

1. Mr. B decides to cut short a class discussion to summarize the results. He compliments the class, calling the discussion "wonderful, just wonderful," but explaining that he wants to summarize results in case anyone got left behind. Doug raises his hand to say, "I don't see where you think that was such a good discussion. I thought it was horrible." The teacher begins to ask for specific objections, then changes his mind and says, "We don't have time for that now. If there are any more objections, just write me a note. You don't have to sign it."

2. Mr. D asks for comments and questions on a lecture from the preceding day. Eugene remarks that the lecture seemed to him to be poorly organized, irrelevant, and lacking continuity. The teacher answers that he was looking for more substantive comments and that Eugene probably misunderstood the lecture anyway. "Maybe," Eugene mutters resentfully. Mr. D then turns to some other topic.

3. At the beginning of an early session, Mr. D asks for opinions of a film on autistic children. When two students seem confused, he defines autism and symbiotic behavior, then reports his shock at some symbiotic behavior exhibited in the film. Morton argues, "Yeah, but the boy was completely autistic when he came in. What we saw was a great improvement." Further discussion reveals that Morton has worked with such children and seems to know more about them than Mr. D does. The teacher turns aside what he seems to consider a threat to his leadership by accepting the information Morton has conveyed but belittling its importance. Then one student begins angrily condemning the hospital in the film for allowing autistic children to spend their nights at home with the same parents who were largely responsible for the children's condition. When Mr. D attempts to point out that it is legally impossible to keep children from their parents in most cases, Audrey remains angry and unimpressed, sounding almost as if she blamed Mr. D for this state of affairs.

Student Factor VI

VI+	VI−
Support	*Unresponsiveness*
Major positive loading	*Major negative loading*
Accepting	Withdrawing
Minor positive loading	
Moving Toward	

The positive pole of Student Factor VI finds the students expressing support for the teacher's person and policies. The factor pattern includes a great deal of Accepting, most of it quite active, and a smaller loading on Moving Toward. The students are responding warmly and positively to the teacher and to various aspects of the role he plays.

This performance may be caused by a number of events. One is the attempt of several students to disassociate themselves from the carping of one or two members. Another may be the teacher's direct request for feedback on some issue or decision. Alternatively, the students may pick up from the teacher's manner some trepidation about whether some course of action he is pursuing is popular or even whether the students consider him to be a potent or likeable person. In many such cases, class members often jump in with statements of support and legitimation for the teacher.

Still another possibility is simply that a large number of students agree with the validity of some intellectual position or the wisdom of some procedural decision and defend it against some resistant member. Finally, support may come spontaneously as an expression of warmth and respect built up in the course of the term's association.

Many segments that score high on Support make obvious the underlying goal of winning the teacher's approval by appearing to be on his side or to be his kind of person. The expectation is that the teacher will feel more favorable to those who place themselves in agreement and help to legitimate his power. This is especially true during the early phases of the term when he is just getting to know the students and can use the support of specific members in strengthening his own confidence and in helping to set up a favorable educational climate in the classroom. Beyond the desire of some students for approval, we sometimes detect a symbolic wish to fuse with the teacher and share his power and charisma. The most salient antecedent for this situation is that of sibling rivalry within the family. The student attempts to get closer to the teacher than his less adept classmates.

Unresponsiveness, the other pole of Factor VI, includes a distinct lack of support from the class. The teacher's plans and ideas are most likely here to meet with withdrawing, a passive refusal even to contend with the issues raised. Long silences follow the teacher's questions; students act sleepy and apathetic.

We may easily indicate a few of the situations in which students become unresponsive. Often, the class simply fails to engage the students' energy because they find it boring or irrelevant. The problem may be with the material, or their involvement may be blocked by an alienated reaction to the teacher. At other times, the material presented raises too much distress to seem worth dealing with. In all of these cases, Unresponsiveness may involve a process as simple as avoiding replying to a question when one does not know the answer, or as complex as passive resistance to important elements of the classroom situation.

One of the advantages of Unresponsiveness for the student who does not feel like going along with the teacher's plans is that it calls much less attention to his personal resistance than does a contentious response. The students may undercut the thrust of the teacher's actions while appearing fairly innocent and avoiding any true confrontation. Moreover, moving away when the teacher tries to initiate something is a very effective weapon in that it usually causes the teacher to feel depressed and leaves him no easy way to fight back. The teacher is exposed, but the student is not. As one of our samples of teachers says in the transcript reproduced in Chapter 3, "Don't you know that the worst thing you can do to a teacher is to sleep in his class?" "I'd rather have you come after me with a gun than sleep in my class."

Unresponsive students seem to perceive the teacher as very powerful. Dependency and Enactment are both ruled out by his injustice, incompetence, insensitivity, or irrelevance, and Contention is also blocked by students' perception of his superior power. Unresponsiveness presents itself as an alternative in these cases. It gives the students only a negative say over what happens in the classroom, but it does give them some power while leaving them in comparative safety.

A SUPPORT SEGMENT

1. Mr. B has recently given a test in which he told the students what the questions were to be well in advance. Amy and Beatrice

complain that this method provoked tremendous anxiety. After the teacher responds that his intention was actually to reduce anxiety, several class members come to his defense. They praise the procedure on the grounds that it elicited more depth of thought than a regular hour test, that it was less work and worry than a take-home exam, and that they were spared restudy of irrelevant material.

SOME UNRESPONSIVENESS SEGMENTS

1. Mr. A asks who would like to moderate a discussion about the novel *Lord of the Flies.* When no one answers, he appoints Frank, who asks for comments, but finds none forthcoming. "Don't all speak at once," he cautions. Eventually, a halting discussion begins. At one point, the teacher asks how the class would feel about trying to equate the characters in the novel to subsystems in the personality, taking Jack to equal the id, for example. A long silence ensues, broken temporarily by one boy's rather irrelevant comment, then resuming.

2. During a long argument concerning the grading of a multiple-choice question, Mr. C attempts to bring the students to express directly some of the personal feelings surrounding the conflict. Toby, one of the most bitter contestants, reacts with the disclaimer, "I was just trying to pick up a few extra points, that's all."

Student Factor VII

VII+	VII−
Exhibition	*Low Exhibition*
Major positive loadings	*Minor negative loading*
Expressing Self-esteem	Showing Dependency
Moving Toward	

Our final student factor, like many factors for both students and teachers, occurs primarily in the early part of the term. Students enter the classroom with a large variety of available strategies and responses, a number of which will soon drop in importance because they are ineffective in the developing classroom situation. Exhibition is one of the best examples of such a response. Students typically display it once or twice, then decide it is not accomplishing anything and stop using it.

The motive of the student engaging in Exhibition is to identify himself with the teacher, to win the teacher's implicit praise and friendship, to distinguish himself from the mass of his indifferent classmates, and to receive special favor. His strategy for gaining this desired state is to show off how smart and competent he is, how well he understands the subtleties of the teacher's views. Once he has established that he is practically the teacher's peer and colleague, he can more directly court him with actions that are usually scored as Moving Toward.

In doing all this, he has attempted to distinguish himself clearly from his potential rivals in the classroom and to set up an exclusive relationship of mutual respect with the teacher. He presents himself as quite above the sniveling dependence exhibited by some classmates or the troublesome Contention of others. This attempt has evident antecedents in familial sibling rivalry and, later, in the classroom situations from previous educational experiences. Since the student's first task of distinguishing himself is to assure himself of attention, students displaying Exhibition may often be found talking at great length to gain this attention.

One problem with this strategy is that its failure can leave the student in a very precarious position. He has counted on the support and protection of the teacher. In courting it, he has had to forego to some extent the support and friendship of his classmates. If the teacher fails to respond to his courtship, he will be left exposed and deserted. For this reason, the first act of Exhibition may be rather guarded and tentative. If it fails to gain results, the student may quietly remove himself from the spotlight or try to erase his image of a hopeful teacher's pet by radically changing his mode of activity. Those of his classmates who were themselves considering trying this strategy may note his failure and become less likely to employ it themselves when a future opening arises.

Like many of the early strategies that students and teacher employ, Exhibition has a rather magical quality to it. The feeling seems to be that somehow, by means of a few easily performed acts, one can henceforth assure himself of a favored position within the classroom. Teachers often appear to display a similar belief in the factors of Warmth and Display. The teacher seems to feel that, provided he can win the students' friendship and admiration at the outset, the term's success is assured. The ineffectiveness of such magical attempts to fulfill such hopes leads to their sharp decline with the passage of time.

Exhibition does appear in scattered acts later in the term, but in a much changed form. Members of the class may now display behavior falling into the categories of self-esteem and moving toward as a celebration of a job well done. The students may, by this time, have established more solidarity, and one student may express pride on behalf of the whole class achievement. In contrast to early acts of Exhibition, these celebrations typically follow the teacher's praise instead of being a ploy to win it.

SOME EXHIBITION SEGMENTS

1. To illustrate theories of conditioning, the teacher has initiated a discussion of how he learns the names of students. He asks the class to provide some ideas of mechanisms whereby he learns their names. Robert's answer is as follows.

> *Robert:* If you happen to know someone else in previous experi-
> ence with the same name, say you have a very close friend
> whose name was Robert, you might learn my name first, or
> something like that.

2. Roger is leading a discussion about the book *Jordi.* The class is bogged down over the issue of why Jordi became schizophrenic, with Roger offering a number of ideas. Mr. B remarks that the book gives very few clues to the genesis of the schizophrenia and is much stronger on the description of it. "It certainly is an intriguing question, though," he notes. "I know," says Roger, "I've been trying to figure it out myself."

3. The teacher has been profusely complimenting the class on their stellar performance on some assignment.

> *Mr. C:* Really, they were very good. Very, very good. How did
> you find them on the whole? Were they tough?
>
> *Nancy:* Oh, very simple.
>
> *Class:* Laughter.
>
> *Mr. C:* It was really very good. I could see you put a lot of work
> into them.

This concludes our survey of the affective domain. Ahead of us lies the assignment of showing how the scoring system can help in understanding the nature of work in the classroom. We turn first to a case study of one session where we can see in detail both how these research operations are carried out and how the task and affective aspects of the classroom are intertwined.

CHAPTER 3

A DAY IN THE LIFE

W<small>E</small> have two goals in mind for this chapter. By presenting and discussing the transcript of one session from one group, we hope to show the scoring system in action. Perhaps in this way the various meanings of and boundaries between the categories will become clearer. However, our major goal is to return to our investigation of the interplay of affective and task issues in the classroom.

If the proper goal of the classroom is work, then the analysis of a particular session should include both the affective interaction, captured here by the member-leader scoring system, and the task interaction. In the first chapter we proposed that the task goals of both teachers and students could be viewed in terms of the teacher-as typology. This typology isolated for analytic purposes six distinct aspects of the teacher's role in the task group: the teacher as expert, formal authority, socializing agent, facilitator, ego ideal, and person. Before turning to the transcript, let us present briefly a scoring system (used systematically only in this chapter) which is designed to keep track of the impact of each act for the task group interaction between teachers and students.

As our discussion of the teacher-as typology has already suggested, teachers not only function as experts or facilitators or whatever; they may also send clear messages either that they do not wish to operate in one or another capacity, despite the students' preferences, or that they insist on filling and being seen as filling one or another aspect of the total teaching function, despite the students' resistance. Thus there are at least four possibilities within a dynamically coherent time span; the teacher may ignore ( ), act as (+), reject (↓), or insist on (↑) each of the six teacher-as functions. In graphic form, then, an act initiated by a teacher who (1) was not addressing himself to either the ego ideal or person aspects of the teacher, (2) was proceeding along smoothly as the expert, (3) was rejecting student pressure to be more of a facilitator, and (4) was overriding student opposition in order to continue as formal authority and socializing agent might be shown like this:

	Task					
	X	FA	SA	F	EI	P
Teacher Act Number	+	↑	↑	↓		

If we turn now to the students, we can employ the same graphic format to capture the ways in which students can and do relate to the task issues in the classroom. Assuming that the individual student is addressing himself to the particular teacher-as function, he can validate and cooperate with the teacher's efforts in that direction (which we shall symbolize graphically by a +); he can criticize or deprecate the teacher's efforts indicating general dissatisfaction (−); or he can urge that the teacher do or represent more (↑) or less (↓) of the particular function. Thus, if a student throughout a class period implied consistently that not only was the teacher dull (ego ideal −) but that he should deemphasize his role as formal authority in favor of his potential role as person, the interaction from the students' perspective would look something like this:

	Task					
	X	FA	SA	F	EI	P
Student Act Number	+	↓			−	↑

The + sign under X would suggest that the student was rewarding or at least validating the teacher's performance as expert.

The question of how the teacher-student interaction looks at any given moment can be answered in part by simply joining the teacher and student components together, but this would leave out the affective domain. A more adequate summary would include some estimate of what the teacher and students were feeling, in terms of the member-leader category system. Thus a portrait of the task and affective interaction between teacher and students might be represented in this manner:

	X	FA	SA	F	EI	P	Affect
							Task
Teacher	+	↑	↑	↓			Showing Dominance Guilt Inducing
Students	+	↓			−	↑	Accepting, Counterdominance, Guilt Inducing

This graphic display of teacher-student interaction suggests that while there is some stability to the expert area, there is a direct clash over the teacher as formal authority. Futhermore, with each side in this tug-of-war resorting to Guilt Inducing, it is clear that feelings are high and both the task and the affective domain portray a fluid and unstable moment in the developing relationships.

As we move from hypothetical examples to the real data of this study, we may address ourselves to the next crucial topic for investigation. We may attempt to understand how the teacher-student interaction over both task and affective issues evolves over time. We need to understand the mutual interdependence of the teacher's and the students' task activities, how each of these influence and are influenced by the affective domain. The frozen slice of the group's history within which the complexity of cause and affect might be represented as:

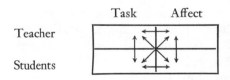

However, a complete analysis of classroom interaction involves a clear sense of how the series of such segments fit together. In trying to understand a particular moment, we need to know how previous task and affective interactions have altered the possibilities open to teacher and student. We turn now to the verbatim transcript of one session of one class. The transcript is divided into seven major segments, and each segment is separated by clear transition points in the personnel and tone of the interaction. Each segment is further divided into from two to seven subsegments, and these define what appear to be dynamically homogeneous episodes within the segment. These smaller time periods can be described in terms of the task and affective messages characterizing the teacher and students in that interaction, and the analytic job facing us here is to show how, even in one session, the task and affective domains constantly influence one another, contributing to the dynamically complex but nonetheless coherent entity we know as classroom interaction.

Introduction to Session 19.   The immediate external precipitating event for much of what happens in session 19 of Mr. C's class was the test given in session 16 and returned in session 17. It is also clear that many of the issues explored and alluded to in sessions 17, 18, and 19 had been part of the underlife of the class for some time. When Mr. C handed the tests back to his students he also called for a discussion of the test items and answers. Mr. C made it a practice to review all of the multiple choice and short essay questions because he felt the discussion could be helpful to the students. He wanted to share with them some data on how good or bad the items were, and he also wanted some similar feedback from his students in order to improve the test items.

The early moments of session 17 proceeded rather uneventfully, with the exception of a few short bursts of Contention and Challenge which centered around minor disagreements over definitional or factual issues. These outbursts seemed to attract little sustained energy and they tended to recede rather quickly. The challenging of test items or of Mr. C that did emerge seemed to be mainly concentrated in the discussion of two items which dealt with Negro-white differences in intelligence and functioning and the heredity-environment issue, a theme that came up later as well. One item in particular led to critical disagreement on the part of several students. The session ended with a sense of unfinished business, but with a promise of more to come. The seeds of confrontation had been planted.

In this spirit Mr. C opened session 18 by announcing that he was ready to do battle. He acknowledged that some students had given him a bad time in the previous session, that he had very mixed feelings about coming to class today, but that he was prepared to confront the issues raised by the students and that he hoped that the class would not hold back. He then temporarily backed off by handing out some dittos and briefly discussing them. Shortly thereafter he returned to a consideration of the remaining multiple-choice items. This was accomplished with only a moderate degree of resistance.

The really serious and intense confrontation, at least on the substantive or content level, focused around a short essay question. The reader should be familiar with the wording of this question, since it is referred to on several occasions in the transcript, and it will enable him to gain a feeling for when the discussion really has drifted away from substantive issues. The item reads as follows:

> "Deutsch studied two New York City schools in lower class neighborhoods—one predominantly white, the other predominantly Negro. He found that Negro children (matched for age, sex, social class) showed consistently lower school performance and more anti-social behavior than whites, these differences increasing with higher grade level. Give three different plausible explanations for Deutsch's findings."

Mr. C took the initiative in clarifying the issue as to content. Before this question came up for consideration he mapped out on the blackboard an extensive chart summarizing many of the potential genetic, prenatal, postnatal, and other environmental, social, or interpersonal factors which may account for the Negro-white differences noted in the question. Mr. Warren, a very bright student who actually did quite well on the question, fired the first salvo. He challenged Mr. C by stating the position he maintained for some time, that the differences are *all* the result of discrimination against Negroes.

In response, Mr. C affirmed his position for the record. As a social scientist, he argued that he could not discount the possibility of constitutionally determined racial differences in potentialities for intellectual functioning. At present, however, it was impossible for him to separate the potential impact of genetic determinants from the known deleterious and class-linked effects of prenatal influences. Until one can extract the impact of prenatal experiences and identify the remaining contributing factors, Mr. C maintained that one should focus attention on the available data, meaning that one should evaluate and attempt to interpret the numerous studies which point to the impact of different environmental conditions. As a matter of personal faith, he added that he did not believe that significant racial differences in intellectual potentialities existed, but he was open to further information.

Mr. Wicker, one of the main antagonists in the next session, challengingly reminded Mr. C that there was also no definitive evidence available against the argument that Negroes were genetically inferior to whites. At first Mr. C responded with considerable anger and accused Mr. Wicker of trying to establish the existence of something like "Jewish blood" or a "Polish temperament." Mr. Wicker was not too visibly disturbed by the attack and suggested that the relevant genetic structures may be identified one day. Mr. C backed off and attempted to outline the kinds of arguments one would have to make and the kinds of data one would need if this were so. Mr. C was still very annoyed and frustrated, and he chastised the class (really Mr. Wicker) for falling back on personal opinions and stereotypes and not using the material which they had read and which he had presented. In a denigrating and distancing tone, he added that on the basis of the material presented in class, they should have had little trouble with the question.

Mr. C then switched the focus of attention by suggesting that some people were probably having trouble with the issue for personal reasons, and that helpful information was being ignored or denied. He also shared his feeling that a personal disagreement had developed between him and Mr. Wicker. He called for other students to present their impressions of what had been going on. Several responded that they did not see a personal disagreement, but rather a disagreement about facts. They also suggested that more information might be helpful. Mr. C then reviewed all of the data he had listed on the blackboard as if to terminate discussion of the issue at the substantive level once and for all. He also placed the responsibility for explaining those findings on the students who rejected this kind of interpretation. The session ended with Mr. C reminding his students to check with him if they were to collect some extra points.

By translating the events and developments in sessions 17 and 18 into Teacher-As terms, we gain some insight into the kinds of themes which could be carried over into session 19. Probably the most pervasive and persistent issue to note is that both Mr. C and a number of students were quite disturbed by his functioning as a formal authority. This was the first test of the term, and it raised for some students including Mr. Wicker and Mr. Warren the painful spectre of evaluation as well as the question of how one deals with potentially arbitrary authority figures. Much of their challenging contentious behavior revolves around these kinds of concerns.

It is also fairly reasonable to assume that Mr. C experienced considerable discomfort in functioning as a formal authority. His desire to share and receive feedback on the test items, his granting of extra points, and his admission that he is fallible and can write very poor items all have a reparative quality to them. In one sense, these all sound like an attempt to make students who were forced to undergo the painful experience of a test and his arbitrary power feel better by giving them soothing gifts. At the same time, by calling for feedback from students on the exam items, he was making himself vulnerable and in a way he may have been trying to undercut the students' resentment. One also has the feeling that behind all of this was an attempt on Mr. C's part to convince his students that he was a fair, trustworthy, and caring person rather than just another impersonal, arbitrary authority figure. Thus, Mr. C seemed to want to play down the formal authority aspects of his functioning, and indirectly he was trying to undo some of the deleterious consequences of having administered a test and of having exercised some of his power.

Much of Mr. C's anger in session 18 reflected his sense of frustration in functioning as a socializing agent. There are really two considerations here. On the one hand, he wanted to communicate how professional social scientists operate when faced with a potentially heated issue; that is, they try to arrive at a conclusion that does justice to most of the data; they are clear about what qualifications are required; and they leave open the possibility that new findings may force a reassessment. On the other hand, he also had a great deal invested in socializing some members of the class in the direction of a more empathic, "liberal" view on the race problem. He sent his message over and over again. The argument that Negroes are intellectually inferior to whites because of hereditary factors is too simple and cannot be proved or disproved at this point. It also enables whites to disown their contribution to the problem. Rather, we have a considerable amount of data on the deleterious impact of different environmental, social, and interpersonal circumstances in Negro development and functioning. Mr. C kept inviting the students to appreciate and understand the implications of this information. Both Mr. Warren and Mr. Wicker, two rather rebellious males who were probably speaking for many other members of the class, rejected Mr. C's socialization efforts.

Much of Mr. C's efforts at socialization involved heavy reliance, at least at first, on a consideration of straight factual material. Functioning as an expert in the service of socialization goals brought Mr. C up against two issues. First, there was the realization that the problem was not resolvable at this level, since there were powerful personal concerns over autonomy and independence, as well as over alienatation from one's old values. Mr. C also recognized his own need to share with the class his sense of frustration and discomfort with what had been happening as well as the need for some of his students to become a little more aware of the extent to which their strong personal feelings were making it difficult to understand not only the substantive questions, but also what was going on in the class. Mr. C's sporadic efforts to open up these issues by adopting a facilitative strategy were primarily in response to these concerns. Finally, we note that much of his functioning as a person was also tied to his efforts to facilitate the class' movement in this direction. The class entered session 19 with these unresolved issues and burdens still with them.

In presenting the scoring of individual acts, the following abbreviations and symbols are used.

For the teacher-as scoring of the task domain:

   X = expert
FA = formal authority
SA = socializing agent   to take one example, the expert (X)
 F = facilitator   function
EI = ego ideal
 P = person

For the member-leader scoring of the affective domain:

MA = Moving Against   DN = Dependency (students)
RS = Resisting   CD = Counterdependence (teachers)
WI = Withdrawing   IN = Independence
GI = Guilt-Inducing   CD = Counterdependence (students)
RP = Making Reparation DM = Dominance (teachers)
ID = Identifying   AE = Anxiety Expression
AC = Accepting   AD = Anxiety Denial
MT = Moving Toward   SE = Self-esteem
                     DE = Depression Expression
                     DD = Denying Depression

For the teacher:

X or X+ = acts as expert
 X↓ = rejects expert role
 X↑ = insists on expert role
    = ignores expert role

For students:

X = relates to teacher as expert
−X = criticizes teacher's performance as expert
+X = rewards teacher's performance as expert
X↓ = pressures teacher to deemphasize expert role
X↑ = pressures teacher to emphasize expert role more
    = ignores teacher as expert

The Analysis of Session 19[3]

Session 19 begins before Mr. C arrives.

1. *Mr. Monk* to Mr. Motley: Have you heard about the latest coup in Viet Nam? The Catholic group is taking over . . . (-FA) (MA,CD,AE)

2. *Mr. Motley:* There are revolutions per minute down in South Africa. In *Time* magazine some German professor burned himself dramatically in protest. (-FA) (MA,AE)

3. *Miss Jewel:* Yeah, I saw that picture. Did he die? It said he was in the hospital . . . It was a beautiful shot . . . (MA,AD,DD)

(Mr. C arrives)

Segment A-1

4. *Mr. C* to Miss Smith: I will have these (referring to dittos outlining a research project) run off. They will all be ready by Monday, and I'm going to be handing out a whole mess of material then. (Low depressed tone) (FA) (RP, DM,DE)

5. So if you want to go ahead and think about an area that you'd be interested either in doing some research or doing some review articles—that's about as far as you can go with your paper. OK? (F,FA) (RP,DM)

6. *Mr. C:* All right, uhm . . . there were several people in this class who had an . . . extra point on that item number five . . . and I added them in and so there are some changes. (FA) (RP,DM,DD)

7. If there's anybody else who has an exam . . . outstanding with those five points please speak to me after class or with that five, because I'll include it. (FA↓)

8. Let's see, that's Stall, Straus, Warren, and Wicker, and Avins, Tuft, and Mr. Monk, Reed, Brewer, Fields, Miss Dabbs, that's it. (FA) (DM)

9. Anybody else hand them in and we'll handle them afterwards. Ok? (FA↓) (DM,DD)

10. *Mr. C:* Now . . . uh . . . we've lost our front row today, I see. (FA↓,P↑) (CD,DE)

11. (Loud) Uh . . . I must admit that you people . . . a number of you . . . raised a very powerful argument on this first question (referring to the first short essay question). I was thinking about some of the things you were saying quite seriously . . . (FA↓,F↑) (GI,RP,CD,AE,DD)

12. for a while . . . (FA↑,EI)

13. *Class:* Laugh. (FA,EI) (AE)

14. *Mr. C:* and uh . . . the thing doesn't just go in one ear and . . . uh . . . I say "well, that's it and we turn you off?" (FA↓,EI,P↑)

15. Uhm . . . and . . . mm it's clear that the word "plausible" means "plausible." (F↑) (RP,DM,DD)

16. So very clearly, from that point of view, in reevaluating it, I think there is a basis for a case. (FA,F,EI) (RP,IN,DD)

Segment A-2

17. *Mr. C:* And what happened was that both of us (referring to Mr. Wicker and himself) all of us . . . including myself, didn't look at the question, and were arguing with each other. (FA↓,F↑,P↓,EI) (GI,RP,CD,DE)

18. *Mr. C:* And I get the feeling that I was very involved and you were getting involved and we were sort of ramming each other down the throat. (F,P,EI) (RP,CD,AE,DD)

19. So . . . mm after I guess I had cooled off a bit I looked at the question. (P,EI) (GI,DM,DD)

20. And it struck me as very uhmm . . . you know . . . funny that there was a part of the question that all of us missed. (F,EI) (CD)

Segment A-3

21. *Mr. C:* And the part refers to the fact that these differences are increasing with higher grade level. (X↑,F↓,P↓) (DM)

22. *Mr. C:* Now, what does that mean? . . . Well, what does it mean? (X)

23. What can happen if increases are taking place with higher grade level? (X,SA↑)

24. *Mr. Monk:* Environmental. (X,SA) (AC,DN)

25. *Mr. C:* Something in the environment is going on because we can't . . . is it reasonable to assume that genetics suddenly start getting activated with age? (X) (AC,DM)

Segment A

	Task						Affect
Segment	X	FA	SA	F	EI	P	
(A1) Teacher		↓		↑			Making Reparation
							Denying Depression
(A2) Teacher				↑	+	↑	Counterdominance
(A3) Teacher	+						Dominance

Despite the fact that the teacher does all the talking in segment A, the students' presence and pressure on the teacher are very much a part of the total interaction we would try now to understand. What is less clear is where in the tangled snarl of causes and effects one might best start. One effect, which is soon to be a cause for other actions by the students, is the teacher's clear move to deemphasize his role as formal authority. We might begin our analysis of segment A by viewing it as a series of efforts by the teacher to replace the formal authority aspect of his role with facilitator, then with ego ideal and person, and finally with expert functions. The teacher, in these opening gambits, is trying to undo some of the negative consequences, as he perceives them, of his prior activities as formal authority, especially the giving and grading of the exam.

What might these negative consequences be? We need to look at both the students and the teacher for the answer to that question. The relevant and disturbing input from the students seems to include a rise in anxiety and dependency in some students, a rise in resentment and rebellion in other students, and a general withdrawal to which the teacher refers in noticing that no one is sitting in the front row. Mr. C's answer to each of these changes in the students is to play down the formal authority role, offering either a more student-centered and personal approach or a more objective, impersonal approach. Both alternatives are offered within this brief interaction.

In the first segment, even before a student has contributed anything to the overt interaction, the mutual influence of teacher and student is under way. As a matter of fact, given the exam question and the subsequent discussion on racial differences, we should not overlook the effect of Mr. Manley's absence. Mr. Manley, the only Negro in the class, evidently had had enough. His absence did more than deprive Mr. C of an ally in the struggle against ignorance and bigotry. It raised the uncomfortable thought in Mr. C's mind that he had failed Mr. Manley in some way. To recognize this factor of the teacher's doubts and uneasiness, added to the residue of the exam grading, helps explain some of the uneven, unsure quality of the first segment.

Our analysis of this segment would be incomplete and shallow if we let it rest with the reconstruction of (student reactions to teacher as formal authority) → (teacher's efforts to deemphasize formal authority role). This would neglect two aspects of the teacher: his feelings about himself as formal authority and his several task goals at that moment. Much of Mr. C's behavior in this segment is scored Making Reparation, and the expression and denial of depression and especially of guilt or blame figure prominently in this segment. Although we can never be sure of such things, we sense that Mr. C is reacting negatively to himself as formal authority not simply because he is under pressure from the students but because seeing himself as formal authority is likely, at least under certain conditions, to lead Mr. C to see himself as the harsh, authoritarian figure he does not wish to be. Clearly, two teachers can perform the same act (give an exam) and stir up the same effect in the students (anxiety and resentment), but one will remain untroubled about himself while the second will need very much to reassure himself that he is still the benevolent, humane person he hoped to be (as a teacher).

Beyond these dynamics we must point to one further issue which will become abundantly clear as the session goes along but is important even at the outset. It is simply not true that Mr. C was attempting to be the "good guy" only as a way of atoning for or neutralizing the effects of the exam. His move toward being the facilitator and especially his move toward being the expert are bound up in the great struggle over values which had broken out in the previous session. Mr. C and at least some of the class are in the midst of a battle over what to conclude regarding the genetic heritage of Negroes, and this battle has cast Mr. C in the role of socializing agent. Thus we would need to remain aware of this key issue as we ask why Mr. C is trying to deemphasize the formal authority aspects of his role. In the context of a struggle against especially one student whose attitudes seem to Mr. C to be racist and unscientific, it becomes especially important to Mr. C that the battle not become one in which "What the teacher says goes" simply by virtue of his power to grade the students. Segment A seems to represent Mr. C's desire to clear the decks, to focus primarily on himself as expert and, for reasons soon to be made clear, as facilitator, the better to pursue his more basic teaching goal as the socializing agent.

Segment B-1

26. *Mr. C:* Go on, Mr. Wicker. (FA) (DM)

27. *Mr. Wicker:* Well, the decreases become more noticeable. It says . . . isn't it that they become more noticeable? (-X) (RS,CD)

28. *Mr. C:* It says that these differences are increasing with higher grade level. (FA↑,X) (DM)

29. *Mr. Wicker:* The differences between this person (the Negro) and the normal person. But that differences . . . (-FA↓,-SA↓,X) (RS,CD)

30. *Mr. C:* The differences between the Negroes and the whites increase over time. (FA↑,SA↑) (MA,DM)

31. *Mr. Wicker:* Yeah, now is that in IQ or in achievement? (X,-FA↓) (RS,CD)

32. *Mr. C:* In antisocial behavior and school performance. In other words, uh . . . (X,FA↑) (DM)

33. *Mr. Wicker:* In school performance. But . . . ok . . . then naturally as you learn . . . as the material gets more and more complicated the performance of this person is going to be more and more noticeable and more and more deficient . . . not necessarily because of environmental differences, but because of the complications of the material. (-X,-FA↓) (MA,CD,DD)

34. *Mr. C:* Ok, Miss Jewel. (FA↑,X↓) (DM)

35. *Mr. Wicker:* At least that's the way I thought about it. (-FA↓,-F↑) (CD,DD)

Segment B-2

36. *Miss Jewel:* Well, I don't know . . . I don't know if I should argue this point now because I don't know if it's a matter of disagreeing with him or not. (FA,-F↑) (RP,DN,AE,DE)

37. *Mr. C:* Well, whatever you want to say, just go ahead. (FA,F↑) (DM)

38. *Miss Jewel:* No, I just think it's environment, primarily. (X,SA,F) (AC,DN)

39. *Miss Jewel:* But . . . well for one thing, as you grow older your social ostracism is more pronounced. And I know it is . . . you know . . . in . . . even in whether it's lower class or upper class or middle class or Negro or white. (X,SA) (AC,DN,AE)

40. And so the kids would become more and more regressed, socially . . . that's socially. (X,SA) (AC,DN,DE)

41. And also, academically they're going to become regressed because they didn't have opportunities when they were younger. I don't know . . . like they come to school with very very little in many cases. (X,SA)

42. And I know like a lot of our families . . . you know something going into school. Most of us knew how to read when we were eight years old . . . and a lot of these little Negro kids didn't get this. (X,SA) (AC,DN,DD)

43. And that's environment . . . because say they have nine kids in their family and the mother's not around. (SA)

44. *Mr. C:* Well, that could fit the conception of the environment that we've been talking about. (X,SA) (AC,DM)

Segment B-3

45. *Mr. C:* What about . . . uhm . . . all right, let's assume that this is not such an unreasonable argument that you are raising, Mr. Wicker. (F↑,EI) (RP,DM)

46. It's possible that the material does get more difficult and that the original deficit that was genetically endowed does come through consistently. (F,X) (AC,DM)

Segment B-4

47. *Mr. C:* Uhm . . . Okay. Go on . . . go on . . . (FA,F) (DM)

48. *Mr. Warren:* Well, the difference in the nature of the material changes because like when you're in kindergarten or say

first grade, they're not so much teaching you academics as uh . . . as uh . . . (X) (RS,CD,AE)

49. *Mr. Warren:* You know what I mean . . . (-FA↓,-F↑,X) (DN,AE)

50. there's not too much difference in the children, but as you go on say you're in eighth grade, it's more how you can study . . . how you can learn. (X,F)

51. You know what I mean . . . (F,-FA↓)

52. Like when you have to start doing homework and studying by yourself. I think IQ comes in more there. (X,F)

53. *Mr. C:* So we could interpret this as again going back to the original deficit in endowment . . . if I follow your argument. (X,F) (DM)

54. *Mr. Warren:* Yeh, also I think . . . uh . . . you can . . . I uh . . . the difference is compounded because of the environment too. (-X,-FA) (RS,AE,CD)

55. It's also compounded because of heredity and . . . (X-SA)

56. it's hard to give three answers that all fit . . . it's sort of an interaction of the three answers. (-FA,X) (GI,IN)

Segment B-5

57. *Mr. C:* OK, Mr. Alkin. (FA) (DM)

58. *Mr. Alkin:* One other point. There's also definitely differences . . . Well, they have found differences in some studies . . . in rate of learning. (X) (RS,CD,AE,DE)

59. If there's a difference between the two races then this would certainly have something to do with actual rate of development . . . (X,SA)

60. Well, it's different between two sexes, too, really . . . that . . . uhm . . . the males don't really accelerate while this is more psychically . . . but the males don't really accelerate until a couple of years after the females . . . (X,SA) (RS,CD,DE)

61. *Mr. C:* Mm, hmm. (X,F)

62. *Mr. Alkin:* and this I think . . . this same difference in growth rates . . . different periods of time can be used to explain what we were discussing and also the difference in potential. (X) (AC,DN,DE)

63. And this difference in growth rate can just indicate this difference in potential. Also, it could indicate for a better environment . . . but this is an argument for heredity. (X,SA) (AC,DN,DD)

Segment B

Segment	X	FA	SA	F	EI	P	Affect
			Task				
(B1) Teacher	↑						Dominance
Mr. Wicker	↓						Counterdependency, Resisting
(B2) Teacher	+		+	+			Dominance
Miss Jewel	+		+	+			Dependency, Accepting
(B3) Teacher				+			Dominance
(B4) Teacher				+			Dominance
Mr. Warren	+			+			Dependency, Resisting, Accepting
(B5) Mr. Alkin	+		+				Depression, Counterdependency, Dependency

In segment B the students join the teacher at center stage, and the immediate effect of their presence on the teacher is quite striking. Compared to the apologetic, slightly depressed teacher who twisted and turned throughout segment A, here we find the teacher in full control. He is "drawing the students out," and this combination of what in factor terms we might see as Reaction and Formality permits the teacher to settle down, to become gracious and encouraging, and to recover his poise.

The stagelike quality is heightened if anything by the brief contribution made by the four students who join the conversation. Each one enters, says that which he will say over and over again for the rest of the period, and yields to the rest. Thus, with as yet muffled intensity, four students made their initial contact of the day with the teacher. Two of the students, Miss Jewel and Mr. Alkin, make themselves heard in a way that is somewhat supportive of the teacher and, more clearly, a plea for attention and esteem. Mr. Wicker snipes from a distance, avoids direct confrontation, but manages to leave the teacher vaguely unsettled about the state of their relationship. Finally, Mr. Warren enters in a more intellectual and more critical vein. Thus we are in a position to take a peek at four key members of the class under conditions where little of the underlying intensity has had a chance to build up, so comfortably does Mr. C play his role as moderator and paraphraser of the class discussion. The whole interaction is so smooth that one could slip right past probably the most important act in the whole session, at least the most condensed indicator of one basic issue which will concern the class for the rest of the period: the issue of bigotry or racism, as it now might be called.

When Mr. Wicker, in act 29, equates being white with being normal and being a Negro with being abnormal, the smoldering issue raised in the previous session and in Mr. Wicker's answer to the exam question flares up, only to be covered up at least for the moment. Mr. C quickly reasserts that the discussion is about *whites* and Negroes, and the petulant, "Well, why couldn't he . . ." tone of Mr. Wicker is lost in the overlap of Miss Jewel's support and Mr. Warren's attack on Mr. C's competence.

A closer examination of Mr. C's task strategy in this segment suggests that although he was able to preserve his composure by staying within the accepted style of teacher as facilitator and occasionally as expert, his underlying strategy centered around his function as socializing agent. Ever so gradually the teacher was working his way back to Mr. Wicker, and the point of his interest was hardly to draw Mr. Wicker out, but to isolate and chastise him for being the class bigot. However, Mr. Warren and Mr. Alkin intervened and pursued points of interest to them. The fight with Mr. Wicker was postponed for a brief duration. Segment C begins with a direct challenge to Mr. Wicker, as if B4 and B5 had simply been distractions from the pursuit of the teacher's basic goal of relating to Mr. Wicker over the value issue underlying the exam question and the debate over genetic inferiority.

Segment C-1

64. *Mr. C:* All right. What about the antisocial behavior? Why should that increase over time? Why should the discrepancy increase over time? (X,F,SA↑) (GI,DM,DE)

65. *Mr. C:* (quietly) Mr. Wicker. (FA,F) (DM)

66. *Mr. Wicker:* Well, it's because his lack of mental ability becomes more and more noticeable to him. He comes to feel more and more uncomfortable among the whites. (X,-SA↓) (RS,CD,AE,DE)

67. *Mr. C:* (calmly) Why does he feel more uncomfortable among the whites? (SA↑,F↑) (GI,DM,DE)

68. *Mr. Wicker:* Because his intelligence isn't up to their level. (-SA↓,-F↓) (RS,CD,DE)

69. *Mr. C:* But why should this bother him? (SA↑,FA) (GI, DM,DE)

70. *Mr. Wicker:* (loud and anxious) He feels out of place among them. They start talking about things he doesn't understand, their level of reasoning's above him; they're learned . . . (-SA↓,-FA↓,-F↓) (RS,DN,AE,DE)

71. *Mr. C:* So, what happens when somebody starts talking about things that you don't understand? (SA,F↑) (GI,DM)

72. *Mr. Wicker:* It depends on whether I'm interested in it. (-FA↓,-EI) (GI,DN,AD,DD)

73. If I'm interested in it, I'll try to find out more. If I'm not interested in it, then I just . . . (-FA↓,-EI↑,-F↑) (RS, CD,AD)

74. *Mr. C:* But where does the impact come from? (FA,SA↑,F↑) (GI,DM,DD)

75. *Mr. Wicker:* What impact? (-FA↓,-F↓) (DN,AE)

76. *Mr. C:* Well, why should this bother, I mean if, you know . . . (F↑,SA) (GI,DM)

77. *Mr. Wicker:* (loud and angry) Well, you just don't feel comfortable talking to him, so you don't associate with him. (-FA↓,-SA↓,-F↓) (MA,CD,AE,DE)

Segment C-2

78. *Mr. C:* Um . . . Mr. Monk. (FA,F↓) (DM)

79. *Mr. Monk:* You don't feel as good as they are. (SA,-F↑) (DE)

80. *Mr. C:* All right, but what determines . . . why don't you feel as good? (SA,F) (GI,DM)

81. *Mr. Monk:* I suppose because of pretty clear comparison. (SA) (DE)

82. *Mr. C:* Where's the comparison? How do you know that you're no good? Where's the comparison? (SA,F) (GI,DM)

83. *Mr. Monk:* Because of parents . . . (SA) (AC)

84. *Mr. C:* All right. Go on Mr. Alter. (FA,SA) (DM)

85. *Mr. Alter:* You don't feel as good because of your environment, because of your social role. (X,SA) (AC,DN)

86. *Mr. C:* You've got to compare yourself to somebody, don't you? (SA,F) (AC,DM)

87. How do you know? (F) (DM)

88. I mean, if we live in a vacuum, right, if I grew up in a vacuum I'll never find out whether I'm dumb or whether I'm smart. (F,EI)

89. All right, is this reasonable? How does somebody find out that they are not as good as somebody else? How do you find out? (SA↑,F↑,EI) (DM)

90. *Miss Jewel:* Interaction. (SA) (AC)

91. *Mr. C:* How do you know where you stand in this class? (SA↑,FA) (GI,DM)

92. *Mr. Alter:* By comparison. (FA) (DN)

93. *Mr. C:* By comparison with what? (FA,F) (DM)

94. *Mr. Monk:* With somebody else. (FA,F) (AC,DN)

95. *Mr. C:* Somebody else; some standard out there; information people give you. (FA,SA,X) (AC,DM)

96. I tell you on your test: "This is pretty good thinking, Mr. Wicker," I give you a grade. I give you a poor grade. Whatever it is. (FA↑) (RS,AC,DM,DE)

97. *Mr. C:* Am I part of the environment? (SA,F,FA) (GI, DM,DE)

98. *Mr. Wicker:* Yeah. (FA,F) (AC,DN,DE)

Segment C-3

99. *Mr. C:* Mr. Motley, you had a comment? (FA,F↑) (DM)

100. *Mr. Motley:* No, uh . . . (FA↓,F↓) (WI)

101. *Mr. C:* Mr. Warren. (FA) (DM,DE)

102. *Mr. Warren:* Well, uh . . . the thing is when . . . they're younger they don't know . . . if this whole thing is based on their being discriminated against . . . when they're younger . . . (FA,-SA↓,-F↓) (RS,AE,DE)

103. They're not . . . there's actually no discrimination and . . . because the little kids . . . you know . . . they associate with don't discriminate against them. (-SA↓,-X↓) (RS,CD)

104. *Mr. C:* How early would you guess the beginnings of racial awareness come into play? (FA↑,SA↑,X) (GI,DM,DD)

105. *Mr. Warren:* Well I'd say it might start as soon as say school starts but still it's not . . . (-SA,-X) (RS,DN,AE,DD)

106. they are kind of young and they don't realize . . . you know . . . the little white kids don't . . . don't have social prejudice against them and the little and the Negro kids don't . . . (-X↓,-SA)

107. you know . . . don't understand anything, and as they grow older the prejudice becomes more and more and they . . . and . . . you know . . . say, hatred increases and they start realizing that they're being discriminated against and they don't like it. (X,F,SA) (AC,DN,AE,DD)

Segment C-4

108. *Mr. C:* Mr. Brewer. (FA,F) (DM)

109. *Mr. Brewer:* I'd say racial prejudice starts in the . . . 4 or 5 years old. I've seen some kids playing together, Negro and white, calling some kids white and other kids black. (X,F,SA) (AC,DN)

110. *Mr. C* (fast): What if I were to tell you that there are a series of studies around which show that prenursery school children of 3, 4, and 5 years old . . . both Negroes and whites when presented with a choice between a white and a black doll will both select a white doll? (X,F↓,EI) (GI,DM,DE)

111. (quietly) What would this mean to you? (SA,F) (GI, DM, DE)

112. Mr. Monk, anyone? (FA,F) (DM)

113. Just call it out . . . . (FA↑,F,-EI) (MA,DM)

114. *Mr. Monk:* Something to do with the fact that maybe white is a superior color or something or what? (-FA,-SA) (RS, DN,DD)

115. *Mr. C:* How does a kid find out? (SA↑,F) (DM,DE)

116. *Mr. Meadow:* White suggests being clean. (X,SA,F) (AC, DN,DD)

117. *Mr. Monk:* They're rewarded for being clean. (X,SA) (AC, DN)

118. *Miss Jewel:* Also, they're all living in a white world, you know . . . all the television and white characters . . . uhm . . . advertisements are white people, and white Christmas. (X,SA) (AC,DN,DE)

119. *Mr. C:* So you think it's a mater of frequency than . . . (X) (GI,DM,DE)

120. does the Negro live in a white world? Ever been to Harlem? (F,SA↑,EI)

121. *Miss Jewel:* No, I haven't. (EI) (DN,DE)

122. *Mr. C:* White stands out like . . . ah . . . like the devil. (SA,EI) (GI,DM,AE,DE)

123. *Mr. C:* Mr. Reed. (FA,SA) (DM)

124. *Mr. Reed:* I was going to say it's environmental conditioning . . . I mean . . . they're conditioned in relation to . . . ah . . . to people, (X) (AC,DN)

125. they're conditioned in relation to white is considered good, black is considered bad . . . not in relation just to people but to other things as well . . . and it's just a conditioned response, I suppose is what I'd say. (X,+SA,EI) (AC,DN,DD)

126. *Mr. C:* Well, you're bringing in the information that we have been trying to read . . . that's good (laugh). (X↓,EI) (GI, AC,DM,DD)

127. I don't know what the process is . . . that's part of it, that may be part of it. (X↓,F) (DM,DE)

Segment C-5

128. *Mr. C:* Well, what's coming out of all this, you see? (X,F↓) (GI,DM,DD)

129. Uhm, I guess what I'm suggesting is that the data is . . . this is the point I've been making before . . . the data clearly show that there is no basis for rejecting or accepting at this point the genetic interpretation solely . . . (X,FA↓) (RP, DM,DE)

130. which means that the suggestion that a plausible answer is a genetic interpretation is very clearly a reasonable one. But . . . built into the question is additional information. (FA↑, X) (GI,DM,DD)

131. And this is where we got hung up, you see . . . because you were yelling "yes! yes!" and I was yelling "no! no!" (FA↓, F↑,EI↑,P↑) (RP,DM,DE)

132. *Class:* Laugh. (EI) (AE)

133. *Mr. C:* and all this kind of business. And both of us didn't look at the question. And the question provides information which can't be denied. Now why does this thing change? (X,F↓) (GI,DM,DD)

Segment C-6

134. *Mr. C:* Even if we assume on the side of intelligence that it is a product of the material as you [Mr. Wicker] and Mr. Warren and probably a number of other people are suggesting, that is a reasonable argument. (X,SA) (AC,DM,DE)

135. But somehow or other . . . however you want to attack the antisocial bit, you have to somehow or other bring the environment in *somewhere* . . . (X,SA) (GI,DM,DD)

136. Unless you assume a genetically-determined difference in antisocial behavior completely independent of the environment. (X,SA) (GI,DM)

137. In other words, right from birth you've got to say . . . you've got to argue, that Negroes or Germans or anybody else who is racially—if I can use this term, aggressive has this thing coming through genetically. (X,SA↑,EI)

138. And that's a powerful assumption to make. (X,SA) (GI,DM)

139. So, does this . . . how does this sit with you, Mr. Wicker? (F) (RP,DM,AE)

140. I'm talking to you because we've been talking. Now I'm sure that you're speaking for a lot of people too. (F,FA↓)

141. *Mr. Wicker:* I agree . . .

142. *Mr. C:* So I'm not singling you out. (FA,F) (RP,DM,AE)

143. *Mr. Wicker:* I agree with you on that . . . I think that the only part of it that would be stated as environmental . . . would be the part about antisocial behavior . . . (X,FA) (RS,AC,DN)

144. *Mr. C:* So there would have to be in approaching the problem some reference to this kind of interaction. (X,FA,SA↑) (AC, DM)

Segment C-7

145. *Mr. C:* I guess . . . you know what concerned me . . . it wasn't so much the fact that the genetic argument came through . . . but that we missed this part . . . both of us, not just you but me . . . we ignored it completely. (F↑, EI↑,P↑,FA↓,X↓) (RP,IN,DE)

146. We got wrapped up in yelling down at each other. You know . . . (P) (GI,IN,AE,DE)

147. and I get the feeling that what was going on was more than just dealing with the question. (F)

148. You know . . . some of you people are annoyed with something . . . Now it's either me, or it's the course, or it's the classroom or something . . . and I felt this is what was coming through. (F↑,EI,P)

149. *Mr. C:* And I'd like to hear about it. I mean I'd like to know, you know. (F,P) (MT,IN,DE)

150. If you want to discuss it this is the place to do it. (P↓,F) (IN,DE)

151. Uhm . . . I got the feeling there was an undercurrent . . . because I got sucked into it, if you know what I mean. (F,P) (MA,IN,DE)

152. And I was getting mad . . . you know. I was getting angry. You know . . . what's coming off here? It was a personal argument rather than an argument about . . . or a discussion about . . . now . . . what's the right answer to this question. (P,F↑,EI) (MT,JN,AE,DE)

Segment C-8

153. *Mr. C:* I don't know if you had that feeling, but I had that feeling . . . and that feeling bothered me . . . you know . . . about myself. (F↑,P)

154. And I was getting mad. I felt like going up there and saying, "Okay, Wicker and the rest of you, let's put the gloves on . . . you know . . . enough of this business." (FA↓,F,EI, P) (MA,DM,AE)

155. *Class:* Laugh.

156. *Mr. C:* Did that feeling sort of . . . I mean . . . was this part of what some of you people felt as well . . . or . . . ? (F↑) (AC,IN,AE)

157. *Mr. Wicker:* I was just trying to pick up a few extra points. (-FA,-F↓,-P↓,-EI↓) (GI,RP,DN,AD,DD)

158. *Class:* Laugh. (-FA) (AE)

159. *Mr. Wicker:* No, I was just trying to see if I could persuade you the other way . . . that's all. (-F↓,-FA,-SA↓) (RS,DN, DE)

160. *Class:* Laugh. (AE)

161. *Mr. Wicker:* At least to see my viewpoint. (-FA↓,-F↑) (RS, RP,DN,AD,DD)

Segment C begins with the teacher directing a question to Mr. Wicker, proceeds to the argument implied by that question, and ends with what seems to be Mr. Wicker's resignation from the battle. To look first at the task strategy implications of this argument, there can be little doubt that the teacher is functioning more as a socializing agent than anything else. The teacher makes use of his expert function to support his position and makes use of his facilitator function especially to draw out those who support his argument, but the bone of contention between Mr. C and Mr. Wicker is inextricably bound up with Mr. C's conception of how a "Liberally educated man" thinks about racial differences.

Nowhere are Mr. C's efforts to press home his points more clearly indicative of his socializing goals than when, faced with Mr. Wicker's stubborn insistence of Negro inferiority, Mr. C proceeds to place Mr. Wicker in the role of the scorned, pressured student. We can see that Mr. C, while not insisting explicitly that Mr. Wicker espouse his liberal views on race, does insist that empathy is a necessary ingredient of a good analysis of the racial scene. One must know how the Negro child feels in school, and therefore the bigoted student

Segment C

Segment	Task						Affect
	X	FA	SA	F	EI	P	
(C1) Teacher		↑	↑	↑			Dominance, Guilt Inducing
Mr. Wicker		↓	↓	↓			Counterdependency, Resisting, Expressing Anxiety, Depression
(C2) Teacher		+	+	+			Dominance, Guilt Inducing
Students		+	+				Dependency, Depression, Accepting
(C3) Teacher		+					Dominance
Mr. Warren	−		↓				Resisting, Accepting
(C4) Teacher			↑	+	+		Dominance, Depression, Guilt Inducing
Students	+		+				Accepting, Dependency
(C5) Teacher	+	↓		↓			Dominance, Making Reparation, Depression, Guilt Inducing, Denying Depression
(C6) Teacher	+		↑	+			Dominance, Guilt Inducing, Making Reparation, Accepting
(C7) Teacher	↓			↑	+	+	Independence, Expressing Anxiety, Depression
Mr. Wicker		↓					Dependency, Making Reparation, Denying Anxiety, Denying Depression

is driven more and more to sense the parallelism between his position in class and the position of the oppressed Negro child. The net result of this pressure is that Mr. Wicker becomes angry and upset, but he clings all the more tenaciously to his original position regarding genetic inferiority. At least in segment C1 the teacher's socializing pressure is resisted effectively.

Given this impasse, the fight begins to escalate. Mr. C turns, as he had once before, to the loyal students, the liberal-minded students who agree that a harsh environment is a detriment to learning. In act 95 Mr. C adds the unnecessary threat of his power to grade Mr. Wicker in the struggle. Mr. Wicker concedes one small point and withdraws. Toward the end of the segment the struggle takes on a new form as the teacher implies more and more insistently that under the surface there might be issues of a personal nature. Perhaps, he implies, there are students who are angry at him or at the class. Perhaps it has become a personal grudge match. At this point, given the rather total aversion of Mr. Wicker to any form of personal involvement with the teacher, the argument collapses. Mr. Wicker chooses the least painful path, that of laughing it off as an effort simply to pick up a few more points.

If we back off and look at this fight from Mr. Wicker's viewpoint, it is clear that while his early opposition to Mr. C as formal authority and socializing agent was reasonably comfortable, the whole purpose of the fight, to disrupt and disorient the pompous authority figure, was thwarted by Mr. C's invitation to redefine the argument as a deep, personal animosity. He got neither his extra points nor his satisfaction of upsetting the teacher, but Mr. Wicker's retreat proved to be only temporary, as we shall see.

One other student whose action in this segment should be noted is Mr. Warren. It appears that he, too, is arguing against the teacher, but with one crucial difference. He shares the teacher's underlying values on racial discrimination and differences. For him, as for Mr. C, it is the environment's fault; prejudice is bad. The issue Mr. Warren wishes to raise goes to the question of Mr. C's expertise and his ability to write an answerable question. Since this effort by Mr. Warren to upstage Mr. Wicker and to redefine the issue as one of expert and formal authority functions, rather than socializing agent functions, will be repeated, it is worth noting that students can be made uncomfortable by the way other students are reacting to the teacher. The loyal opposition, Mr. Warren, and the loyal supporters, Miss Jewel, for example, appear to be annoyed with Mr. Wicker's choice of issues and his mode of provoking the teacher. Therefore they are as eager to enter the discussion with their preferred way of relating to the teacher as the teacher is eager to have them take the floor.

Thus far our major analysis has been in terms of the task strategies employed by teacher and students. However, the teacher's performance in these interactions, especially with Mr. Wicker, is highly punitive. For the most part, Mr. C expresses his anger in ways we would score as Guilt Inducing, but the anger comes through in the teasing, almost taunting way Mr. C reminds Mr. Wicker of the grades or suggests that they might be about to "put the gloves on." Although this anger remains very much under control, and despite the frequent efforts at making reparation, the cumulative effect of Mr. C's performance in this segment is too much for Mr. Wicker to face directly. But, then, it is Mr. Wicker's elusive, hit-and-run style which makes him so provocative.

The more Mr. C tries to confront him with the underlying racism of his comments or the underlying fight between him and Mr. C, the more Mr. Wicker retreats into the flippant, "con man" defense of his actions. It is sometimes hard to keep in mind that a student can threaten the teacher, that deeply personal issues can be aroused by a student, but this is clearly the case. Not only does Mr. Wicker resist Mr. C's socializing efforts and undermine his authority; he manages, by his elusiveness, to become the bigot against whom it is difficult to retaliate. Given Mr. C's identification with the Negro child in the discussion, and given Mr. Wicker's casual references to whites as "normal," we can understand Mr. C's anger as a derivative of more than the immediate teaching situation. By means of that shifting interplay between past and present, Mr. Wicker becomes the insensitive bully, the bigot, and the enemy. Segment C begins with a direct challenge to Mr. Wicker over the exam question. It ends with the traditional challenge and resignation of the verbal street fight: "What was that you said, kid?" "Oh, nothing, nothing. I was just talking about a guy I used to know." Mr. Wicker's retreat in the face of Mr. C's evident willingness to "share feelings" and to become personal was not unexpected by Mr. C, one might surmise. At least part of his motivation, we would conclude, was not to bring Mr. Wicker out but to scare him by the *tour de force* at the end of the segment, in which Mr. C's personal power was added to his formal authority, and the combination was simply too much for Mr. Wicker. We offer this analysis in terms of Mr. C's feelings not as a substitute for our earlier thoughts on task strategies but as a supplement. The teacher's sense of his educational goals and his private, emotional reactions to particular students influence each other and, in turn, the resultant of these forces influences the students.

Segment D-1

163. *Mr. C:* Was this . . . uhm . . . did a couple of other people in the class feel there was a bit more sort of than just a kind of anger that we're sort of describing. (F) (DM)

164. You know . . . like him pushing and me holding and me getting angry and him getting a little annoyed . . . and this kind of thing. (F,P,EI)

165. Was this a common experience? Or is this something that I'm just reading into it? Yeah . . . (F,P) (GI,DM,AE)

166. *Miss Smith:* Well, I don't feel like . . . I didn't get the idea at all. (-F↓,-P↓) (RS,RP,CD,AD,DD)

167. I seemed to feel that it was like you read about some people leaning more toward . . . like toward the genetic interpretation and others toward the environment and I just had the feeling that, you know, it started to separate the people you know that were . . . more leaning to one a little bit more . . . (-X↑) (RP,CD,AE)

168. *Mr. C:* Any other comments on this? (X↓,F↑) (DM)

169. So you're arguing that it was sort of an intellectual kind of separation, in terms of people taking different positions. (F)

170. Mr. Stall, there was a note of recognition or smile on your face. Would you like to share that thought with us? (FA,F, EI) (GI,RP,DM,DD)

171. *Mr. Stall:* No, I just thought . . . (-F↓) (RS,CD,AE)

172. *Mr. C:* If you don't want to you don't have to; I'm not trying to push you. (FA↓,F↑,EI) (DM,RP)

173. *Mr. Stall:* I just thought it was a good argument. I like to sit back and listen to it. (-F↓,EI) (WI,DN,AD)

174. *Class:* Loud laugh. (-FA,EI) (AE)

175. *Mr. C:* Did you feel like getting in there and pitching? (F,EI) (GI,DM,AE)

176. *Mr. Stall:* No. I want to stay on the sidelines. (-F↓,-EI↓) (WI,AD)

177. *Mr. C:* How many of you wanted to get in there and pitch but sort of just held back? (F,EI) (GI,DM,AE)

178. *Class:* Silence. (-F↓,-EI↓) (WI)

179. *Mr. C:* No takers . . . (EI,P) (GI,DM,AE)

180. *Class:* Laugh. (-EI) (AE)

Segment D-2

181. *Mr. C:* It's awfully hard to attack a teacher, then, I guess. Is this the message that comes through? (F,FA,EI,P) (RP,IN, AD,DD)

182. Yes, Mr. Motley. (FA,F↑) (DM)

183. *Mr. Motley:* Well, it's sort of like fighting City Hall. (-FA,F) (MA,AC,DN,AE,DE)

184. I mean you made up the test and I don't like to argue because usually you . . . you've got an answer which is in your mind; like "that's what the good argument was" and normally a teacher won't change his mind. (-FA,-P↓,F) (GI,DN,DE)

185. *Mr. C:* How about that number five? (referring to the test item) (FA↓,P↑) (GI,IN,DD)

186. *Mr. Motley:* Although that number 5 . . . that was an exception . . . that number 5 was an exception. (-FA,-P) (RP,DN,DE)

187. But most of the time you can't fight . . . I mean, a multiple choice you couldn't fight at all. There's nothing too much you can do. (-FA,-P,-F↓) (DN,AE,DE)

188. And also, you get the feeling that you . . . you hate . . . hate to change your mind anyways. It's sort of saying that "well I goofed," . . . and I think that's along where the big argument came in . . . the big fight came in. (FA,-EI,-P) (GI,IN,AE)

189. But I don't know . . . maybe you don't . . . maybe you don't feel that way but I think . . . you know . . . you sort of hated to say "well, maybe there was more than one answer." (-FA,-P) (RP,DN,AE)

190. *Mr. Motley:* You tried to make a test where there's only one answer. (-FA) (GI,CD)

191. *Mr. C:* Right. (FA) (AC)

192. *Miss Smith:* I'm not sure that it's so much changing your mind as that the questions you asked and the answers you expected back on them were kind of the way that you've been gearing the course in the last couple of weeks anyway. (+FA) (AC,DN)

193. And it wasn't a question of right or wrong. It was just that . . . you know . . . this was what you had explained to us and . . . uh . . . unless anyone had done real extensive reading on their own and . . . you know . . . had come up with a complete opposite viewpoint which I think you would have accepted if they had had enough to support it (X,+SA,FA) (AC,IN,AD)

194. It was just that I don't think . . . maybe . . . oh maybe one question would be better than another but just the fact that this is how you had been gearing the course . . . and what you had provided us with . . . and it's not that you have to change your mind and that we try to get you to change your mind. (+FA,P) (AC,DN)

195. *Mr. C:* So there's a little bit of rigidity coming through. Uhm . . . said very nicely, but a little bit of rigidity coming through on my part. (EI,X↓,FA↓,F,P↑) (AC, CD, DE)

196. *Class:* Laugh. (EI,P) (AE)

197. *Mr. C:* Is this sort of general . . . uh . . . feeling or is this a consistent kind of thing. You know, like we hold the fort

regardless of what happens. I don't know. (F,EI,P) (GI,IN, DE)

198. Mr. Motley, you're shaking you head. This is how it comes to you? (FA,F) (DM)

199. *Mr. Motley:* By rigidity you mean that . . . uh . . . you're . . . what you're telling us in the class is . . . (FA,F) (DN, AE)

200. *Mr. C:* The Law. You know . . . it's the Ten Commandments, follow those. (FA↓,F) (GI,IN,DE)

201. *Mr. Motley:* I get that somewhat but I . . . (-FA,F) (GI, DN,AE)

202. Now when I think about it, it would have to be that way somewhat. Because you're our teacher . . . (+FA) (RP, DN,DE)

203. Where if we use our own, a lot of those questions could have been answered by . . . you know . . . "well let me think it out" and what we had before we came into the course . . . (-X↑,FA,-F↓)

204. If we're actually going to get anything out of this course I think we'd have to follow close to what . . . the way your . . . your plan of thinking on different questions. (+FA, -F↓) (AC,DN,AE)

205. *Mr. C:* Uh huh. Miss Jewel. (FA,F) (DM)

206. *Miss Jewel:* Well, I don't get that impression at all. I think it's completely open . . . on the exam, especially . . . just draw from your past knowledge almost entirely, I thought. (+FA,+F) (AC,DN)

207. And anyway, in our class discussions it was pretty open. I mean you weren't saying "this is it." I didn't get that impression at all. (+EI,+FA,+F) (MT,IN)

208. *Mr. C:* Um . . . we have a disagreement. Mr. Motley, you disagree with Miss Jewel. (FA,F↑) (GI,IN,DD)

209. *Mr. Motley:* Well . . . well . . . when you say past knowledge we're . . . this is Psychology 101 and we can't draw from our past knowledge of before . . . uh . . . our opinions maybe. (-X↑,-FA↑,-F↓) (RS,DN,DE)

210. But our opinions must have been geared toward what was . . . what . . . toward Psychology 101. (-FA↑,-X↑,-F↓) (DN,AE)

211. *Miss Jewel:* I know. If we have some intelligence, our opinions are backed up already, aren't they? (+SA,+F) (MT,IN,SE)

212. *Mr. Motley:* Uh . . . Well, we have a . . . we have an in-

sight to it but I think that the opinions should be developed
in the course and what the way to think . . . in the way I
mean . . . the right . . . the thing about the right way to
handle it. (-X↑,-F↓,-FA↑) (GI,DN,DE)

213. I don't think I had too much insight into it . . . the question
on the test before I came in here. I think from past knowledge I don't think I had . . . to answer the questions the way
you wanted them as we got them in class. (-X↑,-FA↑,-F↓,
-SA↑) (DN,DE)

Segment D

	Task						
Segment	X	FA	SA	F	EI	P	Affect
(D1) Teacher				+	+		Dominance, Guilt Inducing, Accepting
Students				↓			Counterdependency, Withdrawing, Accepting, Denying Anxiety
(D2) Teacher	↓			↑	+		Independency, Depression, Denying Depression
Mr. Motley	↑	↑		↓		−	Guilt Inducing, Making Reparation, Dependency, Expressing Anxiety, Depression
Misses Smith and Jewel	+			+	+		Accepting, Moving Toward

Segment D is rather brief and, in many ways, it is a continuation
of Mr. C's earlier move toward self-criticism and toward the encouragement of student criticism of himself and the course. Interestingly
enough, it is really a reversion to the first monologue, at least insofar
as the task strategy is one of downplaying his role as formal authority
and emphasizing his role as facilitator. Just as the monologue in segment A derived from the effect of the exam, so too this segment
is related to the just completed fight with Mr. Wicker. As we have
seen before, Mr. C is capable of regaining both his control and his
composure while playing the facilitator role, and there is some reason
to believe he needed some time to recover from the interchange
with Mr. Wicker. There is, however, one important new element

in this segment: the teacher as ego ideal. What form does this ideal take, as portrayed by the teacher? What is the heroic and courageous thing to do at this juncture? The answer lies in the teacher's evident willingness to be open, to be emotionally vulnerable. He invites students to criticize him for being rigid and authoritarian. The fact that they refuse his invitation for the most part is another matter which we will come to shortly. The questions before us at the moment are: What are the teacher's task strategies at this juncture? How are they related to his feelings toward the students?

At one level it appears that Mr. C is simply opening things up for the students to ventilate some of the grievances, and this does tend to cast him in the heroic role of being "able to take it." At another level, however, when looked at in the context of his recent victory over Mr. Wicker, this segment suggests a slightly different picture. Mr. C is, in effect, asking students to criticize him for qualities only recently shown to be true of Mr. Wicker: qualities of rigidity, authoritarianism, and an unwillingness to respond sensitively to others. The message in this segment for Mr. Wicker seems to be, "See, kid, this is how a good person looks when he is under attack; he's brave and receptive. Now you try it."

The conjecture that segment D is at least in part a continuation of Mr. C's fight with Mr. Wicker is supported by the evidence that the students were unable to connect with Mr. C's sudden new mood of excited openness. Miss Smith and Mr. Stall, for example, struggle mightily to deny the personal animus either in themselves or others. Mr. Motley enters only to insist that the issue is not personal but a matter of formal authority. But the key act is the general silence and unwillingness of the students to enter on the teacher's terms. Withdrawal, anxiety, and the effort to freeze out the teacher as facilitator (in the realm of personal feelings at least) are characteristic of most of this segment. The students' efforts to focus attention on the teacher as formal authority, and within this context to express mainly feelings of dependency and loyalty, clash rather dramatically with Mr. C's heroic efforts to portray what it means to be open and brave.

In one sense the teacher's invitation to the students to be critical or even "annoyed" amounts to an invitation to side with Mr. Wicker, to express the personal animosity Mr. C seemed to think Mr. Wicker and others were harboring against him. Given Mr. C's recent treatment of Mr. Wicker and Mr. Wicker's forced retreat, it is little wonder that no one volunteered to be lumped in Mr. C's mind with Mr. Wicker. In this context the teacher as facilitator is a distinct threat. He seems to be trying to flush out angers or criticisms which he says he can absorb, but the evidence of his previous tangle with Mr. Wicker suggests caution. Thus the teacher as facilitator is ignored, and the teacher is thrust back to the impersonal and safer world of exam question and teacher's expectations in the cognitive domain. Not all students react this way, but the overall impact of the students' unresponsiveness is to thwart the teacher's efforts at being the heroic, open, and vulnerable target of their resentments.

Segment E-1

214. *Mr. C:* Mr. Wicker. (FA,F↑) (DM)
215. *Mr. Wicker:* I think some of the readings stimulate your own ideas, and from this reading maybe you'll disagree with some of the things you'll read . . . I mean it's part of Psych 101 . . . Psychology 101 too if while you're reading this stimulates other ideas. I think you should be able to bring these in too. (-FA,-F↑) (MA,RP,IN,DD)

Segment E-2

216. *Mr. Meadow:* Well, when I encountered the question I worried for awhile whether we were supposed to include the stuff that we had read or not in answering . . . because if you had . . . (-FA,-F↓) (RS,RP,DN,AE,DE)
217. well . . . from what we've read the difference in intelligence might be two or three I.Q. points if you move the social class and environment close together . . . (-X,-FA) (DE)
218. and so I sort of felt that we couldn't use that . . . that's what we've learned in our reading . . . that they can't show that there's any difference, or the difference was small. (X, -FA) (RS,IN,DE)
219. *Mr. C:* You felt that the consensus of what you had read led to the conclusion that if you hold environment constant then the differences which are usually quite great fall down to the point where you could say it's due to some kind of chance error and not really any meaningful kind of thing.
220. *Mr. Meadow:* Yeah . . . or even if there is a difference it couldn't cause the effect that is suggested in the question, that's a very large difference. (X) (RS,DN,DE)
221. *Mr. C:* Mr. Warren. (FA) (DM)
222. *Mr. Warren:* I think . . . I think the whole thing comes from the question because actually you asked for three plausible reasons and it all boils down to the fact that the only differences between the whites and the Negroes is that the

Negroes are discrim . . . discriminated against . . . and . . . (FA,-X,SA) (RS,CD)

223. *Mr. Warren:* uhm . . . you know . . . and that's where the whole difference comes in. (X)

224. Maybe, like one reason would be . . . uh . . . say they were discriminated . . . uh . . . before the child was born and the mother had a rough treatment . . . and you could say well they had . . . he had . . . he was disc . . . the, the Negro hospitals are worse and uhm . . . the child was born with more brain damage. (X,SA) (AC,DN,AE,DE)

225. Or, the Negro teachers are worse; but it all boils down to the same thing: that they're discriminated against. But . . . (-FA, X,SA)

226. You know, I mean . . . it doesn't seem like . . . (-FA,X)

227. I really don't think it's a very good question. Because uh . . . because I think it's all three examples of one thing. (-FA) (MA,MT)

228. The way I see it . . . you know what I mean? (-F↑)

229. because I don't see where . . . heredity versus environment comes in . . . it's all discrimination. (-FA,X) (RS,AC,CD)

230. *Mr. C:* But Mr. Wicker disagrees quite strongly. You see, he interprets the question to the effect that genetics can play . . . uh, very strong part. (FA,F↑) (GI(DM,DD)

231. *Mr. Warren:* You know . . . that's the whole thing . . . I put down . . . uh . . . two answers . . . what I said about discrimination is . . . that . . . well . . . another one is . . . you know . . . no good so I'll just . . . well maybe it's due to heredity, 'cause it's it's . . . (F,-FA) (GI,AC,CD,DD)

232. and that's another thing, the word "plausible" is really a bad word because I mean almost anything is plausible. (-FA) (RS,AC)

233. *Mr. C:* Mr. Meadow. (FA) (DM)

234. *Mr. Meadow:* Well, when I put down my three answers I made them all according to environment but I can see how if you really wanted to pick it apart you could say they were all the same answer, just worded differently and I was really hurting for different reasons. (-X,F,-FA) (RS,AC,DN, AE,DE)

Segment E-3

235. *Mr. C:* This is what happened to you, Miss Straus (mispronounces name as "straws") as well? Miss Straus, have I mispronounced your name, Miss Straus? (FA,F) (MT,RM,AE)

236. What *is* your name? (P)

237. *Class:* Laugh. (P) (AE)

238. *Miss Straus:* Straus [she pronounces it as if it rhymed with house]. (FA,P) (MT,DN,AE)

239. *Mr. C:* Miss Straus (incorrect form "Straws" again). No wonder I haven't been getting to you. (F,P) (MT,CD,DE)

240. *Class:* Laugh. (F,P)

241. *Mr. C:* My original association to your name was . . . sure, was "straws" (incorrect form again). Isn't that strange. Okay. (P)

242. I'm sorry; I apologize. (P) (RP,CD,DE)

243. You were shaking your head there and I . . . you were shaking you head in sort of agreement with what Mr . . . is this the sort of a feeling that you had about it then? (FA,F) (AC,DM,AE)

244. *Miss Straus:* Yes, I think there was one interpretation of the answer and it was just "try to find three different ways of saying that it was all due to environment." (-FA,F) (AC, DN,AE)

Segment E-4

245. *Mr. C:* Uhmmm. All right, Mr. Alter. (FA,) (DM)

246. *Mr. Alter:* I think that you . . . I don't think that you really can say that because see . . . there are different factors in environment and they weren't just . . . it's all environment and blocked together it's . . . (FA,X,SA) (AC,DN,DD)

247. There is one specific fact, for instance, prenatal factors, and . . . then, there's ah . . . the social role that which he's supposed to portray and so forth. There's . . . entirely separate answers and I think there were more than three. (+FA, X,SA)

248. *Mr. C:* Uhm . . . I think I follow your conclusion . . . your point to its logical conclusion. You're saying that under some circumstances one aspect of this environment may be the crucial kind of thing. (X,SA,F) (AC,DM,DD)

249. You know, it could be that everything you're picking up is the result of prenatal difficulties or everything you're picking up is the result of a very harsh kind of discrimination, or it may be a combination, or interaction of a variety of things. (X,SA)

Segment E-5

250. *Mr. C:* Yeah, that's on the environmental side of the coin. That's a reasonable interpretation of the environmental side of the coin. (SA) (AC,DM)

251. *Mr. Warren:* Well, I mean that's all right what he said but the whole difference is due to discrimination . . . that's the only difference . . . that's why you used Negroes and whites: because that's the only difference between them . . . except that one is treated inferiorly . . . and uh . . . because they're treated inferiorly there's a difference that of all through life . . . and just . . . (X,SA,-FA) (RS,CD,DD)

252. You know what I mean? (-FA,F)

253. They get worse treatment all along. (SA)

254. Do you see . . . what I'm saying that . . . a . . . that the whole thing is that . . . there's discrimination and all you have to do is pick out three examples of where . . . of where . . . a . . . a Negro child would get a worse deal than a white child. (-FA,F↑) (GI,DN,AE)

255. *Mr. C:* All right . . . This is a . . . uhm . . . statement in the sense of the central issue along the environmental side because all the other environmental issues that arise, have something to do with this kind of thing I think I would . . . uh . . . (X,F) (AC,DM,DE)

256. *Mr. Warren:* Th-th-that way you're saying that . . . uh . . . all difference is due to environment . . . 100% of it. (-FA,X) (RS,CD)

257. *Mr. C:* Well . . . uh . . . (FA,P) (DM,AE)

258. *Mr. Warren:* Because like when the . . . when the . . . like I said before the child's born . . . you know . . . (-FA,-P↓) (GI,DN,DE)

259. or while the child's being born the mother's going to get worse treatment . . . because she's going to be coming from a worse hospital . . . and it's all . . . it all goes back to discrimination. (X)

In segment E the class seems to be recovering from the antagonisms and intensity of segment C. The teacher is back in the comfortable role as moderator, and, except for a brief exchange with one student over how to pronounce her name, the interaction in this segment is considerably less personal than in the previous segments. In fact, everything is so smooth, and everyone seems in such full accord regarding the minimal role of heredity in the poor performance of Negroes, one might almost forget Mr. Wicker's presence

Segment E

Segment	Task						Affect
	X	FA	SA	F	EI	P	
(E1)							
(E2) Teacher		+					Dominance
Mr. Meadow and Warren	+	−					Resisting, Depression, Accepting
(E3) Teacher			↑			↑	Moving Toward, Counterdominance
Miss Straus						+	Dependency, Expressing Anxiety
(E4) Teacher	+		+				Dominance, Accepting
Mr. Alter	+	+	+				Dependency, Accepting
(E5) Teacher							Dominance
Mr. Warren	+	−					Resisting, Counterdependency, Guilt Inducing Dependency

and the recent fight. And perhaps that is precisely what the participants in this segment are trying to do. For the second time in this session Mr. Warren has moved in to press his version of how the teacher has erred, and Mr. Warren's version clearly grants the supreme importance of environment. That's the problem, as he sees it. How can anything more be said after one has said the answer is the environment? As before, the issues which stir up Mr. Warren's contention center around Mr. C's failure to perform well his role as formal authority, and he leaves some doubt as to whether these failures might not be caused by some deficiency in Mr. C's ability to think abstractly. However, Mr. C fails, as before, to respond with much vigor to Mr. Warren's assertions and insinuations. Perhaps Mr. C was about to respond when Mr. Wicker, now at least partially recovered from the earlier round, returns to the battle. With his return the shifting but not very intense acts of segment E give way to another round of the battle over values (and two points).

Segment F-1

260. *Mr. C:* Well . . . go ahead Mr. Wicker. (FA) (DM)

261. *Mr. Wicker:* Well, this may be a little far out. (FA) (RP, DN)

262. *Mr. C:* Go ahead, try it. (FA,F,EI) (DM,AC)

263. *Mr. Wicker:* The only reason that he is being discriminated against is because of his heredity. (-SA↓,-F↓) (RS,CD,DD)

264. and couldn't you use . . . because of his Negro heredity . . . and couldn't you use this to go on farther and say that perhaps that this is the reason that he's antisocial . . . because of his heredity? (-SA↓)

265. *Mr. Meadow:* But we know it isn't true because they were brought in from Africa and made slaves and they were taken from their environment and made slaves and . . . they were lib . . . . liber . . . (X,SA) (AC,DN,DE)

266. *Mr. C:* Liberated. (FA) (DM)

267. *Mr. Meadow:* liberated . . . and there's a lot of prejudice against them, right? (X,SA) (AC,DN,DE)

268. *Mr. Wicker:* Yeah, but today a person walks in the door and if he's a Negro he's discriminated against . . . discriminated against solely on account of his heredity. (-SA↓) (RS,CD, DD)

269. *Miss Straus:* Well the color of his skin is influential. (SA,X) (AC,DN)

270. *Mr. Wicker:* Well, the color of his skin is part of his heredity. (X,-FA,-SA↓) (RS,CD,DD)

271. *Class:* Laugh. (-FA) (AE)

272. *Mr. Wicker:* And therefore because of . . . it's because of his heredity that he later becomes antisocial. Because he's discriminated against. (X,-SA↓) (RS,CD)

273. *Miss Jewel:* That's environment. (X,+SA) (AC,IN)

274. *Mr. C:* Go on . . . speak any time you like (to Alter who has his hand up). (F) (GI,DM)

275. *Mr. Alter:* Ah . . . I think that . . . well . . . it can be because of his heredity that he's discriminated against but it's by his environment. This environment is the means through which he is discriminate . . . discriminated. (X,+SA) (AC, DN)

276. *Mr. Wicker:* But still the basic cause is . . . I mean . . . if his heredity was different there wouldn't be any environment to affect him . . . (X,-SA) (RS,CD)

277. *Mr. Alter:* Well if he had no environmental influences in regard to his heredity his heredity wouldn't make that much difference. It's his social role which is environmental. (X,SA) (AC,DN)

278. *Mr. Wicker:* I agree with everything he said (to Mr. C).

279. It's . . . but it all traces back to his heredity though. (-FA↓, -SA↓) (RS,CD,DD)

280. *Mr. C:* Where do we go? (FA↓, F↑,P) (MT,CD,DE)
281. *Class:* Laugh. (FA,P) (AE)

Segment F-2

282. *Miss Smith:* It's based pretty strongly on our scale of what's superior and what's inferior. (SA) (AC,DN,DD)

283. I mean, you know . . . like we were saying if you gave . . . you know . . . maybe some of our IQ tests to say someone from China, that they would come out differently just because their whole way of thinking is different . . . and this might be part of it. I mean, it's our standards, it's our tests that we're administering. (X,SA,FA)

284. *Mr. C:* Let's follow that point a little further. (X,FA,F,SA) (AC,DM)

285. This is part, again, that you're pointing out Miss Smith . . . it's part of the environmental thing . . . in the particular test situation where there's a built-in bias. (X,SA,F) (DM)

286. In other words you know . . . over and above the fact that the test is written in English rather than Chinese (humorously). (X,EI) (DM,DD)

287. *Class:* Laugh (loud and long). (AE,DD)

288. *Mr. C:* Clearly it's not an experience that a . . . that a Chinese had and that really taps what is functional intelligence from their point of view. Well, let's look at it this way, (X,SA) (DM,DE)

289. all right, go on Mr. Brewer. (FA) (DM)

290. *Mr. Brewer:* Uhm . . . I think . . . uh . . . I agree with her (X,+SA) (AC,DN)

291. because . . . a . . . I had a teacher from England once in in Canada who uh . . . a . . . taught the way they do in England and . . . especially in our math test . . . uh . . . if you get an American teacher you're pretty well assured that you're going to get something without tricks, 80% of the time . . . whereas in England every question those kids get have a trick in it. (-FA) (GI,DN,AE)

292. And so I think they just get an entirely different way of looking at a question . . . looking for something to catch them up rather than some basic principle to apply. I think you can apply that to an IQ test. (-FA,X)

293. *Mr. C:* Yes, Mr. Monk, you were up before. (FA,F) (DM)

294. *Mr. Monk:* But in the question you stated to us that the IQ's were actually different, didn't you? You said nothing about tests so we just had to take it from you that you took all

these things into consideration and gave us the correct . . . (-FA) (RS,CD)

295. *Mr. C:* No . . . all I stated . . . all the item stated was that the school performance and the antisocial behavior differed, uhm . . . social class, sex, and age were controlled for, and these differences increased with grade or age . . . (FA↑,X) (GI,DM,DE)

296. The older the kid got, the worse off the Negroes got vis-à-vis the whites in terms of performance and in terms of antisocial behavior . . . they had poorer performance and were more antisocial behavior. (X)

297. *Mr. Monk:* So we're talking now about the ability of the Negro to adapt himself to a certain way of conducting class or taking a test. (X,F) (RS,CD)

298. *Mr. C:* This might be . . . part of it . . . (X) (AC,DM,DE)

299. this is the suggestion that Mr. Brewer is coming up with is that coming from a certain kind of environment . . . (X,F) (DM,DE)

300. that is, being a minority group or being a member of a lower class as well, has certain built-in kind of experiences that may not be tapped on an IQ test or school performance than if you're coming from a middle class environment or coming from an English environment or Canadian environment . . . may not train you for the kinds of things that you're being tapped on. (X,SA↑)

Segment F-3

301. *Mr. C:* Let's carry Mr. Wicker's point and . . . or was it suggested by Mr. Alter . . . a little further. (F↑,FA) (DM)

302. That is . . . there is a genetically determined color difference and this is what the environment responds to, so this is genetic kind of . . . if I'm interpreting your point correctly? This is a genetic kind of interpretation. (X,F)

303. Well . . . uh, let us . . . uhm . . . raise the question of a similar kind of differentiation that takes place . . . uhm . . . in . . . uhm . . . uhm . . . in a different kind of situation. (X,F) (DM,DE)

304. Uhm . . . yeah go on (to Mr. Motley). (F,FA) (DM)

305. *Mr. Motley:* No, I didn't have anything. (-F↓) (WI,DE)

306. *Mr. C:* Okay. How many of you have seen the film *Exodus?* (FA)

307. *Mr. C:* All right, you know that in that "Exodus" there is a scene in which . . . a . . . Paul Newman is . . . a . . .

approached by Peter Lawford, I think it is, uhm . . . in which Lawford is communicating certain opinions about . . . uhm . . . the nature of a . . . a . . . differences between . . . uh . . . Jewish individuals and non-Jewish individuals, and that he can differentiate a Jew from a non-Jew on the basis of very subtle kinds of criteria. (X,P) (GI,DM,AE,DE)

308. And in the film this is very different, I mean it's played up very big, obviously. (P↑,FA↓) (RP,CD,DE)

309. But . . . uh . . . here is Paul Newman dressed in a British Army officer's uniform. He also happens to be the leader of the particular terrorist movement, uh . . . the Israeli terrorist movement. And . . . uh . . . he is conning Peter Lawford out of trucks and some other stuff, and it's very clear that . . . uhm . . . Lawford is not aware of the fact that he is looking . . . (P,FA) (GI,DM,DE)

310. Uhm . . . well, in fact what Newman does to . . . magnify this thing . . . he says, "Geez, you know I have something in my eye here. Would you care to look in my eye?" (P,EI) (MA,DD)

311. Now supposedly Lawford can sniff out a . . . a . . . some Jewish individual just by looking at him . . . and . . . uh . . . you know the whole impact is . . . you know . . . this poor prejudiced bastard and this kind of thing. (P,EI) (GI, DM,DE)

312. *Class:* Laugh. (-P)

Segment F-4

313. *Mr. C:* Uhm . . . but . . . uh . . . and also, I don't know . . . is this uh . . . let me raise another question. (P↓,X↑,FA) (MA,DM,DD)

314. Why was it so necessary . . . uhm . . . during the war . . . uh . . . to have . . . uh . . . Jewish individuals walk around with identifying signs in terms of armbands and this kind of thing? (X,P,FA,SA) (GI,DM,AE,DD)

315. *Class:* Silence. (-SA↓,-P↓) (WI,AE)

316. *Mr. C:* Now . . . you see if the difference is because the pattern of discrimination that we're talking about is a very similar one, in many ways. And . . . you know when you do move into various situations where . . . uh . . . you do get a hot kind of discrimination all across the board, then it goes against minority groups in a similar manner at times . . . (X,P↑) (GI,DM,AE,DE)

317. But it varies obviously because the thing is very complicated. (X,F) (RP,CD,DE).

318. But why were these symbols necessary? (X,F,SA) (GI,DM, DE)

319. *Mr. Wicker:* They . . .

320. *Mr. C:* Try to speak up. (FA,F) (GI,DM,AE)

321. *Mr. Wicker:* They couldn't tell, they felt they wanted to know who the Jewish people were. (F,P,-SA) (RS,DN)

322. *Mr. C:* That's right. They wanted to make sure that there were clear identifying signs. (X,F,SA↑) (AC,DM)

323. *Mr. Wicker:* So that they could discriminate against them. (F,SA,X) (AC,DN)

324. *Mr. C:* That's right. (F,SA) (DM,AC)

325. So what role does the environment or the genetically given signs play in a case of this kind? (X↑,F,SA) (GI,DM,DD)

326. *Mr. Wicker:* Well, in that case the genetic difference isn't as noticeable. (-X↓,-F↓,-SA↓) (MA,CD,DE)

327. I mean . . . I don't, I don't quite see what your . . . (-SA↓) (WI,AE)

328. *Mr. C:* Well, let's explore the thought. I think this is a good example. Let's see what kinds of things come up. (F↑,SA) (RP,IN,AD,DD)

Segment F-5

329. *Mr. Alter:* Wouldn't the color of his skin . . . of a Negro's . . . be the same as the armband of the Jewish person? (+SA,+X,+F) (AC,DN,AE)

330. *Mr. C:* This is . . . it serves the same intention, I think. (F,SA) (AC,DM)

331. *Mr. Alter:* Well . . . I actually don't see any difference between the two. They're both signs on which the environment has to react. (F,SA) (AC,DN,AE)

332. *Mr. C:* It . . . are you suggesting that it's a sign that the environmental grips on to and uses in terms of focusing whatever . . . the environment being the people and all things . . . whatever there is mobilized in the society to let go. (X,F,SA) (AC,DM,AE)

333. Does this make a . . . a . . . sensible kind of thing here? Does that fit? Does that broaden sort of the notion that you're suggesting? This is what I'm getting at, Mr. Wicker. (F,SA↑) (GI,DM)

334. *Mr. Wicker:* I . . . I don't see any relationship to what . . . it's just the same thing . . . I don't see any broadening of the notion. (-F,-SA↓) (RS,CD)

335. *Miss Smith:* Yeah . . . Aren't you saying well that it's partly genetic, partly environment? I mean that one kind of starts up the other. I mean you can't say it's genetic just because a . . . you know . . . perhaps a Negro's black. (X,F,SA) (AC,DN)

336. *Miss Smith:* That you know, therefore it's all genetic because of the way people react to him, because when . . . uhm . . . I think it was a couple of weeks ago when we were standing in Angell Hall you were talking about Allen and the fact that it's an interaction between your heredity and your environment, and they kind of work pretty closely. (X,SA, EI) (AC,DN)

Segment F-6

337. *Mr. C:* I think we can clarify . . . (F↑,X) (AC,DM)

338. see Mr. Wicker what you're saying . . . you see, you're labeling your position a genetic position and it's really not. (X,FA↑) (GI,DM)

339. *Mr. Wicker:* Yeah . . . what I . . . what I was saying . . . I don't believe this . . . I mean I was just bringing it out as a point that it it . . . you could . . . that's why I said it was sort of way out. (FA,-F) (RP,DN,AE,DD)

340. That you could point out and say that this person is . . . ah . . . wouldn't be treated this way if it wasn't for his heredity. (SA,-P↑) (RS,CD,DD)

341. But of course . . . I mean . . . it's reacted through his environment I think.

342. *Mr. C:* The words you used . . . let me quote you . . . "you wouldn't be treated this way unless it was because of his heredity." (FA,F) (GI,DD)

343. *Mr. Wicker:* Yeah. (FA) (AC)

344. *Mr. C:* These are the key terms in interaction. (X) (GI)

345. *Mr. Wicker:* A person walks in this room . . . comes in here . . . (SA,F) (RS,CD)

346. *Mr. C:* Right. (SA,F) (AC)

347. *Mr. Wicker:* and sits down. (SA,F) (RS,CD)

348. *Mr. C:* Right. (SA,F) (AC)

349. *Mr. Wicker:* And if he was white he'd be treated one way . . . but because his heredity is different he's treated another way. (X,-SA) (RS,CD)

350. *Mr. C:* That's right. (X,FA,SA↑,F↑) (AC,DM,DD)

351. *Mr. Wicker:* And that . . . that was the whole issue. (-F↑, -X↑) (RS,CD)

352. *Mr. C:* Well . . . this you're describing beautifully, beautifully an interactional position. (X,SA,EI) (RS,AC,DM,DD)
353. This is what interaction is . . . that given certain differences genetically, be it early or later maturing, be it . . . uh . . . Jewish characteristics versus non-Jewish characteristics, versus —a—given a Polish name versus non-Polish name, uhm, Negro skin versus white skin, ah . . . Chinese slanted eyes versus ah . . . American slanted eyes . . . whatever it is. (SA↑,EI↑) (GI,AC,DM,DE)
354. *Class:* Laugh. (EI,SA) (AE)
355. *Mr. C:* The environment responds differently to these different kinds of physical or biological givens, right? (X,SA,FA) (RS,AC,DM,DD)
356. *Mr. Wicker:* Uhm. (X,SA,FA) (AC,DE)
357. *Mr. C:* And what you're describing is beautiful in the sense that that's an interactional position. (X,EI) (GI,RP,DM,DD)
358. *Mr. Wicker:* Okay. (X,FA,EI) (RS,AC,DD)
359. *Miss Jewel:* You won. (FA,EI,SA,P) (AC,DN,DD)
360. *Class:* Laugh. (FA,EI,P)

Segment F-7

361. *Mr. C:* I think you were screwing yourself up in labeling the position that you're defending wrongly. (X,F,EI↑) (RP,DM)
362. In other words, you're saying "I'm saying it's all genetics" but what you're talking about is a very nice interaction which is 100% accurate between genetics and environment. (X, SA,F)
363. You may say in the beginning that Negroes may start off genetically endowed less than whites, that's reasonable, that's plausible . . . but still this endowment must interact with some kind of environment, which is what you were describing. (SA,F↑) (RS,AC,DM)
364. There's no real disagreement on an intellectual level. What I was sort of raising this whole thing for is because I felt there was a lot of ah . . . you know . . . sort of "let's kill each other kind of thing" (X↓,F↑,EI↑,P↑) (MA,RP,DM,AE)
365. and that's okay. (F,FA) (DM)
366. I mean . . . you know . . . there's got to be a swift argument going on. Otherwise you're going to sit back and you're going to sleep . . . and I'd rather have you taking off at me with a gun than to have you sleep. (FA↓,F,EI↑,P↑) (RP,CD,AD,DD)

367. That's the worst thing you can do to a teacher . . . is sleep in his class. (P,EI,FA) (GI,DM,AE,DE)

368. *Mr. Wicker:* Whenever I was arguing this last point I was using it in no relationship to our argument the other day; I mean, you know, it was just a point that occurred to me. (-FA,-P↓,-X↑,F) (RP,DN,DD)

Segment F

	Task						Affect
Segment	X	FA	SA	F	EI	P	
(F1) Teacher		↓		↑			Dominance
Mr. Wicker	+		↓				Resisting, Counterdependency, Denying Depression
Students	+		+				Accepting, Dependency
(F2) Teacher	+						Dominance, Depression
Mr. Monk and Brewer			−				Resisting, Counterdependency
Miss Smith			+				Accepting, Dependency
(F3) Teacher						+	Showing Depression
(F4) Teacher	+		+	+			Guilt Inducing, Depression, Denying Depression
Mr. Wicker			↓				Resisting
(F5) Teacher			+	+			Dominance, Accepting
Mr. Wicker			↓				Resisting, Counterdependency
Mr. Alter			+	+			Accepting, Dependency
(F6) Teacher	+		↑	+			Accepting, Denying Depression, Guilt Inducing
Mr. Wicker		+	+				Resisting, Counterdependency, Denying Depression, Accepting
(F7) Teacher				+	↑	↑	Making Reparation

Mr. Wicker returns to the battle with, as he put it, "a point that just occurred to me." By the end of the segment, however, Miss Jewel can report to Mr. C, with obvious justification, "You won." Perhaps others would view this interaction differently, but we are struck by the fact that Mr. Wicker never really had a chance. His choice of argument, his disruption of the growing consensus within the class, his earlier claim that all he wanted was a couple of extra points, all these factors combine to make the outcome of the argument easy to predict.

How did Mr. C "win?" The sequence immediately prior to Mr. Wicker's final "Okay" suggests one answer, that Mr. C neatly managed to redefine Mr. Wicker's racist heresy as really no heresy at all. The problem, it turned out, was that Mr. Wicker was a true believer all along and simply did not know it. Thus, Mr. Wicker's argument that discrimination is causd by skin pigmentation was found to be an acceptable aspect of the "interactionist" point of view, and therefore the teacher as socializing agent was able to announce another success, as if to say, "Well, class, I'm happy to announce that Mr. Wicker has decided to join our happy band of liberal interactionists." But the teacher's ability to redefine Mr. Wicker as "in" rather than "out" rested on the expert function, on the teacher's greater command of the boundary definitions of the various intellectual positions in the field.

As one reviews the entire segment, however, and not just the acts immediately preceding Mr. Wicker's capitulation, one can find other very important antecedents of the final outcome. For one thing, the socializing issue had become abundantly clear, as had Mr. C's involvement in the whole fight, when Mr. C made clear symbolic equations between Negroes and Jews and shifted the enemy to first the British and then the Nazis.

Mr. Wicker was once more invited to claim, if he dared, that the "poor prejudiced bastard" or the German SS was not responsible for what happened to the Jews. The issue here is hardly one of expertise. With almost the whole class declared as on his side, the teacher is now far less anxious than before that Mr. Wicker is speaking for a large number of silent, angry students.

Mr. C evidently cannot resist one brief allusion to the possibility of personal animus between Mr. Wicker and himself, to what he calls the " 'let's kill each other' kind of thing." As he had earlier, Mr. Wicker feels threatened by the insinuation and struggles to deny it. In this brief interaction, as in the larger fight which preceded it, Mr. Wicker seems determined to avoid personal contact with the teacher. What, then, are his goals? Above all, his repeated efforts to challenge the teacher seem designed to show up Mr. C as an arbitrary and narrow-minded teacher but, at the same time, by trying to arouse the more impersonal aspects of the teacher's role, this student seems also to be trying to block the teacher from getting too close to him or anyone else. The petulance and the needling, the dogged persistence even when isolated and argued down, and the

strange indifference which accompanies the sudden capitulation
—these are characteristic of a very complex set of motives and perceptions. The task and affective strategies set in motion by Mr.
Wicker, which have played so central a role in this session, are not,
however, derived simply from the private world of Mr. Wicker.
Mr. C, Miss Jewel, Mr. Warren, and even Mr. Wicker's lone ally,
Mr. Monk, all have a part in creating Mr. Wicker's performance.
Next to him the loyal students look more loyal, the bright students
look brighter, and at times the teacher looks like a very patient man.

Mr. Wicker became the scapegoat in one sense: he became
(partly through his own provocations) the target for Mr. C's mistrust
and hostility. What made the struggle legitimate, however, was the
infusion of the value issues, the legitimacy of combatting bigotry
and insensitivity. One wonders, then, in retrospect, whether value
issues are not often used, as they were here, to cover over the antagonisms and mistrust generated simply within the formal authority
domain. This session began, it will be remembered, with a primary
focus on the exam grading. Was it not useful, then, to find a value
issue that could serve as the pretext for the expression and resolution
of anger and mistrust issues within the classroom?

Segment G-1

369. *Mr. C:* All right . . . yeah . . . Mr. Warren. (FA↑,F) (AC, DM)

370. *Mr. Warren:* You . . . can *you* give three . . . ah . . . correct answers? (-FA,-X↑) (GI,DE,AE)

371. *Mr. C:* Can I give three correct answers? I'll give you the
ideal correct answer . . . Yeah. (X,EI,FA) (DM,DD)

372. *Mr. Warren:* But but . . . see that's the whole thing. There's
. . . there's . . . I mean you can give one correct answer
. . . I . . . if you asked for one answer it would be real
easy to just say, oh, well, first of all it's possible that the
Negro is born inferior and . . . ah . . . as he goes on this
increases because he's discriminated against because he's inferior. (-X,-FA,-EI↓) (RS,CD,DD)

373. *Mr. C:* That's right. That's it. (X,FA) (DM)

374. *Mr. Warren:* But that's one answer. But then . . . ah . . .
you can't give any more answers after that. (-X,-FA) (RS, CD)

375. *Mr. C:* Well sure you can. Sure you can. (X,FA↑,EI) (RS, DM,DD)

376. Your general thesis is that . . . uhm . . . uhm . . . there is a possibility that Negroes are less endowed at birth than whites. All right, but the environment comes in and manipulates this kind of potential that's given. That's a general thesis. (X↑,SA) (DM)

377. Now, since it's difficult to establish whether whites and Negroes differ in . . . on genetic endowment, uhm, the only reasonable evidence we have at this point is for the environmental uhm . . . depression of this endowment whatever it is. Sometimes along these lines, (X) (DM)

378. All right. (F,FA)

379. Here are three central environmental presses that are exerted on the Negro that could account for the differences. And then you could argue about the prenatal thing . . . anyone of the 15 things I've listed on there is a reasonable . . . uhm . . . accounting of what we know about it. (X) (GI,DM, DD)

380. We don't know anything about the genetics but we do know a lot about the environment. (X) (DM)

381. So you put your money on the ones that you think are the most important. (X,SA↑,FA)

382. *Mr. Warren:* Aren't those . . . aren't those . . . are those three things . . . are those 100% environment, though? (-X, -FA) (RS,CD)

383. *Mr. C:* Uhm . . . those are on the environmental side of the coin . . . yeah . . . (X,FA) (DM)

384. *Mr. Warren:* I mean if you say . . . uhm. (-FA) (RS,CD)

385. *Mr. C:* Well you could . . . you mean . . . sure you could say . . . that all along there's a genetic-environmental interaction. (FA,X) (DM)

386. *Mr. Warren:* So you could . . . so you could only give one answer that's . . . without . . . you know . . . saying the same thing in different ways. That it interacts heredity and environment. (-X,-FA) (RS,CD)

387. *Mr. C:* This is the basic principle behind the answer. (X, FA↑,SA) (DM,DD)

388. *Mr. Warren:* All right . . . so then you want specifics so . . . you have to . . . your specifics . . . you either have to give specific answers that are 100% environment or 100% heredity. (-X,-SA,FA) (RS,CD)

389. *Mr. C:* No . . . why can't you say that . . . ah . . . Negroes are constantly discriminated against and . . . ah . . . because of their genetically endowed . . . ah . . . intellectual . . . a potential or less potential . . . you could

argue that way but there's no basis for arguing against it. (SA,FA) (RS,DM)

390. *Mr. C:* They cannot . . . they respond to this kind of discrimination differently than let's say a white would. (X,FA)

391. *Mr. Warren:* Wait. (-FA↓,-F↑) (RS,CD)

392. *Mr. C:* So all along the scale you see get this two . . . kind of meshing of genetics and the sort of interactional effects. (X) (DM)

393. *Mr. Warren:* I just don't see where you can get three answers. (X,-FA,-SA,-F↑) (RS)

394. *Mr. C:* Well, you can give any number, any number. (FA,F↓) (DM,DD)

395. *Mr. Warren:* I think you'd just say the same thing over again. (-X,-FA,-F↑) (RS,CD)

Segment G-2

396. *Mr. C:* No, you're not. You're not. I mean . . . then you can say well it's all environment . . . you know, that's the end. Let's quit this course. Let's stop now, (FA,P) (RS,DM)

397. we're saying behavior is a function of genetics and environment, and we can stop, let's go home, you know? (X↑,P) (GI,DM,DE)

398. But no, our job is to see what are these environmental issues specifically. These are important. (SA↑,FA↑) (GI,DM,DD)

399. Not only are these environmental issues, but what are some of the interactions that take place? (X,SA) (DM)

400. Otherwise we can quit. Okay, you've gained the main emphasis here: behavior is a function of the person and the environment . . . goodbye, everybody got an "A" and that's it. You know. (X,FA↑,SA,EI) (GI,DM,DT)

401. *Class:* Laugh. (-SA,EI) (AE)

402. Our job is . . . all right, what are these crucial issues? (SA, EI) (GI,DM,DD)

403. What do we know about the person? What do we know about the environment? (X,SA) (DM)

404. What kind of characteristics of the environment? How do these two intersect? (X,SA)

405. You're a . . . you're fishing for premature closure. (FA, EI,SA↑) (GI,DM,DE)

406. *Class:* Laugh. (EI,SA) (AE)

407. *Mr. Warren:* I . . . I just . . . I just don't know . . . I

just don't like . . . I don't like the question. The more I think about it the worse it gets. (-FA,P) (RS,CD)

408. *Class:* Laugh. (-FA) (AE)

409. *Mr. C:* That's . . . that . . . that's your right, that's your right. (FA,F) (RS,AC,DM)

410. Uhm . . . it's possible. There are questions that people don't like. There are . . . oh . . . ways of teaching that people don't like. (FA,F,EI,P) (GI,DM,AE,DE)

411. There are issues that people don't like, and there are teachers that people don't like. That's your right as a student. That's perfectly okay. (FA,F↑,EI) (GI,AC,DD)

412. But let's be clear. You may not like the question, but there are three reasonable answers to it. They are two separate issues. (FA↑,F,X↑) (GI,AC,DM,AD,DD)

413. *Mr. Warren:* I still can't see it. I'll take your word for it though. (-FA↓,X) (RS,CD)

414. *Mr. C:* No, no, no. Think about it. Don't take my word for it. (F↑,FA↓,SA) (GI,DM,DD)

415. *Mr. Warren:* I did. I . . . I don't understand what you said about . . . I didn't understand your . . . 'cause you started mixing things up. You gave me one example . . . you know what I mean? (-X,-FA) (RS,CD)

416. *Mr. C:* Mm . . . hmm . . . (X,FA,F↑) (DM)

Segment G-3

417. *Mr. Warren:* Well first you said you could give your basic . . . uh . . . uh premise, that there's an interaction. (-X↑, FA) (RS,DN)

418. *Mr. C:* Right. (X,FA) (DM)

419. *Mr. Warren:* Then you give three examples of how Negroes are discriminated against. (X,-FA) (GI,AC,DN,DE)

420. *Mr. C:* How . . . how the environment impinges on it's . . . that . . . that particular, let's say, genetic endowment. That's right. (FA↓,X) (DM,AE)

421. Because we don't know anything about the genetics, we really don't. We cannot sit down and say give me a Negro child at birth . . . in utero . . . and I will measure his genetic potential for intelligence. (X,SA) (GI,DM,DE)

422. This is what we would have to do. And then I would take a group of whites and I would measure their genetic potential for intelligence in utero before the prenatal factors have a chance to start messing things up. (SA↑,X) (DM,DD)

423. *Mr. Warren:* No . . . I understand that . . . I just . . . that's the whole thing. I agree 100% with what you're saying. (FA,SA) (AC,DD)

424. I just don't see where you can give three correct answers . . . and . . . I . . . I . . . three . . . three. (-FA,-X) (RS, CD)

425. *Mr. C:* Well, let's look at it this way. We're talking . . . let's take something very . . . we'll stick to for a while, okay. We'll stick to academic performance. (X,FA) (GI, DM,DD)

426. *Mr. Warren:* All right. (FA) (AC,DN)

427. *Mr. C:* We take two groups of people; a group of Negroes and a group of whites. We get a ten-point discrepancy on some valid measure of academic performance. (X) (AC,DM)

428. Okay. Give me one thing that might account for that discrepancy, just one . . . off the top of your head. (X,FA,SA) (DM)

429. *Mr. Warren:* That . . . the . . . the Negroes had worse training. (X,FA) (RS,CD)

430. *Mr. C:* The Negro suffered some kind of cultural deprivation. (X) (AC,DM)

431. Okay. Stop. That's a perfectly valid explanation, plausible. (X,FA) (DM)

432. *Mr. Warren:* Isn't that 100% environment? (-X,FA) (RS, DN)

433. *Mr. C:* Sure, that's an environmental explanation. (X,FA) (AC,DM)

434. All right give me another one, that could account for those results. (X,FA) (DM)

435. *Mr. Warren:* All right, the . . . the Negroes are stupider than the whites. They have less . . . a lower I.Q. (-X,-SA, -FA) (RS,CD)

436. *Mr. C:* All right. They're . . . well they have a lower I.Q. We're really saying what goes into getting a lower I.Q. (X,FA) (RS,AC,DM)

437. Could . . . couldn't I explain without ever relying on . . . well accept, we'll put and sort of lay the genetic issue to rest for the moment. All right. (FA) (DM,AE,DE)

438. *Mr. Warren:* Right. (FA) (AC,DD)

439. *Mr. C:* We accept that it's possible but we just can't say much about it. We can recognize it as a possibility but we have no evidence one way or the other. (X,SA) (DM)

440. *Mr. C:* So let's lay it to rest. Let's stick on the environment

because this is where we seem to be in trouble. (FA,X) (GI,DM)

441. Can we attribute the difference in two things to the fact that . . . uhm . . . the Negroes because they were tested by a white tester get more anxious in that test and consequently performed poorer? (X,FA,SA↑) (GI,DM,DE)

442. Is this reasonable? Is that a reasonable explanation? Is it different from the first one when we talked about culture deprivation? (FA↑) (DM)

443. *Mr. Warren:* Yeah. (X,FA) (AC,DN,DE)

444. *Mr. C:* Okay. Let us say that it's possible that . . . uhm . . . the Negroes because of poorer medical facilities end up with a higher incidence of brain damage which affects intellectual performance. (X) (GI,DM)

Segment G-4

445. *Mr. Warren:* That's cultural deprivation. (-X) (RS,CD,DE)

446. *Mr. C:* Well, it's not . . . not at all, no, no. (X,FA↑) (RS, DM)

447. Cultural deprivation refers to the fact that the experiences that these people are exposed to are different than the experiences that other people are exposed to. They are not . . . let's say, you know . . . (X,EI↑) (DM)

448. what is cultural deprivation? (X) (DM)

449. It means you read books with the Bobbsey Twins—Do your parents use Spock?; does your mother read you these little books . . . you know on "Choo Choo the Wolf" . . . and uh . . . "Johnny the Train" . . . you know . . . these little stories when you're three years old? (X,EI) (DM,DD)

450. Does your mother encourage you to start writing very young? Do you have lots of crayons to play around with? (EI)

451. Sort of . . . do you have all these opportunities for learning? Does your old man take you to the Museum of Natural History when you're four . . . so you take a look at a brontosaurus dinosaur? (EI)

452. Did you ever have a four-year-old kid come to you and say that's a brontosaurus? It throws you for a loop. But that's what cultural deprivation means. (EI)

453. *Mr. Warren:* I agree . . . I agree it's sort of like do you have the opportunities of being born in good medical facilities? It could be . . . (-FA,EI) (RS,AC,DN)

Segment G-5

454. *Mr. C:* That refers to another aspect of the caste system . . . cultural deprivation goes along with it, but that's not cultural deprivation. That's deprived medical or inadequate medical facilities and its logical consequences. (X,FA↑) (GI,DM)

455. *Mr. C:* So are these three different yet plausible explanations on the environmental side? (X,FA↑)

456. *Mr. Warren:* Right, but that won't take into account heredity. (-FA↓,-X) (RS,CD,AD)

457. *Mr. C:* That . . . well, then you can always point out that it's possible that all along with these things there is the genetic kind of thing coming in as well, interacting with it. (FA,X) (DM)

458. *Mr. C:* In other words, that even if these kids you could say . . . even if these kids did get all these books read to them and everything, because of this basic initial genetic differences, they still wouldn't perform as well. (X)

459. *Mr. Warren:* Isn't it . . . isn't it sort of what you're saying when you say that their heredity . . . heredically they have a lower IQ? (-X,FA) (RS,CD)

460. *Mr. C:* No, no, no. We're saying that genetically and in terms of environment both things operate. (X↑,FA↑) (RS,DM)

461. I mean, your lowest kid is going to be the kid who's got the least to start off with and the one who hasn't had any of the experiences. He's going to come up the poorest. But you can take a kid who has the same at least to start with and provide him with lots of good experiences and he's going to make up some of that deficit. (X) (DM)

462. Or let's take the other one. You take a kid who's got 210 at birth . . . you know, he's raring to go. (X)

463. And you stick him into a real deprived environment and you'll end up with a kid with a depressed IQ. (X,SA↑) (DM,DE)

464. And that shows you the way the two work and intertwine simultaneously, side by side. (X) (DM)

465. And this is what we want to get across. (X,SA)

466. Now we know more about the environmental end, this is all I can say: in Negroes and whites we know a heck of a lot more about the environmental end . . . and the genetic end in identical twins in terms of relative I.Q. (X,SA) (DM)

Segment G-6

467. *Mr. C:* Well . . . ah . . . well (sigh) I guess that's about it. (FA↑) (DM)

468. I'm going to start . . . I wanted to go very quickly into learning the first part, classical conditioning, I'll go through very quickly on Monday. It shouldn't cause you too much trouble. (FA) (GI,DM,DD)

469. *Mr. C:* Uhm . . . we'll go over the first part of that assignment sheet that I handed out, too, so that we'll probably get some generalization from that. (FA) (DM)

470. We'll also try to go into a little bit of reinforcement theory or operant conditioning. (FA,X)

471. The bulk of our time in learning will be spent on this . . . either the Mussen and Conger or the Hall and Lindsey. (X,FA)

472. Now for those of you who are in trouble on the Mussen and Conger or the Hall and Lindsey there is another reference that may help. That's given in Hall and Lindsey and that is in Miller and Dollard, *Personality and Psychotherapy* or something like that. (F↑,X)

473. There's about 20 pages, excellent discussion of learning theory. You know, cue, drive, incentive, and some of those four terms are discussed there. (X)

474. So between your book here, the Mednick, between the Mussen, Conger, and Kagen, or the Hall and Lindsey, or if you want to go back to this original source . . . that is Miller and Dollard, which is referred to in many of these places, Chapter 4 or something like that . . . a very short chapter, about 15–20 pages covers the whole deal. (X)

475. We'll try to go through this next week and then I want to move into psychosexual theory. (FA,X)

476. We're moving much slower than I had anticipated, but we're raising hot issues and we can't put them aside without dealing with them. (FA) (GI,DM)

477. Okay. (FA) (DM)

In contrast to Mr. Wicker, who seems to say to the teacher in various ways, "Who says your point of view is the only point of view?" Mr. Warren's message implies more directly that Mr. C has done a poor job as formal authority. He has failed at the crucial task of writing a good question, one which has a clear answer. Since this segment represents the fourth effort by Mr. Warren to raise this same objection to the exam, obviously something is going on that matters very much to him. Each time he raised his point it would seem that one very important factor is that he manages in each case to replace Mr. Wicker at center stage. We know from interviews with Mr. Warren that he considered Mr. Wicker to be annoying.

Segment G

Segment	Task						Affect
	X	FA	SA	F	EI	P	
(G1) Teacher	+	+					Dominance, Denying Depression
Mr. Warren	−	−					Resisting, Counterdependency
(G2) Teacher	+	↑	+	↑	+		Guilt Inducing, Depression, Denying Depression
Mr. Warren		−					Resisting, Counterdependency
(G3) Teacher	+	+					Dominance, Guilt Inducing, Dependency, Denying Depression
Mr. Warren	−	−					Resisting, Counterdependency, Accepting, Dependency
(G4) Teacher	+	−				+	Dominance
Mr. Warren	−	−					Resisting, Accepting
(G5) Teacher	+	↑					Dominance
Mr. Warren	−						Resisting, Counterdependency
(G6) Teacher	+	+					Dominance

Mr. Warren's contention was not designed to get him more points; he had done very well on the exam. It was designed to challenge the competence of the teacher. Not only did Mr. Warren raise no objections to the teacher as socializing agent but his focus on the teacher as expert and formal authority manages for the first time to draw out the teacher. For the first time we really hear a prolonged, content-laden speech from the teacher. Thus, in effect the message from Mr. Warren is: "There's nothing wrong with claiming that you are more knowledgeable or more powerful, as long as you prove your claim." Finally, after all the effort directed toward other aspects of the teacher's total role, the teacher is challenged to function as the competent expert.

Although Mr. C's response is a bit punitive and blame-avoidant at first, before long he is involved in responding to the challenge to give three good answers to his own exam question. Mr. Warren, by so challenging Mr. C, thereby creates the outcome so characteristic of the desire of many students: the outcome in which teacher and students are more like peers. In one sense at least, what could be more leveling in its effect than having the teacher struggle with his own exam question under the evaluative probing of a bright student? Mr. C fares rather well in the interchange. Mr. Warren is forced to abandon his central argument, and in the end he seems to be accepting the teacher's performance as one which earns him the right to continue in power.

By the end of the session the teacher appears quite on balance, and with little hemming and hawing he moves into the formal authority role he had treated so gingerly at the outset. As is his right within the formal power structure of the class, Mr. C proceeds to map out the future of the class. In the final few acts he is clearly the expert and the formal authority. Two challenges to his functioning have been dealt with, and he has had the support of most of the students in the more serious of these struggles.

What happened in session 19 of class C? What do we gain from the dual perspectives of examining the task strategies as well as the affective responses? Let us review briefly how one might answer the question of what happened.

For the teacher, session 19 evoked every one of the six task strategies. The central issues of the session involved the teacher as formal authority and as socializing agent. The exam had precipitated acute tension and conflict over the teacher's authority, whereas Mr. Wicker's prejudiced statements on that exam and subsequently had precipitated the socializing issue. One clear example of how simultaneous pressure on two aspects of teaching can disrupt the teacher's performance can be found right here. The teacher wanted very much to unhook his authority from his value position, the better to argue against Mr. Wicker's prejudiced viewpoint (without seeming to be insisting on it by pulling rank). In order to pursue the socializing agent's goals of either changing or isolating the deviant, Mr. C adopted the outward appearance of the facilitator, whereas in reality his drawing out of Mr. Wicker was designed more to give him enough rope to hang himself than to further any autonomous development at that time. At other times Mr. C's use of the heroic, potent style of the ego ideal or his efforts to personalize the fight with Mr. Wicker also served the goals more properly associated with the teacher as socializing agent.

Mr. C's performance gave evidence of more than the feelings aroused by his fight with Mr. Wicker. For the faithful students, including the argumentative Mr. Warren, Mr. C operated on quite a different set of strategies. He was occasionally warm and responsive to some of the students, and his struggle with Mr. Wicker had some clear implications for the rest of the class. Having defined the argument in terms of bigotry and having found out that the most loyal females and even the most rebellious males were basically on his side, Mr. C could function as the champion, and as the potential ego ideal, of the great majority of the students. Miss Jewel's admiring "You won" at the end was like the rose tossed down to the matador by the lovely donna.

However, probably the greatest progress was made in clarifying Mr. C's role as expert and formal authority. With a clear victory behind him in the socializing area, Mr. C could more comfortably move into the argument with Mr. Warren and act the part of "the one who knows" and "the one who decides." As Mr. C indicated in the closing remarks, this session marked the end of a reactive phase and beginning of a lecturing, proactive phase, and one can only guess at the importance of this session in establishing the teacher in the expert role. It may well have been that for Mr. C to move comfortably and effectively into a phase of proactive, expert strategies it was necessary to emerge from the postexam battle as the champion of manifestly legitimate values and as a patient and decent human being.

If these were the task issues, what about the feelings of the teacher? How did they influence and how were they influenced by the unfolding task interaction? Two aspects of the teacher's feelings are sufficiently noteworthy to be included in this summary. First, recall that his first monologue betrayed a considerable amount of depression over his performance as formal authority. From these misgivings over his effect on the students flowed reparative efforts, apologies, and quite a few attempts to deny the guilt and place it instead on the students' shoulders. One effect of the session, then, was to alter these feelings considerably, and, although the authority-denying, facilitative style was his initial task response to these feelings, we are more struck by the effectiveness of the socializing strategy for relieving the incipient doubts and guilts of the teacher.

The major affective quality of Mr. C's performance, aside from the rather constant dominance and formality, was his punitiveness. By the time he had cast Mr. Wicker in a not too subtle way into the role of the "poor prejudiced bastard," his punitive, guilt-inducing style had become crystal clear. But even earlier there were numerous indications that Mr. C was angry, that he had identified with the Negro child against the insensitive and judgmental white (alias "normal") environment represented by Mr. Wicker. All we need to say in recapitulation is that clearly this anger and identification made a contribution to Mr. C's task strategies. Mr. Wicker and his lack of empathy became an object lesson partly out of retaliation, because he had a personal meaning for Mr. C which went beyond Mr. C's role of educator at that moment.

The question, What happened in session 19? is not to be answered by looking only at the teacher. Clearly one could well begin one's summary of this session by noting that it contained an extraordinary amount of challenge and contention, much of which the teacher absorbed with rather good grace. One could note the inevitable fanning out of the students into their more or less established patterns of relating to the teacher, some being petulant, some being simply anxious, some closing in via hostility, others moving away via bland acceptance. However, it would be doubly instructive to note as well the implications of these various reactions for the task relationship between the teacher and the students.

One clear trend throughout this session is that the teacher as facilitator, especially if this is combined with moves in the direction of the teacher as person, stirs up a whole host of negative and stress-indicative affect. Things can get too close, too hot, or too potentially embarrassing, and as a result the teacher as expert or even formal authority can look like a safe shelter from the interpersonal storms that rage or threaten to rage in a classroom. For other students, of course, the opposite is true, and any moves by the teacher in the direction of expert and formal authority will at least be severely tested.

Round and round and round goes the analytic process of understanding how the teacher-student interaction unfolds. There are, undoubtedly, no two sequences of classroom interaction which are exactly alike, and the best we can hope for is that some of the somewhat congruent sequences will emerge from the maelstrom and serve as guides for our subsequent efforts to understand the classroom. The least we should hope for is that our frame of references, our concepts and research operations prove in subsequent inquiries to be illuminating and useful in the effort to understand even very different classroom scenes.

CHAPTER 4

THE STYLES AND
ADAPTATIONS OF STUDENTS

As the case study of even one session makes clear, students are so different from one another that it is awkward to speak of simply "the students." To understand the nature and process of work in the classroom, we need to focus our attention on the students to find out not only what they have in common but what are their major subgroups. Let us assume for the moment that there is some repetition among the ways students act and feel, and that one can talk meaningfully about more than each unique student. We may then seek to find the most important differences and the most important similarities among them.

Our emphasis here remains on the affective-interpersonal issues of the classroom. The major question we shall ask concerns (a) the various histories, both familial and educational, which the students bring with them, (b) the expectations and hopes which the students have for the class, (c) the development of the student's view of his teacher, the class, and of his own performance, and (d) the one or more ways in which the student tries to adapt to reality as he perceives it. Throughout this study of students and their interpersonal styles, we shall try to point out aspects of the student's past or present which influence his experience of the teacher, the material, and the course as a whole. Clearly, if we can begin to understand how differently students press on the new classroom situation and how differently they are affected by it, we can formulate the different meanings of work for the various students. Even if we recognize that in all probability students are different and need different kinds of teaching in order to learn, we still need a way to pin down which differences matter the most. While colleges have focused mainly on such variations as ability and preparation, we shall try to understand the interpersonal issues that differentiate students from one another. We would assert that in order to understand the diverse meanings of work in the college classroom one must study the diverse needs, perceptions, and affective responses that students have in a given classroom. This effort led us to the cluster analysis of student differences presented in this chapter.

We have divided the students in the four classes into eight groups, or clusters, based on their behavior in the classroom; and we have formulated descriptions of these clusters from the data we have about the member students. We hope these descriptions will make it easier for teachers to think about their students as complex individuals. The clusters are also meant to be helpful in giving an idea of some of the reactions a teacher is likely to create by actions he may take in the classroom. Of course, classes vary, students change, and no person ever fits perfectly into a typology. If teachers want to be closely attuned to their own students they will obviously need to go beyond typologies. But we hope this can be at least a beginning point, one compromise between complexity and clarity.

In deriving the clusters, we wanted to be careful to avoid typing students simply according to their personalities on entering the classroom, since we felt that such a typology would ignore the importance of the happenings and interactions in the classroom. We felt that personality was indeed important, but that we should give primary consideration to the students' feelings during the course of the term as recorded by the member-to-leader scoring system. Only after we had divided the students into clusters on the basis of this classroom behavior did we look at other kinds of data which would give added depth to the portraits of the clusters. Thus the cluster descriptions are at an intermediate level where we can view the ways in which students vary one from another as reflections both of their enduring interpersonal styles and their reactions to the class.

Since the clusters are derived from the interaction process in a particular class, we would not expect that a given student would necessarily appear in the same cluster in his other courses. Students have radically different reactions to different teachers and subject matter, and their interpersonal styles also change with growth over time during their college careers. If Mr. D was both an attractive and frustrating teacher for a given student, and the student reacted with discouragement, we need not assert that this student is a "discouraged type" but can rather note with interest the option open to and chosen by the student in his difficult struggle with Mr. D. We can assert with greater assurance that x, y, and z are among the ways that students react to teachers and classes than that particular students found to be representatives of pattern x or y or z will always react that way in other classes. We can and shall attempt to see in what ways the students who actually chose one path are different from the students who chose the other paths, but this *ad hoc* analysis can only indicate the meaningfulness of the choice, not its inevitability. Our interest here is not in describing personality types, but in delineating some of the interpersonal styles found in the college classroom.

The clusters were derived through the use of a statistical technique called cluster analysis. The category distributions of each student's scored acts on the member-to-leader scoring system were transformed into estimates of the seven student factors and then the cluster analysis was utilized to find natural groupings among the students. This technique generated a number of ways of defining these groups. It provides no unique solution. Therefore, some judgment of how many clusters seemed appropriate and other technical matters was necessary. After generating the seven clusters we collated as much data as possible on the students falling in each of the clusters. This included, in addition to summaries of act-by-act scoring, questionnaire data collected before, during, immediately after, and two years after the course, as well as interviews obtained during the term. These data, when correlated with the tape and transcript material on which the category scores and factor estimates were based, formed the basis of our portraits of the student clusters. More detailed information on the generation of the clusters, the data used in describing them, and the significant differences between the clusters on the various measures can be found in the methodological footnotes in Appendix A.

The presentation of each cluster will begin with a table showing those categories and factor patterns which are significantly higher or lower for that cluster than for all the other clusters combined. The level of significance is indicated in parentheses after the category of factor patterns.

Cluster 1: The Compliant Students

Factors:	HI:	Enactment (.01)	LO:	Challenge (.01)
		Consent (.01)		Discouragement (.01)
				Concealment (.01)

Categories:	HI:	Identifying (.01)	LO:	Moving Against (.01)
		Showing		Resisting (.01)
		Independence (.01)		Guilt Inducing (.01)
				Showing Counter-dependency (.01)
				Expressing Depression (.05)
				Denying Depression (.05)

The first cluster fits perhaps better than any other the picture of the typical "good student" in the traditional classroom. Its members, 7 females and 5 males, seemed quite contented with their classes, their teachers, and themselves. They were consistently task-oriented, only rarely experiencing any of the kinds of emotions that might interfere with their pursuit of that task. Most of all, they took part in no rebellion and seemed to feel no inclination to do so.

These students seem to fit Rank's (1945) conception of the "average man." They have chosen to deal with the pain and guilt caused by differentiating themselves from their parents, their society, and other authorities by adapting themselves to the will of such authorities and learning to follow their dictates. In other words, they easily and naturally conform to the standards of an authority figure without evidently considering the possibility of questioning these standards.

When we look at the backgrounds of these cluster 1 people, we find some antecedents to their lack of rebellion. In some cases these students described their parents as quite strict, so that it seems rebellion would have been too dangerous. In these cases, the lack of rebellion involves an acceptance of the standards of strictness; for example, they plan to raise their children in a similar fashion. More usual, however, is the pattern of indulgent parents who would be disappointed in their children if they did not accept or live up to their standards. In this case guilt becomes the main factor inhibiting rebellion. Thus, Pamela said in her interview, "Mr. C [her teacher] would idealize a daughter and so does my father," and "My father has very high standards but they are realistic." Eve said that her father does not like to see her grow up, and Elaine transferred this kind of situation to her teacher in saying that Mr. B would be an affectionate father who would make definite rules and might be overprotective.

For almost everyone in cluster 1 this combination of affection and high standards produced a strong reluctance to consider the possibility that authorities, or in this case their teacher, might be argued with or doubted. A typical statement of this attitude was by Barney, who said that the students and the teacher were on the same team "because the class doesn't know enough to be able to argue with him." It seems likely that the class never would know enough in his eyes as long as the teacher was in a position of authority over them. Only one student in this cluster showed signs of conflict over her conforming behavior. Jean stated that she was "too cowardly to be rebellious," that "she conforms to society" and "keeps her own thoughts." For most of the others any tendency toward rebellion was firmly suppressed, and it seems that the thought literally never entered their minds.

The lack of rebellion in these people did not seem to make them at all unhappy. Their parents were affectionate, and this seemed to have helped give them a relatively high level of self-esteem. When asked to list adjectives describing themselves, they almost always sounded quite contented with themselves; one example was Elaine who described herself as "understanding, friendly, lively, neat and considerate."

Among the reasons why these students had a pleasant experience in their class was their affinity for the social sciences. Most of them were planning to major in fields outside the natural sciences; their verbal SAT's were higher than their math SAT's, and they generally stated that they found the material in psychology especially interesting. Another notable factor is that a number of them were preparing to be elementary or high school teachers. This bears on their lack of rebellion in that they probably identified with the role of the teacher and did not look forward to having troublesome students themselves. It also seems that psychology would be a personally relevant subject to those interested in teaching, and this would tend to help them enjoy the material in the course.

The compliance that is part of a general interpersonal style for these people brings with it a reliance on extrinsic motivation to stimulate their learning experiences as students. They work because their parents expect them to, because they are preparing for the future, because the teacher will grade them and, particularly for some females in the group who find the teacher especially attractive, because work will bring them praise and attention. They tended to do the work they were supposed to do in the course, no more and no less, and they achieved at about the level one would expect given their ability. One gets the impression that were it not for these outside motivators they would have been pleased not to have to do any work at all, even though they did find this work interesting while they were doing it. Thus, in a discussion of different plans for weighing paper grades, Kurt pointed out that with one plan people could slough off on the last, most important paper; and Pamela once stated: "When I get praise [from parents] I know I really desearve it. Mr. C hands out praise a little too readily. With Mr. C's early praise, they may quit." In a discussion of whether people should be called on in the discussion, Doreen said that it would be a good idea because sometimes she has to be forced to put her ideas together, that "it's like studying for a test, you don't do it unless you have to." Also, two students in cluster 1 brought up the question of whether class would be held the next time in Mr. B's section, since there was to be a special university event. It would, we think, be extremely rare to find one of these studies becoming so engrossed in a fascinating problem in one course that he would let another course slip, or so caught up in a lecture or a discussion that he would not notice as soon as the hour was over. These students, although good students, could not be called intellectuals. The major portion of their excitement about life is devoted to areas outside the academic sphere. In class they fulfill the requirements steadily whether or not they are especially interested in them and they have their real fun elsewhere.

This cluster is predominantly female, which is consistent with traditional role expectations which define females as passive and nonrebellious. The females in this cluster do tend, in fact, to take rather traditional views of themselves. They are not likely to be devoted to careers, and if they do mention careers, they are in such traditionally feminine spheres as teaching. In the classes, they tended to play an important part in discussions of feminine issues such as child rearing and maternal deprivation and to make feminine comments such as Donna's exclamation about Skinner's baby box, "Did he do that with a *child?*" The use of a strategy that is usually considered female does not seem to distress the males in this cluster or make them feel inadequate. They seem to view the classroom in a traditional way and to see their proper role as a rather passive one. They did not tend to participate very much in these classes. Those males who did participate more seemed to want to see the teacher in somewhat more colleagual terms than did the high participating females. But for most of the males, this is just one sector of their life and they do not feel any threat to their maleness elsewhere in taking a traditionally passive, student role in this class.

While this cluster seems to be able to get along and continue with the task in almost any class situation, there do seem to be two kinds of classes that disturb these people to some degree. One of these is the class that does not reward them even when they are doing their best. Their intellectual ability is only about average for the university they attend, and when, as in class D, a teacher comes along who goes too fast for them in presenting material and is scornful of many of the contributions they make in class, so that they are not receiving their customary extrinsic rewards, they will become somewhat distressed, as is found in some of the interviews with people in that class.

Another kind of class that may upset them is one in which the teacher has, in their opinion, relinquished too much control. In this case they may feel that the requirements of the course are not clear enough. Thus, in the two classes where there was a good deal of student discussion, the cluster 1 people, while they enjoyed the discussions, also tended to say that they wandered too much or were too trivial. They want the teacher to take more control and make sure all the material was covered. They tend to do most of their participation and most of their enactment at the times when the teacher is most in control. They are most comfortable when the teacher is proactive, when he talks a lot. They enjoy learning in a rather passive manner the things the teacher has to tell them, and do not trust their fellow students to talk about important things. Judith was rather typical of this cluster in saying that her ideal teacher has "all the answers." In conjunction with this feeling, they also want to maintain the traditional distance between the teacher and the students. Some may be attracted to the teacher, and this helps motivate them to work, but they are content to keep this at a distance and would be uneasy if it shifted. Richard stated in his interview that he would not be uncomfortable on a train with the teacher because he would know that what he said would not affect his grade. Eve said that she was afraid to get too close to the teacher because she was afraid of buttering him up. This concern with the role of the teacher as dispenser of extrinsic rewards prevents them from seeing him as a person with whom they could enjoy a relationship which might have its own quite different rewards.

This cluster does much of the routine work when the classes are going smoothly. They ask and answer questions, volunteer information, and volunteer to be discussion leaders when that is a part of the classroom structure. After class, they sometimes ask for dittos if they have missed any, or stay to "clear up a few points," as Richard said. On the whole, they do not become very involved with other than cognitive work in the class, and they rarely express any strong emotion.

The main concern of this group seems to be understanding the material. They served an important function in their classes in that they usually did understand it rather well. The teacher would sometimes check with them when he was afraid that he might have lost the class, and they were fairly certain to have been paying attention and to be able either to reassure the teacher that he was clear enough or else tell him where he was not. They did the reading and the other assignments and understood them, so that they could answer questions on them in class. They also seemed to have a good sensitivity to the cognitive goals of the teacher, to understand the rationale behind his method of organization and presentation of the material. Thus, in class D, during a discussion of what classes should be like which was filled with a number of emotion-laden comments expressing anxiety and hostility, Walter suggested as class goals: "appreciation of the science" and "presentation of a climate of thinking on the subject." Both of these were accepted with great relief by the teacher, as they reflected rather well what his conscious goals were, and they seemed to have aroused little disruptive effect in Walter.

This emphasis on understanding goes hand in hand for this group with a propensity to accept the statements of teachers and authors without questioning their accuracy or usefulness as long as they are easy to understand. The clearest example of this came when class B started to discuss a lecture on sexual symbolism in the Cinderella story. This was a lecture which aroused a great deal of emotion in most of the class and led to a spirited discussion which challenged the assumptions of psychoanalysis and, by implication, the teacher. The discussion started when Mr. B asked the class what they thought of the lecture. Donna raised her hand and said, "I thought it was a good lecture, it was easy to understand."

In addition to their reluctance to question authorities, the members of this cluster show little inclination to fight with their fellow class members. They gain their status in the teacher's eyes not by defeating other students, but by being loyal and understanding and not causing trouble. Their low need to fight was evident in their questionnaires where they said that they were not very distressed, and neither were the other students; unlike some other clusters, they felt no need to derogate the other students in order to feel good themselves.

This group is not solely interested in understanding things. They also find the material interesting from a personal point of view. The females who were high participators (the group on the average was not very high on participation but a few members were quite high) were likely to bring up personal examples and to have some desire to be analyzed by the teacher. This is partly connected to the fact that they are attracted to the teacher, and this passive-receptive but personalized model of learning is very pleasant for them.

Since the students in cluster 1 tend not to differentiate themselves from authorities, they are left to rely heavily on those authorities for their own ideals and ideas. They cannot, without pulling away on their own, develop creative reintegrations of themselves and others, of their own thoughts developed from their own experiences and the thoughts of teachers and writers and psychologists. They may apply things, but they are not good at innovating. They will not be the people who will come up with an idea that goes beyond the teacher's theory or integrate it in a new way with someone else's theory. In fact, since they are not so much interested in the material for its own sake but rather for the rewards which it can bring them, they do not tend to read things outside the course; they do not try to look at the field from any perspective other than that chosen by the teacher. Their understanding of that perspective will be helpful in discussions, and certainly they can take a part in the work of the group. But in their own cognitive worlds, their suppression of negative affect prevents them from being very creative or original in thinking about the ideas with which the class deals.

We might add that it may be relevant to keep in mind while thinking about this cluster that most of them are freshman, and it is possible that they are just beginning to experience the process of differentiation which Erikson calls the identity crisis and which seems to be a crucial part of the first few years at college for many students. In later classes they may be members of different clusters.

Cluster 2: The Anxious Dependent Students

Factors: HI: Anxious Dependence (.01) LO: Exhibition (.01)
                 Consent (.01)   Concealment (.01)

Categories: HI: Showing Dependency (.01) LO: Resisting (.05)
                 Expressing Anxiety (.01)   Showing Indepen-
                 Expressing Depression (.05)   dence (.05)
                 Level One (.05)   Showing Counter-
                                                  dependency (.01)
                                                Denying Depres-
                                                  sion (.05)
                                                Amount of Partici-
                                                  pation (.05)

With 16 females and 12 males, this is a large cluster, and one which forms an important part of every teacher's experience with his students. Its members are somewhat angry on the inside, but mostly frightened on the outside, very dependent on the teacher for knowledge and support, and very anxious about being evaluated. Their anxiety keeps most of them from doing anything we might call work in the classroom; but for many of them, something about this class becomes an important part of an experience of growth and change and personal learning, of which the anger and fear were a painful but necessary part.

We found in the parents of the cluster 1 students a mixture of parental affection and high standards, a combination which is hard to rebel against but which leads to contentment in the students involved. For the people in cluster 2, the past was not so happy. There were high standards, strict rules, and probably liberal punishment but, as they describe it, the accompanying love was insufficient or absent. Some of them had parents who were often absent, one had a parent die when he was quite young, and for a good many more their parents just did not seem to give them enough affection. Carey, for example says, "My father doesn't relate to children well. He's always pushing us. . . . We have more responsibility than great love." Tod said that he only talked to the teacher one time outside of class but "he probably knows me better than my parents." And in class one day during a discussion of cognitive development in children, Leslie said, "If, like a child when a child is about 2, adults speak softly to a child and they kind of whisper because the baby's sleeping most of the time and, then, all of a sudden they'll do something wrong and they're yelled at and this hits them at that time and the reaction is maybe they'll pick up something and throw it back."

There are a number of possible reactions to the lack of love which these people perceive in their parents, and for this cluster the norm seems to be that a number of these different reactions are mixed in each person. On the one hand, these students feel helpless and dependent; they are easily hurt, and they try their very hardest, over and over again, to win love through accepting and carefully following the standards of authorities. Tod identified with the standards of his parents, said that they raised him well, and thought that young adults were naive; Molly in her interview worried that she ought to keep talking because the tape recorder was going. But this strategy of trying to please authorities by carefully following their standards was never very successful at winning love from these people's parents, and following this strategy does not seem to lead to happiness for them.

Another possible reaction to lack of love or attention is anger, and one can see quite a lot of anger in the interviews with these students. But with strict and demanding parents anger is a dangerous thing, and for children of very religious parents, who make up a portion of the membership of this cluster, anger in themselves arouses great guilt. The idea of actually expressing the anger they feel is a very threatening one for this group. Thus, not only did they tend to avoid any rebellious behavior in class, but they became very anxious when other students expressed hostility, either toward the teacher or toward each other. Their anger is usually not unconscious, but it is kept under tight control, at least at this stage in their lives, out of fear of the consequences which might follow its expression.

Neither bottled-up anger nor anxious dependence leads to a very happy state for these students, and most of them tend to be depressed and dissatisfied with themselves. When asked to name metaphors which would describe themselves, they were likely to use such expressions as "color me blue" or "the dull one"; and a not atypical set of self-descriptive adjectives was "lazy, shy, dreamer, hungry."

For a couple of people in this cluster, there was a special problem because of membership in an ethnic minority group. The special problems of rejection faced by such people and the likely reactions to this problem were well-illustrated by one black member of class C. Marvin said in his interview, "I stopped coming to class . . . I didn't want to talk about race . . . being put on the spot . . . I wanted them to know that I could hate. That they could be bumped off. They do."

There seem to be some important differences between the male and female members of this cluster. This cluster, like cluster 1, is predominantly female, and once again it fits rather well with cultural definitions of the female role. But in cluster 1 the females are satisfied with their role, whereas the females in this cluster give considerable evidence of dissatisfaction. While this is not always true, several of them seem to feel a particular inadequacy in comparison with men and a particular hostility toward men. Leslie is particularly angry with men; in her interview she said that she had two brothers who were favored over her and allowed to do things she was not because she was a girl. Her older brother, who she said resembled her teacher, sat back twice when her life was in danger and did not try to save her. Her father was strict and dogmatic with her, yelled at her, and she still feels that he treats her like a child, but he pressures her to get high grades and tells her that if she flunks out, then that's it, she's through. Evelyn, another female member of this cluster, in a discussion of careers for mothers in class B, said, "Boys will always be bigoted anyway. I never worked with boys before and I thought we were all equal—we're *not*." Others of the females in this cluster are trying to live up to brothers or fathers whom they considered to have superior intellectual competence. Still others are angry because they would like to pursue careers in addition to being mothers, but do not expect to be able to.

These females do not express their anger any more than do the other members of this cluster. But some of them seem to feel to some extent that they are consciously playing a role when they act dependent and submissive, and that manipulation of men is one function which that role serves for them. The interview with Kathryn gives us one example of this attitude; when asked to imagine what Mr. C's wife would be like she said, "She doesn't feel dependent on him, but makes him think she is."

The males in cluster 1 seemed to have their main sources of self-esteem outside the academic world and were not bothered by acting fairly passive and nonrebellious in the class. But this is not true of the males in this cluster. They are more caught up in feeling inadequate and incompetent and in wishing that they could be stronger and perhaps fight a rebellion successfully. They do seem to show a little more hostility toward the teacher than do the females in this cluster, but their rebellion appears ineffectual next to that of the more hostile males in some of the other clusters. Ray, for example, argued with Mr. C about the answer to an exam question and clearly lost the argument. A little later in the same class session he tried to argue about a question which was supposed to be a gift, and which only three people missed. When these people do try to rebel, they are likely to pick issues which make their rebellion easy to put down.

One of the most pervasive issues in this group is the members' feeling of intellectual incompetence. This feeling may have had some basis in reality—their scores on the verbal SAT were significantly lower than those of the other clusters. But their high anxiety level probably played an important part in those low scores. In any case, their feelings of inadequacy are further accentuated by their doubts that they will be able to do well. Thus, Leslie, whose father was pressuring her to get good grades, said "My father may overestimate my mentality. The other kids seem smarter than me." Nora said she was afraid to say anything in class, that what the other students said seemed deeper, and she was afraid of being laughed at. Shirley, when asked to title the class, said "intellectuals—especially the four up front." Tod wondered "if I really have the ability to think as deeply as Curt and Rich do"; and Perry said, "Some students seem way over my head" and later stated that if he were on a train with his teacher, "I'd probably ask questions that would be over my head . . . he'd realize that and give superficial answers. We'd get off the subject of psychology."

This feeling of incompetence, together in many cases with persistent external pressures, especially from parents, combine to make these students tremendously concerned about grades. This concern is so pressing that it often overshadows all other aspects of the course. Perry said, "This is one class I really need a grade in . . . I just need the mark so badly . . . there's so much anxiety from him not telling how he's going to mark." Sarah said, "My parents expect good grades from me. I'm the family failure." Audrey was worried about her grade, saying that she did not think the teacher asked questions on tests that fit with what had been said in class, and that since she could not get the right answers on tests, she would advise a friend to switch out of that class.

Their anxiety about grading tends to make these people somewhat uncomfortable with the discussion mode in class; they are afraid they are not learning enough facts to do an adequate job on the tests. Thus, when asked what hints they would give to friends who were going to be in that class, Katy said, "Take notes on everything he says," and Brad said, "The tests are based on the readings; skip the general discussions except when the teacher talks; there's not much information otherwise." When Mr. B suggested that they change their format to a discussion led mainly by students, Perry asked "Could it be possible at the end of the discussion either to discuss with you as a coordinator or for you to wrap it up at the end? I want to be able to take notes. . . ."

For these students especially, the issue of grades is so crucial that the final grade can cast a happy glow or a pall of bitterness over the memory of the course and can have a great deal to do with whether a person takes any more courses in that area. Two years after her class was over, Katy stated that she "never took more psychology because I didn't do as well in it as I should have," and lowered her rating of the instructor. For other people there is the opposite effect. For this group which is so unsure of itself and so afraid of negative evaluation, grades are a very powerful reinforcer, and are probably taken much more seriously as an indicator of intellectual and personal worth than most teachers would wish.

This discomfort seems to be part of a larger phenomenon which is rather ironic. Some of these people are actually afraid to get involved with the material. They are afraid that if they get very interested then they will want to think about it and talk about it and, if they do that, they will not have the time to learn it in such a way that they can repeat it on tests. Thus, Esther said that Mr. D was not a good teacher for her, but that he would be for others who could follow his thoughts better; she liked the depth with which he covered the material because it was interesting, but it was not good for her grade. Roy said, "As it progressed I got more interested. I fell down on the exams though"; Paul said that his difficulty with the material came because he was thinking about it too much; and Katy said, "If he'd only lecture I'd get a lot more . . . I'm afraid we're not covering what we should be . . . the prime purpose we're here for is grades. I enjoy getting underneath these things, but grade-wise it isn't going to help me."

The performance of members of this cluster in class tends to mirror their dependency and anxiety but not very much of their anger. One of the frequent comments they make is that they do not understand something; they often ask the teacher to repeat what has been said or to clarify it. Sometimes they express feelings of inferiority, as when Candy, in a discussion of whether people should be called on, said that lots of times she thinks what she has to say is not as good as other people's and that is why she does not talk more. They tend to act rather helpless and to emphasize the fact that they need the teacher. Thus, when in the first session Mr. C asked if everybody knew about the reserve book procedure, it was Kathryn, a member of cluster 2, who said she did not. He asked her if she had a friend in class, and she said no.

They show a great deal of anxiety about testing and other evaluative procedures, and many of their comments in class are about those issues—they ask for details about grading, how much things will count, which material they will have to know, etc. They also show their anxiety in discussions of other issues, as when Audrey, in a discussion of teaching machines, asked "Are you tested on this material later? . . . I don't see how you could do an essay and combine all the different things." They generally take careful notes, and this may be disconcerting to a teacher who is trying to be democratic and lead fascinating discussions. When Mr. A asked the class why they wrote down what he just said, it was Audrey who said she did because she had never heard that word used before.

The people in this cluster tend to express their thoughts and even their questions in a very tentative manner and often need encouragement. They are easily silenced by punitiveness on the part of the teacher. Mr. C and Mr. D are good examples of teachers who handle these students very differently. Mr. C had a warm manner; he tended to accept all the students' comments with enthusiasm and to deemphasize grades. He was very willing to help those who were discouraged or confused. This attitude is typified by an interaction with Kathryn. Mr. C asked if there were any questions on Harlow, and said "Kathryn has a questioning look." She said, "I'm just not sure about the independent variable, but I'll get it." Mr. C answered, "We'll see if we can nurture it a little bit." Mr. D, on the other hand, tended to stress his own competence and to be somewhat intolerant of those who were less intelligent or knowledgeable than he. The cluster 2 people in this class seemed by his standards to give wrong answers and to ask a lot of stupid questions. Even when they answered correctly, he might ask them another question which followed from the first, at which point they aften became confused and could not answer. In session 4 of this class, Donna said she did not understand something in the assignment and asked for help. Shortly after this, Mr. D discussed a girl in his last class who did not understand the assignment and got a D on it. (Actually, two people in this cluster in Mr. D's class did fail the course.) An especially anxious comment from Mr. D's class was made by Joe. They were discussing experiments with rats, and he asked the teacher whether rats ever go out of their minds because they are cut off from the experimenter.

Anger is rarely expressed by these students but sometimes it comes out in an indirect way. Roy made a speech to the teacher about how students should not be able to argue about test questions because "it's sort of like fighting City Hall. I mean you made up the test and I don't like to argue because usually you've got an answer which is in your mind; . . . and normally a teacher won't change his mind . . . Now when I think of it, it would have to be that way somewhat. Because you're our teacher . . . if we're going to actually get anything out of this course I think we'll have to follow close to what—the way you—your plan of thinking on different questions." This talk sounds rather guilt inducing and annoyed, especially given that he tried to argue about a couple of questions in a previous session and failed to win his point. Another example of subtle anger came from Candy, who, when Mr. B asked for some negative effects of punishment, said "The person who's being punished could come to hate." But on the whole, these people are very compliant and so anxious about evaluation of various kinds that, at least during class time, they are unable to become involved in the material or to look at it from an independent, task-oriented point of view.

Most of this cluster's participation comes in the first half of the class and, while there is a slight rise in enactment at the very end of the term which may indicate that some of the members of the cluster have become more capable of independence in the class, there is, on the whole, very little enactment.

The most encouraging aspect of the members of this cluster is not what they do in class but what happens to many of them outside of and in conjunction with the class. We have seen that they are not very happy with themselves, and this feeling of dissatisfaction seems to provide them with some impetus for change. Their manner of dealing with their parents was to accept their standards and avoid expressing any anger they might feel toward them. At this time in their lives, they seem to be looking for a different way of dealing with people, one which would allow them more independence, more of a feeling of self-esteem, and more freedom of expression. Probably in part because of their readiness for change, many of the people in this cluster reported that this particular class was especially important to them, that it influenced their development in significant ways. Some of them reported this influence during the course and on the final evaluation. For others, the importance of the course was not obvious to them until later. The ratings of the course and the teacher by this cluster were higher relative to the other clusters after two years than they were immediately following the course.

The reasons why this course was so important for them vary. For some the development of a personal relationship with the teacher came to mean a great deal. They tended to emphasize that the teacher cared about them, that he "went out of his way" for them. Audrey became much more involved in the class after the teacher asked her to tell the class about an experience she had mentioned to him outside of class. Leslie talked to the teacher about her personal problems with her parents and the university in the last week of the term. When Tod was upset about a particularly emotional class discussion, he discussed this with his teacher; the teacher found this important enough to discuss the general issue with the class, and later visited Tod when he was in the hospital. This kind of thing is very important to these cluster 2 people because they have a special need to find older people who care about them. For some of these students the question of whether a teacher will listen to their confidences with sympathy is the most crucial aspect of that teacher's role. Thus, Herb said the ideal instructor should "run the class on a personal relationship level," "encourage you to bring problems to him," and "be sincere." For such a student, finding a teacher who is glad to talk to him can be a very important experience, and it may help him to overcome his anxiety in relation to authorities to some degree so that he can begin to enjoy cognitive academic work.

To some of the students in this group, a factor which especially involved them in this course was an independent project of some kind. Several of the teachers included such a project, usually an experiment designed and carried out by the student alone, in the course format. Many of the cluster 2 students stressed the value of this project on their final evaluations and even two years later. One reason why such an independent effort might be especially important for these students is their fear, in general, of being independent at all. To carry out a major project entirely on their own probably represents for these people an important step away from the pattern of careful adherence to standards of others and fear of individual thinking. We would expect that many of these people were rewarded by the teacher for their hard work and enthusiasm in this regard, and such a reward might also be very significant for people who have grown accustomed to punishment or indifference.

These students are very unsure of themselves in the social as well as the intellectual sphere. Brad, for example, said in his interview, "I very much dread social intercourse." Because of this mixture of insecurities, it is often difficult for them to take part in a discussion, especially in a large group; the fact that they talked in class even as much as they did seems to be a significant accomplishment and an indication of some degree of emotional involvement in the class. Katy, for example, said in her interview that she was a discussion leader early in the course and was involved from then on, that she loved the course and changed her major to psychology. In class, during the discussion of whether people should be called on, she said that this was the easiest class she had known in which one could say "I don't know," that "this is a good place for someone who wants to overcome fears" about saying this.

There seems to be an important relationship between the actual material in the field of psychology and the fact that these persons tended to become very involved in some aspect of the course. One way in which this seems to be relevant is that psychology is not as yet a tightly woven science that builds on itself in a natural progression and that is easy to learn as a list of "facts" to be memorized. It is a collection of various experiments, concepts, and theoretical writings that are difficult to integrate and that offer few solid answers to meaningful questions. These students, on the other hand, have for the most part learned in the past that there is truth and untruth, that things are clear-cut and unambiguous. Not only has it been important for them to accept what authorities say, it has been important for the authorities to be sure of themselves so that they can know what they are supposed to believe. It is important to them that they not be confused in their view of the world. Herb, for example, described himself as a "nondrinker, nonsmoker, not mixed up." Because of this intolerance of ambiguity, these people tend to find it difficult to adapt to the ambiguous field of psychology. Brad, for example, "didn't like the idea that there isn't any proof of id and ego." Donna said psychology was "too unstructured." Sometimes these students try to deny the ambiguity in psychology so they can adapt to it. When asked what he thought about the idea that sex was a motivator in people, Tod said, "Well, why not, it's been used to cure thousands; that's proof enough for me"; and Perry said that he "wouldn't take issue with Freud; it's a bit hard to believe at first, but it's lasted so many years it just can't be superfluous." But this kind of denial is hard to maintain in the face of the teacher's presentation of the field, and eventually these students have to find another way to deal with the ever-present contradictions.

It seems to be important that refusal to accept ambiguity tends to be connected with compliance with parents and other authorities and with belief that they know all the answers. Thus, Nora said, "I'm the sort who will read it and try to understand what he's saying, not thinking about disagreeing." Paul said that if he were on a train talking to Mr. C, "if it was about psychology, he'd do the talking because he knows about it."

The problem of how to handle the ambiguity in psychology is accentuated for these people by the realization that once one acknowledges that nobody has the answers to some questions, then it is no longer possible to believe that authorities have the answers to all questions. This implies relinquishing to some extent the strategy of dealing with parents and others by believing absolutely in everything they say and trying as hard as possible to live up to their ideals. On the one hand, this is a difficult idea for these cluster 2 people to think about but, on the other hand, we have seen that they are really quite angry at some level and they are hoping that they will be able to change in some way. We would expect that given the issues with which they are concerned and their present strategy for dealing with those issues, the field of psychology would influence them to increase their acceptance of ambiguity and to begin to be less afraid to have their own opinions about important questions in their lives. This would be especially true when they feel warmly toward the teacher of the course, as many of these people do. But the number of students in this cluster who change their major to psychology or change their career plans so that they can work in a field which is closely related to psychology as a result of this course seems too high to be explained on the basis of the teacher alone. This group of people seems to feel, in addition, a peculiar affinity with the field itself.

One subgroup of people in this cluster seems to have an additional reason for appreciating the field of psychology. A number of these students were brought up in very religious or at least very strictly moral homes, where they came to think of things as either bad or good, and of themselves as sinful whenever they could not live up to the very strict rules taught by their parents. For them, it must be something of a relief to learn about a field which teaches that the expression of sexual and aggressive impulses can sometimes be valuable, and that their suppression can sometimes have harmful effects. Of course, relief is not by any means the first reaction expressed by such people. The relation between psychology and traditional morality is such that it is very difficult for them to study the field. They are likely to become angry with psychologists and to think, as Roy said, that they are perverted or, as Sue said, that Freud is horrifying. But, as in the case of the ambiguity discussed above, the flexibility which psychology allows on moral issues offers an alternative way of viewing things and, to some of the students in this group who feel a particular need to change, this alternative may be helpful. One example of such a student was Perry, who was surprised and pleased when his teacher allowed him to write a paper about guilt and who wrote on his final evaluation that the course had influenced him by changing his "outlook on religion—it pointed out to me that man is neither good nor bad inherently."

Cluster 3: The Discouraged Workers

Factor: HI: Discouragement (.01)

Categories: HI: Making Reparation (.01)
                       Showing Independence (.01)

It is somewhat difficult to describe this cluster, because it only includes four people; with such a small number there are few significant differences in the paper-and-pencil data, and it is not as easy to see trends in the more impressionistic data. We can make out some interesting patterns, but with such a small number of members it seems that this cluster is probably less important than the others. Having said this, we can still look and find an interesting group of people, three of whom are, in fact, high participators and one or two of whom may be important in a given class. Basically, we would describe these people as depressed but strong, the kind of people who use depression to spur themselves on to further growth and development of their potential. They find special reasons to be discouraged in these particular classes, but they are also especially strong in these classes and especially caught up in the process of growing. They tend to become quite deeply involved in the material and take many more courses in psychology after this one.

The members of this cluster tend to say often that they are dissatisfied with themselves. Libby said, "I don't like things I see in myself in other people;" "I've been persecuted by the way I talk too fast, kind of whine." Thad said many times in class that he was a "slow thinker," that it took him a long time to think about Mr. B's broad, imaginative questions. By the time he was able to back up his opinions and was ready to say something, the discussion would have gone on to another topic.

When things go wrong for these people, they tend to blame themselves and not turn much hostility on other people. For example, while they were very discouraged with the way these classes were going for them, they liked their teachers a great deal and rated them very high relative to the other clusters. Thus, Eugene, while very disturbed at the way he being treated by the teacher, still persisted in saying, "I'm a firm believer in self-improvement." In assuming all responsibility themselves, they may even be upset if their teachers try to engage in self-deprecation. When Libby was asked what she found most annoying about the teacher, she said, "At first it seemed he was apologetic—the only experience he had to draw on was his class last term. He was an excellent teacher."

Concomitant with their tendency to place all fault on themselves comes a general feeling of guilt and fantasies that they may hurt or destroy others, especially children. Dennis, for example, described the girls in his class as "bent physically and bent mentally" and said he only wanted to have boy children. Libby said she was afraid she wouldn't be able to adequately love children, given the "deep drains" they would put on her; and Thad said that he did not want to get married "because I don't want to have a kid. I would probably kill him."

Besides being worried about their own potential for hurting others, this group seems somewhat depressed about human nature in general. This was most true for Thad, who said in a discussion of concentration camps that people think the Germans had a monopoly on cruelty but that it has been going on forever, and who was preoccupied with wanting to discuss *Lord of the Flies* and questions of determinism and free will during class.

The members of this cluster do not expect their depression to end in any short period of time. Their projections for the future are gloomy. Thus, Libby said that in 10 years time she would like to be "serene and pleasant" but that she expects to be "confused and nasty"; Thad said he would like to be happy, but he expects to be dead. The depression seems to be an integral part of their lives, not something which is only part of a particular stage in their development.

In spite of their depression, this group seems to feel that they possess an underlying strength which is considerable. Thad, in response to an interview question on how he and Mr. B would handle an emergency, said that he would be "cooler" than the teacher. Libby said that her teacher could speak to her as someone on the same mental plane, even though she would not be able to make it with him socially. She also mentioned that she thinks she has an aptitude for the social sciences. Finally, there are some adjectives which they used to describe themselves which show a mixture of the strength and the depression—from Libby, "hypersensitive, jealous, relatively intelligent, immature where it shows, mature where it doesn't, ambivalent"; and from Eugene, "intelligent, strong, serious, lonely (in the sense of a center of motivation) honest." The mixture of self-esteem and strength with depression and guilt makes us think that for these people it is important never to be satisfied with themselves because they want to continue to grow and to find new goals beyond the ones they have attained. They seem to be introspective people, which is perhaps one reason why psychology seems to appeal to them especially. Their introspection may be related to the fact that they need continually to reappraise themselves, to think about where they are in relation to where they would hope to be. They seem to be overachievers to some extent, though we have no conclusive data on this. They tend to see themselves as heading for professions which require a good deal of preparation and hard work. Even the one female in this cluster is intent on having a career along with children. In general, they are an independent group, involved in their own concerns and process of growth. They seem to see the material in this course from the perspective of these concerns and find it fascinating from that point of view.

In addition to their general discouragement, the members of this cluster find reason to be particularly discouraged in these classes. Sometimes the reasons for discouragement are primarily connected with the students in the class. Libby's most discouraging moments came in a vehement discussion with practically the whole class, both male and female, aligned against her when she defended mothers who worked while their children were young. She became further alienated when she interpreted a dream as penis envy in class and shocked most of the other class members. It is difficult to discern the reasons for Dennis's discouragement since he talked very little, but it seems that when he did talk the class was prone to reject his suggestions. Thad tended to talk slowly and lengthily and bored most of the class. He also wanted to spend a lot of time discussing the implications of *Lord of the Flies*, and the class was not interested in doing this. Eugene's discouragement, on the other hand, stemmed mostly from a relationship with his teacher. Eugene identified with Mr. D at first and tried hard to win his approval, but Mr. D met his frequent approaches with scorn and ridicule.

In general, we would hypothesize that the problems of this group in class and their depression are linked to one aspect of their independence. One of the motivational sources of their independence seems to be a fear of being hurt or of causing hurt in close relationships with other people. This fear leads then to withdrawing from relatedness with others and becoming preoccupied with their own inner selves. Many of their problems in the classes seem to have stemmed from a lack of sensitivity to others which led to surprise and discouragement when they found that students did not share their specific goals or teachers could not fill some of their needs. But their introspection helps them to understand that their feeling of separateness stems in large part from themselves, so they do not tend to blame others for their discouragement. And they also are able to realize that they are strong in many ways, and to appreciate and profit from much of what other people have to offer them, especially in intellectual areas. Thus they did express pleasure with this course overall, and felt that they had gained a great deal from the experience. They all took many more courses in psychology and seemed to feel that this course had an important influence on them. It does not seem that there is much that a teacher could do to make these students happier—for this group, discouragement is a part of work and growth.

Cluster 4: The Independents

Factors: HI: Enactment (.01)   LO: Discouragement (.01)
                    Support (.01)

Categories: HI: Showing Independence   LO: Expressing Anxiety
                    (.05)   (.01)
                                                 Expressing Self-
                                                 esteem (.05)

Perhaps the most clearly distinguishing attribute of the members of this cluster (which consists of 9 males and 3 females) is their age. They are significantly older than the other students, being on the average between their second and third year of college, while most of the students in this study are freshmen. An important subgroup of them is also especially intelligent. Thus there are certain natural factors which give this group an advantage in these classes and, together with particular personality traits and backgrounds which we shall explore, help account for the independence and security which these students manifest in the classroom. They generally seem quite confident of themselves and are not often threatened by the teacher, the work, or the other students. They remain relatively independent while the other students are confused or anxious or angry, looking at the material relatively objectively and working with it in creative ways.

There seems to be no one background which leads to this independence for all these people. Some, like Mike, reported that their parents gave them enough freedom and there was no need to rebel. They seemed to have been able to empathize with their parents in a somewhat colleagueal way (Edward described his father as "a good man who has had an interesting life"). They felt that they had been able to differentiate themselves from their parents and become individuals without a period of violent separation. Others described their parents as overprotective, like Dave, who said his parents "should learn to be happy when their children go." They tried to separate themselves gently, without anger and with empathic efforts not to hurt their parents too much. Most of them, however, did have stormy periods and, in fact, many were still angry with their parents—usually for being too authoritarian. We would guess that there was a time when these students were angry at almost all authorities and would have been likely to be more rebellious in class, but at this point in their lives they tend to see this teacher as different from their parents and worthy of more respect. Pat, for example, said that Mr. B "would be a fair guy as a father. He'd explain things. My father tells me to do things and since I'm stubborn, I won't. I'm easily won over if anybody tells me things more reasonably." Henry says that Mr. C as a father of a teenager "would not have too many problems with control like some parents. He'd understand. He would not be like my family."

A concomitant of independence for this group is a certain degree of detachment from the teacher and the class. Most of these students have already chosen a major field and plan to limit their investment in psychology. And since they are older than the other students, they may want to maintain a superior position by remaining above the conflicts, dependency, and other emotional involvements of the younger students. Finally, it could be that strong emotional involvement with another person might represent to these people a loss of independence in proportion to the degree of dependence on that person. In any case, they seem to value their limited involvement, and it would be unlikely to find one of them becoming very emotional in class, making friends with the teacher outside of class, or changing his major field to psychology.

This group shows a remarkable uniformity in their philosophy of education. Their ideas parallel their personal independence and the kind of noninvolvement discussed above. Independence is a value as well as a style for them. They like to be, as Henry put it, "free to move around and explore." The kind of class they like best is one in which they are free to discuss their own ideas. They like seminars better than lectures. They seem to feel, as Hilda stated in her interview, that although they like the information the teacher gives them, they can just as easily get that from the reading; the most important thing to them is not the material itself but the analysis of it—which is best done in a discussion. Their ratings of this class were closely tied to their desires for freedom and informality. If they saw it as unusually open to discussion, they tended to like it more, and most of them did, in fact, see it that way. They were significantly high on the item, "Students were free to comment," on the final evaluation form. But if they felt that it was becoming less free at some time, they tended to lose interest and withdraw or express anger. Thus, Henry said that "since the first exam there has been animosity between Mr. C and the class. He became more authoritarian and the class lost interest right then. It's better when he's more democratic."

The desire for freedom does not keep these students from appreciating what the teacher has to offer them. In discussions of teaching machines in two classes, this cluster tended to emphasize that the teacher was an important part of learning, that he had valuable resources and was needed to guide discussions in fruitful directions. While they tend to favor collegueal relationships with the teacher, where teacher and student work together on intellectual tasks, they also want to keep teacher and student roles clearly distinct. For the most part they are not looking for intense personal relations with the teacher outside the class, nor do they want him to become just another peer in class. It is important for them that a certain distance be maintained along with the freedom and informality which they desire.

Having examined some of the background and ideas of these students, we can now look in more detail at their actual behavior in class. Their comments and questions were generally characterized by good integrative ability. They frequently brought up unassigned readings which were relevant to the topic discussed, either readings from other parts of the course or things they had discovered and read on their own. They were also likely to contribute relevant personal experience or expertise, as when Dave played an important part in a class discussion about autistic children because he had worked with them. But they did not rely only on past experience and knowledge to bring new ideas into the class. They were also capable of thinking critically about the new material that was being discussed. They had ideas for new experiments or alternative hypotheses or explanations for data, and additions to theoretical ideas.

The members of this group seem to look at psychology from individualistic perspectives. To some extent these attitudes limit the ways in which they are likely to be influenced by or to contribute to the course but they can also enrich the class by broadening the perspectives of the teacher and the other students. One source of the particular vantage points from which these people view the field is the fact that most of them are already extensively involved with another field in which they are planning to major. Some members of other clusters for whom this is true tend to respond to this fact by derogating psychology for not being as good, as scientific, as concrete, or as interesting as their field. They need to defend their choice by carefully avoiding investment in possible alternatives. But the members of this cluster are able to appreciate both at the same time and to use each to enrich the other. Thus they are able to use their knowledge of other areas to contribute to discussions of psychological questions, as when Frank and Mike both talked about the potentialities of computer programming for use in teaching machines or when natural scientists talked about the construction of good experiments or about physiological aspects of behavior. They can also find psychology useful in relation to their fields, as with Dave, who was interested in its relevance to speech therapy, or Frank, who wanted to learn about industrial relations and production supervision. Even those few students in this group who were planning to major in psychology had already made this choice and had some expertise and investment in a certain subarea of the field such as humanistic or experimental psychology. Therefore they were also in the position of having an individualistic perspective in this respect.

Aside from involvement in another field, there are more general and personal reasons that bring these people to look at the field in their own idiosyncratic way. For many of them, these reasons involve a desire to be able to apply psychology to their lives in certain ways. Thus, on his final evaluation Henry said he wished to "develop a knowledge to prepare for a life I can enjoy," and wanted to "learn more practical knowledge and learn to live in the world." Carol said in class that the object of a good course was to "get people to think about the material and learn to apply it," and Arthur said the best thing about the course was the "opportunity to apply the material to the outside world." Sometimes there are more general philosophical issues which interest them. Mike said that the best thing about the course was "that it made me more aware of some of the seemingly universal predicaments in which man finds himself in relationship to his own self-interests and the interests of others." The worst thing, he said, was that it did not provide enough solutions to the above, Edward felt that his "primary duty" was to understand himself and others and chose history as a field because of this, but also found psychology relevant. As he said, "Anything that helps me understand my environment is good."

Thus, for a combination of personal and professional reasons, this cluster tends to view the course in an individualistic manner, and to make contributions in class which stem from the way of looking at the field which interests them the most. For many, this includes the idea of applying psychology to the outside world and their lives, which they tend to do as a part of the classroom discussion. Other contributions vary from person to person depending on the interests of each.

Relatively speaking, this cluster is not very rebellious in class. They tend to see their teacher as a benevolent authority who would make a good parent; as Rod said, Mr. C as the father of a teenager would "let his son have independence, would give him certain decisions and then work up to full independence." Since they hold this view of the teacher, they have little desire to rebel. In fact, the cluster 4 people are usually supportive of the teacher while other clusters were fighting. But this group is not significantly low on rebellious factors either; they have their moments of disagreement. Sometimes when they do disagree with the teacher, it is over intellectual questions and has little of the quality of a personal attack. Thus, Richard considered himself a learning theoriest and his teacher a Freudian and expected that on a train ride with Mr. C they would have a debate about this. When the debate is mainly over an intellectual or factual issue, this cluster rarely becomes angry.

Generally, this group seems to be opposed to teaching machines and utopian societies set up by psychologists. Thus, Edward said in class, "You spoke of intrinsic rewards in teaching machines—what if a student doesn't feel a reward just from filling in a blank?" Morton said he heard about a utopia which only lasted four years—"and it was supposed to be one of the better ones." As can be seen above, it is difficult to tell when disagreement merges into attack, but it seems that the most rebellious moments for this group come when the teacher is being most authoritarian. When Mr. D was talking about the term paper and stressing his stringent requirements and the high possibilities for failure by the students, Morton asked a series of hostile questions of the nature of "Should it be typewritten?" satirizing the formal authority aspects of the teacher's performance. This example also illustrates a certain kind of composure which some of these students are able to maintain even when they are angry, which allows them to make subtle attacks that are difficult to recognize as such since they do not appear to be upset. It is rare that these students get very angry, however, for when they think the teacher is wrong about something, they can usually back up their claims well enough that the teacher responds to their demands right away. Thus, others of the rebellious clusters argue about exam questions at great length, sometimes winning and sometimes losing. But Morton, rather than arguing, corrected a mistake which the teacher made on the exam, so that it was immediately clear to him that he was wrong, although it was such a subtle point that the rest of the class was baffled. Unlike cluster 1, where for the males the lack of rebelliousness means nonparticipation in the male struggle for power, this cluster is involved in that struggle. They are more likely to argue with fellow students, mainly the stronger males, than they are to argue with the teacher. And they are not averse to displaying any superior knowledge or competence they might have at moments when this contrasts with lesser ability on the part of competitors.

Generally, the members of this cluster like to think of themselves as above the other class members. An example of this was when Morton said, "Do you think these [teaching] machines would be better for younger kids? I found them boring." More extreme was Rod's titling of the students in his class as "those who ask simple-minded questions and those who don't."

It should be said that there are some important differences among the members of this cluster and that some of the characteristics we have mentioned are more noticeable in some subtypes than in others. We can talk about three divisions which seem relevant: the low-participating people, the involved males, and the involved females.

The lower participators of this cluster were not really very noticeable in class. They were independent, and they brought up readings and original points, but they did not talk very often. Although their remarks were helpful they were not often striking. They were younger than the average for this group, but for the most part they did fit in with the trends so far discussed. Most of the information about them had to be gathered from interviews and evaluation forms rather than transcripts. It would seem that it would be hard for a teacher to distinguish them from some of the other low participators in class.

The males who were high participators in class tended to become involved in a special relationship with the teacher. They felt far above the rest of the students. While they were somewhat ambivalent about showing this (Dave described a girl in the class as "caught —like me and everyone else—between wanting to feel good and assert your worth when others aren't quite so good"), they did display their superiority quite frequently in class. They were very ready to answer difficult questions or suggest subtle analyses of data or talk about expertise they had gained from experience. They willingly supported the teacher by answering questions that no one else could, by making discussions more interesting, and by maintaining intellectual work when other students were dependent, anxious, or angry. They sometimes took a mediating position between the teacher and the other students, explaining what each meant to the other.

The teachers involved with these students came to appreciate them and probably even to some extent to "count on them," as Morton put it. Their rebellious moments were infrequent enough so that they were not too threatening. They obviously liked and respected the teachers. They were quite competent and interesting people, but they sometimes carried their confidence a little too far for their teachers to feel comfortable with them. For example, when Mr. B was trying an experiment on the class, Dave would make comments like "Suppose we catch on to what's going on?" and "Was *yes* the reinforcer there?" And Morton, in a similar experimental situation which threatened much of the class, suggested, "What if I got an A in this course?" as a hypothesis. They sometimes began their statements with authoritative prefaces like "The point is here . . ." and they sometimes interrupted the teacher to make a comment without being called on. Finally, they were always very colleagueal and sometimes even a little condescending toward the teacher. Morton said that Mr. D had led a "sheltered life" compared to him and, while he might have expertise, lacked experience. And Dave said that in an emergency, "the teacher has been my superior" so he would let him lead. Actually, he would rather be the leader himself and, in fact, come to think of it, he would only hand over one and one-half reins. This kind of cockiness led the teachers to try to quash these students once in a while. In the second session of class D, for example, Morton volunteered an answer to a difficult question. Mr. D was pleased enough that he asked him to explain it to the class, and then complimented him on his explanation. But when Morton tried to answer the next question without being called on, the teacher ignored him and looked for someone else. Mr. B oscillated all semester between accepting Dave's contributions with pleasure and ignoring them; as Dave said, "I'm not sure how he'll react to me. He's sometimes very pleasant; other times he'll slap my wrist and bark at me." But such obstacles did not seem to bother these students too much, as they maintained their confidence throughout the semester. Generally, they were able to maintain a good relationship with the teacher; they saw themselves as working together with him and the teacher appreciated the quality of their work. They did not tend to get to know each other outside of class, but in class they felt more identified with each other than is true with most students and teachers.

The most crucial fact about the involved females in this cluster is that they are very much attracted to the teacher. Hilda, for example, when asked what the teacher's wife would be like, said, "Good Heavens! That's the $64,000 question." This may be explained partly by the fact that they are not very much younger than the teacher. Also, while they are very intelligent and proud of their ability to do intellectual work, they feel angry at men and have some trouble feeling that work and relationships with men are compatible. (Hilda did not want to get married because, she said, she did not want to be subordinate.) In this teacher they find a man who, in his role, is likely to appreciate their competence. In any case, they are very strongly attached to their teachers but are careful to keep this hidden and to maintain their overt relationship with the teacher at the traditional distance. Like the other members of this cluster, they do not get to know the teacher outside of class. What they do is to put a great deal of energy into the classroom or into work for the course outside the classroom. They try to gain a special position of favor with the teacher through their intellectual capacity and hard work. Margaret felt that she had suceeded with this strategy in class. She felt that the best thing about the class was that her teacher liked her and mentioned that in handling another girl's crush "he was smug about it and gave me a knowing look." She felt a special rapport with him, described him as "shy" and looking "very young when he smiles." She could be colleagueal toward him, as when she had suggestions which might have helped him in the course. It does seem as if Mr. D appreciated her efforts and felt a special identification with her not unlike that with the involved males of this cluster. Hilda also seemed to work out a successful relationship with her teacher using a slightly different strategy. While she did not participate as much in class, she must have worked very hard outside of class, for she got one of only two A's in class B. These females succeed in pleasing the teachers intellectually. In that sense, the use they make of the energy derived from their attraction to the teacher is adaptive. But they are not entirely happy with the results because the teachers do not get involved with them personally. While this would not really be expected, given the strategies they were using, we would guess that they still had some fantasies that a covert romance would somehow develop.

Before beginning our description of cluster 5, we should point

Cluster 5: The Heroes

Factors: HI: Contention (.01)
                   Challenge (.01)
                   Enactment (.05)
                   Concealment (.05)

Categories: HI: Moving Against (.01)   LO: Showing Depend-
                   Showing Counter-   ency (.01)
                     dependency (.01)   Expressing Anx-
                   Resisting (.05)   iety (.05)
                   Denying Depression (.05)
                   Amount of Partici-
                     pation (.05)

out that clusters 5 and 6 were together in the original cluster analysis and that we split them at the midpoint of their scores on factor one: Enactment. Since this is the case, they share many common characteristics, the most noticeable of which is their common rebelliousness. But it also seems that each of them has many distinctive characteristics. Thus, having given this reminder, we shall proceed to treat each as a cluster in its own right.

For the members of cluster 5, all of whom are males, classwork is inextricably tied to rebellion. Both are manifestations of a deep involvement with the teacher and the course work. Unlike cluster 4, whose involvement with a given course is necessarily limited by a commitment to other matters, students in cluster 5 have the potential at the beginning of a course to be some of the most deeply involved in the class. But involvement has for them certain implications which tend to lead them not only to very productive and creative work, but also, in the same class, to extreme hostility and resentment.

The members of cluster 5 tend to see themselves as exceptional people. We can see evidence of this in the class sessions where they seem very confident in themselves, sometimes almost arrogant. Curt, for example, once explained to the class, "You've got to keep in mind that Skinner is a rat man, here in his fullest bloom." Further evidence is provided by the adjectives which they choose to describe themselves on the follow-up questionnaire. Words like "intelligent," "versatile," "competent," "well-read," "good-looking," and "mature" are common in their self-descriptions, and they sometimes veer toward "proud," "unimpressed," "arrogant," or "aloof."

The feelings of superiority that are an important part of the identity of these students are accompanied by expressions of contempt for ordinary or common people represented here by most of their classmates. They are particularly contemptuous of people whom they seek as weak, conforming, and afraid to be independent. George, in arguing for the feasibility of utopian societies, said, "You've overlooked the fact that some people have an immense fear of breaking the status quo." Ned, in a discussion of whether people should be called on, said, "There's enough bull already without calling on scared people." They do not like people who they think are talking to please the teacher. Peter said about Pamela, "She tries to clear up facts. She always has something to say even if it's the same as Mr. C. She's obnoxious." Ned, when asked what the worst thing about the class was, said "a few students (like Doug) who buttered up the teacher and put him on the spot with ridiculous questions."

The last part of this statement is an example of the discomfort of these cluster 5 students with their association with the other rebels in the class, those in cluster 6. They tend to be scornful of them, to think, as Peter said about Toby, that they "make stupid comments" and "challenge the teacher on trivial points."

The strength of the assertions of confidence and contempt for others by this group seems to indicate to some extent that they feel a need to deny both depression and tenderness in themselves. Their depression seems not to center around the question of whether they are adequate in relation to most other people, whether they are acceptable or respected by other people, but rather around the question of whether they can be true to themselves. They know that by other people's standards they are intelligent (they had the highest scores on the college board examinations of all the clusters) and creative. They were also highest on the creativity scale of the OAIS (see Appendix A). But they seem to have inner standards which require a good deal more of them than acceptability in the eyes of others. They tend to be introspective, and self-respect and a sense of integrity seem to be very important to them. They want their motivation for action to come from themselves, not from the desires or the potential sanctions of others. Bruce, for example, said, "I'm impulsive. I do things I like to do, otherwise I don't. Studying, for example—I don't do it for a grade. I play piano and guitar." They want to be able to feel that their creativity springs from within themselves, that they are not simply accepting the dictates or the advice or the findings of their parents, their teachers, or their society, that they are creating something new and better. One good example of this kind of attitude is Floyd, a black student. When the teacher was leading the class in a discussion of which of several different alternatives would be the best way to go about raising a Negro's social position, Floyd argued with the teacher saying things like, "What if he doesn't want to have his social position raised? Maybe blacks don't accept white's standards of what they ought to be." In a discussion of utopias, he asked, "What if people want to strike out? Do the people in control think enough of the individuals and their attainments to give the reins back to them?"

There is some tendency for them to see their lives in romantic or poetic terms, to conceive of themselves as living intensely and deeply. Roger is more like this than any of the others. In his interview he described himself as "Johnny Appleseed. I have theories on trees. Love is like trees. The pine tree is love for beauty . . . Love starts from an acorn into a great white oak. Help people to love in their love. Sequoia as pine—beautiful love of beauty." Roger is also the best example of the intensity with which this group is likely to involve themselves in certain aspects of their lives. During the semester of this class he was very involved in a relationship with a girl and at the same time with philosophical questions about the meaning of life and the direction in which his own life might go. As he describes it, he was so caught up in these problems that he let all his courses go and slept 24 hours a day. By no means all of these students describe themselves with such intensity, but they seem to share a view of themselves as heroic figures, as leading lives which are somehow apart from and beyond the common. They are proud of their uniqueness and individuality, proud of the ways in which they are alone. Probably one reason why it is important for them to deny the warmth they feel for others is that such feelings might imply that they were on the same level as those others. But their contempt for others does not extend to all people. They do find other people for whom they feel a great deal of affection and with whom they are likely to feel an immediate and almost magical closeness. These others are people who are similar to themselves, who also feel different from and above most people. The members of cluster 5 tend to greatly enjoy the company of those whom they feel are also somehow special or elect in their own right.

Students in this cluster are all males, and maleness seems to be one of the bonds which ties them to those with whom they feel especially close. When this group mentions females, it is usually in the context of a purely sexual relationship, and is more or less facetious. The answers to the following questions are typical: "Would you have felt any differently if your teacher had been a female?" From Edgar: "I would only hope that she was a good-looking one." From Ned: "I would have been more interested if she was good-looking (I mean this as a serious response)." "What names do you remember from class?" From Ned: "Katy. She had nice legs." "When was the class most interesting?" From Curt: "It was most stimulating when all the pretty girls were there." These comments would seem to indicate a lack of interest other than sexual in females. This evidence is somewhat counterbalanced by what we already know of Roger's deep involvement with a girl and by the introspective and somewhat artistic nature of this group, which would seem to lend to them something of an understanding of feminine concerns. We also can see them competing with other strong males in what could be a display for the females in the class, or symbolic fights about who should take possession of them. It seems likely that as women become more liberated from their culturally-defined roles, there will be more female heroes, and the kind of males found in this cluster will be more involved with these females. But at this point, it seems that the main loyalty of this group is to their fellow males. In fact, their display is more for the benefit of the males, perhaps even the ones with whom they may be fighting.

One of the ways in which maleness is displayed by the students in this cluster is by showing that they are not afraid to talk about topics that might arouse anxiety in other less confident people. In a psychology class the anxiety-arousing topics may center around unconscious motivations, sexual and otherwise, which people do not like to recognize in themselves. There seems to be some tendency for this group to accept the idea of unconscious motivation more readily than some of the other clusters. More specifically, Ned brought up two such anxiety-producing topics when, in the first session, he gave "fear" as an example of a primary motivator, and later when he said, "I would disagree with the idea of a standard sexual response because the sexual drive can be met in a lot of ways." Comments such as this may be designed in part to test out the teacher as a male, to see if he becomes anxious or uncomfortable. This teacher responded with, "Yes, for example, it can be satisfied by perversion, and then there's natural heterosexual behavior." Peter was one of the most successful at the kind of male display engaged in by his cluster. He said in his interview, "I went in for a project. I didn't have any ideas . . . the correlation between breast size and academic performance (this was in front of the girls) . . . the psychology of kissing . . . homosexuality . . . the height of grandmothers with steel production"; and in class he once asked, "Isn't that part of a female . . . being attracted to men?"

The issue of homosexuality seems to be salient for most of the members of this cluster. They are likely to bring it up in class and seem to feel somewhat attracted by the idea at some level. For most of them this probably is not a conscious fantasy, but one member of this group seems to personify this aspect of their personalities. The following are quotes from the interview with Bruce. "Mr. C is intelligently, sexually pleasant . . . he has a big square chin like in *Playboy.* I'm not on the make for him. There's no homosexual thing there. He's coarse and base in a relaxed sort of way . . . I didn't develop much of a personal relationship with Mr. C. I did with a philosophy fellow. He was plain looking—had my sense of humor. He was also preoccupied with sexual intercourse. Mr. C is married." The idea that this cluster would be interested in homosexuality at some level has some intuitive appeal, since we have already mentioned that, at least at this stage, they generally seem to feel closer to males than females.

An important implication of the characteristics of this cluster that we have described thus far is that the teacher is likely to be one person with whom these students might be interested in developing an involved and close relationship. The teacher in all of these classes is a male. He is above the rest of the class and likely to be quite intelligent. Besides this, he has additional magic because of his position of authority and his added age and experience. There seems to be some tendency for these students to describe their fathers as either authoritarian or frequently absent or both. It seems likely that they would be somewhat interested in developing a personal relationship with an older male and, indeed, this seems to be the case. They tend to find very appealing the relationship of favorite son to their father-teacher. They make some attempt to set up a situation where their teacher is almost like a guru, where the teacher and student are close to each other and learning is through the personality of the teacher as well as through his ideas. They tend to fantasize and work toward what might almost be seen as a co-teaching model, where they and the teacher work in tandem to teach the ordinary students, where they help the teacher when he needs it and act more as colleagues than as underlings.

It seems somewhat paradoxical that a group that places a high value on private work, work according to their own inner standards and not under pressure or sanctions from authorities, should also have the potential to be most involved with a field and its ideas when they are at the same time involved with an authority figure who represents that field, that is, the teacher. However, for one thing, this group is very ambivalent about father figures, and for another they tend to relate to the teacher as a person, another male who is similar to them, who can understand them, and with whom, since he is additionally a teacher and a father figure, they can identify and learn how to develop their inner strength. Since this is the kind of relationship that they seek, it is very important to them that the teacher be what they consider a strong person. If they see signs that he might be what they consider a weak, silly, or dependent person, or if he seems to need to depend on the strength associated with his role as an authority rather than on his personal strength, then they will not be interested in seeking a special relationship with him, nor will they be as likely to be involved in the course as a whole. Ned, for example, worried that his teacher might be weak or effeminate. In his interview he said that he would give the follow-ing hint to a friend: "Don't take the teacher as being effeminate. He gives an effeminate image, but he isn't like that at all." In discuss-ing what the teacher's wife would be like he said, "It's tough because it's hard to tell if he could be dominated by her or if he is just being democratic. Hopefully democratic, but it could be dominated." On the follow-up study he said that what he liked least about the teacher was that he was effeminate.

Much of the work which these students do in the class is directly related to their relationship with the teacher. At the beginning of the class, they do not tend to be anxious and dependent like many of the other clusters. They are likely to be exploring the potentialities of a relationship with the teacher. They are usually the first to break out of emotions that are typical of the early sessions and begin an enactment phase. Part of this enactment takes the form of a willing-ness to help the teacher when he is feeling somewhat uncomfortable. If he asks a question that no one can or will answer through fear, resistance, or lack of knowledge, it may be a cluster 5 who will step in and give him the answer he wants, even though it might not be the kind of question in which they are particularly interested. Or if, as happened in class A, the teacher has somehow set up an embarrassing situation where he is not able to give the students the degree of freedom that he had implied, it may be a cluster 5 (in this case it was Edgar) who extricates him from the difficulty by proposing an integrative solution that satisfies the class. This group can show a remarkable empathy with the goals and emotions of the teacher. Especially at the beginning when most of the students are too involved with fears of their own to consider how the teacher might be feeling, these students can be very helpful.

There is another kind of work which is somewhat more in charac-ter for this group and only related to the teacher insofar as it is motivated by the involvement with him and helps make his class better. This is the creation of new ideas in class. Cluster 5 tends to enjoy the discussions in class, especially if they feel close to the teacher. Curt, for example, said in his interview, "I like the material. I've done a lot of reading on my own . . . I love participating in class." They, like cluster 4, tend to bring in outside readings and experiences and apply them to the material in class. These contribu-tions are likely to be quite impressive. But they also go beyond this kind of application more than cluster 4 is able to and expend a great deal of energy in the course of the class itself thinking about the material, discussing it, and creating new ideas continuously throughout the term. They tend to play a major part when the discussion is freest. If the teacher turns the class over to the students for a day, or if he introduces a structural change which allows more student participation on a more colleagueal basis, then the cluster 5 students are likely to participate more and become very involved in what are likely to be excellent discussions. They tend to feel an identification with the teacher when they are enjoying the class this much, as when Floyd said to Mr. D, "That's what I noticed myself doing while I did it; what you just said." They also may volunteer to be discussion leaders more than once, as Ned did in class B.

The work which these people do outside of and in conjunction with the class reflects their concerns about integrity and working for themselves rather than pleasing anyone else. From the teacher's point of view, it must seem very erratic. They are likely, on the one hand, to fail to hand in written assignments or read the assigned material or to do clearly inferior work on assignments. They will skip lectures which they are supposed to attend and come in late to class without seeming to feel very guilty or worried about any of these unorthodox kinds of behavior. But, on the other hand, if they are involved with the course and the teacher, they continually surprise him with unassigned work that they have discovered. One day, when Mr. C said that he had forgotten to tell the class about a special lecture, he learned that two of the cluster 5 members had found out about it and had gone. Another day in the same class, two of this group had not handed in an assignment that the teacher was giving back, but a third one had read an article which the teacher had never been able to understand himself, and had written an excellent paper on it. They are likely to remember things from the textbook during class discussions that the teacher has forgotten and to be able to explain things to the class that he does not know about. When they do work on papers or readings they tend to become very interested in their work, to work very intensively, and to turn in exciting, creative products. Theirs are the kind of papers from which the teacher learns something he never knew or through which he thinks about a problem or issues that had never occurred to him. The problem from a teacher's point of view is that this group is sporadic in their production of this work, so that they may not become involved in this way in any of their classes in a particular term. Their involvement, once again, depends to some extent on their relationship with the teacher.

We come now to the other face of this cluster, the rebellion which for them must inevitably accompany creative enactment. We have seen that it is important for these students to be different from other people, to be alone in an important way, in order to maintain their personal integrity as they see it. A somewhat schizoid nature may be an essential aspect of this cluster, for a separation from other people and a unique perspective probably are important factors in their ability to be creative, to think of new ideas and integrations.

We have also seen that the teacher is likely to be one of the people with whom members of this group feel a magical union and closeness. But it seems that this kind of closeness, while very important to this cluster, is at the same time very threatening to them. They seem to be afraid at some level that if they become too close to another person it will mean for them a loss of integrity, a betrayal of their loyalty to themselves and their ideals. It is very important that they be able to maintain their right to withdraw from even these special relationships at any time they wish. If the teacher calls on them to answer a question for which they did not volunteer, they are likely to answer it in a contemptuous fashion, making it clear they would rather choose their own times to talk. Ken seemed to be somewhat uncomfortable with Mr. C because, as he said, Mr. C as a father "would be hurt if a boy said, 'I don't have time to talk to you, Dad.'"

Although this group has special, positive feelings reserved for older authority figures, these figures also represent a special threat. An important part of the meaning of authorities to this cluster is their desire to force others into their mold, to use the sanctions available in their position to take away the freedom of others to grow in their own way and to force them to change in the directions which they, the authorities, believe in. This cluster tends to see the school and university system as a whole a repressive one, one which allows them neither to develop their creative potential in their own ways nor to develop relationships with teachers which are not centered around formal role-oriented teacher-student behavior. In a new class, this cluster needs to test out whether they will be allowed to be independent and creative, and they tend to be mistrustful of early claims by the teacher that this will be the case. When Mr. B changed the class into a circle and invited increased student participation in discussions, Ned needed to ask more than once whether the discussion would be graded. If it were, he would not have been able to enjoy taking part in it because the implications would have been that he was doing it for the grade, not for his own reasons. This group on the whole tends not to trust authorities, and it is important for them not to comply with their regulations to avoid punishment. They might, in fact, go so far as to be counter-dependent enough to do the opposite of what they originally wanted to do if it meant going against the wishes of an authority.

It is important to this group that the teacher be a human being and not try to maintain a front that he is perfect or all-knowing just because he is the teacher. They want him to be strong, but part of strength is acknowledgement of failings. When they talk about the teacher, they are not reluctant to see his limitations themselves. On the interview question of what the teacher would do in an emergency on a train, they saw him as being strong, but not unselfish, and usually no more heroic than they themselves. Bruce, for example, said, "If there was enough danger he'd organize people. But in an extreme situation he'd save himself first." Peter said, "If the train was on fire, he wouldn't come back 10 times, but he'd help." They are also not averse to reversing roles and interpreting the teacher's behavior in psychological terms. Peter, for example, said about Mr. C, "All his sex examples are reaction formations. He repressed it when he was young so now he can talk about it."

This group is happiest in a colleagueal relationship with the teacher. They know that they have good ideas, and on the interview question of what they would talk to the teacher about on a train, they seem to savor the possibility of meeting with him on an equal level and comparing their theories. Curt said, "There are many things I'd like to talk to a person with his training about. Anything involving behavior with people intrigues me—I have pretty good explanations. I'd like to complete them." Peter said, "I'd sit and ask him his plans. Ask him about his specialty. Ask him what course to take next semester. Ask him about work he's done. Tell him about some of my own theories."

On the other hand, if the teacher is not willing to encourage or allow colleagueal kinds of relationships, if he stresses the aspects of his role that involve the invocation of his authority, the cluster 5 students tend to be unhappy with the class and angry with the teacher. They are insulted if barriers are set up which define the teacher as alone and unreachable and above all the students. They want to have a chance to be seen as people, so that they can then show that they are themselves superior and deserve a special place with the teacher. They do not like to be condescended to; if they are arguing with the teacher, they will reject any implications that they are just being silly, or that they are incompetent or do not know enough yet to be ready to argue. They want to be seen as competent individuals who are capable of disagreeing with the teacher in a colleagueal, intellectual fashion. One of the most striking examples of an action by a teacher that angered this group, occurred in class B. After Mr. B's innovation of the circle discussion group, the members of cluster 5 were working very hard and taking a major part in the discussion. They were also spending some time arguing with other students about psychological issues, such that Mr. B was prompted in one session to comment that he and some of the males in the class were probably scaring some of the class members by their strong talk. When several sessions later the strong talk of this cluster turned to an attack on one of the teacher's most cherished tenets, Mr. B made a long speech about the "subversion" of the discussion which had been carried out by the members of cluster 5. He said that students should first learn things, then understand them, but not criticize until these first two steps were thoroughly mastered. After this session, he began to spend more time lecturing and was more continuously in control of the class discussion. These students felt that their freedom had been betrayed. Their teacher had retreated from a colleagueal into a more formal authoritarian position. Ned was especially affected by this move. In the next session, he asked, "Why is it you say that you should let anger out when other people admire people for hiding it?" Later, in a discussion of activism on campus, he said, "The people who object are going to pull out anyhow." In fact, he participated less after this incident and was less involved in the class. In his evaluation of the course, he mentioned as a criticism another incident which had similar implications. After the class changed into a circle and Mr. B began to call the students by their first names, Curt asked Mr. B what his first name was. Mr. B answered that he preferred to be called by his last name. This was important enough to Ned that he mentioned it after the course was over.

The fear of becoming too close to others and the need to withdraw even while approaching, in combination with mistrust of authorities and the actual unwillingness of these teachers to maintain purely personal and colleagueal relationships without exercise of their formal authority, leads these students to rebel in the classroom. Attacks made by this group can be very broad and sweeping and extremely hostile. This is especially true early in the class when they want to test the teacher's reactions. Peter, for example, when the teacher was trying to do an experiment on ESP with the class in the second session said, "I don't see how this will prove anything. It's just guessing numbers." Ned, when Mr. B was talking about sublimation, said, "Is beating up on a doll really constructive though?

Wouldn't that give a person some stress and he'd go around beating up on furniture and all?" A little later he asked, "Is it just a hasty generalization that the children of psychologists are all screwed up anyhow?"

Usually this cluster is happier if the teacher is skillful in most areas of teaching, if he is strong in expertise, runs good discussions, and is well acquainted with the various aspects of his field. But the function of the teacher that they do not like and that they are most likely to flaunt and attack is that of the formal authority. They do not want to be forced or pressured into doing or believing anything that they do not want to. Ned, for example, in answer to a loaded question from the teacher, stated, "I think we can all tell what you're looking for, but I don't see how it would be. I don't see how you can assign that term to such an action." One frequent method of attack by this group is to ask in a resentful fashion about the details of the requirements for an assignment. This is an especially adept weapon, when, as with Mr. C, the teacher is trying to present it as primarily a learning, not a grading assignment and does not want to face its formal authority implications.

This brings us to another aspect of the revolt of these students, that is, the skill with which it is carried out. The empathy of this group with the goals of the teacher enables them to be very helpful to him at times, and also means that they are sometimes able to express feelings which the teacher in his role is not able to communicate but is likely to feel, such as contempt for certain kinds of students. But this same empathy also gives these cluster 5 students a particularly effective mode of attack when they are angry. They can guess which issues the teacher is very sensitive about and which kind of attack would make him very uncomfortable or angry. Combined with their skill in sensitivity is a more general intellectual skill which is also useful in attacks. Thus their ability to apply and create which can contribute so much to the class also enables them to defeat the teacher in arguments, to refute claims that he might have made, or as happened fairly frequently with this cluster, to catch him on a questionable or wrong answer to his own exam question.

One aspect of the rebellion of this cluster which distinguishes them from some other clusters is that they refuse to be defeated. Just as it is important for them that their arguments be taken seriously as intellectual, colleagueal differences and not be belittled as lacking in knowledge or ability, it is also important to them that they not be clearly beaten in an argument with the teacher. They are able, fairly often, to win such arguments but even when they seem to have lost, they never admit it. An example of this can be seen in Peter's argument with Mr. C in session 19, the transcript of which is included in Chapter 3. In the session before this one, Peter had actually succeeded in convincing the teacher that he should accept different answers to one exam question. But in this session he had an argument about a different question which Mr. C was not willing to accept. The debate continued for a long time, and finally ended with Peter saying, "I don't know. I just don't like the question."

The erratic nature of the private work of this cluster and the mixture of rebellion with their work in class makes it difficult for most teachers to appreciate their presence in the classroom. And the demands, in most classrooms, for steady work and a willingness to learn what the teacher thinks is important make most institutionalized educational experiences unpleasant for this cluster. They are very clearly underachievers, having, in spite of their superior intelligence, an average grade point of just over a C. In most cases this group was not entirely satisfied with their experience in this particular class either. Their participation tended to be the highest in the beginning and to drop off at about the point where the teacher tended to take more control of the class. This cluster seems to feel at some level that this process of taking over is something of a betrayal, implying that the work that they have been doing is inadequate in that it reduces their freedom and relegates them to the position of just another student in the class rather than a special aide and friend to the teacher. In their evaluations they tend to say that the teacher was inadequate as a person with whom they might become close. On the scales that were significant, they said that he was not enough of an expert in class, that he did not act as a person in relation to his students enough, and was not good at facilitating student initiative. They also implied that he did not allow them as much freedom as they wanted. On significant items, they said that "Students were not free to comment and criticize" but that "Students did volunteer their own opinions," implying, it seems, that while they did express themselves, this expression was inhibited by the teacher. Displeasure with the course was by no means unanimous in this group. They seemed to appreciate especially classes B and C, where there was the most discussion by students and the least emphasis on grades. In class C, where their rebellion was treated as worthy of serious consideration and discussion in class (see the transcript of session 19) some of these students became very involved, felt that they had gained a great deal from the course, and made contact with the teacher after the course was over. It seems to be generally true that this cluster had strong reactions to these classes. Sometimes, if a good relationship with the teacher had developed, their evaluations were strongly positive, as with Peter and Roger, who both rated the teacher superior and planned to make their careers in psychology. Sometimes the reaction was very negative. George, for example, commented on his evaluation form that "the course should be abolished" and described it as "tired, bored, uninterested students enduring another rather meaningless hour"; and Edgar stated that, "After taking the course I felt that Psychology was designed to keep a number of people busy while the rest of us worry about making the world go around." Finally, some students, like Ned, maintained an ambivalent attitude throughout the course. He stated that the course was "superior (though the lecture reeked)" and that what he liked most about the teacher was "his knowledge (as a person I despised him)."

When asked about their expectations for their future, cluster 5 seems to be quite optimistic. They expect to be able to work through their anger at authorities in such a way that they will be able to be creative and productive persons, maintaining their integrity in the process.

Cluster 6: The Snipers

Factors: HI: Contention (.01)
                  Challenge (.01)
                  Discouragement (.01)

Categories: HI: Moving Against (.01)   LO: Level One
                  Counterdependent (.01)
                  Reparation (.01)
                  Resisting (.05)

Since clusters 5 and 6 were together in the original analysis they have much in common. The members of both groups are underachievers; they are counterdependent, rebellious, and likely to direct hostile comments toward the teacher. But there are important differences as well. While students in cluster 5 want very much to be involved with the teacher, the cluster 6 students more often state that they are not involved, and that they do not care very much about the teacher or the class. In addition to reasons for low investment in this particular class, the noninvolvement of the cluster seems to be related to a low level of self-esteem and general pessimism about the possibility of fruitful relationships with authority figures.

The combination of low investment and high rebellion leads to a kind of sniping at the teacher from a distance. They frequently level attacks at the teacher, but they do not move close enough to argue in a way which expresses relatedness, nor do they identify with the teacher and intersperse their rebellion with enactment as is the case with cluster 5.

There seem to be some relevant commonalities in the backgrounds of the students in this cluster. They tend to describe their fathers as authoritarian, but also somewhat weak. More often than not they said in their interviews that their mothers "wore the pants" in their family and that they were able to have their own way. Sometimes they also described circumstances that caused them unhappiness as children. They might mention parents who died or lived overseas, or the loneliness of being an only child in the country, or jealousy of brothers or sisters. The females more often talk of feeling neglected by parents, but the males, too, tend to at least imply it, though they do not seem to wish to talk about it very much.

These students do indicate in the Interpersonal Outcome Inventory that they rebelled against their parents and they certainly rebel against their teachers but, on the other hand, they are very ambivalent about authorities and authoritarianism. It is striking that seven of the members of this cluster specifically mentioned in their interviews that the teacher did not take enough control over the class or that he would not be enough of a disciplinarian as a father. And several who mentioned that their fathers were authoritarian said that they planned to bring up their children in a similar manner. Dale, for example, said that he would be "conservative and traditional" as a father, using "moderate to strong discipline." Some of the members of this cluster want to follow very directly in their father's footsteps in other ways as well. Gary, for example, whose father was a minister and grandfather a doctor, wanted to be a medical missionary. Some illustrations of the need of this group for dominant authorities can be found in the discussion of whether to change class B to a more discussion-oriented format. Members of cluster 6 made comments like Gary's: "Since this is the beginning of the course I think we should get more information," and Peggy's: "You've had a few more courses than we have." Then, after the chairs had been arranged in a circle, Doug said, "I don't like it." One interaction from class B involving two different cluster 6 students illustrates the two sides of the ambivalence rather well, as well as one way in which teachers may respond to the rebellion of these students.

Mr. B:	What are some of the possible consequences of punishment?
Doug:	The tendency for rebellion.
Mr. B:	Yes, the possibility of rebellion and other negativistic behaviors which really interfere with the learning from the experience . . . What are some of the benefits of punishment?
Class:	Silence.
Mr. B:	Anybody.
Gary:	A lot of times you don't know what's good for you.

It seems somewhat paradoxical that some students would be rebelling against authorities precisely because they are not authoritarian enough, but for this group this seems to some extent to be the case. Of course, this is not always true, and they will join with the cluster 5 students in attacking the formal authority aspects of the teacher's role, but they also tend to become upset if he seems to them to be relinquishing his authority. Some of the issues they chose to argue with the teacher were related to authoritarian issues like prejudice and intolerance of ambiguity. In session 19 of class C, the transcript of which is found in the next chapter, Toby attacked Mr. C for maintaining that racial differences were environmental. Dale wrote on his follow-up questionnaire that what he liked least about the teacher was his section in civil rights, and he also said, "If the teacher had been a female, I would have strongly disliked the course."

An unwillingness to be introspective, to think about ideas that are new or personally threatening, or to discuss ideas that are more ambiguous than hard facts is also fairly common in this group. Typically the material on Freud is the best example of this aspect of psychology in these courses, and the students in this cluster tend to express anger at psychoanalytic theory. Dale, for example, said in his interview, "I think Freud is a crackpot in some cases. I don't think people are that way. If people were as Freud says, everyone would be sex maniacs." In answer to Mr. B's question about the lecture on symbolism in Cinderella, Doug said "I thought he read too much into it." When the teacher asked if he thought he was justified, he said "No." Perhaps the comment which best illustrates the fear of introspection seen in some of these people is from Gary who said, "If you know too much, there's no use in being a human being."

An issue that seems to be related to fear of introspection for these students is the fact that they tend to feel more guilt than most other students, as seen, for example, in their high scores on reparation and discouragement. Because they are liable to feel guilty about their motives, impulses, and actions, it may be difficult for them to look too deeply into themselves, for they might find things that would make them feel even more guilty. The guilt that these students feel seems to be related to their backgrounds in that many of them were probably taught that there were strong moral laws which must be obeyed. It also seems to be relevant that they saw their fathers as weak, and must have felt fearful of hurting them with their rebellious behavior and guilty about their hostility toward them.

There are many examples in the interviews and transcripts of the guilt these students feel and the reparative gestures that they make. In describing class A, Frances said, "I don't understand the class, the teacher wants to let it go but . . . we don't come through." Arthur, on his follow-up questionnaire, wrote a note at the end saying he was sorry that it was late and that he could not remember more, but he hoped it would do some good anyway. And Toby, whose argument for hereditary racial differences had been a major source of discomfort for Marvin, a black student, said in his interview, "Marvin knows what he's talking about. He has good ideas. He's the only one." Finally, in class B, in the session after Mr. B had told the students (mostly cluster 5 and 6 males) that their excessive arguing had subverted the class discussion, two cluster 6 students made comments about their guilt. Doug, in discussing Milgrom's experiments and Nazism, said "I'm feeling guilty; one of the biggest effects it (a movie on Milgrom) had on me was when it was talking about who was responsible, and I realized it was all deep in my personality." Peggy, in the same discussion, said, "You can't blame everything on society."

One way in which these students can make reparation to the teacher for their attacks is to give him high final ratings and, in fact, they rated the teacher much higher than they rated the course. They seem to want to feel that their attacks are not directed toward the teacher as a person, but only toward issues in the classroom. Their need to separate things in this way is probably accentuated by their feeling that the teacher, like their fathers, is weak and could be damaged by their hostility. In fact, on the metaphor checklist data, they rate the teacher significantly low on the activity-potency factor and significantly high on distress.

The guilt of the students in the group seems to be related to a generally low level of self-esteem. One student who illustrates well the mixing of these two phenomena is Gary. When asked to describe his ideal self in adjectives, he used "responsible, considerate, honest,

Christianlike, unhypocritical." When asked what he thought he was actually like, he said, "quiet, withdrawn, hypocritical, worrisome, proud." Their lack of introspection seems also to be connected to a low regard for self, in that they are afraid that if they looked too deeply into themselves they would be unhappy with what was there. Peggy, for example, said on her final evaluation form that the worst thing about psychology is that you find out things about yourself that you do not like. There is little doubt that the students in this group feel dissatisfied with themselves, as seen in the adjectives they use to describe themselves. Ron wrote that he was "unmotivated, undisciplined, wishing to make friends yet unreasonably 'closed.' " Arthur said he would like to be "at peace with the world" but that he was "discontented, sad and lonely"; and Doug described himself as "confused." They also express a lack of confidence in themselves in the classroom. Lawrence stated on his final evaluation that he sometimes did not talk because he thought his ideas would seem utterly absurd. Doug felt incompetent when he was a discussion leader and felt that the other students were not contributing to his discussions because they were hostile to him. Ron said in his interview that he did not like the class because he was nervous with people looking at him, and at the end of the interview he was worried that he might have made a bad impression on the interviewer.

Not only do these students feel dissatisfied with themselves as they are, but they also tend to feel relatively pessimistic about the possibility of successful resolution of their problems. When asked what they would like to be doing in 10 years and what they expect to be doing then, this group tended to talk about magical or unrealistic hopes and anger resulting from low expectations of reaching them. Doug, for example, said he would like to be "an experienced world traveler, a writer, as free and open-minded as I feel I am now," but that he expected to be "settled in some career, with a stable life pattern, having made my compromise with society." Toby said he would like to be "marooned on a TV-equipped South Sea island" but would be "still filling out forms."

These students do not feel any more hopeful about establishing an enjoyable or worthwhile relationship with their teacher. When asked what they would talk about on a long train ride with the teacher, they indicated that they would not enjoy such a situation. Lawrence said he would not talk about psychology. Frances said that she and the teacher would both be uncomfortable but would not let each other know, and that the teacher was a psych major and would pick her apart; and Toby said on a train with Mr. C he would "sit down. It would depend on what I had to do. I'd talk or read. If I had work to do, I'd do it."

One reason why these students do not look forward to being with the teacher as a person seems to be that they tend to see him so much in terms of his authority that they are unable to understand or be very interested in other aspects of his personality or role. Their reactions to authority figures include much hostility and ambivalence, but not much empathy or involvement with the teacher as a person outside of his position of authority, and not much optimism about potential outcomes of their relationships. They can easily imagine a scene in which they and some authority fight over a long period of time with no real resolution or development of a satisfactory relationship. Toby, for example, when asked what kind of a father Mr. C would be to a teenager, said "There would be problems, a diversity of wills. Both would be pretty stubborn. It would be around independence. There would be quite a lot of conflict over ideas, more conflict than in most homes. He's stubborn. Both would think they are right. Sometimes the father would worry, sometimes the son. There would be no real victory or defeat. The conflict would linger."

The actual outcomes in class for this cluster do not tend to be any more satisfactory than those they imagine with other scenes involving authorities. They rebel against the teacher's authority, but even when they have a chance to lead something themselves, they do not feel comfortable doing it. This is especially obvious in class B, where this group hardly ever volunteered as discussion leaders and sometimes begged off when requested to fulfill this function. Peggy explained her reticence by saying, "I like to argue too well and you're on the defensive too much as a discussant. I like to be on the offensive." In fact, however, this group seems in an important way to be on the defensive much of the time. When they rebel, they do not seem to have in mind a particular outcome or state which they hope to achieve. We have seen that they are very pessimistic about outcomes, to the extent that it would be difficult to hypothesize that they were rebelling because they were unhappy with one situation and reasonably expected that their rebellion might produce a much more satisfying state of affairs. Instead, it seems that their rebellion is more expressive and defensive than is that of cluster 5. It serves the purpose of providing an outlet for their pent-up dissatisfactions with themselves and others, and at the same time it defends them from outside forces, such as psychology teachers or theorists who might be pressuring them to think harder about threatening aspects of themselves. Unhappily, what this group's rebellion does not accomplish is to lead the way toward resolution of the problems that are the source of their discontent. Thus, while the rebelliousness of the cluster 5 students is related to a desire to form a close relationship with the teacher and a class situation where they can feel comfortable and be relatively free of authoritarian constraints, the members of cluster 6 feel much less hope for such good outcomes, and tend to rebel in a way that helps them to maintain a safe distance from the teacher and the classroom experience.

The members of the cluster need to proclaim frequently to themselves and to others that this course is unimportant to them. This is partly a distancing mechanism which they need because of the factors discussed above. There also seem to be particular aspects of this course which are important in understanding their need for distance. Many of them state that they took it mostly to fulfill a requirement, not out of interest in the subject matter. Also, one would expect that the subject matter would be difficult for these people; they tend to have higher math than verbal aptitude scores and, in addition, insofar as the study of psychology encourages introspection, it is likely to be threatening to them. In any case, it is very important to this cluster to make it clear that they are basically indifferent to this class. One way in which they express their noninvolvement is to emphasize that they really did not want to be in this class or sometimes even in the university. Frances said she did not have a choice, that she had to come to this university, and Peggy said something similar, that she had come because she really needed to get away from the people she had grown up with, not for intellectual reasons. And Gary said he was not fond of school, that it was too much work, but he had not thought seriously of giving it up because the currency value of the degree was important. As far as the course goes, Dale said he took it because he was considering switching programs and this would fulfill two different requirements, and Toby said that "the only relationship this course has to my overall goals in college is that it is required for a teaching certificate, which is only a secondary goal anyway."

This group also tends to say that since they are not committed to the course or the field, they do not work very hard in it and they do not intend to. When asked to describe themselves in the course, Arthur answered, "Vacation—I'm taking it for fun . . . the work is not nearly as hard as engineering," and Toby said, "trying to get by—do as little work as possible and still get a decent grade without getting wrapped up in the course. In reading courses you don't have to get involved." Lawrence, in his interview, described the discussion as "asinine" and said he never did the reading until a week after the discussion. We would guess that this group would tend to hand in assignments more regularly than cluster 5, to avoid repercussions, but that their work would be of a lower quality than they could potentially produce and that they would hardly ever become excited enough to produce an extraordinarily good piece of work. Also, they do not tend to become very involved in the discussions and are likely to denigrate the accomplishments of the rest of the class in this area. Doug, for example, once said in class, "I don't know where you got the idea it was such a good discussion—I didn't get a thing out of it."

Direct statements from this group that they are indifferent to this classroom experience are frequent throughout our data. Anna stated on her follow-up questionnaire that she "started sleeping in that class very early." Toby said he had "almost forgotten the course entirely." Dale said in his interview that "the material made little shift in my attitude. You can understand his ideas without believing them." And Lawrence said that "the material is boring" and, when asked what hints he would give to a friend about the course, he said, "You don't miss much not coming to class." Finally, comments from the observers of these classes seem to indicate that these students do cut class quite often compared to the others.

Given their own need to remain uninvolved in the course, these students' opinions about the teacher's involvement are interesting. Some of them seem to want to think that he is not involved either, perhaps so they will feel less guilty about attacking him. Toby said that in an emergency Mr. C would be "pretty cool, calm. He doesn't let things get him down" and, when asked to describe him, said, "Happy-go-lucky—seems not too deeply involved or bothered by it." While there is this component of denial of the teacher's involvement, this group on the whole seems to feel that the teacher was more involved than they would have liked. In our measure of students' opinions of different aspects of the teacher's role, this group tended to say that he did too much of everything, and they were significantly high on saying he was too personal.

Since this group wants to avoid strong emotional involvement, they may be upset when they see other class members involved in highly charged confrontations. Gary, for example, stated that he thought the arguments among students in class B were annoying and useless, and Doug stated that he found the heated discussion about motherhood in that class "disgusting—we came to the same conclusion that we started with. It's all right to talk about it but there's no sense to argue."

When these students say angry things in class, which they often do, they tend to deny the implications of their statements and try to avoid confrontation. If someone whom they are attacking responds to the emotional content of their message, they usually deny that they meant anything personal. Ron, for example, was asked by Mr. B if he would mind being called on in class, and he answered that he sometimes did not mind but that if he did not like the question he might become antagonistic and answer a different question. When the teacher asked if he ever became antagonistic in this class, Ron said he did not. Doug, in the same session, asked about the seating change, "Is this in any way connected with that little machine [the tape recorder]?" When Mr. B asked if he was particularly concerned about that, he answered, "No, I haven't noticed it, it's just that she [the observer] sits there every day." Toby, in the session of the major confrontation in class C, said about his position, ". . . what I was saying . . . I don't believe this . . . I mean I was just bringing it out as a point . . . that's why I said it was sort of way out." Later he denied the relevance of the argument to his relationship with the teacher saying, "Whenever I was arguing this last point I was using it in no relationship to our argument the other day, I mean you know, it was just a point that occurred to me." In his interview Toby said about that argument, "I was just trying to get points." (Interviewer: "Was Mr. C mad?" Toby: "No, it was not a conflict of wills, but of viewpoints.") Peggy said something similar to this in her interview. When asked if the teacher knew her, she said, "I hope he didn't take me seriously. I was just arguing for the sake of arguing . . . I have to have one class I'm more aggressive in than the others." The idea of personalized anger directed toward the teacher seems to be too threatening and too involving for the group. They want to believe that they are carrying on a content-oriented debate, and they deny the messages about feelings which are part of their communication with the teacher.

In what seems to be another manifestation of their need for distancing themselves from their experiences with the class, this group tends, even within the content area of their contentiousness, to avoid major substantive issues and concentrate more on peripheral issues such as the physical aspects of the situation. One of these aspects was this study, and the tape recorder and questionnaires frequently came under attack by this cluster. Arthur said on one questionnaire that the worst thing about the course was the "white tornado of forms to fill out." Dale said, "The old Chinese proverb, 'the longer the spoke, the greater the tire,' applies to course evaluations as well as speakers," and "Does the department do anything with the undergraduates besides use them as guinea pigs?" Finally, Doug under "further metaphors" on one of the forms wrote, "The whole thing is ridiculous."

There are other kinds of peripheral issues that provide targets for this group. One example is the preoccupation that Dale had with the poor technical quality of the films the class saw. He asked in class, "Why do they pick movies with such bad photography?" and on his evaluation wrote that the films were "absolutely the worst done pieces of work I have ever seen, including home movies," and repeated twice that he could not understand the audio. But what is especially interesting in this case is that on the follow-up question-naire two years later he mentioned especially that the film "Night and Fog" impressed him. It seems that the content did have an effect on him through his denial, and that this may be true in some cases for other members of cluster 6 as well.

Most of the attacks on the teacher from the students in this cluster have to do with his position as an authority, particularly specific details about the formal requirements of the course. From the first day of class, when, for example, Arthur remarked, "I take it we're not going to use the textbook" and "Would it behoove us to take it back to the bookstore then?" they tend to pick at the teacher's authority and to try to make him uncomfortable about it. Dale's remark in class A that the paper was due the same day as the exam, and Toby's question to Mr. C, "If we do the research project and still have to take the final, will we still have to review the whole course or will it only be part?" are fairly typical of questions on the details of evaluations asked in angry tones by this cluster. When in class C the teacher suggested a plan where two people could work together on a project, Toby asked if it would have to be teams of two, and when Mr. C answered that it could be any number, Arthur asked "How about teams of 15?" There is a testing quality to these interactions such that it is difficult for the teacher to respond in a way that will satisfy them. If his answer either strongly asserts his authority or tends to relinquish that authority, these students will not be happy. One way in which they express their ambivalence about the teacher's control is to read authoritarianism into comments by the teacher in which he meant to let the students have freedom. When Mr. B asked the class informally to think about some aspects of an experiment the class had been working on together, Gary asked, "You don't want that written out, do you?" And when Mr. A, worried about being too much of an authority, asked why people had written down what he just said, Dale said that Mr. A had mentioned earlier in the term that they would have to know the terminology of the field. In fact, Mr. A had said that terminology would not be very important. This kind of pressure on the teacher, pushing him into a more authoritarian position at times when he is already uncomfortable with that role, is more typical of cluster 6 than of cluster 5. The latter are more likely to support the teacher when he tries to move out of his position as an authority because they are less ambivalent about being in low structure situations than are the cluster 6 people.

A clear difference between these two related clusters is that members of this group sometimes collapse and obviously lose arguments in class, while cluster 5 students almost never admit that they have lost. This probably has to do with their investment in the course and in their relationship with the teacher. The cluster 5 students are less likely than the cluster 6s to deny that the argument was important and withdraw if defeated. Another relevant factor in the tendency of the members of this group to allow themselves to be humiliated in class may be that they tend to feel more guilty about their hostility than do the students in cluster 5, and they experience some alleviation of guilt by being punished. One concomitant of the different attitudes toward defeat is that cluster 5 students usually enter arguments on more solid ground. It frequently happens with members of cluster 6 that they have not read the material relevant to an argument in which they are taking part, and the teacher and the class together can easily expose a lack of sophistication in their point of view. The cluster 5 students are more likely to argue about an issue when they have in their possession some data or ideas which go beyond what they were required to know.

One example of cluster 5 refusing to give in and cluster 6 being defeated is session 19 of class C (see Chapter 3 for transcript) where Peter (cluster 5) and Toby (cluster 6) both argue about a test question. We have already quoted Toby when he denied at the end that he really believed or was committed to what he was arguing for. It is interesting that just after he said this, a girl said to Mr. C, "You won." Peter, on the other hand, under similar pressure from Mr. C, ended his argument with "I don't know, I still don't like the question."

Another scene between Mr. C and Toby illustrates beautifully the defensive, nonintrospective quality of the rebellion of cluster 6 as well as their tendency to lose arguments. In session 29 of class C, the following interaction took place.

Toby (to Mr. C):	Are you sure this oedipal thing is so extensive?
Mr. C:	That is an issue we're going to discuss.
Toby:	'Cause I don't believe it.
Mr. C:	You don't have and never had any feelings toward your mother?
Toby:	No, or my father either.
Mr. C:	(Talks about how the oedipus complex is not the same for everybody and how everybody represses it, and some people must massively repress it.)
Toby:	Wouldn't the relation between the parents have something to do with it?
Mr. C:	Yes, and siblings, too. (He explains that when a child cannot handle it and massively represses it, you find that neurosis or sexual problems, hand-washing compulsions, etc. result.)
Toby:	Will we have some readings on this?
Mr. C:	Yes, do you want them?
Toby:	Yes, we haven't had any.
Mr. C:	Yes, we have. (He tells what.)
Toby:	But we haven't had any experiments.
MR. C:	(Asks Toby if he read a specific book.)
Toby:	Yes.
Mr. C:	(Asks if he read a specific article in it.)
Toby:	No.
Class:	Laughs.

The question of the different reaction of teachers to the clusters 5 and 6 students cannot be answered simply. On the one hand, the teachers often become angry and punitive toward the students in cluster 6. Mr. C, for example, forgot Toby Wicker's name at least once, and then later accidentally started to call him "Miss Wicker." And when, in an ESP experiment, Arthur asked if he wanted them to write down the suit and number of the cards, Mr. C answered in a hostile tone, "Yes, if you're going to read my mind exactly, you should be able to do that." In class A, the teacher asked who had not done a certain reading, and chose Dale out of the group to illustrate a point. And Mr. B, when he saw Peggy on the street one day, pointed his finger at her and said "Bang!" When she asked him about this in class, he said he must have been feeling some hostility toward the class.

There are many understandable reasons why this group could make teachers angry. They can be very hostile, but they rarely move toward the teacher, and they are elusive when the teacher wants to confront them directly on an issue. Unlike the cluster 5 students, they do not usually mix their rebellion with Enactment, so there is little for the teacher to appreciate in their performance. In addition, they do not tend to support the teacher at times when he needs it, as may those in cluster 5. One indication of this is the distribution of the students across classes. The teacher in class A was probably the one whom this cluster perceived as weakest and most often distressed. Dale described Mr. A as "not a cool guy, not a hero type," Anna said he "seems afraid," and that "every time he does something he asks the class to analyze it." But while they saw this distress, and some positive aspects of the teacher (Anna also described him as a "nice man" and "sincerely kind and helpful to individuals"), this did not seem to alleviate their attacks on him. Their other comments about this teacher were on the order of: "He doesn't stimulate you." "It's the worst course I've had." "What he does is nothing to get excited about." And in the class, a cluster 6 person, Dale, was the highest participating student. In class D, on the other hand, where the teacher seemed extremely strong and sure of himself, there were no cluster 6 people at all. For some reason the group seems to find it easier to attack those whom they see as fairly weak. One observer also commented that these students tended to attack the teacher when he was already feeling down. Perhaps one reason for this is that if they are not too invested in forming a personal relationship with the teacher, it is not worth the risk to attack a teacher like Mr. D who is capable of responding punitively.

The tendency of the group to attack at times when the teacher is distressed probably adds to the teacher's negative reactions to them. However, there are important reasons why these students could be less threatening than the members of cluster 5. Since they are less involved with the teacher as a person and less sensitive to his inner conflicts and desires, their attacks are less skillful and less upsetting. There is a great deal of denial in their claims that they mean nothing personal against the teacher in their attacks, but those statements also express something important. The kinds of attacks they make probably would tend to apply to almost any authorities, whereas the cluster 5 attacks are usually very personally directed toward unique aspects of this particular teacher.

Another reason why this group may be less threatening than cluster 5 is that they are easier to defeat. If the teacher is attacked but can, in the course of the argument, clearly prove his superiority, he probably will not feel too bad about it. And, as we have seen, this occurs fairly frequently with cluster 6. There is also a related factor that makes it easier for teachers to deal with them, namely, that these students do not tend to be very well liked by the other students in the class. Sometimes the teacher does not have to defend himself because other members of the class will do it for him, and sometimes a teacher will purposely utilize the feeling of the other students in his defense. In session 8 of class C, for example, when Toby objected to a statement made by the teacher, Mr. C asked the rest of the class what they thought about it, and they answered that Toby was wrong. At this point, Mr. C could content himself with telling Toby that if he had been right he would have had a good point.

There are three females in this cluster, and they differ in important ways from the males. Their feelings of inadequacy, their distancing, and their rebellion are all closely tied to their feminine identity. They tend to feel that women in general are inadequate and to be jealous of and angry with men for considering them inferior and discriminating against them. Usually they want to pursue careers but feel that they might not be able to because of the attitudes of men. Peggy, for example, sided with Libby in defending working mothers when the students in class B were arguing about maternal deprivation. Anna, when asked what she thought she would be doing in 10 years, answered, "I'll be married with five children." To the question of what she would be doing, she answered, "married with five children, still able to use my degree." One of the ways in which their anger at their presumed inferior status is expressed is in a tremendous sensitivity to condescension by men. When Frances was asked what kind of a father her teacher would be to an adolescent, she answered, "He would be understanding. It would make me mad. He wouldn't take me seriously." She also mentioned in her interview that Mr. C slipped once and called the class members "children." And Frances complained that her teacher did not give students credit for thinking, that he was "constantly explaining and over explaining" and that his grading scale was "deprecating—so big and broad and condescending."

If males were the sole source of the idea of the cluster 6 females that women are inferior, they would be less unhappy than they are. But in fact they seem to believe it to some extent themselves. They tend in some ways to like and respect men more than women. When asked how they thought they would have liked the course if the teacher had been a woman, Peggy answered, "I would have been less interested," and Anna said, "I probably would have been even more ready to criticize." Their chosen style in the classroom is also closer to a traditionally masculine style. They are competitive and rebellious and want to be seen as successful in the intellectual sphere. Their desire to be part of and successful in the men's activities seems to be related to a feeling that men are more interesting than women and that the things that they do are more worthwhile. Given that they do believe these things, it is not surprising that they would feel inadequate and defensive about their sexual identity.

There is another problem, however, which seems to be even more central to the sense of self-esteem of these females. Not only do they feel that females are inadequate, but they feel that they are inadequate females. They know that they cannot be males, and beyond this they feel that they cannot even be good females. Two of these girls described themselves as unattractive. Related to their concerns about their attractiveness is the fact that approval from peers is important to them. Frances, for example, commented in one discussion that social reinforcement was important, that people needed the appreciation of other students; and Anna was worried that her friends thought she was too calculating with them. But they tend to feel that they cannot obtain the approval of and especially that they cannot be attractive to men. On the form asking for adjectives describing themselves, Peggy wrote "physically unattractive," and Anna "shoddy and dowdy." And the observer (male) in class A described Anna as "old before her time, mature, controlled, and not able to be sexy or sexualized."

These students are rebellious and distancing in a similar way to the males in this cluster. One example of their rebelliousness is Peggy's comment in Class B, "There're various degrees to which things have been proven, too. Gravity and electrons are pretty safe, God is pretty nebulous, and so are id, ego, and superego." They do seem to be somewhat more sure of their intelligence than the males. Peggy described herself as "bright." Anna said that instructors would describe her as "intelligent" and "having potential," and she also said, in a discussion of teaching machines, "Aren't you kind of cheating people who could learn it quicker?" But they are more sensitive to their interpersonal inadequacies than the males, and these are an important motivator for their behavior in class.

One important aspect of the class for these students is that they find the teacher attractive, but have hardly any hope of being found attractive by him. Some evidence of the attraction comes from Peggy, who wrote that more females talked in the class "because of the rewards of talking to a man" and who in class said "Well!" in a sexy tone when Mr. B slipped and said "Psychiatrists under every bed." Their reaction to the belief that the teacher is not attracted to them is also well illustrated by Peggy. Shortly after the teacher's slip mentioned above, she asked him what the relationship between anxiety and frustration was. He turned the question around to her, and she, sounding frustrated, said she did not know. At another time in that class the teacher forgot her name, and she said that was all right, that she did not mind, and he said that she should mind. Finally, Peggy was very upset when Mr. B saw her outside of class and said "Bang" to her. That was one of the most salient events in the class for her.

Since the group feels that they are unlikely to become close to the teacher in a female way, they, like the males, tend to withdraw to a safe distance in class, cut class more than most people, and direct a great deal of hostility toward the teacher. One way in which they handle their attraction to the teacher is to deny it and focus their feelings on more distant, more unattainable objects who will not have the opportunity to reject them. Anna, for example, wrote that the most exciting thing about the class was the observer. And Peggy said she was very attracted to the lecturer, and that he reminded her of a teacher in high school who was her friend. Their need to find an older man to whom they can feel close is probably accentuated by the fact that they seemed to be dissatisfied with their relationships with their fathers. Frances's parents lived abroad so she was alone in this country at the time. Anna said that her father was too controlling, and needed to have people depend on him. And Peggy's father died when she was ten.

For both the males and females in this cluster, it is difficult to determine how much of their behavior in the class is related to the fit between them and this particular teacher or class and how much it is similar to their behavior in other classes. If, for example, many of them did take the course because it was a requirement, perhaps we should not be surprised that they were angry. And if they feel, as Doug did, that they "come from another culture" than that which is represented in the class, for whatever reason, one would expect them to feel somewhat alienated.

Also, it is not clear how much of their behavior can be attributed to our seeing them at a particular point in the development over time of their life style. One of the crucial things about the students in this cluster is their inability to find satisfactory resolution and integration between different aspects of life. For the females, the attempt to integrate masculine and feminine aspects of themselves has so far been relatively unsuccessful. To the males, a worthwhile and fulfilling relationship with a person who is in a position of authority seems impossible at this time.

Cluster 7: The Attention-seekers

Factors: HI: Exhibition (.01)
                        Concealment (.05)
Categories: HI: Moving Toward (.01)
                        Self-esteem (.01)

The members of cluster 7 tend to have a predominantly social rather than intellectual orientation in these classes. They are very concerned with their relationship with the teacher and other class members, especially in the sense of wanting to please them. One way in which they do this is by trying to seem attractive by frequent talking, showing off, bragging, and joking, the kind of behavior represented by factor seven, Exhibition. Another way is best represented by the category Moving Toward; students in this cluster may move toward by complimenting other people, expressing positive affect toward them, flirting with them, or quietly admiring them. Generally they tend to express positive feelings toward others and to deny negative ones. But they are contentious at times. If they feel they have been rejected or, on the other hand, if they are very confident of their position in a relationship, contentiousness may become an important part of their style, although it is still usually expressed in a denying, joking manner. One problem faced by these cluster 7 students is that their interest in people and their need to be accepted by people tends to overshadow their interest in the more cognitive aspects of work and inhibits their intellectual development. This group does not seem to lack intelligence, but sometimes their concentration on the affect in a situation and their willingness to be pliable in order to please others keeps them from being as creative as they might be in their contributions in class. They also tend to lack some depth in their thought about themselves and about intellectual issues because they tend to deny aspects of life which might cause them to experience anxiety or depression.

When we look at what the members of this group tell us about their backgrounds, we find there is a much greater involvement with mothers than with fathers, and also a great deal of concern with the issues of nurturance and control. An important theme running through their interviews is that of mothers who are dominant and much more vivid in their minds than fathers. Fathers tend to be seen as either distant or weak, and to be perceived as having played a minor role in the nurturance and discipline of this group as children. Cindy, for example, said that her mother was dominant and hypothesized that her teacher would be weak as a father and would delegate authority to his wife. Alfred described his father as "reasonable and democratic" and "not usually home." His mother, on the other hand, "runs things while he's away and . . . she has her ideas and is not about to change for anybody. Like she questions drinking. In the summer at night I just stay home. It's ridiculous. She's Pennsylvania Dutch and she still has their ideas." The most extreme example of the preoccupation with mothers is Rod, who talked about his mother as follows: "She is 'maternal' and has a strong will about things she has a 'feeling' about . . . She is hard to talk about. Some might think she is schizophrenic. She is either a nasty bitch or real nice." This description of a mother as either "a nasty bitch" or "real nice" seems to be related to a major problem faced by these students. They are very ambivalent about the issue of being controlled by authorities, and this seems to be related to inconsistent control and loving by their mothers. On the one hand, they tend to feel that they have been spoiled. The observers in the classes describe most of them as physically attractive and charming, and we can easily imagine their being rewarded for their performance as "cute" little children showing off for and charming their elders, and avoiding punishment by this means. In what seems to be a reaction to this kind of pattern, they tend to be sensitive to the possibility that other parents might spoil their children too much or that authorities might allow too much freedom. When asked what kind of a parent his teacher would be, Roger said he would "have a tendency to spoil his children" and would be too lenient about drinking. Lois seemed to be approving of him when she said he "wouldn't let his kids walk all over him—he'd exercise his authority." And Alfred said he would "spoil a little child," that he would "understand a little more the problems of the teenager" but still "might be too democratic." Some of their comments in the classroom are in the same vein. Alfred described Mr. C as " 'The Good Sailboat who needs more canvas.' He has everything; he's a good teacher, but he seems indecisive about certain things. He doesn't keep control of the conversation." And Lou, in a discussion on the control of aggression, said that aggression cannot be allowed to run rampant, that "otherwise if I was in a classroom and the teacher said something I didn't like I'd take a chair and start beating it on the wall." This was, of course, partly a joke but it expresses the feeling of this group that they do not have adequate internal control and therefore need to be controlled by others. There is other evidence of this need for control. Cindy, for example, stated that she functions best in school if she is under pressure, and others seemed to feel this way too; both Mary and Lois, in a discussion of Skinnerian utopias, seemed to like the idea of the strict and consistent controls which would be exercised in such societies. Mary said it was good that Skinner gave the children frustration when they were old enough to handle it, and Lois said that planned frustration was not "any more inhuman than the way people treat their kids in everyday life."

The idea of strict control by parents seems to have several different meanings for these students. When they talk about spoiling and the need for control, they seem to feel that if a parent fails to control a child carefully he or she is also failing to love the child enough. They seem to be quite concerned with inadequate nurturance by mothers. Lou, for example, stated in class that children may suffer speech impediments if they change mothers at an early age. And Rod, who had described his mother as vacillating between being a nasty bitch and real nice, also said in his interview that he had "all the symptoms of an oral fixation: always something in my mouth, very extroverted, but I try to avoid being dependent. I know that I am too dependent." For him the issue of nurturance and the fear of bad and dangerous mothering were also relevant in class. The metaphors he chose to describe his teacher were "scolding mother" and "sharp scissors." It seems that the situations where these students were spoiled have come to mean for them at some level that their parents were lazy and did not care enough about them to bother to control them. But these feelings represent only one aspect of their attitude toward control. Many times they seem to say that parents or authorities are too strict, and this makes them angry. Cindy furnishes some examples of these feelings. She said she had a lot of conflict because her parents were strict and she was independent, so that it was now hard for her to go home for week-ends. She said she would not join a sorority because they "impose discipline for discipline's sake." Roger thought his teacher as a parent would push his kids too hard to get good educations when they might not want to. And we saw before that Alfred and Rod resented their mothers' willful insistence on certain kinds of control.

It seems that either insufficient or excessive control can mean rejection to these people. Perhaps one reason for their concern with both extremes of this control issue is a particular kind of situation in their backgrounds. One guess we could make from what they say is that their mothers, compared to those of other clusters, were more capricious in the giving of both discipline and love. This kind of background would help to explain one of the most pervasive traits of these students in this class, which is their unusually high need to be reassured by others about themselves. It seems that if parents did not react to certain behaviors with love or punishment in fairly predictable ways, it would be difficult for those children to learn to build enduring internal standards for themselves of what is good or what is lovable. If they had difficulty in finding reliable standards which would help them predict reactions to their behavior, then we could expect that they would need to be checking frequently with others to see if they are pleasing them, to be reassured that they are liked, and to figure out if they are controlling their impulses in proper ways. This kind of continuous orientation to and performance for others' reactions is probably what they were rewarded for the most consistently in the past.

At the time of our study we find that this group of people is very much oriented toward other people in their thoughts and actions. They tend to like and need to be with other people and speak often about the subject of friendship. Gloria, for example, wrote that her goals in taking the course were "to better understand and get along with others." Cindy, when asked about career goals, said she was "going to work with people—in nursing, social science, or something". Pat said she transferred from another college because the people there were unpleasant. And both Andy and Lois talked about the importance of their friends. Roger told the interviewer that he had many friends who came to him and confided in him. ("Their parents aren't around, and these kids have to tell their problems to someone, so they tell them to me.") And Lois said about friendship, "I enjoy school, but I go home a lot too. My best friend is at home, and we have so many interests in common."

Another way in which the general orientation toward other people is expressed for this group is in always keeping in mind the impressions they are making on other people, feeling that they are being judged by other people, and worrying about whether other people like or love them. For example, Pat became upset in a discussion in class C of material versus nonmaterial rewards from parents to children. She said, "I don't think you can separate those. My parents love me, but they gave me a dollar reward for a good report card."

And in talking about other people, Gus said he "feels uncomfortable with people," especially strangers. When asked what the worst thing that could happen would be, he responded "doing something that would make me look clumsy, like I am a real clod." Also, some of the responses of these students on the forms we asked them to fill out illustrate their preoccupation with the way they appear to others. Mary copied over a whole paragraph on a form because the first one had been a little messy, and Roger wrote under "additional comments," "I hope my answers don't look unbelievable; I was generally quite honest." In talking about their classes, these students tended to be especially concerned with the impression they would make on the teacher. Gloria said she was afraid of doing or saying things that Mr. D would find stupid, and she was often afraid to ask questions because of the possibility of sounding dumb. Mary said that she would enjoy a train ride with Mr. B because "We'd both be more relaxed. He's being judged too." Gus said about his teacher that "If you give the wrong answer, he thinks you are an idiot, and you think you are too. I feel embarrassed and guilty unless I get the right answer."

This group also tends to look to other people to provide incentive for their actions and to want to be pressured to help them make decisions. Lisa, for example, said that for best learning you should always be "a little afraid of the teacher, you should respect him and not have a friend relationship with him, because with a friend you could lose your incentive to work hard." And Roger, when asked why he took the course, said, "I should take it, I have two sisters majoring in psychology." One way in which these students use others to provide incentive for them is to measure their own worth or progress in terms of how well others are doing. They are unusually concerned with competition and jealousy. Thus, Gus argued against teaching machines by saying that competition between students is necessary. Mary suggested that status was a primary drive in people, and when asked to elaborate on that, said she meant competition. And in a discussion of utopias, Lou said, "I don't see how they would get around competitiveness like in marriage." Margaret seemed concerned about competition with siblings when she said, "I have one older brother and an older sister. I'm caught in between. Sis went to U of M and was in the 'bad element.' Brother is frat. Little Margaret is caught in between." And Roger seemed to be expressing jealousy in answer to the interview question of what student name comes to mind first. He said "Curt stands out. He's older. He has everything all thought out ahead of time. He has a little moustache and wants to be noticed—'this is my home—welcome, people.' He smokes regular old small cigarettes. I could tell you all his mannerisms in class."

It is very important to the students in the group that they be approved of and reassured by their teachers. One way in which they express this need is by a whole cluster of behaviors which could be loosely lumped under the category Moving Toward. This group tends to have warm feelings toward the teacher, to want to please him, to perceive him as a strong figure, and to support him in class. These things are more common with the females in this cluster, but they seem to be present to some extent in all the members.

These students give many indications that they are interested in a personalized relationship with the teacher. One example is their tendency to come up after class, especially early in the term, to talk to the teacher, to ask for special favors, or to set up special relationships in some way. In the second session of class B, for example, both Roger and Mary came after class to ask for special favors. It was important to Lois, as another example, that Mr. D let her enroll in the class when it was already full. Lou came after class to talk about an independent experiment he was working on, and Robert came to see Mr. D and confided to him some important problems and happenings in his life.

The support which these students give to their teachers is expressed in a number of different ways. When they talk about him they often express warmth toward him and approval of him. Thus, Lois said the worst thing about the course was that there was "not enough time," and she also said in her interview that she liked Mr. D and that "everyone does." Alfred said, "There should be more teachers like Mr. C," and Gus said Mr. D was the most competent teaching fellow he had ever had. Sometimes the members of this cluster, especially the females, became protective of their teacher in a somewhat maternal way. Lois, for example, said what she liked least about Mr. B was that he "sometimes accepted criticism he didn't deserve." Pat commented about the discussion of the first test in class C, "It was his test; he didn't have to defend it." Gus criticized Mr. D but then also apologized for him saying "ridicule is not his aim." And Cindy said that her teacher "wants response from the class and deserves it, but he doesn't get it." Other ways in which these students support the teacher are by acting weak and perceiving the teacher as strong and also by reassuring him when he has doubts about the worth of his own contributions. They may be tentative in their asking of questions, as with Gloria, who raised her hand

and said, "Can I ask a question please?" They may want to be encouraged to speak, as when Mr. B asked Mary, "You were going to say something?" or when Mr. D said to Lisa, "It's all right, don't be afraid." They may act naive and express a need for help in understanding things, as when Lois told Mr. B she was confused when some males in the class were talking about protons and electrons. But they also are reassuring in return, as when Mary told Mr. B that his test was not too hard for her, or when Pat and Alfred both reassured Mr. C about his nurturance by saying in answer to his question that a father would be more likely to come to the aid of an infant at night than a mother.

It is very important to these students that the teacher be nurturant for they are sometimes quite dependent on him. They seem to feel somewhat uncomfortable if the teacher shows signs of leaving them to their own intellectual devices. Lois and Lou, for example, were both concerned with the change in format in class B, wanting to make sure the teacher would still be teaching the important material. When Mr. B turned the class over to the students for a discussion, Lou asked, "In what light are we supposed to discuss this?" But the main kind of dependence on the teacher is a need for attention and approval. One comment which Lois made again and again about her teacher was that he was sensitive to the feelings of the students. And Mary seemed to be expressing a desire for this kind of sensitivity when she said she wondered if some people wanted unconsciously to be called on. She also expressed the need for nurturance when she said that one thing she had learned from the course was that a child needs cuddling. Often the students in these classes seemed to feel that the teacher had not been warm enough to them and they felt rejected. Rod said he was bothered by his teacher's "indifference" and "lack of patience." Gus was upset that his teacher did not seem to like him very much, only consoling himself by saying, "If he thinks I am a complete clod, I wouldn't have done as well on the exam."

The need for dependence and nurturance in this group leads us to another issue, that of the sexual relationship between the females in this group and the teacher. Most of the characteristics we have been discussing as part of Moving Toward have been much more heavily represented by these females. The males tend to have different strategies for pleasing the teacher which we have yet to discuss. But before we leave the females it seems important to deal with the issue of sexual attraction. It is helpful at this point to subdivide the females again into the relatively low and high participators. We shall describe those females at the high and low ends for whom sexual attraction is most relevant, but it seems to be important to some extent for all the females of this group. The low participating females tend to be described by the observers as less physically attractive than the high participators. They tend to be highly dependent on the teacher and very high on the Moving Toward category. Some of them state explicitly that they have or have had crushes on the teacher, and this sexual attraction seems relevant to the others as well. They seem to feel rejected by the teacher and to be quite unhappy about this. Gloria is the best example of a student with this kind of problem. When asked who in the class had a crush on Mr. D, she said "All of us did in the beginning, but we restricted it." The adjective she chose to describe the class was "frustrated." When asked which student in the class came to mind first, she said, "Robert—he's depressed, he doesn't like getting cut down; Shirley—she's sad, for being mocked during Mr. D's experiment; Joe—he's sad and depressed." On her final evaluation she said it was "not easy to get along with the teacher; I used to enjoy the class but not any more" and that the teacher's "moodiness bothered me; he could be sarcastic and rude." But she rated the course "very good," and two years later described herself as having been "very enthusiastic." Then she said she was "fed up with the superiority complex" of the teacher, but that "the instructor was a creep but I learned in spite of him," and "Even though I couldn't stand the teacher, I became interested in psychology and took three more courses." The ambivalence expressed here seems to be mostly the result of her feeling of being sexually attracted to but rejected by the teacher.

The high participating females in this cluster were able to work out much more satisfactory relationships with their teachers. The observer reported that these females were quite attractive, and the teachers apparently agreed, for they tended to give them special attention and seemed to enjoy their flirtatious behavior. These students, who are best represented by Lisa and Cindy, seem to be intrigued with the strength and status and knowledge of the instructor and to enjoy flirting with him. Both Lisa and Cindy used the word "fascinating" to describe the field of psychology, and the word seems relevant to their feelings about the teacher as well. Lisa said about Mr. D, "He never smiles unless he is talking about psychology . . . he must have a deep love for it." She thought he would see the class as "very young, groping in the dark; he is trying to help us." The task of learning from and relating to such a strong and intriguing figure is pleasant for these females, partly because they are confident of their ability to please him. While he is distant from them, they also can feel that he is not too unattainable, at least for the kind of relationship they want to have with him. Cindy, when asked what she would do on a train with the teacher, said, "I would enjoy it. The teacher is young and informal. I'd feel at ease with him." And Lisa said, "It sometimes made a difference being a female in the class" because "the instructor was young and good-looking and frequently referred to when he was in college, which wasn't very long ago." The confidence of these females in their relationship with the teacher reminds us of favorite daughters who can afford to be imperious with their fathers. They seem to feel that they have a special right to make certain demands on the teacher. Thus they may ask him to explain things again for them or to give examples so they can understand better. They sometimes interrupt the teacher, and they contend with him in a flirtatious way. They are not afraid to argue with the teacher and may carry on such arguments for a fairly long time, frequently saying, "No I know that, but . . .". They may, though, sometimes argue for a naive position and allow the teacher to disillusion them, as when Lisa said about race prejudice "But it's gotta end someplace, it can't be that hopeless." Cindy, for example, complained about her teacher's language. She said that she didn't like swearing, that it did not seem natural, it was vulgar, and it lowered her opinion of him.

Perhaps the statement which best illustrates the confidence of this group is from Cindy, who said, "Mr. A depends on me personally for answers, so I have to prepare." Indeed, these teachers do seem to appreciate the presence of these students, who are on the whole loyal and supportive as well as seductive. Mr. D's comment to Lisa, "It's all right, don't be afraid," encouraging her to continue her comments, was rather unusual for him. And a fairly typical response to one of these females came from Mr. A, who after a hostile comment by a cluster 5 student, said, "Cindy, do you have any response to that?" This subgroup of cluster 7 females, while they are attracted to the teacher and enjoy playing a flirtatious and supportive role in class, do not seem to be as deeply involved with him as the lower participating females we described before. Cindy, for example, rated the course only "good," and Lisa described herself as "interested but not enthusiastic" and said two years later, "My evaluation has gone down after becoming acquainted with different courses and teaching methods."

The males in this cluster tend to express the concerns of the group by somewhat different kinds of behavior. Their strategy for gaining the attention and approval of the teacher is more involved with the Self-esteem aspect of the Exhibition factor than with the more female Moving Toward strategy. Of course, there is a good deal of overlap. The males do move toward the teacher and, in fact, their kind of exhibition is often an indirect way of doing so. And the Self-esteem part of Exhibition is important in understanding the females, particularly the high participating females we just described. There are also members of both sexes who combine the two strategies almost equally. But, generally, the males in the group are more likely than the females to manifest an exhibitionistic style of interaction involving bragging, joking, showing off, and talking a lot.

While the members of this group often support the teacher in the moments when he displays his strength, they can also be quite threatened by that strength. The males especially may see it as a threat to their own potency. Gus, for example, described in his teacher "a feeling of power behind him, like a gun or a sword." Robert seemed threatened when he chose the metaphor "sharp scissors" to describe the teacher. And Alfred seemed to be expressing some castration anxiety when he suggested as an emergency with the teacher on a train, "like if somebody stuck their foot through the bottom of the train." These students' fear of the teacher's power is augmented by an exaggerated and magical view of the potency of the field of psychology, which they sometimes see as his weapon. Cindy, for example, described psychology as "a very powerful tool, often flaunted by those who have only had one semester of it." Lois said she felt as if she knew Mr. B well "because of the material in class—we express feelings that reveal our personality." Lou said in his interview "I can't remember anyone's name, probably because I don't like people. That's what psychologists say." They were concerned with the tape recorder as a representative of psychology too. Pat said about it, "People don't like to be guinea pigs or statistics," and Roger said in his final evaluation that the had learned "to beware of experimentally taught courses." Finally, Pat said about the field of psychology that "it does something to you when you major in it."

The exhibition of the cluster 7 students seems to be closely tied to their fear of the teacher's potency; they do not wish to exhibit their fears and weaknesses to others or even to themselves. They do not want to admit that they are afraid, that they care very much about what the teacher and others think about them, and that they need reassurance of their worth and could be hurt by rejection. They prefer instead to try to present themselves as highly confident in their own strength and worth. Thus we find that they are prone to bragging. Lou, for example, said that in an emergency the "teacher would lose his poise, but I wouldn't, I'm heroic—I'm also conceited." And Pat displayed a bragging and contentious tone thoughout her interview, for example, when she said, "Child rearing practices: I'd beat em up. Freud is too much to stomach," or when she described her teacher as "a cherry-red and round and smiling and happy. He's going to snap someday—snap a stem off a cherry."

This kind of bragging is a way of indirectly expressing hostility toward the teacher as well as trying to appear confident in themselves. The feeling of being dependent on and threatened by the teacher evokes a great deal of hostility in these people, but they do not tend to react to their hostile feelings by engaging in direct angry confrontations. Instead, their hostility becomes a part of their exhibitionistic style. The joking or half-joking comments which are very frequent for this group usually touch on areas loaded for them with both anxiety and hostility. One of these areas is, of course, the fear of rejection by the teacher. One comment made by three different females, for example, was that education or therapy carried on only in the daytime was insufficient. Gloria made the class laugh when she asked, "But if you educate the kids and they go home to stupid parents, won't there be conflict?" And Lisa argued that having patients only in the daytime was not enough because "the family could do horrible harm to them." Roger wrote some bitter half-joking comments two years after the class which had to do with the rejection he felt from having received a low grade. He said that the course had "great influence" on him because he had "given up psychology completely" and described his relationship with the teacher as "comical, yet sad." Also, the observer in class D described Robert as having been rebuffed in a very early attempt to become close to the teacher by confiding important secrets to him, and as thereafter resorting to clowning and bitter joking in class as a means of expressing hostility and at the same time denying that he cared about Mr. D.

The other main area on which their joking and contention touch is their defensiveness about the field of psychology and their fear of what they think are its implications about their personalities. Pat, for example, said in a hostile tone to Mr. C, "You seem to be equating narcissism with egocentricism and I don't agree with that. I mean, you view things through yourself." Another thing which is very frequent with this group is turning the tables on the teacher by jokingly interpreting his behavior. Thus, Robert ended an argument with Mr. D with the comment "You're just rationalizing," and other students, especially the males, made similar comments throughout the term. There seems to be some warmth involved in this game of interpreting, and some identification with the teacher as well, but there is also a component of reacting angrily to the threat of his perceived interpretative powers.

The degree of participation of various members of this cluster is an important factor in understanding their tendencies toward exhibition. Some members especially, and to some extent the whole cluster, tend to have a very low threshold for deciding to say what they are thinking. There was one member of this cluster in the four highest participators of each class, and no one in the group was very low in participation. They tend to be very willing to carry on much of the everyday conversation of the class: asking questions and answering them, giving examples when the teacher asks for them, presenting thoughts, and sometimes debating issues. If there is tension that is causing much of the class to be retentive, members of this group often help the teacher out by being ready to say something. They will answer questions after resisting silences by the rest of the class, make jokes to relieve tension, and generally try to help keep at least the appearance of a smooth-running class. An important reason why they engage in the kind of participation seems to be wanting to please the teacher, to move toward him and gain his approval.

One mechanism implicit in the strategy of exhibition and pervasive throughout the cluster is that of denial. Much more than any other cluster, we found that this group tries to deny thoughts which they find threatening. Sex is one of these things; Lois, who had children of her own, stated that the class had gotten off the track when it discussed breast or bottle feeding and said that when a baby was sucking on a nipple hunger was involved, not sex. Similarly, Roger complained that another student had tended to make comments "which didn't belong" and gave as an example a day when the students talked about homosexuality. They also want to deny the strength of aggressive impulses in people. For example, in a discussion of Milgram's experiments where people followed the orders of the experimenter even when they thought they were hurting people, Roger commented "I don't think it was fair to stop the experiment where he did, he should have carried it out further and given the people a chance to think about what they were doing." And Lou, in talking about a hostile class argument about working mothers said, "When we were ripping up Libby—I like to do that. I good-naturedly rib people a lot." Finally, it is very important to these people to deny the threats which they feel in class. Robert, for instance, said about Mr. D, "I have no impression of him as a father or tyrant," and "He thinks I'm an oddball but that doesn't bother me." Lou's response when Mr. B suggested that perhaps the class was being reticent because they were afraid of being challenged was, "I love to be challenged." Gus, who had previously associated Mr. D's power with a gun or a sword, stated that in class "people are not afraid to say something and get chewed out for it," and later described the class as "a casual discussion group, with a generally relaxed atmosphere." Finally, in a striking example of denial, Alfred, when asked to describe his relationship with the teacher, said, "It seemed like he was afraid of me."

The interpersonal styles of the cluster 7 students tend to cause them some difficulty in a classroom situation. The members of this group do not seem to lack intelligence in some broad sense, but they do not often seem to be able to desire or enjoy difficult intellectual work. Their tendency to orient themselves so much to other people and their frequent use of denial do not seem to lend themselves to very deep thought either about themselves or about more external intellectual issues. Therefore they have more difficulty than some other people in certain aspects of the intellectual work of the class. This seems to be particularly true with essay questions on exams, where they are required to develop their own ideas and to use abstraction to integrate things in creative ways. Roger, for example, said, "I failed the last test. I know I know the material. Everything seems too obvious. I'm lost when it comes to essays. I have to be guided through an essay test." The exaggeration and oversimplification of the power of psychology which is common with this group seems to be related to a similar kind of problem. They tend to be preoccupied with the appearance of things and have trouble understanding the more complex aspects of psychological study; as a result, they tend to see any ability to look at many difficult levels of personality as a simple application of some magical principle derived in mysterious and wondrous ways. Given this assumption, they tend to be afraid of psychological knowledge, joke about its application to them, or deny it easily without trying to think very hard about it. Roger once said in response to Mr. D's query about Freud, "He broke down the complexity of the person into id, ego, and superego, and of course I disagree with it."

This group's preoccupation with appearances seems closely tied to their reliance on others' standards in forming their own judgments.

Since they are afraid of displeasing others, they also tend to be afraid of thinking too much or too deeply about issues, since they might come to conclusions which would offend whichever reference group was most salient for them at the time. They are more likely to pay attention to the appearance they are presenting to others and take their cues for their performance from some of the more superficial aspects of those others' beliefs. Thus, Gus was very worried about looking like a "real clod." Both Gloria and Lois complained that some people in their classes were "rude." Lou said that the hint he would give to a friend who was going to be in this class would be: "Read the material. Participate in class. Be interested and intelligent and friendly." Roger commented in class that he thought most children wanted to be firemen or something else exciting, and Lou said that he hoped in ten years to "have two kids, and be making at least $15,000."

The intellectual ability of this group is hindered in some ways by their high social orientation but, on the other hand, other people provide much of the motivation for the work which they are able to do. They do not seem to have much motivation within themselves to work hard in classes. On their evaluations they frequently complained about the work load of the course. Lisa said, "After about the first two days I wanted to transfer to a different section. He was going to demand a great deal of work . . . I was overwhelmed by the 20 page independent research paper." Gus said the worst thing about the course was "the terrible amount of reading." And Lou said, "I'm in school for sports. I'll play any game invented. There's an awful lot of pressure up here . . . I'm too lazy to study enough." When this group does work it often seems to be as a way of either gaining the approval of other people or avoiding their displeasure. One way in which this is expressed is in concern about grading. Thus, Mary said that the worst thing about the course was "the quizzes, because I didn't do too well." Lisa said that "besides getting a D," no worse thing could happen to her in class. And Cindy said, "I'm grade-oriented. Low grades lower my self-esteem. I have to do well all the time." This statement illustrates the way in which the grade issue is part of the larger issue of wanting to work to please others. The teacher is seen by them as appreciating certain kinds of intellectual work, and it is important to them to try to live up to what they perceive as his standards.

The question in the interview about what kind of a father the teacher would be is revealing in this respect. Roger answered the question as follows: "He would want his children to be intelligent—he'd push them—he'd be expecting kids to go to school, and would be happy to see that his children were normal. If they didn't want to go to school (me) he'd be crushed. He'd try to convince them." And Mary, to the same question, said, "He'd stress education—a college degree . . . he'd be sorry at rebellion from school—they wouldn't do that—it would make him too disappointed." The question about what hints they would give to a friend is also interesting. Lois said, "Class participation—he likes it when you ask an intelligent question. Ask yourself questions while reading." And Mary answered this way: "I'd tell her not to say anything until she's more sure of what she's going to say. Every time she says something it should be worthwhile so every time she raises her hand, he'll call on her."

One result of this group's attentiveness to others' reactions is that they gain some insight into some of their own failings. Especially in a class where the students and teacher become very involved in work in class, these students are likely to feel left out and to look harder at themselves to try to discover why. At the beginning of the classes in this study, these students held a very important place. They helped to relieve the early tension and to keep the discussion running smoothly, and they tended to be seen as charming and likeable people. But as the classes developed and were able to work better and with more depth than in the early attempts, the need for very high participation by this group seemed to drop, and they talked less later in the term. Insight into themselves and their interpersonal style is important when we consider their potential for change. The members of this group, for example, are quite uneasy about their tendency toward exhibition and their high participation. Some of the uneasiness may appear when they are being rewarded less in class, but for others it was important enough earlier to keep them from talking very much throughout the term. There are many examples of this feeling. Lou said in his interview that his participation had decreased because "I don't like to talk unless I know what I'm saying. I'll take over if there aren't any leaders." Alfred described himself as a "turtle sitting in his shell who doesn't come out unless he wants to do something worthwhile. I don't say anything unless I really feel like it." Mary said, "I end up talking when I shouldn't," and Lou said in class, "I talk a lot but that doesn't mean that I think it's more important than other people's, it's just that I'm more egocentric." There is also an awareness in this group of their tendency to not want to work hard intellectually. Roger proposed "sleep" as the basic drive in class B. Pat described herself as "unmotivated," as did Cindy. And Lou said he was "too lazy to work hard."

It seems that since members of this cluster are capable of observing themselves and to some extent are highly sensitive to the reactions of others, they do have the potential to change in the course of a class. And the evidence is that they did in these classes. For many of them this change might only have involved a decrease in participation and a vague feeling of discomfort with their role in that situation. For others it seems that there was an increased understanding of themselves. And some members of this group seem to have been able to learn to enjoy intellectual work much more than before. Alfred, for instance, became fascinated with the field of psychology in class C, chose a very difficult area, and wrote a good paper on it. It seems that a discussion class where peers as well as the teacher put pressure on students to work might have the most influence on these students.

Cluster 8: The Silent Students

The last cluster of students that we shall consider are characterized less by what they do in the classroom than by what they do *not* do. They do not participate verbally. For many teachers, the quiet, inactive people in class often form the most mysterious and at times the most disconcerting cluster. When members of a group do not participate, they can only be known by one's projections, both benign and malevolent, on them. To some extent, then, they continue the phenomena typical for the first day of class, when the teacher's perceptions of his students were most primitive and autistically determined. The teacher's only reality links to these students come, perforce, through exam results or written papers and also, hopefully, through outside contact during office hours and the like. For our four teachers, for whom class participation at various times represented a kind of idealized goal which defined one as a "good teacher" in the teaching subculture, the issue of the "quiet members" was particularly salient.

A rather large group of 21 students (second in size only to cluster 2) "qualified" for cluster 8 by having less than 20 scorable acts over the course of the entire semester. (The average number of scored acts for these students is somewhere in the neighborhood of 9 to 10 per student, with the median being about 5.) Since our factor analysis was based on 20 acts as the unit of analysis, individual factor scores cannot be derived for these students. It should be pointed out that these people were not evenly distributed across the four classes. Mr. A, who lectured more and allowed less discussion, had eight cluster 8 people in his class, fully one-third of his group, while Mr. B, who had students give reports to each other in class, had only two students who were in cluster 8. The predominant quality of all cluster 8 students, whether male or female, is their tremendous sense of helplessness and vulnerability in relation to the teacher. By and large, their relationship to him as they describe it is distant and remote, and this seems to be a result of their perception of him as either threatening and/or manipulative. The teacher is seen very often by these people as not acting from the highest motives but rather as acting out of his own needs and in the process ignoring or being indifferent to the needs of the student. A great many of these students are therefore suspicious and guarded in the classroom, and part of their silence clearly springs from this. For example, Eileen in Mr. C's class described him as "too interested for his own good"; Louise, in the same class, saw the teacher as democratic on the surface but "ultimately authoritarian." In some students, this suspiciousness borders on something like paranoia. Thus, Nancy did not like Mr. B's "constant psychoanalysis of us either by watching us or expressing himself verbally—and suppressing his own reactions for those he thought would be more psychologically appropriate." She also described him as both a compassionate and threatening father, since "underneath he has a powerful temper which he keeps well-hidden."

The males in this cluster are often angry and defensive and take a certain sort of malicious pride in having maintained their autonomy in a situation in which the teacher was clearly out to overwhelm them. For example, Tim in Mr. C's class, struck a familiar theme for these people when he suggested that he was going to study only if it was personally interesting to him and not because he was "hot and bothered" by what the teacher thought was important. He explicitly suggested that he was "cooling it" and "being his own man." Like other males in this cluster, he would very much like to present the teacher with something of value but, at the same time, he feels that the teacher is prying too much into his private affairs, and that if given a chance (that is, if he moves too close) the teacher will be dominating. It is interesting that many of these males see their silence as a kind of counterattack on the teacher's perceived intrusiveness. Howard said that when he first saw Mr. A he thought, "This guy is going to teach me something because he knows how to teach, or he is not going to teach me anything and I'll have to teach myself using his outline." When asked what events in the class had the most impact on him, he said, "I met the girl next to me and we dated a few times." When asked what he liked most about the class, he said, rather angrily, "I usually don't like anything or anybody the most."

The impression conveyed, then, is that the teacher poses a real danger to these students' identity. They are engaged in a battle with him to maintain their sense of who they are. But there is much more to it than this, since at the same time there is a deep but seemingly hopeless yearning for the affection and attention of the teacher. Thus, Tim, who asserted his freedom and ability to resist the blandishments of Mr. C, at the same time said he would want Mr. C as a psychiatrist and also bought a jacket just like his. In the midst of a highly symbolic discussion of maternal deprivation centering around the mother's ability to provide gratification, Tim, in one of his rare statements in class, suggested, "I don't think mothers feel the same toward adopted sons at all . . ." This comment stirred up enough anxiety in the class to make us suspect that Tim was really saying something about himself vis-à-vis the teacher, namely, that it was highly unlikely that Mr. C would be able to, or would want to, gratify Tim's nurturance needs. But there is a difficult paradox here. If the teacher moves closer to the student, this is perceived as a narcissitic and manipulative intrusion on the students' sense of self; yet at the same time the student yearns for the psychological supplies one receives through interpersonal closeness. It is no wonder that these males retreat into a passive-resistant stance, since this expresses both the fear of manipulation and the resentment at not receiving the needed supplies. For the males, it may also be true that this counterdependent assertiveness is a defensive response to acting in a way traditionally defined as feminine, that is, silent, unassertive, and unaggressive in a group situation.

Among some of the females in this cluster, we find a stance which, while superficially different, bears a good deal of resemblance to the passive-resistant stance of the males. These females present themselves as "the good little girl who is seen but not heard." Their relationship with the teacher is somewhat sexualized and flirtatious, and they seem somewhat hysterical in their tendency to deny negative feeling toward patients or teachers and in their idealizations of these older people. At the same time, they are very antiintrospective and are quite disturbed by the idea of unconscious motivation. Unlike the males, the females in this cluster tend to express directly their sense of dependency and helplessness. They are also more likely to describe themselves as "shy" or "inhibited," although at the same time they also describe themselves as somewhat stereotyped "good girls." The females also rank significantly lower on the Creative Personality scale of the OAIS (see Appendix B), a scale which is related to verbal fluency. However, it should be noted that cluster 8 students are not significantly different from other clusters on our intelligence measures (although in terms of a rank ordering of clusters they do tend to be toward the bottom). We find, then, that females in this cluster show a greater readiness to express their dependency and helplessness, while males are more likely to repudiate it. Part of their silence in class, then, comes from the playing out of a stereotyped feminine sex-role and part from a passive-submissive stance toward the teacher.

For the cluster 8 students, a stance of passivity has come to be seen by them as perhaps the only viable mode of interacting with a powerful authority. Not surprisingly, we find this also to be true in regard to the reported interaction between the cluster 8 students and their parents. It appears that these students had parents or older siblings who had high standards of evaluation, as did the parents of students in clusters 1 and 2. However, the parents directly or subtly punished expressions of intellectual independence and at the same time seemed indifferent to the child's attempt to articulate his own needs. Tim had a father who was very intelligent and a top-flight architect, who could not be beaten in an argument ("He tears your argument to shreds"), and who always had the facts to back up what he was saying. Audrey described her father as having "high standards," and when you "say something" he then "interprets it in his own way." Like other cluster 8 people, she did not remember talking much with her family at home, and she described the class as a "bull session which I have never had." Cora had three older brothers who were highly evaluative of her ideas, although she was quick to say that "they protected me and didn't bully me." And Carey remembered her mother telling her specifically that girls should be seen and not heard.

A few of these students have had to struggle with parents who clearly seemed to be using the child to gratify their own needs at the expense of the child (although this is something most cluster 8 students *suspect* about their parents). Eileen, in Mr. C's class, was the only child of a widowed father who, from her accounts, wrote her twice a week, sent her "articles and stuff," and pushed her to read and discuss them with him. She was quite upset with this, experiencing it as an intrusion on her life, as stifling her independence, and, in a more subtle way, as having not-well-understood sexual connotations. Eileen clearly felt that close friendships are bad, since they encourage dependency, and that close relationships between people of the same sex (as between Mr. C and another teacher with whom he collaborated) border on the perverse: "There's something wrong there, something unhealthy." Here we see clearly how high (or impossible) expectations for performance, parental narcissism, and parental indifference to the child's needs combine to produce a suspicious, resistant person, determined to fend off any attempts by teachers to establish relationships. However, in the muted way so characteristic of these students, Eileen expressed yearning for real affection and love from Mr. C. She noted at two points in her interview that she would really like to see Mr. C alone in his office, away from the rest of the class. But her mistrust level was very high, and it is doubtful that she could make the move.

In the descriptions of these students, parents appear to be either emotionally distant or physically absent. In this sense, they resemble the parents of students in cluster 2. However, while standards of intellectual achievement were clear and quite high, the evaluation attached to any intellectual performance was not clear in the sense that parental sanctions seemed directed not at the person himself but in a more impersonal way at his intellectual products. Many of these students note that while they often felt put down by their parents intellectually (usually by the father), the parents never seemed to get mad or angry at them. Thus, not only have these people been exposed to high standards and repeated negative reinforcement for expressing their own opinions, but they were often at a loss to discover what these evaluations might mean about them as people and about the powerful person's feelings toward them. However, it does seem clear to these people that judgment of one's personal worth depends very much on the quality of one's intellectual products. We might speculate that self-worth for these people is deeply tied up with the worth of an intellectual production.

These circumstances seem to have a number of effects on cluster 8 students which are not, by and large, conducive to work in the classroom setting. First, it makes the game of "finding out what the teacher wants us to say" a deadly serious one for these students, since so much affect in their interaction with parents has been funneled into the area of intellect and thinking. This seems particularly true for females in this cluster. More so than in other clusters, they are likely to agree that it has been important, and will be important, to learn older people's standards of conduct so well that they can be adjusted to without specific directives and that it will be important in class to be careful not to violate the teacher's standards of mature and dignified behavior. There are some quite amazing examples of these students' sensitivity to "what the teacher wants." For instance, Mr. B demonstrated the principle of operant conditioning by asking a student to say three letter words, and then reinforcing her with a verbal "yes" when she used words that had the letter "b" in them. Nancy, who produced no more than three or four scorable acts all semester, was the first one to guess correctly what the operant was, and she did so with a good deal of assurance in her voice. Another example: Mr. C put a great deal of stress on the heredity-environment controversy, coming down very hard on the primacy of environmental determinants. Audrey, who from her voice, seemed quite shy and frightened, mustered up courage to produce four acts during the semester, two of which came when the teacher was clearly trying to elicit the "correct" response from the students about environmental determinants. She seemed almost grateful for the opportunity to say something which she knew would be approved by the teacher. But it is interesting that she replied only when there was close to perfect assurance of teacher approval.

A second effect of the parent-child interaction for cluster 8 students centers around a fear of failure and consequent rejection by potentially nurturing adults. Again, as in many other ways, cluster 8 students here seem similar to students in cluster 2. That is, they are people with relatively high sensitivity to evaluation and a strong fear of rejection. Indeed, we find that some of our cluster 8 students can be characterized as "covert 2's." Carey's father, for example, was the "classic example of the father who lavishes his kids with gifts but no affection," and who tended to withdraw such affection as was there when he disapproved of what Carey did. Mr. D, her instructor, closely fit this description—a strong, attractive authority figure who remained aloof and showed little or no affection. Carey was certain that she would not say anything in class unless Mr. D approved. But, at the same time, she felt that Mr. D did not like her because she did not participate.

There are complications here, however, which appear to have to do with the problem of competition and the tendency of these people to equate verbal interaction with hostility and anger. Practically all of the students in this cluster have siblings whom they judge to be "smarter" than they are, which, of course, implies more valued by the parents. For example, Tim had a brother majoring in architecture at the University of Michigan (his father was an architect and Tim had dropped out of architecture school). Cora had three older brothers who "were very articulate" and whom she could not beat in an argument. Members of this cluster often see the active participators in class as a bunch of show-offs who are crudely trying to dominate the scene and grab the teacher's attention. For example, Fred said that "so many kids in classes just talk to hear themselves talking, to show off their intellectual abilities—to impress people and hear themselves talk . . . it has to do with the fact that classes up here [at the University] are so competitive that so many people are opponents. They're here to really impress the class, particularly the instructor." The classroom, then, may be a re-creation of an earlier family scene in which siblings competed for the attention of the parents, and in which the cluster 8 person perceived himself as coming out on the losing end. These students may be telling us that they would rather not get involved in a "battle" in which the probability of attaining the objective is not great.

Silence, then, may represent a counterexhibitionistic maneuver, something which Fenichel (1945) sees as a basis for stage-fright and similar phobias (see also Paivio, 1965). That is, the cluster 8 person *does* want to be centerstage; he *does* want to bask in the glow of the parent's approbation; he *does* want to be reassured about himself. But the imagined consequences of "moving center stage" are so overwhelming that it seems safer to remain silent.

We have carried out an empirical study of student differences, and it has yielded seven kinds of active participants and an eighth cluster of low activity students. Clearly, one next step would be to explain how the teacher might respond most effectively to each cluster of students, since each seems to need a unique approach. Each seems to be alienated or upset by a different set of teacher behaviors. We shall return to these matters, but not until we have pressed deeper into a matter of great importance in the study of groups, the matter of history. We shall turn next to a consideration of how the classroom develops over time. Hopefully we can make use of our understanding of the different clusters in our analysis of the changing teacher-student relationships. And after this investigation we shall return to the question of how the process of learning to work varies according to the needs, feelings, and interpersonal style of the individuals involved. Our picture of the process of teaching and learning is getting more complicated. Hopefully, it is also getting more accurate and more useful.

CHAPTER 5

A CASE STUDY OF
TEACHER STRATEGIES
AND STUDENT RESPONSES

THE life history of a college classroom is often broken into coherent segments by dramatic or deliberate alterations in the teacher-student interaction. The occasional visitor might, upon returning, have little sense of how these changes had been produced, but he would certainly sense that some marked shifts had occurred. These changes, whether for the better or for the worse in goals of the educational tasks of the classroom, are of great importance to us in our study of the teacher-student relationships because adding the time dimension to our analysis increases our ability to understand classroom interaction. As one comes to appreciate how each participant is speaking not only from some set of immutable predispositions but is, as well, trying to alter the status quo, one begins to appreciate both the complexity and the coherence of the classroom as a system. If a sequential analysis of the participants' efforts to change various aspects of the educational-interpersonal relationship was feasible within one session, as in Chapter 3, then how much more one might learn from the more explicit maneuverings over the course of an entire term.

A case study of group B holds the promise of several gains. Group B was a great success in terms of the satisfaction of the teacher and nearly all the students. Even two years later students reported highly positive recollections of this class and useful effects on their subsequent education. However, more important to us at this juncture is that whatever success was achieved came about not by some immediately effective teaching strategy but only after some painful and instructive detours. It is precisely this erratic course, at times altered by teacher fiat and at times by unplanned but crucial events, which now interests us. Specifically, we wish to know whether the analysis of task and affective issues can clarify the gradual and the abrupt shifts that occur over 40 or so sessions in the life history of a single class.

In order to accomplish these ends we shall introduce the teacher as we find him in the very beginning of the term, since so much of the rest of the term represents a gradual unfolding of the diverse goals and needs that Mr. B brought with him and expressed in his early performance. We shall then present the quantitative data, the changes over time for the teacher and for the students, and begin a more systematic narrative of the four main blocks of sessions. Throughout, we shall try to show how the changes reflect the problem-solving efforts by teacher and students to find a satisfactory outcome in both the task and affective domains.

The first few sessions of group B demonstrate that Mr. B was in great conflict about his role as the term began. Mr. B's first action in the class was to collect a class card from each student individually, repeating the student's name for pronunciation as he took the card, and checking the name with his list. If the name was not on the list, he inquired about the student's "eligibility" for that section and said he would check with the main office. As more and more students came into the room, Mr. B made several remarks about how large the class was. Later, he told the class that he hoped to learn their names within two weeks. This small episode about the class cards and the names is evidence of a persisting conflict for Mr. B. On the one hand, he valued a teaching style which involved being considerate of the students' needs and providing them with an environment of warmth and acceptance. On the other hand, perhaps more than most teachers he needed to be liked. His concern about being liked, however, was linked to several disruptive fears about being drained by extreme closeness and being left powerless and robbed of control by the students. He suspected that the students would try to take advantage of him, to undermine his efforts, or to expect too much of him. A whole set of personal needs and fears seemed to run counter to a teaching style based on openness and respect for the student and a belief in the students' ability to learn, independent of the teacher. The need to protect himself against the strangeness of the class and to reassure himself that the students would like him was expressed in the name learning and in the gesture of taking the card from each student personally. These acts fit into his open, student-centered model of teaching. The use of the class list as the final authority and his anxiety about the number of students were evidence of Mr. B's fears and of his tendency to protect himself from the blame or hostility of the students while still maintaining control. The combination of Mr. B's doubts about his strength, his suspicion of the students' motives, and his personal and philosophical needs to be accepting and honest stood in the way of finding a stable and satisfying role for at least half of the term.

Mr. B's ambivalence about the students was demonstrated in several ways during the first session. In describing his goals for the course, he mentioned first that he wanted everyone to learn to spell "psychology." Then he said that he wanted everyone to feel comfortable, that there was no "party line," and that people should feel "maximally free to participate." Thus he was belittling and scornful of the students while at the same time he was accepting both of their interests and their privacy. The combination of his scornfulness and his fear of the students made his attempts to engage their participation somewhat bumbling and ineffective. In the middle of the first session, Mr. B asked the students if they had any particular interests that they hoped to discuss during the course. As each student mentioned some topic, Mr. B responded by fitting that interest into the outline he had already prepared for the course. A few students who mentioned problems that did not fit into the course plan were told they would probably not deal with those issues fully. A little later, Mr. B asked the class how they felt about take-home exams: "Let me get your opinions . . . I won't be bound by it . . . your feelings on the take-home essays." These two incidents demonstrate how difficult it was for Mr. B to follow a philosophy of teaching that emphasized responding to the students' needs so long as he had doubts about his own control of the class and doubts about the students' capabilities and motives.

Finally, Mr. B's personal definition of work for the class was quite ambiguous in that it derived from conflicting needs and ideals. From the early sessions, it is clear that at first Mr. B considered student participation to be essential. On three different occasions, when describing his goals for the course, the kind of class it would be, and the grading system, Mr. B mentioned the importance of participation. Yet, he insisted that no one *had* to participate. As he went over the reading list with the class, he stressed understanding of the basic concepts. He gave several warnings about the ambiguity of the material, advised the class that there were no clear-cut answers, and invited the students to help him "tie things together." However, he also mentioned that on one test he had given to his last class he had asked for a definition of normal personality that he had given in class. When he talked about the quizzes and tests, he said, "The quizzes are not to see if you are keeping up to date. I can see that in class. They are more for me than for you." If we take a close look at that combination of statements, it becomes obvious that we have no real idea of what work might mean for Mr. B. The class period was essentially a time when the group could discuss the readings. The style of that discussion was often of the question and answer type. Mr. B asked a question and the students gave all the answers that were appropriate. Often, Mr. B had a few specific answers in mind and he would continue accepting answers until those he had thought of were given. At other times, Mr. B lectured on some of the material in the readings, clarifying or explicating it with different examples. There were two quizzes, two papers, two hour exams, and a final examination during the semester; the class time was not to be spent in determining whether the students really understood the material. Nor was it to be spent exploring further implications of the material.

The students were very suspicious and resistant in the early sessions. They were busy protecting themselves from being taken in by a man who said he was really interested in them and yet made derisive remarks about their ability. Mr. B was anxious and uneasy that the students were not going to the mass lectures or doing the readings. And he was challenged by the contentiousness he found in the class. Every doubt he had about the students' abilities to deal with the material was associated with some doubt he had about his own capacity or potency. Every effort he made to encourage student participation was accompanied by some tactic that inhibited or decreased the quality of the students' performance. The guessing-game approach, the guilt-inducing about not participating, the decision to follow an interesting case study (Hartley Hale) with all the jargon of learning theory, each of these approaches had built into it the maintenance of suspicion and the possibility of reconfirming Mr. B's doubts about his students. The issue of mistrust was so strong in the early part of the course that nothing resembling serious thought or close interaction between Mr. B and the students could have taken place.

Before opening up the far more complex issue of teacher-student interaction, let us pause for just a moment to consider Mr. B and his opening presentation of himself and his goals for the class. In terms of the teacher-as typology it is clear that Mr. B is in some conflict about which of several paths to pursue. Each path seems to him to lead away from some other important goal and toward a mixture of negative as well as positive outcomes. For example, should he pursue the goals implied by the teacher as person? If he does, this might be satisfying for his own needs to be liked and to the similar needs he attributes to students, but with what limits and at what cost? Perhaps getting close would undermine his other goals of having his authority respected regardless of the costs in terms of personal feelings. Similarly with the teacher as facilitator: how can Mr. B encourage participation (for its own sake, as a good thing) if this seems to block him from making it very clear that he is very competent in matters psychological and, in fact, has quite a bit he would like to get across? Perhaps the nub of Mr. B's confusion in the early session lies in the simple fact that Mr. B has grave doubts about the students' abilities, and he fears being taken for a ride. Thus it is hard to open up full throttle in the expert area, since this will risk showing how scornful he, the former Ivy League honors student, feels about his Big Ten class. And any effort to be either the teacher as facilitator or the teacher as person would be doomed to failure once his scorn had been made known. Even in the first few classes the intensity of the multiple pressures on the teacher and his multiple misgivings are clearly evident. Unable either to relinquish or to assume control, unable to keep from spoiling whatever overtures of warmth he could manage, Mr. B is a clear case of how one's task strategies are inextricably bound up with one's affective preoccupations. Fortunately for Mr. B, he did not have to solve this problem all by himself. The students, in their equally complex search for task and affective satisfaction, contribute the essential ingredient: new options, genuine reassurances, and even distraction from the teacher's private definition of the situation. We need, then, to turn to the full picture of this class as it evolved over time.

The issue that makes this class a particularly fascinating one to study is the unusual relationship between the formal structure of the class, the underlying emotional concerns of the teacher and the students, and the teacher's goals. In an attempt to reduce the tension of the early sessions, Mr. B suggested a structural change at session 11 whereby each member of the class would be responsible for the discussion of a particular topic and Mr. B would become more a resource person than the central authority. The group moved their chairs from rows into a circle, and Mr. B began to call students by their first names. Mr. B hoped that the change would challenge the students to pay more attention to the group and its interactions as a source of material for discussion. He also hoped to increase participation and to reduce the contention he faced from the students by stepping out of the position of direct control. The important point about this change is that it did not lead to increased satisfaction for Mr. B; neither did it reduce expressions of discouragement from the students, although it did limit the expressions of contention and challenge for a while. Revision of the formal structure which might have led to open discussion of the early hostility and mistrust did not, in fact, produce that result because Mr. B's goals for the class remained in conflict. In other words, it is obvious from this case study that the conflicts and goals of the particular teacher are directly related to the distress and work periods of the students regardless of the formal structure of the classroom.

Before describing particular events or sessions, it is important to point out that Mr. B was entirely free to run the class any way he pleased. He had full responsibility for the course readings, the questions on the exams, the paper assignments, and the nature of the class sessions. Once a week, all sections of the course met for a mass lecture or panel discussion which was planned in part by the teaching fellows. The other three class sessions each week were under the sole direction of the individual instructors. Since much of the following discussion involves inferences from the structure of the class and the nature of the discussions concerning needs and conflicts of both Mr. B and the students, it must be recognized that these structural decisions were made by Mr. B himself and not planned by some supervisory or departmental authority.

The factor trends were derived from the taped sessions which were scored according to the member-leader category system described in Chapter 2. The factor trends were isolated by creating moving averages of the session factor scores, combining four sessions to make a single data point. Thus the session-by-session vacillation was reduced and the strong trends were emphasized. Figure A is

Teacher Factors for Group B

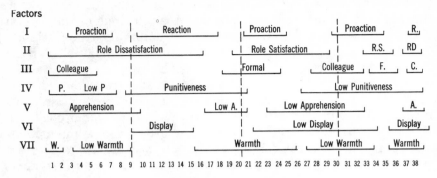

Moving Average Points

Student Factors for Group B

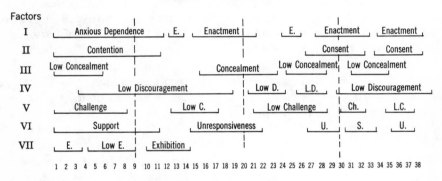

Figure A   Teacher and student factors for group B.

a summary of the teacher and student moving average factor scores for group B. This graph will allow us to keep the total student and teacher interaction in mind as we focus on some of the sessions.

Now let us look at the factor patterns from Figure A. In the early sessions (data points 1–9) Mr. B did most of the talking. He tried to be casual and to encourage student participation, as indicated by the high levels on the Colleague factor, but the Punitiveness, the Apprehension, and the general Role Dissatisfaction are evidence that these early efforts at egalitarianism were unstable and probably not fully felt. Rather, they served as a model for the kind of relationship Mr. B *hoped* would develop. The early sessions find Mr. B asking a lot of questions which he would then follow by long answers to his own questions. This dominance was accompanied by suspicion of the students, hostility toward them, and a long period of uncomfortable depression. It is interesting to note that one way Mr. B reacted to his own role discomfort was by punishing the students. He confronted them time and again with having failed to take over the responsibilities he gave them. Nonetheless, his doubts about the students' motives and abilities did not alleviate his discomfort but became entangled with it.

In order to understand the students' participation in the early sessions and throughout the semester, it is important to keep in mind that the high factor scores on each factor do not necessarily reflect the total group acting in unison. Instead, they may be the result of different subgroups who responded in different ways to Mr. B and to the class situation. For instance, it is not the case that all the people who spoke in the early sessions were both challenging and supporting. Some were challenging and some were supporting. If we look at the early acts, however, it is clear that almost everyone who did participate was expressing anxiety and dependence. Then, too, we have no way of monitoring the feelings of the silent students during those early sessions.

There was an initial period of denial and insincere closeness by the students in the first and second sessions which paralleled Mr. B's early Warmth and Colleague style. The brief periods of Low Discouragement and Exhibition are evidence of this "so glad to know you" game. The long periods of Anxious Dependence, Contention, and Challenge, however, were the most serious and disruptive responses for Mr. B to handle in the early sessions. The students' support was so closely linked to dependence that Mr. B was unable to accept it as a trustworthy sign of alliance. For the males, the issue of trust was closely linked to a kind of testing to see if Mr. B really was the powerful male in the group. For the females the issue of trust became linked to the problem of intimacy. How close could they get to him as a person before he reverted to the formality of the teacher role?

The tension of the early sessions can be seen clearly in session 9. Mr. B's Role Dissatisfaction, Punitiveness, Apprehension, and Display were responded to and elicited by the students' Anxious Dependence, Contention, and Discouragement on the one hand and by Support and Exhibition on the other. The session began with a critical discussion by the students of the panel discussion they had heard. Evelyn had a criticism, but when Mr. B wanted to call on her, he could not remember her name. Mr. B encouraged the class to bring up any questions they had about the reading or the panel discussion, but he responded to most of the questions with, "Wait and we'll get to it." He invited the class to bring back any unanswered questions at some later time. The discussion was on avoidance conditioning, and Lou asked if punishment was the same as avoidance conditioning. Mr. B seemed unable to answer, but Libby offered an answer for him. Mr. B was very grateful. Different instances of avoidance conditioning were discussed, and the class, led by Evelyn, began to criticize an experiment in which Alfred, a little boy, was conditioned to fear white, furry things. The students argued that it was cruel to leave Alfred afraid of something of which he had no fear before the experiment began. Curt criticized the whole process of conditioning as shallow to which Mr. B responded by insisting that we are always being conditioned. No matter what example Mr. B gave to illustrate concepts of drive, frustration, and conditioning, there was always at least one student who found an objection to it.

The class' criticisms of the panel discussion were indirect criticisms of Mr. B, testing his competence and his control. In this session, the group seemed to use the injustice done to one of its members, Evelyn, as a springboard for their attack. Particularly at a time when the class was discussing unconscious motivation, and finding that notion so difficult to accept, Mr. B's inability to remember Evelyn's name was interpreted as an act of hostility. Thus, this insult, coupled with Mr. B's rejection of the very questions he had asked for, increased the group's sense of anger and frustration. When Libby responded to Lou in Mr. B's stead, she gave the group the strength it needed to begin to blame Mr. B for his injustice and for unfairly exercising his role as teacher. The blame that Evelyn wished to put on Mr. B for having forgotten her name was carried by others into a general resistance. The case of Alfred was symbolically the case of all of them. They saw themselves as confronted by disquieting concepts like unconscious motivation and left in the hands of a controlling authority who did not fulfill his responsibility as a leader, counselor, or mother. Mr. B's support of a behavior point of view quite at variance with his own personal views was a sign of his helplessness in the face of challenge.

The change in structure that came from Mr. B's suggestion in session 11 was not planned from the beginning of the term. Rather, it was a response to the first three weeks of class. The plan was designed to increase the informality of the class, to bring students into contact with one another, and to increase each student's feeling of responsibility for the work that was to be done. Mr. B proposed the plan with a great deal of apprehension and reminded the students that he would not be satisfied if the discussion turned into a general bull session. It was as if he were caught between his need for control and his need to be liked, between his intellectual value on learning concepts relevant to psychology and his personal discomfort with the distance, hostility, and challenge of those early weeks. The structural change was Mr. B's way of dealing with the conflict between his intellectual and emotional needs. On the surface the plan was in harmony with the goal developing among teaching fellows that the classroom be a meaningful interpersonal experience. On closer inspection, however, the structural change was not supported by any strong conviction on Mr. B's part. He was not comfortable dealing with hostility in the classroom and did not change in this respect after session 11. Furthermore, he was uneasy about the students' ability, and the new system provided an increased chance for that uneasiness to grow. Giving the students responsibility for the discussions meant that he could not be certain that all the material he had planned for the course would be covered. In order to compensate for that uncertainty, Mr. B gave two quizzes, two hour exams, two papers, and a final. In evaluating the quizzes and exams, Mr. B continued to compare the performance of this class to his other section which was a straight lecture-discussion format. Mr. B had not changed his work goals, he had not revised his opinion of the students, and he had not dealt with or resolved his personal needs when he proposed the change. Thus a format designed to promote openness and to encourage independence did not, in fact, have those effects in class B.

The factor scores for data points 11–20 are evidence of continued wariness in the class. In line with the proposed change in structure, Mr. B switched from a Proactive to a Reactive style but his Role Dissatisfaction continued. The discussion format became a forum in which Mr. B supported those students who participated and punished those who did not by reminding them of their responsibility for the success of the class when students led the discussion. Mr. B restrained himself from participating and entered mainly to give a summary or to settle a dispute. He thereby removed himself from the position of control which had elicited hostility from some of the students. It is clear that, following the change, the students' Challenge and Contentiousness declined. Having agreed to the change, the students tried to make this new plan succeed by taking the role of discussant or by cooperating with the person who was the discussant. During this period, however, Mr. B gave a quiz, a paper, and an hour exam. The message which gave the students difficulty was Mr. B's ambivalence about how independent he could or would allow the students to be. Students who enjoyed independence were discouraged by Mr. B's continued efforts to control the class. Students who wanted Mr. B to remain in control were discouraged by his seeming willingness to let students make some of the decisions and by his restrained participation. Thus, while student Challenge and Contention dropped out, discomfort is demonstrated by the continuing undercurrent of Discouragement, the decline of Support, and the lack of Consent, which accompanied their early period of Enactment. A central problem to be considered in this case study concerns the change from this early enactment which was unstable and linked to student distress to later enactment, which was not accompanied by discouragement and coincided with student consent.

We sense a large amount of compliance in these sessions (11–20) both by students and by Mr. B. Students volunteered to be discussants and took the responsibility when it was their turn to lead the class. The other class members remained rather passive in their participation during these student-led sessions. Mr. B, for his part, complied with the scheme by remaining relatively quiet during the student presentations and providing only a short summary at the end of those sessions. Students who had volunteered felt discouraged because of the lack of student participation. Other students were both angry and discouraged by the quiz in session 13. They felt that the format of the quiz and the format of the class were incompatible. Seeing the results of his quiz, Doug's response was "I hope we're not an experimental group . . . I'm more concerned with my grade point than with learning." The students had a sense of being abandoned to which Mr. B responded by reassuring the class that he would not have tried such a change if he did not think the class was capable. He also insisted that it was up to the class to take the responsibility for making the class periods valuable.

The last two discussants in this period, Libby and Lois, bore the brunt of the students' uneasiness. They were supposed to present material about perception in sessions 17 and 18, but they were unable to engage the class in discussion about this topic. The interaction was mostly between the strong males in the class, challenging and struggling with each other. The content of the articles was lost amid disagreements and quarrels over small points. Occasionally Libby looked to Mr. B for help and he spoke up in an effort to clarify or make peace between two class members. Finally, Mr. B took over the discussion by reviewing the content that had been covered and by commending Libby and Lois for their fine discussion. At that, Doug, one of the boys who had been quarreling, said, "I don't know where you got the idea that it was such a good discussion. I didn't get a thing out of it."

In the second of these two discussions on perception, Mr. B tried to open the discussion up to what had happened the time before in order to find out how the class felt about the changes in format as a whole. Lois began to say how discouraged she was about the discussion when Dave broke in to ask when they would see the trapezoid illusion. Later in that session when Libby confronted the group with issues of participation and responsibility, Dave interrupted again to ask a content question about Gestalt Psychology. In the face of this failure to bring the issues of participation out, Libby and Lois became discouraged and turned to Mr. B for more and more assistance. The male students seemed to take over the class, either by more fighting or by telling personal anecdotes only tangentially related to perception and memory. At the end of the session, Libby asked Mr. B to summarize, but he seemed very withdrawn and said that all the material had been covered.

The importance of these sessions is that they showed Mr. B that the new structure would not bring about the sort of interaction that he hoped would be possible in this class. Mr. B was fond of Libby and Lois and he was discouraged at having allowed them to meet with disappointment and frustration. Furthermore, he was faced with the recognition that he lacked the skill needed to make use of the kinds of interactions that take place when there is low structure. Finally, he was hearing competent people ask for his help and dominance which strengthened his earlier notions about the necessity for a teacher to be in control. These sessions of student distress without direct challenge toward or contention with Mr. B set up an atmosphere in which Mr. B felt freer to be dominant and controlling. He had created a situation in which his strength could be seen as a way of coming to the aid of students and responding to their demands rather than imposing control.

In session 20, Mr. B took the opportunity to find out how the class felt about his strength and his role in the class by asking the students what they thought about being called on to participate. This session provided a chance to hear all the students' opinions about the amount of control they wished Mr. B to have and the amount of autonomy they wanted to preserve for themselves. Some students wished Mr. B to keep the procedure the same, letting those who wished to speak do so and those who wished to remain silent be silent. Other students wished that there were more pressures on them to talk. Ned said he thought it would lead to even more needless discussion if there was pressure to participate. Curt pointed out that there was no opportunity to ask Mr. B points on the readings when there was a student discussant in charge of the session. Although this was not really the case, Mr. B accepted his complaint. What he did not accept was Doug's pressure for Mr. B to tell the class his opinion about the nature of the participation in the class. Finally Peggy remarked on the quality of the interactions of the class: "We've got a long way to go, we're still plenty inhibited." It is clear that participation meant very different things to different members of the class. For some it was a sign that work was getting done, for others it was a way of "snowing" Mr. B, for others it was a way of getting close to Mr. B in a more personal sense, and for still others, it was a way of engaging Mr. B in challenge.

The sessions between 11 and 20 served to reassure Mr. B somewhat that the students could deal with the material and also that they both needed and wanted him to take an active part in the class. Furthermore, the next part of the course was to cover psychoanalytic theory and psychosexual development, areas in which Mr. B was both interested and invested. It was a combination of the students' expressed need for his dominance and his own concern that the material be adequately covered and understood that produced Mr. B's change of role in sessions 21–29. These sessions were characterized by Role Satisfaction combined with a dominant, formal style of interaction with the students. The Punitiveness of the sessions immediately following the change in format dropped out. The most comfortable sessions for Mr. B were during this time in the class when he was Proactive and Formal. He met the students' anxiety over the material by taking an expert stance toward the class, combining a drop in emotionality with concentration on the details of the theory. Mr. B lectured during part of six of nine of these sessions. It should be noted here that Mr. B's comfort was not matched by simultaneous comfort for the students. Although student discouragement faded after session 20, there was still anger and mistrust which lingered into this third quarter of the semester, particularly in session 21 when Mr. B discussed the hour exam, 22 when the males and females fought over the role of women, and in 24 when Doug and Curt struggled over the problem of psychic determinism. In addition there was general anxiety over the material, particularly the sessions on dream interpretation and psychosexual development. During this period, the students learned how Mr. B wanted them to deal with these kinds of threatening issues. He taught them to resist expressing their anxiety in order to work on substantive issues. He let the class know that he could be very pleasant and effective if they did not demand that he respond either to their anxiety or to their dependency.

One of the concerns that continued to trouble Mr. B was whether this class was learning as much of the material as his other section despite the difference in structure between the two sections. Rather than adjusting the second hour exam (which was held the night before session 29) Mr. B held a cram session in the evening to review the material. He announced the exam in session 22 and referred to it again in sessions 25, 27, and 28. During session 29 it was clear that Mr. B had strongly identified with this class over the issue of the test. When asked how this class compared to his other section, Mr. B referred to this class as *we*, the other class as *they*. There was a considerable amount of argument and criticism over the items on the test. Mr. B was too ambivalent about the structure of the class to assure the students that they had done well. His evaluation of their performance was, "Either the test was easy, or you really knew it." That comment could not satisfy those students who needed a definite response to assure them of their competence. So the concern and distress continued to be expressed until Mr. B asked the class why they were so anxious about the test.

Mr. B's uncertainty over the value of the class structure and about the students' competence elicited uncertainty among the students about those same issues. When they expressed these feelings, Mr. B was unable to reassure them because he was further discouraged by their increased dependence and distress. His response was to communicate his own ambivalence and to deny the students' anger by switching the subject of discussion to their opinions on take-home exams where he got a lot of support and consent from students on his point of view. Mr. B's style remained consistent during the sessions, moving quickly from affect to task issues, permitting the expression of some hostility among the students, but rarely using these moments of anger to look at the class process or the feelings of the students toward him. The resulting mood of the sessions of the 20's was somewhat impersonal, restricted considerably to task role interactions. The discussants discussed, Mr. B lectured, and only occasionally did hostility burst out and then die down within the framework of the discussion. Feelings about other students, about Mr. B, or about the class structure were never examined as the legitimate work of the class. The fundamental issue was one of competence rather than legitimacy as it had been earlier. Mr. B was proving to the class that he was competent, and he was testing the students to find out if they were as competent as he had claimed they were in session 11.

The last 12 sessions, 30–41, include the second student enactment phase accompanied by fading role satisfaction for Mr. B and continued proactivity. This final period in the group development involved a shift away from role relationships to personal relationships. A combination of several events allowed students to perceive Mr. B much more as a person than he had been perceived previously. Session 30 had been scheduled as a time when a movie would be shown, somewhat in compensation for having had the hour exam at night. Because of some mixup in scheduling the movie never came so Mr. B (who came to class for the first time in Bermuda shorts) and those students who wished to stay just sat around and listened to Mr. B joke about grading the exam, the money he had collected from the class to pay for the movie, and the class in general. Mr. B was informed and relaxed. The students who stayed seemed to be eager for this opportunity to move closer to Mr. B. When it was clear that the movie was not going to come and Mr. B suggested that they could stay and talk, Mary asked: "Will you psychoanalyze us?" She was clearly eager for this chance to interact with Mr. B on a personal level, if only to satisfy her own curiosity and fantasies.

The other "personalizing" events were an evening meeting at which Mr. B showed slides of his trip to Russia and several class meetings when Mr. B talked about the professional opportunities in psychology and about the value and failings of psychotherapy. On all of these occasions, Mr. B was clearly the central figure; they were not times of mutual self-disclosure. These meetings allowed the students to know Mr. B outside of the context of the classroom struggles and allowed them to relinquish some of their stereotypes about him. It seems appropriate to infer that the periods of student independence that occurred in this last quarter of the term were made possible by the emergence of Mr. B as an independent person in the students' eyes. Mr. B's willingness to respond to the students in a personal way seemed to encourage a sense of responsibility and concern for the class that was linked earlier to Mr. B's punitiveness and distress. In these later sessions it is important to point out that student enactment sessions were not the result of one or two students' leadership but of a great deal of student involvement in student-led discussions.

The paradox of these last sessions is that while the students seemed to have a resurgence of energy, Mr. B was withdrawing energy and enthusiasm after a long and exhausting struggle. In an interview after session 33, Mr. B expressed his position: "I'm tired of the doubt about it. I've felt very insecure many times during the year and I wish it were over." "I've had to prove something all term long. It would have been easier with one class. Then I wouldn't have to compare them." "It's not really discouragement, it's more like brain fatigue! I've had it." This sense of low energy accompanied a new position for Mr. B. He left the final series of presentations much more up to the students to plan. He wrote two final exams: one for 8:00 A.M. class and one for this section, relinquishing his previous insistence on comparing the two groups and his investment in mastery of the content. Of course, this independent style had its own dangers. Some students who began to feel increasingly strong and comfortable made moves toward closeness or frankness that Mr. B was not willing to accept. In session 38, after a short quiz, the students were talking about a future school event. Everyone was talking at once until Lou asked Mr. B teasingly: "Do you feel left out?" Mr. B responded: "I didn't feel left out when you were taking the quiz." Mr. B was still very sensitive to any moves that looked like disregard of or threats to his authority, even in this final period when students were both performing well and consenting to his control.

The final session was an interesting demonstration of the interpersonal sensitivity that had developed in the class. The topic for discussion was learning and the need for structure. Although Elaine was supposed to be the discussant, Mr. B took that opportunity to present an apology and justification for the course. It was clear that he felt quite distressed at this final meeting, trying to describe his mixed feelings to the class and to apologize for some of the failures in covering the material. The students responded to Mr. B's distress with a series of unique and meaningful positive reactions. Even Doug chimed in, "Who cares about facts, it was the exchange of ideas that counted." The class struggled to reassure Mr. B with all the techniques of denial and support that they had learned from him over the semester. However, Mr. B who was still struggling with his discomfort and mistrust of the situation could only respond by reiterating his doubts. It was only after Curt, an older student who continually expressed a sort of condescending disbelief and criticism of the material and of Mr. B, confirmed the value of this course relative to an earlier psychology course that Mr. B resumed his usual sunny outlook and agreed that the experience had been a good one for him and for the group.

The term ended with a great deal of support from the students and some sessions of comfortable student-teacher interactions on topics in which both Mr. B and many of the students were interested, issues of psychotherapy, psychological testing, free will versus determinism, and the implications for child-rearing and education of *Walden Two*. Mr. B, having tired of the continuous struggle to watch himself and his control of the class, moved comfortably into a dominant position which he relinquished to the discussants when they were in charge and which he resumed when he wanted to with the students' consent. The brief regression to the uncomfortable, mistrustful tone of the early sessions was probably the result of Mr. B's concern about the students' reactions to the course as they would appear on the student evaluation forms given out during session 40.

One may infer from the data that Mr. B's notion of work solidified as a function of his increasing commitment to the subject matter. The sessions that most represented the goals Mr. B valued were during this last quarter of the term in which students interacted with a high degree of effective involvement on content issues which Mr. B had chosen as appropriate to the course. They were sessions like session 39 when the students took a major role in introducing points of view or criticisms, where the students supported rather than abandoned each other, and where Mr. B was free to interact without either becoming the sole focus of attention or shifting the discussion on to his comments. When the students found ways to help each other, Mr. B was not needed as a source of energy or protection. During this session, it was not necessary for Mr. B to take control in response to feelings of discomfort about the quality or level of understanding involved in the discussion. The content was felt to be legitimate, the students were able to rely on and control each other, and Mr. B was not threatened by direct anger or dependence.

As with the analysis of a single session, it would now be possible to review the varied course of this class over time in terms of the task issues, the affective issues, and the mutual influences on each other of these two components of the total interaction. The one single most dramatic event in the group's development was, of course, the teacher's unilateral move to produce a discussion group sitting in a circle and addressed mainly by students. What produced this change in structure and how did the change work out?

The first phase of the group, roughly the first nine sessions, were characterized by the usual good form between teacher and student together with a mounting resistance to the teacher as both expert and formal authority. The compliant, but basically anxious and clinging, student gestures combined with increasing levels of contention and challenge to produce an increasingly intolerable situation for the teacher. Although Mr. B began with a heavy emphasis on his expert and authority functions, this was a tenable strategy only if the outcome was reasonably pleasant and reflected well on himself as a benign, stimulating, and likeable teacher. The change in structure, then, represented an effort to step out of the role of expert, against which so much resistance had been mounted, and into the role of facilitator.

By presenting himself suddenly as merely a resource person, as an adjunct to the student discussant, Mr. B confounded but did not solve the fundamental issue of authority. How indeed can any teacher "solve" by himself what is after all the result of a developing relationship between teacher and students? Thus the second set of ten or so sessions was characterized by a very mixed set of messages regarding the teacher as formal authority. While it seemed that Mr. B had "removed himself," thus conceding to the more rebellious and autonomous students, neither these students nor the more dependent, structure-seeking students were satisfied with the outcome. The challenge of the first phase was replaced by discouraged, low energy compliance with the new arrangement. Some students felt annoyed at the considerable amount of control still held by the teacher, while others felt annoyed that the teacher was not playing his proper and dominant role. In terms of the teacher's own affective status as well, the change had produced role dissatisfaction rather than the sought-for harmony and self-esteem. Caught between the complaints of the two sets of critical students, the teacher came more and more to feel that to reassert his role as expert and formal authority was legitimate, necessary, and even his best chance of making people happy.

If the altered structure was short-lived, it had nonetheless served several important functions. Mr. B emerged from this phase more reassured regarding the students' competence than when the phase began. He had heard how well they could do, and he felt needed not so much as the fountain of all knowledge as the one who can prevent silly arguments from upsetting his best students and "distracting the class from its goal." Thus the development of greater respect regarding the competence of at least most students permitted the teacher to move more forcefully himself. This paradox hinges around the fact that his early mistrust of the students and his fear of inevitably becoming scornful and hurtful had been reduced considerably. He was to that extent able to imagine being competent in the expert area without abandoning his wish to be supportive and encouraging. Evidently, the discovery of even a few competent students can make a big difference. One can speak to them, reward them, and as in the case of discarding the student presentation format, one can even act in their behalf.

The third phase of the class shows how, as the teacher moves more comfortably into the expert function, he can pick up momentum and support by managing to function as the socializing agent and ego ideal. The teacher's rising role satisfaction and the increased task orientedness of the active students seem directly related to the personal and intellectual excitement associated with the subject matter of his lectures. The fourth phase is equally significant in that here we find an upsurge of the teacher's ability and willingness to function as person and to pull back from his role as formal authority. The six aspects of teaching seem at the end not like incompatible goals, not like paths stretching out in opposite directions. Now the teacher can move smoothly from person to socializing agent to expert to facilitator and so forth. The students are equally free to move back and forth across functions, making new combinations out of what had previously seemed like either/or propositions. The final dozen sessions are characterized by a real burst of student energy, enactment, and satisfaction. When at the end the teacher suffers a momentary attack of doubt, even the most rebellious student is able to provide the necessary reassurance about the success of the class.

Each change from one phase of the group's development to another has been related to the central thesis of this and the earlier chapters, that each choice or alteration of task strategy reflects as well the pressing affective preoccupations of the teacher and the students. The effectiveness of each strategic move cannot be divorced from its affective consequences. Mr. B meant well when he let the students run the discussion, but he really was not all that interested in what they had to say. He was insufficiently trustful of how his favorite students would fare, and he was unwilling to let students mangle his favorite topics in the course. Thus he aborted his own innovation, but not until he had learned enough to view the students with greater respect and to comprehend more explicitly what he had to offer to his class.

This case study has raised certain issues regarding the course of a group's development which we may now examine across all four classrooms. In the process of expanding our frame of reference to all the groups it will be necessary as well to pay more attention to the students (as they are described in Chapter 4) and especially to the variations among the students as they respond to the task strategies and affective messages initiated by the teacher and by their fellow students.

CHAPTER 6

THE NATURAL HISTORY
OF THE CLASSROOM

Now that we have presented some of the intricacies of the developmental history of one of the classrooms, it would be interesting to widen our perspective once again to include all four of the classes in our sample. The kind of questions we wish to include: Are there uniformities in the way teachers alter the stresses they place on various aspects of their roles as the term proceeds? Do the members of the various student clusters have their periods of greatest Enactment at similar phases in the development of all classes? Can we find meaningful similarities in the developmental patterns of all the classes?

Each classroom, of course, has its own peculiarities. There are the various teaching styles and personal histories of the individual teachers, the differences in composition of the group of students, the variations in the structures the teachers impose on the classroom situation, and even such realities as the time of day at which the class is scheduled to meet. However, our hope is that we may somehow transcend such unique circumstances as Mr. A's leaving his class in the middle of the term while he participated in a civil rights march, Mr. B's particular problems in dealing with a counterdependent older student, or the fact that Mr. B gave four hour exams to Mr. D's one. We hope to delineate a few developmental trends common to all the classes. We are looking for some of the common themes around which the individual classes create their own unique variations.

One aid in this search is the category scoring of single sessions, combining all student acts on the one hand and all teacher acts on the other. We first determined what percentage of the total acts fell into each of the 16 member-leader categories. This array of percentages was then converted into factor scores, seven for each teacher and seven for each class for each individual session. Finally, these scores were standardized within each of the four classrooms so that they would have a mean of zero and a standard deviation of one. This strategy serves to obscure differences between classes in the total frequency of a given pattern and allows us an easier comparison between developmental trends in the four classrooms.

When we plot for each classroom the 14 factor curves from the data as prepared above, we are first struck by the wide swings from session to session, and it is certainly not surprising that major developmental trends do not fully determine the events in a single session. Various events, such as handing out an assignment, the surfacing of some issue which is particularly important to an individual student, or the teacher's depressed mood deriving from some problem external to the class caused many deviations which run counter to the dominant momentum of long-term trends during that period. An additional process which may cause such swings is the teacher's occasional tendency to try to counterbalance the extremes of one session by going to the opposite extreme in the next session.

Despite these short-term swings, the factor scores do reflect definite developmental changes. In order to make these clear, we have transformed the data by means of two additional steps. The first of these is the computation of four-session moving averages. This operation consists simply of pooling the scored data for sessions one through four to form the first data point, then pooling sessions two through five to form the second data point, then three through six to form the third, and so on. This has the effect of smoothing out the factor curves by muffling unique, but transient, effects.

In order to obtain a still clearer picture of long-term deviations about the mean, we further transformed the moving average data points for entry into the charts seen in Table 6–1 and 6–2. In these tables we have given to each data point that received a score greater than +1.00 (that is, any score more than one standard deviation above the mean) the designation ++. Scores between +.50 and +1.00 receive only one +. Similarly, scores lower than −1.00 are represented by −−; those between +.50 and −1.00 by −. Finally, data points scoring within half a standard deviation of the mean are left blank.

The advantage of such a picture is that it allows us a very quick and direct comparison between the four classes. Thus we can see immediately that all four teachers begin the term on a note of higher than usual Apprehension, that this lasts longer in some classes than in others, but has dropped into a stable period of low Apprehension in all four classes by the 15th data point. We can also observe more general trends; for example, while the periods of occurrence do not exactly correspond, all four teachers register much greater Role Satisfaction during the second half of the term than during the first. These periods of generally high or generally low scores have been highlighted by entering the factor pattern titles below the appropriate data points. It is also possible to distinguish individual deviations from common developments, as when we see that a general trend toward a nonpunitive stance in data points 25–39 is broken by Mr. A's burst of Punitiveness around point 30. Such developments are much easier to discern once the factor scores are standardized and moving averages are computed.

To study the parts that the various clusters of students play in the development of the classroom we treated the data in similar ways. We obtained graphs of factor estimates for the clusters on the seven student factors for moving average data points across all classes (see methodological footnote in Appendix A for further details on this procedure). For ease of presentation we have here converted the summary graphs of all four classes to a table (Table 1–3) in the same form as Tables 6–1 and 6–2. The pluses and minuses signify the same degree of departure from the mean. It is important to remember in reading the table that each cluster has been standardized within itself so that the high or low moments for that cluster can be compared to its normal level on a given factor can be seen. This means that for some clusters the high points on a given factor may be lower than the low points on that factor for others. In Table 6–4, as a reminder of the relative differences between clusters, we have listed the factors that are significantly high and low for each cluster compared to the others.

These tables suggest an affirmative answer to the question of whether we can find important developmental similarties across all four classes. Similar trends arise at similar periods and override many of the individual differences that are present. This is, of course, more readily evident during some periods than during others. For example, the early phases with the high loadings on Role Dissatisfaction and

Table 6–1

Factor Scores for Teachers by Moving Average Blocks by Group

Factor	Class	1	2	3	4	5	6	7	8	9	10	11	12	13	14	15	16	17	18	19
1	A				−			−	+	+	+	+	+	+		+	−	−	−	−
	B	−	+		−	−	−				+	+	+	+	+	+	+	+	+	+
	C	+	+	+	+	+	+	+	+	+	+	+	+	+	+	+		+	+	
	D		+	+		+	+	+	+	+	+	+	+	+	+	+		+	+	

Reaction

2	A	−	−	−	−	−	−	−	−		−	−	−	−	−	−		+	+	+
	B	−	−	−	−	−	−	−			−		−		−		−	−		−
	C		+	+			·				−		−	−	−	−	−	−	−	−
	D	−	−	−	−	−	−		−		−	−	−		−					

Role Dissatisfaction

3	A	+	+	+	+			−	−		+	+	+	+	+	+		−	−	
	B		+		+	+	+	+		−								−		−
	C	−	−	−	−	−	−	−		−				−		−	−	−	−	−
	D		+	+	+	−	−		−	−	−		+	+	+	+	+	+	+	+

4	A	−		−	−	−		−		+	+	+	+	+	+		−			−
	B	+	+	+	+	−	−	−	−		+	+	+	+	+	+	+	+	+	+
	C	−							+			+	+	+	+	+	+	+	+	+
	D	+	+	+	+		−		−			−	−	−	−	−			+	+

Punitiveness

5	A	+	+	+	+	+	+	+		−	−	−			−			−	−	−
	B	+	+	+	+	+	+	+			+	+	+		−			−	−	−
	C	+	+	+	+				+	+	+	+			−			−	−	−
	D		+		+	+	+	+	+	+	+	+	+	+		−	+		−	−	−

Apprehension   Low Apprehension

6	A	+	+	−	−	−	−		+	+	+	+	+	+	+	+		+			−
	B							+	+	+	+	+	+	+	+		+	+		−
	C		−	−	−	−	−	+	+	+				+		−	−	−	−	−
	D		−		−	+	+	+		+	+	+	+	+	+			+	+	

Display

7	A	+	+	+	+	+		+	−	+	+	+	+	+	+	+		−	−	−
	B	+	+		−	−	−	−	−	−	−	−		+			+	+	+	+
	C	+	+	+	+	+	+	+	+	+	+	+	+		−		−	−	−	−
	D	−	−	−	−	−	−	−	−				−	−	+	+	+	+	+	+	+

Warmth

		1	2	3	4	5	6	7	8	9	10	11	12	13	14	15	16	17	18	19

Moving Average

Key
++ = > + 1.00 Standard Deviation from norm
 + = .50 > t > + 1.00 S.D. from norm
 − = −.50 > t > −1.00 S.D. from norm
−− = > −1.00 Standard Deviation from norm

```
     – – – –       +   + + + –   – – –     –   –   +   + + +   +   +   +   –
 +       –   – –   –   –     +         – – – – – – – – – –             + +
 –   – – –   – – –   – –   –   – –   – – –     –                 –   – – – – – –
 –   – –         – –   – – – – – – – –       – –       –   – – – – – –
```
Proaction
```
+ + + + + +   +   +       –     – –   –               +   +   +   +         – –
 +   + + + + + + + + + + + + + + + + + + +                 +     +   +   – –
– – – –   –           + + + + + + + + + + + + + + + + + + + + + + + +     +
     –   + + + +   +   + + +   + + + + + + + + +   +   +   + + + +
```
Role Satisfaction
```
     –         + + + + + + + +                   –           – – – – – – – –     +
– – – – –     –   – –   – –     +   + + + + + +       –   – –         + +
     +   + + + + + + + + + + + + + + + + + + + + + + + + + + + + +         +
         –   – – – – – – –         +   +     – – – –       – – –
```
Formality   Colleague
```
     –               –   – –           –       – –   –   – –   + + + + + +   –   + + +
     – –   – – – – –   – –   –   – –   –   –     – – – – –     –   – – – – –       – –
     +   +   +       –   – – – – – – – – – – – –   –   – – – – –         – –       – –
+ + + + +     +   +             – – – – – – – – – – –   –                 –   –
```
Nonpunitiveness
```
 –       –   – – – – –   –       +       + +   +   +             + + +
 –   –   – – – – – – – –     –               –                       +
 –   –       +   + + + + + +         ±   ±   –   –   – – – – – – – – – – +
 –               +   – –   –           – –   – – – – – –
```
```
         –       –                   –         – –                     – –
 –   –   – – – –   –   – – –   –   – –   –           + +       +   +   + +
     –         –   –   –         + + + + + +                         + + + +
+ +   +   –       + + +             – – – –   –   – –   –               –   –
```
```
 –               –   – –   –                   –   – – – –             – –
 +   +   +   +   +   +   +         –   – – – – –   –     –   –     +   +   +
 +     –   –   – –   –   –     – – –   –   –   –   +   + +   +   –   –       + +
 +             – –   – –   –   –                                            Low Warmth
```

Table 6–2
Factor Scores for all Students by Moving Average Blocks by Group

The following is a best-effort reproduction of the symbol chart. Rows are grouped by Factor (1–7) and Class (A–D); columns are Moving Average Blocks 1–19.

```
F  C
a  l
c  a    1  2  3  4  5  6  7  8  9 10 11 12 13 14 15 16 17 18 19
t  s
o  s
r

1  A        +     +  +  +           -  -  -  -  -  -  -     +++++++
   B     - - - - - - - - - - - - -        +           +   +  ++   +
   C     ++++                   -  -- -   -   -   ----          ++++
   D     -     -           +              -       ----   +++++++      +
                              Anx. Dep.                  Enactment
2  A     -- -         ---- -                    +                     +
   B     - - - -   -         - - - - - - - - - -         - -        -                  +
   C       +   +                                           +   -  ----
   D     - - - - -   -           +                         +  ++   +   +
               Contention
3  A          -                -  -        + +++++         +  ++           ----
   B     - - - - - - - - - -             +                           ++++++
   C          -    -    -    ----                                         -
   D               ++++++++++++                -     ---
                                   Concealment
       Low Concealment
4  A     -   -     ++++++++++++    +                    -     -     -
   B     - -         +   +   +   +   +   +++   +   +   ++++++   +   +++++
   C            -    -    -    -    -           +   -   -           +   ++++++++
   D     ++++                 -- -                       -   -           ++++
                                                                Discouragement
5  A                       -  -       -                       +  +       -  -     -
   B     ++++++   +   +   ++++++                                  -     - -
   C     ---               +         +                         ------           +     -
   D     ++++   +   +   +++++++++       ---                         -     - -
                Challenge
6  A     ++++++   +   +             +           -     -----       +   +   +   +
   B     ++++   +   ++   +         +   ++   +   ++   +                   -----
   C     +   +   +   +   +   +++++   +                     +           ++   +   +
   D     +   +   +         ++++               ---   -             +   +   -   -  -
                Support
7  A     ++++++   +   +   +++++   +                 -   -   -   -   -       -     -
   B     ++++               ----   -   -   +++++++                 -   +   +
   C     +++++++++   +   +                             -   -   -
   D     +++++++++++++++++             -   ----   -   -   -   -   -
                Exhibition
         1  2  3  4  5  6  7  8  9 10 11 12 13 14 15 16 17 18 19
                                                    Moving Average
```

Key

++ = > + 1.00 Standard Deviation from norm
 + =   .50 < t < + 1.00 S.D. from norm
 − = −.50 > t > −1.00 S.D. from norm
−− = < −1.00 Standard Deviation from norm

```
+    --      +  +  +        --------  -              ++
        +              +  +  +  +          +    ++++
-  -----  -  ++              +++++++  +                -
-- -  -          --                          +
        Aux. Dep.                          Enactment
     +++++++++          --++--      --  +  -  -------+
          -          +  +    ++++  +  +++  -  -  +  ++++++
---  -  +  +  +  +  +  ++  +  +++++  +  +    +  ++  ----++
+++  +  ++  -              +          +        --------  -  +  +
        -  -  -                    Consent
     -    -  -          ------  ++  +  +  +  -  -  -  -  -  -
++  ++++++          ---  -  -      -    -  -
-----  +++++++++    -  -  ++  +  +  ++---        +  ++
  +  +        -          -----      -  --------
```

```
          -  +  +  +  ---                    -  -  -  -  -  -
++  +++  ---------  ---      -  -      -  -    -  -  -  ----
        -  -    -  +++++++++----  -      -  ---
          +  ++++++  +  -  ----  -  -    -  -  -------
                                Low Discouragement
        --  -  -    ++++++  +  +        -  -  -
-    +      -  ----  ------  -  +  +          ---
  -  +  +  ++    --+++  +  ++---      +  +
  -    -        --  --    -  --------
```

```
        -    -            -  -  -                    ----
--    -  -          -  -  -  ++  +          -------
  ++++  +        -  -  _  --    --------        -
-- -    ----  ----    +  ++++    ++++++
                                Unrespon.
  ---          -  ----  -                    --
-                    -  -  -        -  -  -  -
        -  ------  -            -  -  -  --  --
-  --  -        +  +  -      -      -      -      ---
```

Table 6–3
Mean Factor Estimates for Clusters by Moving Average Blocks

Factor	Cluster	1	2	3	4	5	6	7	8	9	10	11	12	13	14	15
1	1	−	−	−	−−	−					−	−	−	−	−	−
	2	−	−		−				−	−	−	−	−	+	+++	++
	3				++	+			−	−	−	−	−	+	+++	++
	4	−	−	−	−	−	+						−		+	+++
	5	−	−	−	−	−	−	−	−		−	+++	+++	+++		
	6	−	−	−	−	−	−	−	−	−	−			−	−	
	7	−	−	−	−	−		−	−		−	−	+++		++++	
				++ = Enactment						− − = Anxious Dependence						
2	1								−	−	−					
	2	−		−							−	−	−	−	−	
	3							− −						+	+	
	4	+	+	+	−	−		−					−			+
	5			−							−	+	+	+++	−	
	6	+	+		−	−	−	−	−			−		−	−	−
	7	−	−	−	−	−		−−	−	−		+			++++	
				++ = Consent						− − = Contention						
3	1			−								+	+	+		
	2	+++	+			−	−−				−−	−	−			
	3	−	−	−	−	−			+++++		+	−	−			
	4	−	−	−−	+	+	+	+	+++++++++++							
	5	−	−	−−−−−			+									
	6	−	−	−			+	+	+	+	+					
	7			−	−	−		+		+	−					
				++ = Concealment						− − = Low Concealment						
4	1		−	−				+		+	+	+	+	+		
	2	−	−−−−−−−					+								
	3	+	+	+							−	−−	+++++			
	4	−		−				++		+++	+					
	5	+		+	−−	+					+++++++					
	6	−−				+++++++										
				++ = Discouragement						− − = Low Discouragement						
5	1	+++++++++				−										
	2	+++	+		+	+				−−						
	3	+	+++++		−	−	−−−−									
	4	−−+++++++++−			−	−	−−−−									
	5	+++++++++	+	+	+	+	−	−	−	−						
	6	+	+	+	−	−		+	+++++							
	7	+	+	+	+++++++	−	−−−−−−−−									
				++ = Challenge						− − = Low Challenge						
6	1	+	+	+++++	+	+++++	−	−	−−−−							
	2	−	+	+++++++	+	−	−−−−									
	3	++++		+	+	−−−−−										
	4	+++++++	+	+	+++++−	−−−−−										
	5	+++++++++++	−	−												
	6	+	+++	+	+++	+	+	+	−							
	7	+++++++++	+	+	++	−	−−−−−−	+	+							
				++ = Support						− − = Unresponsiveness						
7	1	+++++++++	++++	−−−	−	−	−	−								
	2	+	+	+++												
	3	+++++++++−−−−−−−−−	−	−	−											
	4	+++++	+													
	5	+++++++	−	+++												
	6	++	+	++−	−	+++++	−−−									
	7	+++++++	+++++++++++++	++−−−	−											
				++ = Exhibition						− − = Low Exhibition						

```
         ---   +  +++++    -              +++++++++    -              -
++       ------            -    +              -    -    -   +  +++++      ++
++ ++++                         +                   -----    -  -   ++++
++ +            -    -   +   +  ++++       +         -------
  +    +   +               +++++++++-    -    --         -       +   +   +  +++++
++ ++       -   -   -   -         +  ++++++                         +       +  +

                              En.-Axx. Dep.

   -   --            +    -----         +   ++++++++++   +
+   -   +                   +  +++++++++   +         +   +  ++
+   +       ---------              +    ++                     ++++
+   ++++++          -   ---       +       +       -----              ------
--   ---------+++++++++++         +    ++++++   +       +   +       +       ++
++ +++             ++++++              -         ---    ----

                              Cons.-Cont.

   +++++  +            ++      -   ----   -   -   +   +   -      --
   +   -   -   -    ++++++++   +   +  ++      --
   +   +  ++++++++++        -       ---    -   --   ---
++ +               +       -----              --        -
+   +++++++        --------       +   +  ++++       +     ------
+   ++++++              -------        +++  +  ++------

                              Conc.-Law Conc.

+   +++  +              -   -   --         -   ----    +
+   ++++++             -   -   --              ---    ----
      +   +  ++       ++          -   +++++++++----
         ++++      -   -   +++  ++       ---   -    ----
+++  +              -------    +++       -++              -------
+       +          -   -       ++++    -++              -------    -
                      ++            -------   +   +   +   +        ---

                              Disc.-Low Disc.

--          -       +++         -----------------+   +  ++
   ++     +           -   -   +++   +   +  ---    --
-------           ++++           +++++    -   -   -   -
   --   ---    +       --   -              +          +++
+++     +    ++          -----    +--   +   +        --  -
+   ------              -           -        +   +   +          +   +

                              Chal.-Low Chal.

   +   ---    -              -                  ---    ----
  ---+  +   +     -   -              -                         +       --
   -   -   --  ----+       +  ++   +  +                   -   --
-------           -       +                ---              +
   +++               +              ++++   -------    -   -   --
   -   -----    --              ---    -   --       +   -   --
   --        --              ---   -   -                     +

                              Supp.-Unresp.

-------------    -    -   --              ++++------
   -   -   -    -  +++++++++----    +  +   -   -
-   -   -------    -   --    +++   +++   ---    +   +          -
++ ++-  -   -              -  ---------    -   --   -
-   -   --  ----   +       -   -  ----------

                              Exhib.-Low Exhib.
```

Key

++ = > + 1.00 Standard Deviation from norm

+ = .50 < t < + 1.00 S.D. from norm

− = −.50 > t > −1.00 S.D. from norm

−− = < − 1.00 Standard Deviation from norm

Table 6–4
Summary of Cluster Characteristics

Cluster 1: The Compliant Students (High Exhibition and Consent, low Challenge, Discouragement, and Concealment)

Cluster 2: The Anxious Dependent Students (High Anxious Dependence and Consent, low Exhibition and Concealment)

Cluster 3: The Discouraged Workers (High Discouragement)

Cluster 4: The Independents (High Enactment and Support, low Discouragement)

Cluster 5: The Heroes (High Contention, Challenge, Enactment, and Concealment)

Cluster 6: The Snipers (High Contention, Challenge, and Discouragement)

Cluster 7: The Attention Seekers (High Exhibition and Concealment)

Apprehension for the teacher and Contention, Support, and Exhibition for the total student group allow us to infer that similar issues and reactions to those issues preoccupy all our classrooms soon after their inception. However, differing rates of development lead to temporal lags which obscure the similarity of later phases. All four classes exhibit a conjunction of punitive teaching with student discouragement some time after the group's opening phase, but this begins much earlier in groups A and B than in groups C and D. Finally, the impending end of the group again raises issues common to all four classrooms at an equivalent time period and gives us some more obvious correspondence in factor development than are to be found in the middle parts of the term.

What we would like to do now is to use the most dominant trends apparent in the tables to paint a composite picture of the developmental history of a typical classroom. To do this, we must ignore for the time being many of the individual variations that give each classroom its unique flavor and concentrate instead on the similar trends and on some of the processes that cause them. From time to time, we shall pause in our account to report on individual sessions that typify processes occurring at a particular period, that allow us to view the teacher's actions in the light of the teacher-as typology, and that illustrate the manner in which the classes vary despite sharing many common trends. We shall also consider the particular influence of each of the clusters in the unfolding drama of the classroom. We shall try to indicate the ways in which various clusters exert pressures on the teacher to change the times at which different clusters are particularly happy or discouraged or angry, and probably most important, the conditions under which different kinds of students are most able to work.

The First Phase

We start our account where the classrooms themselves start, with the first session. Our teacher sits at the front of the room as the students dribble in the door in ones and twos. He waits for a full enough complement to start the class formally. Perhaps he has written his name, office hours, or the like on the blackboard. He is nervous; in a few minutes he will have to start performing before this crowd of strangers. A false move, he fears, may start things off in the wrong direction. He looks around at his new charges, rehearses mentally the things he will say, and attempts to look calm.

Most of the students arrive earlier than they ever will again during the term. They sit attentively or they slump down, perhaps with a notebook turned to its first white page, surveying the room, looking out the window, trying to size up the teacher, wondering what the course will be like. As in any new meeting, both parties take a rather defensive stance, carefully maintaining routes of possible escape in case of disaster. In the first few sessions, this need on both sides for unhindered movement will exhibit itself in a tenativeness of action, a willingness to try out seemingly incompatible roles and strategies in an attempt to find one that is both successful and comfortable. We encounter here the most fluid period of classroom life, a time marked by a tendency to extrapolate the smallest bits of interaction into momentous portents for the entire future of the relationship.

At some point, the teacher officially begins the class. If he is at all like the four teachers in our sample, he will start by presenting himself as a formal authority. Apparently, the first order of business is to establish control, to get things moving on the right foot. He introduces himself, calls the roll, goes over the reading list, starts talking about what he plans to do in the course and what he will require of the students. To a large extent, his major aim is to give the students as many clues as possible to what he expects from them. Besides helping him establish control, this strategy may relax some of the tension the students feel in the face of an originally undefined situation.

Woven through this long burst of formal detail, however, are a number of other strategies and messages. For one thing, the teacher is hopeful of producing a friendly, accepting feeling in the students. His main attempt at fostering such a climate shows up in frequent expressions of Warmth. Even as he tells the class how he intends to set things up, he constantly takes steps to reassure them that he is not only the distant, demanding figure he may seem to be, but that he is also a friendly person who is interested in them and on their side. His main object here is to enlist support at this early stage but he may also be trying to placate what he takes to be hostile and disapproving strangers his more fearful fantasies make the students out to be.

One outstanding example of such an interaction occurs during Mr. B's presentation of the reading. "I wouldn't buy Hilgard, if I were you," he informs the students. "We'll only be reading a few chapters of it, and I'm sure Mr. Hilgard can get along without the money." With this statement, he distances himself from the text-book-writing authority and identifies himself with the students whom he sees as hostile and resentful toward such authorities. One implication of such activity is that the teacher is intensely ambivalent toward the students. They may sense this, and many hold themselves aloof from laughing at the teacher's early quips or appearing to be easily won over. And indeed, although the teacher continues his protestations of Warmth during his act of detailing the course's structure, he may also display a variant of Punitiveness by implying that he assumes in advance that the students will be sluggish and balky in the matter of meeting the requirements he sets for them.

In addition to needing to establish control and to impress the students favorably, the teacher also has a need to become better acquainted with the students. He will have to understand them to teach them effectively, but there are other factors involved as well. For one thing, once the students actually begin talking for themselves, some of the teacher's fears about what they are thinking will no doubt be dispelled. In addition, there is a problem that the relationship might become too one-sided. Thus far, the teacher has done all the talking. It's time to let the students have a say and become involved through active participation.

Our teachers' manner of first prodding the students to speak was to involve them in a discussion or exercise concerning the nature of psychology or science. Mr. A, for example, set up a card game which involved the students in hypothesis testing, then asked them to discuss what they had learned. Thus the students had their first statements patterned by their socialization into the field of psychology and the teacher's perspectives on it. In this way the teacher turns more reactive and facilitative without, as yet, relinquishing his almost total direction of the class.

As the students begin to talk more in this and the next few classes, it is obvious that, like the teacher, they, too, desire to gain some control over events, become known and liked, and better acquaint themselves with the teacher. They, too, strive to find a comfortable mode of existence in the classroom.

The desire of some students to have a say about the ultimate direction of the class shows up in common earlier tendencies toward Contention and Challenge. Students engaging in such behavior wish to demonstrate from the first that they will not sit idly by while the teacher assumes total dominance and superiority.

The rebellious cluster 5 and 6 students, in particular, are very involved during these early sessions in testing the teacher's strength and tolerance for student autonomy and particularly for their counterdependent style. They also seem to want to demonstrate to him and to one another that the teacher is not the only powerful male in the room, that they will compete with him on that issue. The traditionally oriented cluster 1 students, on the other hand, may become somewhat anxious if the teacher is too reactive at the beginning; they prefer a more proactive stance in which they will be sure to absorb the right kind of knowledge from the teacher and, if they are frustrated by a reactive phase, they may become more contentious, although they never rebel very directly. The cluster 2 students, who have been accustomed to an anxious dependent stance in the past, probably have some of cluster 1's concerns early in the class, especially since they are so worried about managing to get good grades. But they are more ambivalent. They also seem to be involved in trying out a new form of independence in this new setting, and their scores on Contention and Challenge, which are unusually high in these early sessions, seem to be an expression of these fledgling attempts at independence, as well as of their anxiety about inadequate supplies of information from the teacher.

While Contention and Challenge are prominent in this first phase, they are, somewhat paradoxically, accompanied by high scores for all of the clusters on Support. Many of the teacher's expressions of Warmth during this period are attempts to elicit support, and he typically receives the desired response. While the students may not yet be ready to accept the teacher or his teaching style wholeheartedly, just about all of them seem to be willing right at the beginning to help him out if he needs it, to try to act in ways which will win his favor, and generally to make their own contribution toward starting the relationship out on the right foot. For the compliant cluster 1 students this early Support will probably mean communications of willingness to accept whatever rules the teacher may choose to make in the class. For the heroic cluster 5 students, there will be sincere efforts to become very close to the teacher interspersed with angry attacks on him. For the exhibitionistic cluster 7 students, Support will mean primarily attempts to figure out what will please the teacher and to act in ways that will tend to make him like them. For the cluster 3 and 4 students, who are quite independent, the early Support may involve telling the teacher that they are not like the others of their peers, hung up on anger or dependency, and that they are ready to get to work. In fact, these clusters are the only ones that swing even briefly to the Enactment rather than to the Anxious Dependent side of factor 1 in the first phase. Their attempts at such early enactment are very brief and tend to be accompanied by Exhibition and Concealment, but still they must be encouraging to the teacher as a first partial glimpse of good things which could evolve out of the early confusion.

Our chart shows us two other common tendencies for students in the very early classes. The major one is the high scores on Exhibition found in all four classrooms. Like the Support factor, this performance parallels the teachers' Warmth as a strategy for getting things off on the right foot by winning the others' favor and presenting oneself as confident, likeable, etc. In the students' case, of course, we have the added factor of individuals jockeying for a favorable position vis-à-vis their fellow students. All of the clusters play some part in this early tendency towards Exhibition, but the most conspicuous performers are the high-participating cluster 7 students. They are especially likely to talk a great deal, to have their hands raised to answer any question, to show off and brag about their knowledge, to come after class to gain special favors, and to watch the teacher closely for cues as to how to please him. A teacher often welcomes such patterns early in the term for their value in boosting his ego and getting the student group talking, despite the fact that the same kind of frequent but relatively shallow participation may be less welcome as other clusters join the discussions later in the term. A related early trend for the student group is their low scores on Concealment. This factor is somewhat similar to Exhibition. It seems to reflect a desire on the part of the students to present themselves openly so that they may be seen and known by the teacher and others. Clusters 1 and 2 especially are likely to bring up personal examples in class and in other ways show their desire to be seen as persons by others. Also, since Concealment may often entail joking and avoiding important issues, these early low scores may indicate a willingness to take the business of the class seriously and a fantasy that they will be able to deal openly with all issues that may arise.

Thus we have the outlines of our picture for the actions of the student group as a whole during the first few sessions. In general, those who do the talking act very involved and seem concerned with showing off their intelligence, their compliance, their independence, their willingness to support the teacher, or their readiness to fight him when they consider it necessary. Early in the term students seem primarily preoccupied with presenting themselves in a favorable light and with setting up a social climate in which their needs and abilities will be respected. These efforts may eclipse the teacher-as-expert's goals of developing students' understanding and knowledge. For the purposes of displaying one's intelligence, for instance, old insights are as useful as new ones, and almost any argument or objection will serve the purpose of communicating the message that one cannot be easily dominated. As a result of these developments, many early student contributions seem rather off the mark or uninspired. New teachers often extrapolate this kind of student behavior into the whole future of the course and despair accordingly. As we shall see, this is premature; student concerns and viewpoints will change.

When we look at the *teacher* factors for the first few data points, we find that the tendencies toward Warmth and Apprehension whose presence we noted in the first data point have been joined by a persistent Role Dissatisfaction. This seems to have a number of causes depending on the teacher. The failures of students to manifest greater task-orientation in this phase is often one such factor. The Challenge and Contention that students display may also be particularly annoying. The teacher feels he is trying his hardest to be warm and competent, yet some of the students seem to attack him at every turn. The cluster 6 students attack as if from a distance, and while the cluster 5 students are much more involved, their attacks are even more hostile and upsetting. Different kinds of students seem to be pressuring him to act in incompatible ways. The result is a depressed, hostile reaction which begins to accompany and undermine his warmth. Another factor in this Role Dissatisfaction is the teacher's inability to find and immediately take on a professional role that is effective, stable, and ego-syntonic. Again, not blessed with the foresight our charts give us, the teacher may project his feelings into the future and look forward to a whole term of role discomfort.

The reader might wish to raise an objection here. If we are discussing the Role Dissatisfaction evident in data points one through six, say, how do we explain the statistics for Mr. C, who appears to have been more satisfied than not during this period. We notice in listening to the relevant tapes that one of Mr. C's chief strategies in the first few sessions was to place a special emphasis on Warmth, a fact indicated in part by the duration of the Warmth with which he began the term. His style through this period stressed the roles of friendly ego-ideal and reactive facilitator. He encouraged the students to talk a good deal, being very receptive toward most of what they said. That this strategy worked well at first is shown by the failure of the students in this class to share in the Contention and Challenge of their peers in other classrooms. In contrast, the students exhibited a surprisingly strong burst of early Enactment. The events of this period developed a strong mutual trust and allowed self-presentations to take place in a fairly relaxed atmosphere.

We find, however, as is often the case when issues which are ascendant in most classes are skirted or bypassed in one, that these issues rise to the surface at a later time, long after they have become dormant in other classes. In class C, Role Dissatisfaction finally made its appearance at data point 7 and stayed high for a good time thereafter. Apparently, despite all the mutual warmth, work was not proceeding maximally. Also we find that class C underwent a period of student Contention around data point 16 which is unique among the classes for that period. There is no doubt that much of the peculiar bitterness found during this period is a legacy of the restraint of Contention early in the term. "You presented yourself," the students seem to be saying, "as a fair guy, someone who was on our side, and we went along with you. Now that the test comes along, you prove to be as distant and arbitrary as the rest of them."

In addition to the teacher's early tendencies towards Warmth, Apprehension, and Role Dissatisfaction, there tends to be movement toward greater Reaction as the term gains momentum. Apparently the necessity for gaining control and setting a direction takes some precedence over the teachers' need to get to know the students and to get them actively engaged in the classroom process, for Reaction seldom shows up at the first data point. A reactive style does tend to appear soon afterwards, however. In some classrooms, it is postponed for some time, perhaps because the teacher feels his control would be threatened or because he feels he has to give the students some background in the field before they will be able to contribute productively. To the extent that the first of these reasons is uppermost, a long period of Proaction may be self-defeating. In such a case, the teacher leaves himself scant opportunity to compare with reality his anxious fantasies about student wishes. In addition, when the teacher finally does inch his way into a reactive style, some students may be settled in a deep groove of passivity while others are more than ready to seize this opportunity for an overdue attempt at revolt. Still, all four of the teachers do switch into a more reactive style by the end of the initial phase.

As we mentioned earlier, we supplemented our observations of these phases by careful listening to individual sessions whose factor scores appeared to typify the trends we have mentioned. The sessions chosen for our early phase were the third session from Mr. A's class, the second from Mr. B's, and the fifth from Mr. D's class. Since the teachers' role performances as described by our teacher-as typology are not directly measured by the factors, we paid special attention to this aspect of his performance in scrutinizing these sessions. Hopefully, this will serve as a useful supplement to the information contained in the factor curves.

Mr. A began session 3 by asking whether the students had found it hard to find the readings. This allowed him to appear friendly and helpful while also starting the class with an implicit emphasis on his formal authority role as an assignment-giver. In response to some student questions as to how the class would be graded, Mr. A appeared rather anxious and uncertain. After this, he began to lecture about the differences between "tough-minded" and "tender-minded" approaches to psychology. The lecture stressed his role of socializing agent, teaching the students the proper perspectives from which material is to be viewed, and also exhibited Mr. A's expert knowledge of the subject. In the course of the lecture, it became obvious that Mr. A was himself very conflicted about this schism within the field of psychology, and he became involved in a proactive argument with himself about which viewpoint should prevail. This ambivalence made it hard for him to express the excitement or feelings of competence that one would associate with a successful ego-ideal performance.

Toward the end of the class, Mr. A opened a discussion on the topic of how he might have improved an experiment he performed during the previous class session. Students offered various suggestions, and Mr. A dealt with them purely from the perspective of the expert socializing agent, criticizing them on scientific grounds. Most of the students accepted this orientation, but those whose statements tended in other directions also found that Mr. A was more interested in treating their responses from the point of view of the discussion he had already set up rather than in facilitating the students in any further expression of their own concerns.

Mr. B's class, interestingly enough, also began with some questions about the availability of the readings, led into a lecture on the values of psychology, and ended with an experiment which was used to demonstrate the points made in the lecture. But while Mr. A's expert-socializing agent performance had a monotonous stability, Mr. B, although stressing the same two role functions, continuously changed his role orientations, acting within many different combinations of the teacher-as categories. This flexibility seemed to reflect both Mr. B's active efforts to present himself as a multifaceted person and his tendency to ignore or deny conflict by switching directions whenever it appeared. Another notable difference between Mr. A's session and Mr. B's is that Mr. B was able to muster a great deal of enthusiasm for his subject. Where there was a conflict of values in psychology, Mr. B emphasized that he saw both points of view as valuable and exciting.

The way Mr. B handled conflicts within the field of psychology seems typical of how he handled conflict generally. He presented himself as very facilitative in urging the students to express their own opinions in a discussion on such matters as which human drives are primary, which secondary. However, when arguments arose, he appeared to be bothered by them, tending to cut them off by asserting either that both sides have good points or that there really was no conflict between them. As a result some students came to feel their statements were not taken very seriously.

Mr. D, on the other hand, began his class with a lecture on the topic of conditioning, stressing that the students must learn to master the jargon of psychology. Here, his performance as a formal authority was more closely bonded to his expert-socializing agent lecture than was the performance of the other two teachers, both of whom told the students not to worry too much if they failed to understand all the terms immediately. His style as he lectured included asking the students technical questions, forcing them to search for the correct answers. He also acted rather scornful if they failed to produce the proper response. As the class proceeded, student comments implied that many students would have liked Mr. D to stop stressing his formal authority and become more facilitative of their own interests. He ignored these implied requests and the covert battle of wills resulted in a halting discussion in which the various parties seemed bored and continually failed to understand each others' statements well enough to give any coherence to the discussion. Mr. D exhibited increasing amounts of Role Dissatisfaction throughout the session.

We can see that the teachers in all three of these early sessions exhibit many common tendencies. Some examples are the strong emphases each put on socializing the students into the viewpoints and, in one case, the jargon of the field, their common struggles to integrate various aspects of their roles into comfortable classroom identities, their somewhat apprehensive avoidance of many of the emotional messages conveyed by the students, and their common lack of satisfaction with the progress made during the session. Both Mr. A and Mr. D were dissatisfied with their students' lack of enthusiasm for and understanding of the viewpoints they presented. In Mr. A's case, however, the lack of student enthusiasm flowed mainly from his own inability to present himself as involved or confident, whereas Mr. D's students became alienated by his scornfulness and overemphasis of the formal authority aspect of his role. Obviously the concerns which needed to be resolved before work could proceed optimally would be quite different for the two classes.

By the end of the first eight or nine classes a pattern has been set up, but changes are already under way. Teacher Apprehension is slackening as the worst disasters fail to materialize. Student Contention and Challenge also lessen in most classes as students see that the teacher is not the worst sort of tyrannical monster. Patterns of Warmth, Support, and Exhibition have just about outlived their early usefulness. But probably the strongest spur toward active attempts at change is the teacher's persistent dissatisfaction with the way things are going.

Dissatisfaction and Discouragement

At about this point, we might mark the beginning of a new phase during which the teacher's Apprehension and his reliance on Warmth both gradually fade out of the picture, but he still remains well on the Role Dissatisfaction side of factor 2. The teacher has introduced himself, and the class has begun running along in some kind of groove, but the teacher is bothered by a number of things. The students have been too involved with their own concerns and fears to be able to do much work thus far. They have to some extent begun to identify with him, but they have not yet been able to develop much independence in this setting. The attempts at early Enactment by clusters 3 and 4 were all too ephemeral, and the other students have been very slow to emerge from their early anger or dependency in order to use their energies for work on such things as learning to employ the viewpoint and information necessary for an understanding of the field. The early patterns of Exhibition, in particular, contribute to the teacher's discouragement. The participation of the cluster 7 students gets higher and higher over these early sessions; they are filling more and more time with their less-than-adequate exhibitionistic contributions. As the teacher continues to be unable to bring about a productive classroom atmosphere, he probably becomes increasingly preoccupied with his own ineffectiveness.

His state of depression over these factors spurs the teacher to determine the reasons for these failures and to make whatever changes seem indicated. His conclusions about the nature of underlying problems may, of course, be more or less realistic, but they are certain to reflect many of his preconceptions about what is necessary for a good classroom relationship. If, like those in our sample, he is a relatively new teacher, this period can be particularly trying. Unaware of the slow development of most classes, he is likely to blame any problems in the classroom on his own lack of teaching experience or even defects in his personality, and he may be quick to see the ideas and strategies with which he began the course as inadequate.

Two role performances the teacher is especially likely to emphasize at this point are in the areas of ego ideal and formal authority. One conviction which may affect the teacher's handling of the formal authority role is that the problems are caused by the students' lack of work. It may be increasingly apparent that students arrive at classroom sessions only minimally prepared to make any intellectual progress. To the extent that the teacher feels responsible for this state of affairs, he may identify his own early Warmth as the factor that has kept the students from taking his demands for work seriously enough. "I tried to be nice to them," one might paraphrase his thoughts, "and they just took it as a sign of weakness. Now I had better get tough."

Tough, in this context, means punitive. The teacher tends to start placing increasing blame on the students whenever the class slows down. "How many people have actually done the reading?"

may become a familiar refrain. In addition, the teacher tends to drop numerous references to coming tests as a threat to those who are presumed to be doing an insufficient amount of work. It is interesting to note that the two teachers in our sample who were slowest to swing around to a pattern of Reaction were also the first to take to Punitiveness. Just as these teachers feared that students, freed to participate, might wrest control away from them and overthrow their goals, they also seemed to find reasonable the idea that the class was proceeding poorly because of student laziness and indifference.

Another cause to which the teachers commonly attribute unsatisfying classroom interactions is their failure to get the students really involved in the subject. This belief will lead to different strategies for different teachers, depending on which aspect of involving the students they think they may have slighted. One guess is that the students are not engaged because they have not had a chance to participate, and this leads to increases in facilitating and reactive styles for some teachers. Another is that lack of student interest in the class reflects lack of enthusiasm for the teacher. This belief puts stress on the importance of the teacher's acting as an ego-ideal and may move him in the direction of trying to become a more exciting model for his students. His first attempts at this, however, are likely to be of the rather crude type which show up in the Display factor. The defensive stance of this performance ("You may not think much of me, but I'm really great") indicates that the teacher's plans to use himself as an ego-ideal have been affected by his unhappiness over having been rejected as a person. Indeed, a great deal of the Role Dissatisfaction present may derive as much from this issue as from discontent over the status of work in the classroom, and this may also be true of much of the hostility that finds an outlet in Punitiveness.

Another change in the teacher's behavior which might help make his energy sources more available to the students is a movement in the direction of greater independence and identification. Indeed, we do find two of our teachers making the important switch into a colleagial stance during this period. In the case of Mr. D, there was a very conscious decision behind this change. We should note that such consciously premeditated changes are a hallmark of this period. True, some variations in style arise rather spontaneously out of the instability inherent in the teacher's impatience, but many others, such as Mr. B's decision to change the seating arrangement of his class, come into being after long periods of out-of-class soul-searching.

Also, it should be pointed out that such an unspontaneous appearance of a colleague style as we find occurring in this period is unlikely to include any real willingness to share responsibility for the class with the students.

Another point to note is that in his zeal to improve the classroom situation, the teacher may find himself the victim of new contradictions. One place where this is evident is in his attempts to become at once a stricter formal authority and a more effective ego-ideal. The whole problem with threats and Punitiveness is that they alienate many students. And yet student alienation is the very thing teachers are trying to fight with their excursions into the ego-ideal role. The reparation mixed in with Punitiveness may help, but not sufficiently. Thus the teacher's discomfort is increased by the feeling that the measures he does take to help matters often turn out to make things worse.

Before turning to the behavior reflected in the factor scores for the student group for this period, we might do well to look more closely at the teacher's performance in one typical session. Mr. A, in session 12 of his class, exhibited the kind of tentative and indecisive attempts at reform that mark the most depressed periods of this phase. In the previous session, he had offered the students choices in the matter of how they would like their third paper, an outline of a proposed experiment, to count toward the final grade. The students appeared most inclined towards the alternative of having the paper count if it would raise their grade but not if it would lower it. Mr. A had also suggested that those individuals who wrote good research proposals would be allowed to carry out this research in place of a final exam.

In offering students this choice, Mr. A shifted into a more "Colleagial" and facilitative role in the hopes of spurring greater student engagement. On second thought, however, he began wondering whether this facilitation might not undercut his formal authority. Early in session 12 we find him mentioning these second thoughts and telling the students, "I think it's feasible. After all, I suggested it—but consider this: what if somebody just sloughs off? There has to be some provision that this doesn't happen." And in another statement opposing facilitation to formal authority, he says "I don't know why it couldn't work out . . . . If a proposal was good and if you're really interested in it, this could be a substitute for a final examination—subject to all kinds of red-tape clearance on my part of course."

When the students gave their opinions, they further acted out the conflict which Mr. A had been experiencing. Some attacked the proposal for the manner of grading and expressed their fear that it would allow some (other) students to "get away with" not working. Others supported the proposal and seemed confused by the fact that it was being reconsidered after having been accepted during the previous session. A third group tried to find a compromise that would allow the proposal to stand with the added clause that everyone would be forced to meet some minimum standard, thus hoping to assuage some of Mr. A's fears of students' sloughing off entirely.

During this discussion, Mr. A pointed out that he also experienced some conflict between his roles of facilitator and expert: "I like the idea of having a lot of responsibility placed on your shoulders. A lot of times I can't do this because there's some material I have to cover, for example." Nothing had been definitely decided by the end of the session, and Mr. A seemed to feel depressed and incompetent. The conflicts he expressed at length in the classroom had kept him from an effective ego-ideal performance, an outcome quite similar to that of the early session in his class described above. His final statements, which presented him more in the peer-facilitator role, went so far as to deny his desire to be an ego-ideal. "There are a lot of unresolved issues in teaching," he said, "and all too often too few teachers make this clear to their students, and as a result what happens is that the teacher does not become a teacher at all, but becomes some sort of mystic figure standing up here holding forth on something which he and no one else knows about. There's no magic involved in teaching."

The other sessions we chose as typifying this period portray the teachers as introducing innovations which were designed to reduce some of the affective arousal that was interfering with learning. For Mr. A, as we saw, this involved a change in the evaluation procedures and assignments. Mr. B, on the other hand, restructured the physical arrangement of the classroom and the pattern of discussion, while Mr. C attempted to confront and work through some of the disruptive affect aroused by the first exam. All three, moreover, encountered some degree of student resistance to the changes they attempted to actualize.

One of the most important student factor patterns in this phase is that of discouragement. Like the teacher, students have had hopes and expectations for the class, and at this point they, too, are likely to feel frustrated. They do not, for one thing, feel satisfied with their own performances. Especially if the teacher seems to have put very much of the responsibility for the creation of a productive class on them, they are likely to feel that they have not been able to adequately live up to this responsibility. The other important factor in this student discouragement is their awareness that the teacher is unhappy with their performance. The teacher's assignment of blame may tend to drain much of their confidence and energy, and it diminishes their hopes of ever gaining his favor. Clusters 2, 5, and 7 are the highest on the Discouragement factor in this phase. The anxious dependent cluster 2 students seem to feel guilty for their tentative early challenge and to be worried both that the teacher will not like them and that they will fail in the intellectual work of the class. The punitiveness manifested by the teacher in this phase seems to be most upsetting to this group, whose confidence was none too strong to begin with. The rebellious cluster 5 students are one of the first clusters to become discouraged. They seem to be perplexed by the fact that the teacher has not been able to appreciate their early identification and moving toward because it was mixed with so much hostility, and they are beginning to realize that they will need a somewhat different strategy if they are to succeed in getting close to him. The cluster 7 students' discouragement seems to be centered around the teacher's increasing dissatisfaction with their exhibition as a contribution to the class. At first they tended to be rewarded for this kind of behavior, but it is less and less welcome over time, so they need to search for a new way to please the teacher.

The pattern of high Concealment is also evident at this time in the development of the class. For some, the cluster 7 students, for example, this reflects an attempt to avoid facing the issues of their discouragement and the teacher's dissatisfaction by denying them and joking about them, while continuing to follow their pattern of exhibition and to talk even more. For other students, the Concealment factor seems to have other meanings. We may recall that the issue of illegitimate desires to avoid work and the fear of having these desires revealed in class were among the chief characteristics of the high points on this factor. For cluster 1 students who do the required work in time for the tests, but probably do not often work for the sake of class discussion, this is probably a relevant part of this factor. The independent students of clusters 3 and 4 are also quite high on this factor at this time, perhaps reflecting a slacking off of energy on their parts after their very early attempts at Enactment, as well as a need to invest more energy in their other classes and activities. Finally, the idea of Concealment as a fear of revealing a desire to avoid work is relevant to cluster 7's high scores on this factor, for, especially this early in the class, this cluster tends to be rather lazy.

At the same time that these trends are developing, the teacher's manifest dissatisfaction as well as the students' depression are important in prodding many students toward dropping some of their earlier behaviors. Support and Exhibition by most of the students slacken as it becomes more obvious that neither is enough to win the teacher's favor and esteem. The rebellious cluster 6 students and the exhibitionistic cluster 7 students are exceptions to this trend, as they are both still high on both of these factors. But most of the students have decided that this kind of behavior has outlived its usefulness, and even cluster 6 and 7 drop them somewhat later in the term. Challenge and Contention also tend to become much lower at this time in the class for almost all of the clusters. It seems that the teacher's displeasure with these rebellious performances, combined with a lessening of some of the less rational fears behind them, are enough to cut them way back at this time.

The other developmental trend that comes to the surface here and contributes to much of the flavor of this phase is the students' growing Anxious Dependence. The students have been unable to satisfy the teacher's demands as yet, the term is progressing, and the threat of exams and other evaluative procedures is in the air. Discouragement about the effectiveness of employing their own abilities causes some students to become more anxious than ever and to experience increasing feelings of dependency. Clusters 1 and 2, the most compliant and dependent groups, are especially high on Anxious Dependence at this stage, probably because they were worried all along about the implications of the more reactive strategies on the teacher's part for their grades, and now the time of testing their fears is approaching. Cluster 2, especially when we looked at the graphs for the four classes individually, seemed to become very upset at the approach of any evaluative procedures. Even if they were working very hard up until then, their enactment would decline for awhile and be replaced by a mixture of anxiety, submission, and some manifest anger. Unfortunately, the dependent and anxious behavior that is led by these two clusters, and followed to some extent by other students as well, is likely to make the teacher even more dissatisfied, a pattern contributing to one of the more vicious circles among classroom situations.

About the best thing that can be said about this period is that it cannot last forever. The discomfort shared by teacher and students provides a growing pressure for change, and although this often vents itself in rather shortsighted and irrational attempts at resolving problems, both the students and teacher are slowly gaining a more sophisticated view of some of the processes which are necessary for success within this specific classroom. The students gradually learn the types of involvement and application that constitute work in this situation, and the teacher gradually gives more of his attention to the emotional climate of the classroom and realizes the necessity for a number of changes in attitude even as he is learning to shape his expert pronouncements to the students' level of competence.

A more direct view of the kind of classroom interaction that is typical of this phase can be gained by listening to some dialogue from this period which illustrates some of the depression and fumbling activity on both sides. Mr. C begins the session.

> *Mr. C:* "I have a ditto here—not a problem, it's a help. You have had it in terms of reading lists, I take it. It should be picking up by now. I understand that most of you have been busy with [Fraternity] rush and other . . . um, tensions.
>
> *Class:* Roar of laughter.
>
> *Mr. C:* You should be raring to go now. This is a statistics ditto. My usual statement of don't panic goes tenfold here. This is just intended as an aid.

He leads them through the first couple of pages of the ditto.

> *Mr. C:* Page three is probably the most important one for you. I do want you to be able to understand correlations and the basic idea of cause in correlations. For those who want to go a little further . . .
>
> *Class:* Anxious laughter.
>
> *Mr. C:* Page 5 gives some very good ideas on how to proceed . . . Well, last time we were really flying through a very important area, prenatal and paranatal influences. Let me stop here for a moment. Are there any questions? Are you clear on this behavior? How many of you have had a chance to start on the third reading list?
>
> *Class:* (Five or six raise hands.)
>
> *Mr. C:* How many have not?
>
> *Stan:* You mean start the third reading list already?
>
> *Mr. C:* Yes. How many haven't begun it at all yet?
>
> *Class:* (Ten or twelve raise hands.)
>
> *Mr. C:* Okay, careful, because it's a lot, it really is a lot. So see

	if you can get going on it. Try not to leave it all for the end.
Leslie:	Will this be on the first exam?
Mr. C:	(Wearily) The first exam will cover all the material up to the end of the fourth reading list. The end of maternal deprivation.
Audrey:	(Anxiously) Brenner too?
Mr. C:	You don't like it? Clear or unclear? Well, in all honesty, I can't hold you responsible for Brenner if I haven't covered it in any systematic way in class.
Peter:	What's going on tomorrow?
Mr. C:	Tomorrow? Hill Auditorium. How have those lectures been, by the way? I haven't had a chance to pick up any feedback on it from you.
Authur:	I hear they're five times better than last term. But then again . . .
Mr. C:	Five times zero is zero, huh? Well, five times point one is point five. Let's give it a try awhile longer, huh? Why don't we all sit in the same area?

They discuss for a while where their class will sit in the mass lecture in Hill Auditorium. This reminds the teacher of an incident.

Mr. C:	. . . Crossing the aisle. We'll cross the aisle, like Churchill, you know. Oh, you don't . . . well in Canada, unlike here, a politician can switch parties more easily. And Churchill, when he switched from the Liberal to the Conservative party, was called a rat. But finally Churchill got fed up with the Liberals and switched back again, at which time he said something like, "It takes courage to be a rat, but imagine how much courage it takes to be a re-rat."
Class:	Silence.
Mr. C:	Okay, so we'll sit on the right side, about halfway up.
Richard:	I think that there are actually four sections, not three.
Mr. C:	I'll put up a flag, okay? Any questions now about pre-natal or paranatal. Or are we kicking a dead horse? Shall we move on? (Laughs.) I don't know, cause I got no feedback in terms of: This stuff is great, it's boring, pursue it further, review, I understand, I don't understand—I don't know. Move on? Everybody?
Ray:	I have one. On this test we're going to take, what kinds of questions are they going to ask?

> *Mr. C:*   Oh, crazy, crazy questions.
> *Ray:*   But what? What could they ask us on this birth and
> about this child influence and everything like that?

Mr. C endeavors to answer this and more questions following on specific problems about the topic and questions about the test. He becomes rather depressed that the same things need to be explained over and over, and one can see that he would like to get on to the next topic. We jump about 20 minutes of class time and come to these interactions.

> *Peter:*   Yeah, maybe you're right. I'm just not sure.
> *Mr. C:*   Well, you're not alone. Not by any means. It's a very
> complex problem, a result of all kinds of wild inter-
> actions, and I'm only giving you a few things to
> hang your hat on. Yes, Ken.
> *Ken:*   As far as environment goes in the home, what's more
> important for IQ, an educated father or an educated
> mother? Do you think you could say?
> *Mr. C:*   You know, you're really raising a question of what's a
> good mother, and that leads us to maternal depriva-
> tion (laugh). What happens when you don't have a
> mother. Great! Good transition. I take it we can
> leave prenatal and paranatal effects. Thank you Ken
> (laugh) . . . I was just sitting here waiting for
> someone to toss me the ball. Okay, the kid comes
> out; he comes out with various predispositions,
> sometimes with deformities. He comes out into this
> bloody, bleeding confusion . . .

Mr. C continues, lecturing on maternal deprivation from this point on.

Early Enactment

This period of mutual distress is brought by the sudden student reversal from Anxious Dependence to Enactment. This striking change occurs in all four classes somewhere around data point 15. The question facing us is where, in all the floundering around, can we find the causes for such an upturn. One relevant key is probably that the teachers finally hit on a combination of strategies and styles which help open the door to student independence and identifying. As we have noted, the teacher is likely by this time to have gained a more complicated conception of what activities on his part are best calculated to foster independent involvement by the students. The teacher may also have learned from his previous failures that he must go beyond token changes in style and attitude if he expects the students to change significantly as well. Whether by taking premeditated steps in hope of change or simply by "feeling his way," the teacher is increasingly likely to find his actions bringing more successful results.

An example of such a successful change in style occurs in Mr. D's classroom. Mr. D started the term with a powerful, rather forbidding stance which tended to funnel students' energy into Contention and Challenge or Distressed Dependence while effectively blocking their efforts to identify with him. After becoming increasingly dissatisfied with the progress of his class, Mr. D for the first time realized that a less scornful and superior style might have better effects. The result was that he went into a series of sessions determined to be warmer and more colleagial. His altered behavior gave many students their first view of him as a possible model. The students who had been afraid of his power, typified by the cluster 2 students, were able to respond in a less dependent way when they could see warmth along with his scorn. And the students, especially those in cluster 5, who had bristled and become angry at his overbearing superiority early in the term, were able to cooperate with him when he became more colleagial. Therefore students were better able to approach independence from both dependent and counterdependent stances and, at the same time, become much more identified with Mr. D, thus bringing about the first good period of enactment in the class.

Changes in the teacher's style are not the only factors that can unblock pathways to Enactment at this point. In two of the classes, for instance, hour exams were held at about this time, and the fact that most students got through them without major tragedy no doubt restored much of the confidence that was so wobbly in the sessions just prior to the exam. Also, it is probably true that extra studying done for exam preparation or simply in hopes of avoiding the teacher's Punitiveness gave some students the breadth of information and background they needed for an enacting performance. Finally, we cannot forget that the students themselves have been very discouraged with the progress of the class thus far, and like the teacher they look for new personal strategies that will help make the class more productive for them and for others. They are more than ready to step out from behind images of themselves as lazy and dependent dullards, silly show-offs, or sniping unproductive rebels. Their early strategies for asserting their competence in the classroom have yielded sparse results, their paralyzing early fears and doubts have diminished, and they are ready to work in concert with the teacher to look for more useful adaptations to this particular classroom setting. Thus we see that the most striking thing about the beginning of this phase is not the removal of the various blocks to Enactment, but rather the readiness with which the students turn to it.

There seems to be some tendency for those clusters of students who were the first to become very discouraged with the class to also be the first to move into Early Enactment. This may have to do with their higher expectations or commitments to the class at the beginning. Thus they are frustrated faster than other groups but also have more ideas on how to work their way out of this frustration. The cluster 5 students are the leaders of the early Enactment phase, going up very high on both Enactment and participation at data point 11, while most of the other students are still discouraged and anxiously dependent. For this group, the teacher's tendency to be reactive and facilitative and to encourage student initiative at this time seems to be a crucial factor in reducing their need to be hostile and counterdependent. The reactive style implies respect for students ideas and worth, and that kind of freedom is what the cluster 5 students thrive on. For the anxious dependent cluster 2's the reactive period also seems crucial in bringing out their potential to enact, for they want to try out some independence of their own, and when students are encouraged to think up their own ideas and present them, the cluster 2's seem to welcome this opportunity. The cluster 7 students have by now discovered that their Exhibition and Support will not be welcome to the teacher as the term progresses (the beginning of this Enactment phase marks the final downfall of Exhibition as a student strategy). They turn to Enactment at this period as a more effective way of pleasing the teacher. Part of their new adaptation, though, is involved with lower participation rates, while the participation of clusters 2 and 5 increases with their Enactment. Finally, clusters 3 and 4, the independent groups who were the first to try out a little Enactment very early in the term, are quite comfortable in the setting that is brought about by the teacher's new strategies and the onset of Enactment, and they easily join in and play an important part.

The pattern of Enactment at this phase of the class development does not provide us with a picture of the optimal state a classroom might attain. It is probably difficult for the teacher to appreciate the tentative Enactment attempts of cluster 2; the continuing fears of this group and their lack of practice and skill in independent thinking lead to not very high quality performances. And while the cluster 7 students have realized that they need to try Enactment instead of their Exhibition-Support pattern, they, too, are likely to be unskilled in this at first, and their early attempts will usually be lacking in depth and creativity. Cluster 5 has drastically reduced its contention and challenge for this Enactment phase, but its members are still threatening to the teacher because of their past performances, their occasional flare-ups of rebellion, and their skill in using creative Enactment as a way of competing with the teacher and the other students, for positions of power and competence in the class. The Enactment of clusters 3 and 4 is quite low on threat and high on productivity at this stage, but the cluster 4 students have only limited commitment to the field and thus only a limited potential for contributing to the discussions. The puzzling lack of fit between the cluster 3 students and this particular classroom setting, which will later cause them to be extremely discouraged, is probably beginning to emerge in this early Enactment phase. Finally, cluster 1, the traditional passive students, and cluster 6, the low-Enactment, rebellious students, do not participate in this early Enactment period for a long time. For cluster 1, the need to feel prepared by the teacher for tests and other evaluative procedures is more important than the chance to take part in creative discussions where their own ideas develop, so they are not very comfortable with the combination of the teacher's Reaction and the students' Enactment. The reasons for cluster 6's failure to participate in the Enactment are somewhat different. Rather than being compliant, they are still very much involved in Contention and Challenge. One of their problems is the part of them that is authoritarian and that keeps them from being able to enjoy and make productive use of a low-structure situation. Also, this cluster is very involved in the competitive struggle for power and may feel somewhat upstaged by the cluster 4 and 5 people who are able to display a great deal of competence and gain status in this Enactment phase.

There are reasons, which are general to all students and probably to all classes, why this early Enactment is not as good as later Enactment phases can be. The teacher and the students usually do not know each other well enough yet to work together in highly productive ways. The students have not as yet been very thoroughly initiated into the skills and orientations necessary for really fruitful contributions to a discussion of the field, nor to the teacher's interpersonal style and preferred ways of dealing with the field. The teacher, on the other hand, has not yet figured out the particular ways in which the students of this class differ from others in their needs and their potentials. He may feel at times that he is being told by some students that they are so competent that they no longer need him in a special capacity while he is blamed by others for whatever dissatisfaction they may feel with the class. He has not yet found a satisfactory role for himself which could at the same time allow students to grow and contribute within their own framework. It seems that in some universal developmental sense, the Enactment generated this early in the class, while very important as a step toward what comes later on, will not be as satisfactory as teachers and students might hope.

The teacher's Dissatisfaction starts to trail off during this time, but for the reasons given above it does not disappear completely. The teacher is bound to be happier with this performance than with previous ones, but it still is a long way from being what he would consider a truly successful class. His willingness to employ a reactive, facilitative style during this period may express his desire to protect and nurture the students' first real attempts at independence because they have great potential. But, as we have seen, he may find much of this early student enactment either dull, shallow, or threatening. Also, he is likely to feel that the class is moving too slowly, that there is a great deal to be covered, and that the students' efforts in this direction are rather fumbling compared to the speed and efficiency with which he could present the material. He may see this early enactment as, to some extent, like a child trying for the first time to tie his shoelace when it comes loose on a walk. His mother will be glad to see him make any advance toward self-reliance, but after watching him fumble with the laces for a while, she may decide to do it for him, thinking that for the present it is more important to get on with the trip. Finally, he has not yet been able to find a satisfactory and rewarding role for himself within the context of student Enactment. For somewhat analogous reasons, the student factor of Discouragement persists throughout this phase. This is less true for clusters 3 and 5, who are perhaps most genuinely ready for and comfortable and satisfied with this time in the class, but the other students seem to continue to feel somewhat depressed and apologetic about their own performances and the teacher's reaction to them, as well as discouraged with the overall development of the class.

This student discouragement is also directly related to the fact that the teachers tend to retain their Puntiveness throughout this phase. As always, reasons for this will differ among the teachers. One is that they suspect, perhaps correctly, that their Punitiveness has already played some part in the students' attempts to improve their work. Another point is that Punitiveness has not proved to have the feared effect of totally alienating the students. Finally, the teachers do not want to have to place all blame on themselves for their nagging dissatisfactions and can easily feel justified in shifting some of the blame on to the students. So even as we find the teacher warmly encouraging the students' tentative steps, he is also making certain that they remain aware of the blame that would befall them were they to stop making a satisfactory effort. Especially for the less confident of the students, like those in cluster 2, the Punitiveness increases student Discouragement.

On the more positive side in this phase, one factor that begins to drop out of the teacher's repertoire is the previous high loading on Display. This pattern was a common one so long as the students' response to the teacher seemed cold, but now that students have begun to make a gratifying identification with him, he no longer finds himself as tempted to rely on it. We also find in this period that Apprehension has plummeted to a new low in the face of greater responsiveness from the class.

As a result of some of the problems inherent in student Enactment at this time, this period turns out to be a short one. Nevertheless, it represents an important advance over previous patterns of interaction. While the teacher's dissatisfaction may not have lifted completely, his despair about ever getting the class off the ground has been overcome. And while the students do not exactly have cause for feeling triumphant at this point, they have certainly improved their position a good deal. Moreover, they have had a chance to discover the possibility of Enactment as a way out of the uncomfortable status of Anxious Dependence.

The Teacher Takes Control

The early Enactment period continues for a few sessions, the teacher maintaining his facilitating, primarily reactive style. After a certain duration, however, the teachers make a more or less conscious decision to step in and take a greater measure of control. They seem to feel that the students have been given a chance to develop their ability to work independently and that this ability can be called on later in the term. But because of all the imperfections in student Enactment discussed above, and because of the teacher's dissatisfactions with their own roles in the class, they seem to feel a need at this time to move into a more active, intensive style.

If the teacher is wise, he will avoid doing anything to belittle the students' achievements. He is in the position of the coach who says "Good try. Let me show you one more time, though." Any hint of, "Well, you had the chance to run the class and messed it up—now it's my turn" is bound to drive Enactment underground for a long period. Perhaps even more important is the way in which the teacher deals with the emotions stirred up in the students by his takeover. If he avoids discussing them with the students, it is likely to be much more difficult for the class to create a late Enactment phase, than if he pays serious attention to the students' feelings.

One example of a transition into greater teacher control occurred in Mr. B's class. Everyone had recently returned from a short holiday which broke the continuity of a previous phase marked by student-led discussions. Mr. B had finished handing back a quiz and handling the inevitable arguments about the fairness of the grading.

> *Mr. B:* I would like your permission to close discussion on the quiz, and I would like to lecture uninterruptedly, that is, as a departure, for about ten minutes on child-hood perception, and if you have any questions, I want you to restrain yourselves, and make notes, or . . . or . . . Yeah, Maury.
>
> *Maury:* I have just one request. If you go too fast, can we tell you?
>
> *Class:* Laughter.
>
> *Mr. B:* (Warmly) Yes, you may raise your hand if I'm going too fast, Okay? The reason I'm kind of insisting on this pattern without asking you how you feel about it is that there is information which is critical for our takeoff for discussion. I want to go back to the passage I read from *Look Homeward Angel.*

Mr. B asked for ten minutes, but actually this interaction marked the temporary end of the persistently reactive style he had employed throughout the previous period. Although a few student-led discussions were scattered through the next few sessions, Mr. B became increasingly determined to change his style. A few sessions later, we see him continuing his push toward Proaction.

In the previous session, Maury, a member of cluster 6, had presented some material on unconscious motivation as grounds for a discussion. Before it was completed, however, his presentation had been interrupted by two or three cluster 5 students who had spent the remainder of the session arguing that there is no such thing as unconscious motivation. Mr. B began the next session by telling the students that in considering that discussion, he "was thinking that there was some material that I didn't give you that might make the idea of unconscious motivation easier to accept." After saying this, he lectured for some time about indications of the reality of such motivations.

At the end of that lecture, he discussed further his reactions to the rebellious discussion of the previous session. "I think the problem with the discussion was this," he told them. "Maury was working very hard to proceed from a basic assumption of motivation and not to question this. And I think when we talk about Freud and Erikson this is the way we have to operate at first. We've got to understand what the person is saying, understand their theory. Start with the assumptions and don't question them to begin with. I think you can only effectively criticize and discuss a theory after you've understood how it works. So what I view now, in retrospect, as a subversion of the discussion by those who were—wanted to say 'Well, how do we know there's unconscious motivation?' That's not a bad question, but what Freud was trying to do—which was to work with the concepts that were already given to us; I think this was subverting the purpose of that particular discussion—so I think the points that George was trying to make were very good points and things to come back to, uhm, at a later time. Therefore, I'm not saying that these other directions we were taking were irrelevant. I'm saying temporarily they diverted working with the theory. I'm not trying to say this as something that's—it's not an evaluative judgment . . . I'm summarizing what I thought I heard people saying towards the end—we were kind of, that is, going around in circles. I don't think the discussion was bad, and I think it highlighted an important problem. That is that only after we've worked with it can we go back and say, 'Well, okay, we know how unconscious motivation works—so what?' " After this Mr. B began a lecture on Freud's structural hypothesis, but interrupted it to say, "I'm really changing the format for awhile to do a lot of talking, to lay down certain concepts."

Of course, not every teacher will combine the feelings and strategies indicated by Mr. B's actions. And, indeed, we find generally during this period and the ones following that the number of correspondences in behavior between the four classes become fewer and fewer as the cumulative effect of the group's prior history shapes a unique history for each classroom. As in chess, it is the middle game that reveals the distinctive character of the interchange. Nonetheless, all four teachers evince an impatience with student progress along dimensions of expertise and socialization, and all make moves toward less facilitation and more lecturing.

In general, then, the end of the early Enactment period signals a switch to a whole new pattern for the teachers. They become formal, proactive, and for the first time, move over to the Role Satisfaction side of factor 2. The category that best characterizes the period is the teacher's Showing Dominance, and perhaps the key factor is Formality. The teacher here shuns a sharing, independent style and opts for control and responsibility. The teachers seem to feel confident that they have something valuable to impart and that it is important that it be channeled through formal lecturing at this time.

Looking back, we can see the ways in which both student and teacher behaviors and feelings led up to this transition point. There seems to be a spiraling kind of deterioration that takes place toward the end of the early Enactment phase which leads the teacher and many of the students to feel a need for a change. It is difficult to say what begins this spiral, but we have seen in the discussion of the last phase that there were forces creating some degree of discouragement and dissatisfaction all through that time period. The student discouragement seems to intensify earliest for clusters 2 and 7. They both reach peaks of discouragement several data points before the time when the teacher takes control. It seems probable that the reasons for this discouragement lie in their own and the teacher's dissatisfaction with the quality of their work. Both of these groups have difficulty in maintaining good Enactment without slipping into superficiality or their own characteristic strategies: anxious dependence for cluster 2 and exhibition for cluster 7. Cluster 1 also reaches a peak of discouragement and is low on consent before the takeover. These traditionally oriented students never did enjoy the discussion mode of this early Enactment, and they became increasingly unhappy with it over time. Finally, cluster 6, the low energy and rebellious students, maintain their contention throughout the period and also their discouragement. They do, right at the end, try a little Enactment, perhaps as an effort to compete with the cluster 4 and 5 males at their own game, but this attempt is bound to be unsuccessful, and they maintain their rebellion and discontent throughout.

The independent clusters 3 and 4 students and the heroic cluster 5 students play crucial roles in the downward spiral of Enactment at this time. They are the people who are most comfortable with the process of Enactment and probably most skilled in it as well, so that when they are working hard, their contributions are likely to be among the most creative and productive. But at this time there are problems developing. As the teacher becomes more dissatisfied with student discussions and as his ambivalence impels him toward becoming more controlling, the cluster 5 people begin to change their behavior. They were the first to move into combined Enactment and Consent. As time goes on, they continue to participate a great deal but their Enactment begins to merge into a combination of Exhibition, Contention, and Challenge. We have seen that Enactment could serve for this cluster as a way of proving themselves in competition with the teacher and other males. At this time, having done some good work, they may with this combination of three factors be saying to the teacher, like the young son to the father, "Look, we have done great things, perhaps better than you could have done, and now it is *our* class too and we shall do as we please and need no longer bow to your wishes." There is still much identification with the teacher in the message, but also much threat to him. Another meaning of the Contention and Challenge seems to be a rebellion against the teacher's increasing control. Thus, in the class discussed above, the rebellious performance of the cluster 5 students in questioning the existence of unconscious motivation came after Mr. B had already made several moves in the direction of taking more control. In some classes, like class C, these moves involve tests, and the Contention and Challenge may be aroused by the issue of evaluation. With this cycle of cluster 5 and the teacher, as with the general spiral, each party contributes to increasing the unwanted behavior in the other. As the teacher becomes more controlling and more ambivalent about the worth of his reactive stance and of the student Enactment, the cluster 5's become more angry and exhibitionistic, and the teacher, in turn, becomes more dissatisfied. The cluster 4 students do not join in the rebellion at this point, being less involved with counterdependency and more adaptable to various teacher styles. But they do get discouraged at this time, for they are likely to be disappointed at some of the decrease in Enactment by students. They also prefer unstructured kinds of situations in classes and do not like to see this one end.

At the time when the teacher does take control, there are many radical changes in student factors. First of all, there is, as we might expect, a general decrease in Enactment. Three of the four classes even dip back into Anxious Dependence, as if in response to the teacher's overriding dominance. This decrease in Enactment does not hold for all clusters. Those students who were most invested in the reactive early Enactment period are the most likely to share in this trend. Clusters 2, 4, 5, and 7 all drop very low on Enactment right around the point at which the teacher takes over more. Cluster 1's students, on the other hand, who were not especially happy during the previous phase, fall right into place with the teacher's new proactive role, and begin to enact almost immediately. Cluster 6 follows soon after. They seem to be involved in a number of issues that make this period more comfortable for them. One is that despite their rebelliousness they seem actually to prefer a more directive authority figure, partly perhaps because this situation requires less energy on their part and also assuages their guilt for being rebellious. Another thing that seems to be happening for this group is that the takeover gives them some sense of victory, with the teacher's aid, over their cluster 5 male competitors. Class B, which is discussed above, seems to provide the best example of this process. Maury, a cluster 6 student who had taken little part in the earlier Enactment time, decided to make a presentation on unconscious motivation, a very important concept to Mr. B, at a time when the cluster 5 students were in a challenging mood because of Mr. B's increasing control over the class. Thus, when Mr. B attacked the cluster 5 students for their subversive activity, he was supporting cluster 6 at the same time. On the factor curves, we see that at the point of the takeover, cluster 6 becomes very exhibitionistic, perhaps to some extent crowing over what for them was a kind of victory. They also become suddenly very low on Discouragement, Contention, and Challenge and very soon begin to enact.

Another notable general change in the students' behavior at this time is their high loadings on Consent. Consent provides a great part of the base for the teacher's confident performance all through this period. For clusters like 1 and 6, it seems to indicate a genuine contentment with the way things are going. For others, like the independent cluster 4 students, it means that although they may not prefer this situation, they are willing to give it a try since the teacher seems so invested in it. This cluster reaches a high peak of discouragement at the point when the teacher takes control, but they recover very quickly and move into Enactment. For some students Consent seems more a capitulation to something they are not happy with but see themselves as having no choice about. And finally, the clusters

3 and 5 students who are the most dissatisfied of all do not participate in the Consent at this time and are, in fact, quite contentious.

Student Discouragement is another factor that is important at this period. The teacher is less dissatisfied, since he has been able to redeem his confidence through strong action, but the students have no such path to take at this time. They are likely to feel depressed over the fact that the teacher felt the need to interrupt their own attempts at work and begin to do more of it himself. No matter how tactful he may be at this time they will probably feel somewhat rejected and upstaged by the potency of his performance. The curves for clusters 1 and 6, as we might expect, are exceptions in this case, since these students tended to want the teacher to be more directive. They reach peaks of Discouragement late in the early Enactment phase and then drop off very rapidly when the teacher takes more control. But clusters 3, 4, and 5 have very high peaks of Discouragement right at the time of the takeover. The cluster 4 and 5 students become less discouraged before long, but the change at this time has a more permanent effect on the cluster 3 students. Their Discouragement curve is low up to the point at which the teacher takes control, when it shows a sudden increase and remains high for most of the rest of the class. It looks as if the cluster 3 students, who were enacting right up to the end of the last phase, are disillusioned and depressed by the takeover, feeling that it means they have failed just when they thought they were doing well.

We might ask at this point about the effect of the manner in which the teacher handles this takeover on his later relationships with different students, making use especially of the material quoted previously from Mr. B's class. As we said before, the two most relevant aspects of the teacher's performance seem to be the degree to which he implies that the reason for his increased control is the failure of the students and the degree to which he takes seriously and is able to deal with the feelings aroused by this move. Mr. B, in his earlier steps toward increased control, was tactful and careful not to say anything about student failure. But he did not seem to consider that feelings would be stirred up by his more controlling behavior, and thus when some students started to become discouraged, anxious, and dependent, and especially when the cluster 5 students became angry and rebellious, he was unprepared and responded with anger himself. In class C when there was a good deal of anger and anxiety in the room after the first exam, Mr. C took a session, the one presented in Chapter 3 of this book, to explore and try to understand and deal with those feelings. This seemed to make a big difference to all the students, and especially to cluster 5's, who worked harder later in this class and became closer to the teacher than any other class. But in class B, the teacher just announced the change in session 26. ("I'm insisting on this pattern without asking you how you feel about it.") And in announcing it, he tended to deny his own as well as others' feelings, as when he said, "It's not an evaluative judgment" but, at the same time, called the behavior of some students in the previous discussion "subversive." Also, he seemed to be insisting that not only must they be willing to listen to his point of view but that they must not disagree with him until they were better informed. This kind of attack on the legitimacy of rebellion and even on certain kinds of independence is bound to drive many students away, and in this class the cluster 5 students were angry and withdrawn for a good while after this session.

From the teacher's point of view the period after he takes control tends to bring many improvements. For one thing, the early Enactment phase has played an important part in dispelling some of his worst fantasies about the students. He can no longer imagine that they are a bunch of unresponsive dullards who like his subject little and himself less. They have shown themselves to be capable of involvement and intelligence. And, if their first Enactment is still mixed with many unresolved affective issues or if they are still somewhat unskilled in dealing with this particular field, that is no more than could be expected at this stage of the course.

The teacher now seems more capable of maximizing the potentialities of a number of his roles. The students' Contentiousness has greatly decreased, reflecting a willingness by most of them to defer to the teacher at this time. Thus he is freer to use his own judgment in the formal authority area. Moreover, the experience gained as the term has progressed has given him more competence in this area and in the additional roles of expert and socializing agent, as they relate to the needs of this particular group of students.

The strongest addition to his repertoire, however, is his new ability to make use of the ego-ideal function. At earlier periods fulfillment in this role was blocked by a number of things. The students, being caught up in their own achievements, were not as interested in his own perspective as they might have been. They identified with him and were grateful for his facilitation of their efforts, but earlier his role did not afford him enough opportunity to be a central exciting leader of the class who was both respected and needed. Now the students are willing to let him take such a role, and he can also sense that by now they understand better and share more his intellectual goals. For this reason, his new excursions into the ego-ideal realm have little of the ambivalence and defensiveness characteristic of his earlier bursts of Display. Rather, he appears at home with the function of offering the students a vicarious experience of his own excitement and involvement in the field. It is little wonder that all of these advances snowball into a long-postponed break-through into Role Satisfaction. This satisfaction appears at about this time in all four classrooms and is remarkably persistent from this point on.

An example of the kind of relaxed, effective performance we find some of the teachers giving as they hit their stride during this stage is session 25 of Mr. C's class. At the beginning of the session, a problem arose in that Mr. C had forgotten to bring some mimeographed material to class, but he quickly suggested a solution in a casual, friendly manner. Then he began to lecture on the work of Piaget, in an energetic, enthusiastic manner: "Piaget is to psychology now what Freud was 50 years ago. That kind of depth, thinking—a real trailblazer. And it's very clear that movement in the field now is very much along his lines." As his lecture continued, students occasionally questioned him. Their questions were extremely useful in clarifying the lecture and tying it to other material that had been covered in the course, and Mr. C often began his replies with compliments on the intelligence of the question.

To illustrate the idea that a child lacks the ability for empathy, Mr. C gave the following example: "What do I do in the classroom? I see what I get across by watching. I take a person and I throw myself into that person. I become you and I listen to myself lecture in class and I try to understand what Mr. C is saying. Or, like when it comes to exams you put yourself in my position and try to psych out what I'm going to ask. You see, a child can't do this." In this one example, Mr. C managed to blend effective performances in almost all of his roles. The general tenor of the lecture, of course, is an expert one, with overtones of socializing students into new viewpoints and methodologies for studying the field. In his onrushing enthusiasm and in his taking an example from the immediate classroom situation on which to demonstrate the theory, he shows the excitement and relevance the subject holds for him, thus providing himself as an ego-ideal for the students. The fact that he can use the matter of examinations as an example demonstrates that he feels little of his previous ambivalence about presenting himself as a formal authority. Finally, his personal revelation about how he lectures catapults him out of a frozenly formal role and makes him more of a peer for the students.

One dividend of this period may be an increase in mutual trust between the teacher and the students. Both parties are much better acquainted with each other than in earlier stages, and there is an awareness that each now holds a degree of respect for the other. Of course, this is more true in some classes than others. In some classes, for example, this trust may have been seriously impaired by the teacher's implied belittling of the value of student contributions during his switch to proactive Formality at the conclusion of the Enactment period.

As we have mentioned, divergences among classes are on the increase during the later periods of the term. We could see in our examples of early sessions that the personal attributes of the various participants in the classroom helped precipitate differing types of conflicts in the different classes. Some of these conflicts are resolved or at least lose much of their intensity as time goes on whereas others intensify or lead to new crises. At any rate, there is a whole range of relational issues which may or may not have found some resolution by data point 25 or so. Has Mr. A managed to overcome his feelings of depression and incompetence, for example, or has Mr. D's hostility been integrated into the classroom in a way that does not disrupt all student attempts at work? Or, to cite some more commonly encountered issues, has the teacher realized the potential of the energetic and rebellious cluster 5 people to contribute to the class or does he see them only as unwelcome competitors? Were the teacher's early moves to quiet some exhibitionistic cluster 7 people when they threatened to run away with the conversation deft and easily accepted, or did they arouse fears of speaking freely in all the students? Has there, for another example, been enough interplay among the individual students to make them feel part of an integrated class or do they still feel they are in a group of strangers?

The questions we might ask are numerous, and the answers are as diverse as the number of classes we choose to study. Where few of these issues have been satisfactorily resolved, the class will have little chance of transcending the formal lecture format and may even regress now and then to styles more suited to continued work on problems that were not resolved earlier. In some classes, however, many of these issues have been successfully resolved, and this success has removed many of the original blocks to classroom work and contributed to feelings of competent strength on the part of both students and teachers. In cases such as this, we may find scattered late sessions where increasingly satisfactory classroom relationships occur.

Late Enactment

As the teacher continues through the lecture period, his trust in the class increases steadily. The students are less withdrawn and retentive, they seem to be working harder, and their questions grow in intelligence and maturity. The students, for their part, provided that a number of the issues we touched on above have been solved satisfactorily, are better prepared than ever to assume more responsibility in the class.

The teacher's first tendency, in this case, will be to downplay Formality and begin to act more in keeping with the Colleague pattern. The teacher may continue doing the greatest proportion of the talking, but he begins to treat the students more as friends and equals, to tell stories from his personal history, and to adopt a casual style. In classes such as Mr. C's, where earlier issues have been dealt with well and where the teacher is able to maintain a collegial stance for prolonged periods late in the class, we are struck by the degree to which many different kinds of students can be satisfied at this time. Sometimes teachers worry that with such a variety of students, each having very different needs and desires, one could not possibly conduct oneself in a way that would make use of the uniqueness of each and come close to satisfying all. But in the best of these late Enactment periods in the class, there is room for the integration of many different styles and contributions from both teacher and students. And while not all the different clusters may be working at exactly the same time, they all seem to be able to find productive and satisfactory resolutions at some time during this phase in the good classes. The rebellious cluster 5 students are eager to work together with a teacher who is strong himself and respects their strength as well. The compliant and dependent students who are worried about grades are relieved of much of their anxiety because there is plenty of factual material being presented and discussed. If the teacher has, in addition, been able to reassure them about his respect for their intellect and his interest in them as people, they may be able to try some Enactment as well at this time. Cluster 2, for example, in some classes has a very strong period of Enactment late in the class. Finally, the students who have been relatively independent all along are able within the proactive colleagial framework of this period to enjoy contributing and discussing their own ideas.

Dialogue chosen from various portions of one of Mr. C's classes from this period gives evidence of his shift into a colleagial lecture. We would also note the complexity of the student questions and the teacher's ability as an ego-ideal to give the class the benefit of his own experience and make theory relevant to everyday life. The session has begun with a decision on when to hold the next quiz.

> *Mr. C:* I don't feel any better about exams than you do. I just came back from getting one back today myself. I'm mad at the instructor and everything—I'm going to kill him. (laughter); I've got an appointment tomorrow. I'm going to yell and scream at him . . .
>
> *Students:* Laughter.
>
> *Mr. C:* He doesn't know what he's in for. Everything you do to me, I'm going to do to him . . . Well, onward. Today, I want to tie up a considerable amount of psychosexual theory.

Mr. C lectures for some time, answering occasional questions.

> *Mr. C:* . . . Later in his career, he suggested that aggressive impulses become fused with the libidinal, or sexual ones, and play an important role in the anal stage.
>
> *Catherine:* Did he say anything about biological determination of these changes?
>
> *Mr. C:* Okay, now this is going to represent a problem.
>
> *Catherine:* Well, what did he say determines going from stage to stage?
>
> *Mr. C:* It is, in a sense, the distribution of, or the locus of, sexual energy. Where it is located; where it derives its primary sense of gratification from . . .

He lectures further, explaining the concept of sublimation.

> *Mr. C:* So that's what finger painting is all about. I used to use a lot of . . . I had one kid I worked with, a seven-year-old kid, who liked to use flour and water. We'd take this big batch of flour and water, mix it up together. Then, what the kid wanted to do—and I had no idea why he did this—he would take one of those powdered brown paints, mix powdered brown paint into this flour and water. Now obviously, the

anal implications of this were quite clear. This was a seven-year-old kid. Why brown paint? Why not red, white, and blue? He was just impossible if we ever ran out of brown paint. No other kind would do.

He continues to discuss anal character types.

> *Mr. C:* . . . So he said that the three traits of an anal personality are, let's see, what are they? Parsimony, that's one. Parsimony, orderliness . . . Yes, Richard.
>
> *Richard:* But that seems to me to be just the opposite of the anal thing. I mean . . .
>
> *Mr. C:* So you say all of these qualities are the opposite of smearing, and, and . . .
>
> *Richard:* No, no, not all of them. But some. Like orderliness.
>
> *Mr. C:* Well, now, it's clear that there are really two distinct kinds of anal pleasure . . .

He explains and lectures further, covering the concept of fixation.

> *Mr. C:* So what kind of wife would a guy like this look for. Gee, I see that I'm integrating a cool unit on mate selection. It's not really like that, believe me. But for pedagogical purposes . . . So he might, instead of looking for a girl who will help him move up the ladder, he might look for a girl who can do only one thing—take care of the kids. But, look, to get back to this oral dependent guy. What about the kid who grows up with a mother who's always indulging him? Indulging his every little need. And some mothers are very seductive toward their children. Remember I told you about Paul? Now clearly his mother had a nice sexy relationship with him. Look, I have a relative, who is a brute of a guy, he's about six foot, very effeminate, and he has various problems going along with that, and she just indulges his every dependent bid. Just think of this 16-year-old kid crying because he can't handle the world, and his mother cuddles him, and he puts his head on her breast, and there's all this dependent, sexual . . . you know.

The lecture continues, returning to anal fixation.

> *Mr. C:* So you hear them saying, especially about the middle class, that someone collects money as a derivative of the pleasure of holding feces.

> *Ray:* Hasn't there been some kind of a study done to find out whether more successful people have this kind of toilet training, or . . . ?
>
> *Mr. C:* Well, you will find, you see; the point is, that being somewhat fixated at the oral or anal level is not necessarily so terrible, because a little bit of being anal is . . . Okay, like most researchers who are very systematic and orderly, or accountants, for example, have to be a little bit compulsive. Otherwise, they couldn't function in their job. So it's quite functional. It's not so bad.
>
> *Ray:* How do you handle something like toilet training?
>
> *Mr. C:* Well, how do you handle any of these issues? You've just got to be a reasonable person. You're asking me for a magic formula. I just don't know. I think flexibility is the key issue, the ability to sympathize with and know your child.
>
> *Ray:* Then I guess the main thing would be to avoid extremes.
>
> *Mr. C:* Yeah, I'd say so.

As the teacher moves toward a Colleague pattern, he also finds that the time is ripe for dropping his Punitive thrusts. The students are working creditably, and threats and blaming have become an unnecessary hindrance. At about the same time, partly as a result of this switch, partly because of their own growing self-confidence, most students' Discouragement trails off, never to return. The students have some record of achievement behind them acting as a buffer against the loss of confidence. Since Role Satisfaction for the teacher also remains high, the issue of depression in the classroom has been pretty much transcended as was the issue of anxiety before it. The drop in these disruptive emotions brings a concomitant drop in hesitation. The remaining classes are less tentative, more straightforward, and they accomplish much more than most earlier classes.

The other fact to note is the return of Enactment in some classes. Growing familiarity with the teacher's style and subject have given the students more potentiality for effectiveness in cooperative work, and the teacher's switch into a Colleague stance makes possible its actualization. This late Enactment is clearly evident only in some classes, of course, and even classes that do reach this stage do so only in their best moments. Nonetheless, many classes have their most successful periods during this part of the term.

The Enactment we do find here takes place in a slightly different setting from that appearing in the early Enactment phase. At that time, we found a reactive teacher responding primarily as a facilitator to the statements put forth by the students, using accepting and resisting to shape their output toward greater socialization. This teaching style both reflected a situation where the teacher felt he knew far more than the students and was acting as a guide for them. The teacher also acted rather cautiously at that time, afraid that any thoughtless move could severely harm the young sprouts of student initiative.

Now the situation more greatly resembles an exploration team whose leader just happens to know the terrain a little better. The chief aim is discovery, and anyone who can make a contribution is welcome. The students make use of their ideas and resources; so does the teacher. To this end, he makes his contributions without giving up his proactive style, and these are paralleled by the students' Enactment. This picture is, of course, correct only for the best moments of this phase, but no other period comes nearly as close to this ideal as this one does.

Separation

Whether the classroom in its last stages has neared this ideal or not, whatever issues have predominated in this phase are eventually overshadowed by a new concern, the approaching end of the course. An interesting two-pronged phenomenon occurs here. On the one hand, the *dramatis personae* begin to withdraw from the here and now and to take a longer view. The course is not eternal and all-important, they realize. On the other hand, the last few sessions usually include a drive to cover as much material as possible and to resolve as many outstanding affective concerns as possible before the end of classes and the final exam.

This time in the class is notable for the number of terminal reverses in factor patterns. In some cases, there is a drop in the energy and continuity needed to sustain the work phase; in others, there are radical attempts to correct long-term imbalances while there is still a chance. Sometimes there are regressions to earlier stages in the class' development. At the same time, we find a number of new phenomena specific to this period.

There are great differences among teachers here in the way in which characteristic themes are handled. One example is the way various teachers manage factors 1 and 3. Mr. B drops his Colleagial stance around data point 31, lectures uninterruptedly for about five sessions, then chooses a reactive, colleagial note on which to end the class. Mr. C, on the other hand, retains his role of Colleague almost until the end, then enters in a surge of proactive Formality in the last two sessions as he drives to prepare the class for the final. What is evident is the need both to retain a colleagial style and to cover a great deal of material.

Three sessions from which we chose close to the end of the term illustrate two different ways of dealing with Separation. Mr. B, in his next-to-last session, appears relaxed and casual. He retreats from his nonstop lecturing of the preceding few sessions to the more reactive style he had favored during the late Enactment period. The students respond with an intelligent discussion concerning possibilities for ego development in utopian societies. The session has a warm, friendly tenor and the students appear proud to be working with such great understanding of the values (and jargon) of the field.

Mr. A tries in his last two sessions to transcend, finally, his conflict between his roles as formal authority and facilitator. He accomplishes this by turning the leadership of the discussion over to a student and withdrawing for long periods of time, a radical departure for his class. The student discussion turns out to be enthusiastic, if a bit tentative, and much of it appears to reflect affective concerns springing from the classroom relationship. It is hard to tell to what extent the content of the discussion does relate to the classroom situation itself, but we might remark that many of the content concerns appear to parallel events in the classroom. For example, the students argue about whether Frazier, creator of the utopian society described in B. F. Skinner's *Walden Two*, is really a part of the community he created. Meanwhile, Mr. A sits silently at the edge of the circle, and many seem to be wondering whether he is still the formal authority, or simply another member like themselves.

As the session progresses, Mr. A is inevitably drawn to speak out on one issue. When his statement is followed by silence, he seems at a loss, then says, "Now someone disagree." The students appear to feel they are in the bind they have been in throughout the term, namely, that they are asked to disagree with the teacher but are likely to be squelched by his defensive display of superior knowledge if they do so. Mr. A does seem a bit more sincere about wishing to abandon some of his authority, to play a more facilitative role here, however, and students finally respond to his request for disagreement. Like Mr. B, Mr. A seems much more relaxed than usual in this session. Many of the conflicts that have persisted all term still haunt Mr. A's last two sessions, but faced with the prospect that the term is ending and he has little left to lose, he is much more willing to experiment in hopes of overcoming them.

Three late trends bear remarking. One is the sudden drop in Role Satisfaction that we find in two classes. It seems that some teachers, toward the end, shift their frame of reference from the real possibilities within the classroom back to the ideals with which they began the term. The late phases have been gratifying when compared to the early ones, but the class has been far from an unqualified success. Now it is ending, leaving many hopes unfulfilled. The enthusiasm that accompanied the involvement of the late phase is dying, leaving depression or even a sense of relief in its wake.

We find a more common terminal trend portrayed in the rise in student Unresponsiveness. Both students and teachers have had an increasing share of their thought and energy tied up in the classroom process. Now they must find some way to reclaim it for other uses. There are exceptions, as some students are still very involved at the end and are doing some of their best Enactment before and throughout the separation phase. This seems to be especially true of those clusters, such as 3 and 5, who were most upset by the teacher's taking control earlier in the term and who therefore tend to take longest to recover from it and move from somewhat unwilling Consent into genuine Enactment. Also, cluster 2, under certain conditions, may be enacting at the end. Of course, each class is very different, and if the teacher is trying hard to encourage Enactment by a reactive or a colleagial stance, as does Mr. A in the last session, these three clusters are more likely to respond at this point. But as a more general trend, the class's death is not sudden; the participants have typically withdrawn much of their commitment long before the last bell rings. Unresponsiveness, the student version of Withdrawing, surfaces four or five sessions before the end. The teacher, in keeping with his professional commitment to keep things going and his greater emotional investment in the course, hangs on longer, but his withdrawing also shows through in a reappearance of high scores on Apprehension right at the end.

Even as this process occurs, we notice activity of a different kind in two other factor patterns, Warmth and Display. These are linked, in the two classes where they are most evident, to a decline in Contention. What is happening here is that teacher and students are reviewing the class's progress and are congratulating themselves on a job well done. The work phase is over, the distancing aspects of some previously necessary roles can be relaxed, and there is a celebration replete with warmth, relaxation, and triumph. Not surprisingly, this pattern is most evident in the two classes that had the most sustained periods of the Colleague-Enactment combination, classes in which the students and teachers had managed to create a real and satisfying collaboration.

CHAPTER 7

THE PROCESS OF LEARNING TO WORK

I T is time now to take stock of where we have been and what we have found. We began this study with the assertion that the proper goal of the college classroom is work. This formulation led us to investigate both the task demands of the classroom and the complexity of its interpersonal, affective processes. Clearly our study has explored the affective domain more extensively than the cognitive or task domain; and this imbalance is a weakness we can only hope to rectify in future efforts. In the course of this study, however, our sense of the meaning of work has expanded beyond the simple distinction between task and affect.

The process of learning to work cannot be understood without differentiating among students and without taking into account the development of the classroom over time. Furthermore, it matters which aspect of the task is most salient. By considering the interplay of the following ingredients, we may arrive at a firmer and more sensitive picture of the nature of work: (a) a particular teacher with a particular way of viewing the task and of dealing with students, combined with (b) an array of quite different students each with his own view of the task and his characteristic interpersonal style; to yield (c) a human group which develops its own unique history and its own unique techniques for maximizing (and for blocking) the collective ability to work toward common tasks and affective goals. If these are the ingredients of work, or at least all the ingredients with which we have dealt in this study, then two things follow. First, any statements we make about the nature of work in general will need to be rather vague and abstract. Second, any effort to understand both work and the various impediments to work will need to be quite limited in scope, applying to a particular combination of task dimension, teacher, student subgroup, and developmental phase. Most of this chapter is devoted to the second or intermediate level generalizations. We shall treat each task aspect separately and review our findings on the impediments to work. Before we do that it may be useful to talk briefly about the goal state, the moments of work in the classroom. It may well be that we have spent so much time attending to the unhappiness, anger, or shallowness of the teachers and students in this study that we need first to be reminded that "teaching can be beautiful." As we sift over the data and our own memories, at least three different kinds of work present themselves. We are reminded first of the class periods where, regardless of whether the format be lecture or discussion, the level of task energy is extraordinarily high. The discussion stays on the topic, the students seem especially attentive to the intellectual issues being raised, and one is struck by the low level of distress, quarrelsomeness, or withdrawal. The class seems like a finely tuned motor operating at maximum efficiency.

The first example of work is soon joined in our minds by a slight variation. The second example includes seemingly extraneous material, brief outbursts of irritation or uncertainty, but one is struck here by the ease with which the teacher and/or the students can find the effective thing to say, effective in the sense that one can almost watch the misunderstandings dissolve or the anger and distress become transformed by means of gentle humor, reassurance, or some form of valid and satisfying responses to the emotions involved. In a slightly different sense this, too, is an efficient social institution, one in which there is such flexibility that the teacher and students can spend some time reducing potentially disruptive conflicts and distress without any drop in task involvement and capacity.

We shall return to these two variants of work in the classroom discussion, but only after introducing a third. This candidate for the best session of the term is really quite different. This third kind of interaction, far from suggesting an efficient and flexible task group, might more usually be called the "turning point" or the crisis. To qualify, at least in our view of things, these sessions need to be characterized by more than a vast eruption of emotion, although this may well be part of the picture. Perhaps the contrast in marriages or other intimate dyads between prolonged but unproductive sniping and a genuine fight captures some of the distinction, but the session in question need not be hostile in character. Instead, what seems to cut across these sessions is an intensity of emotional engagement that signals a widespread belief that this digression into nontask activities is purposeful, legitimate, and necessary. Over and over again, as we sift through the important sessions in these and other classes, we come up with periods of quite minimal task activity which seem nonetheless to be directly related to subsequent gains in both task productivity and interpersonal harmony.

If we cast our view over the three sorts of work, what do we find that links them together? In all of them there is a quality of engagement, a serious involvement in what is going on. One's whole sense of time seems altered in a good discussion, of whatever variety. That paradoxic sense of time standing still but in the end seeming to have rushed by is part of these moments. One is free to explore within the present because the future seems so ample, and it appears that no exploration can go so far off course that one will be unable to make appropriate adjustments later on. And yet one is hardly standing still. There is a sense of almost effortless progress and growth.

Looking further into these moments, it appears that behind the intensity and the vivid timelessness there is in each case a high degree of correspondence with the underlying interpersonal realities of the group. The unsteady mixture of task pressures and affective, interpersonal pressures creates a shifting reality for teachers and students alike. The high moment in a class, whether it involves pure task involvement, rage over the teacher's grading policies, or some precise and effective mixture of the two domains, is invariably a moment of high energy liberation. If teacher and students alike are deeply involved in pursuing the intellectual material, then the path of maximum energy will be in the direction of the task, but if the preoccupations of the teacher or the students, or both, run in the direction of unresolved power or intimacy issues, the moment of high energy will be the moment when it suddenly seems legitimate and promising to thrash out issues far removed from the content of the course.

If we define work as a problem-solving process addressed simultaneously to the achievement of task goals and to the reduction of disruptive affect, it is clear that the particular classroom activities we would call work would vary in numerous ways. First, work would vary as a function of which aspects of the task goals were most pressing at the moment. If the teacher and the class were struggling to figure out what Freud meant by primary process, work would look one way, but if the task goal were to facilitate student creativity in choosing term papers, it would look quite different. Second, work would vary as a function of the then-current set of affective or interpersonal problems needing to be faced and resolved. If everyone in the class were really quite content with the focus and progress of the class, the class at work could and would look highly task-oriented, but if the teacher and the class were sinking further and further into mutual distrust and hostility, then to plow on with the content in the same old way would be the very opposite of work. Work is doing what needs to be done, and one point we hope this study has made is that the needs of a classroom group are not addressed solely to intellectual or task goals. Finally, the question of what constitutes work is inseparable from the individual and collective histories of the group members. Work in a class filled with embittered rejects from a callous school system would not be the same as work in a class of docile but self-deprecating college freshmen. Neither would work in a class that has effectively handled its earlier crises be the same as in a class where emotional issues have accumulated and festered to the point where only their direct expression would revive any sense of optimism that they could be solved.

We wish now to address ourselves to the general question: What are the obstacles to work in the classroom? Our analysis of classroom interaction provides us with quite an array of obstacles, and the interaction among the determinants of how the class is going generates a set of obstacles of dazzling complexity. The main argument of the book thus far has been that the teacher and/or the students are deflected from their mutual task goals by the pressure of disruptive affect and by the conflict over task priorities. However, the complexity grows as one begins to take account of the variations among students. Different clusters of students are deflected from their task goals by quite different emotions, and each cluster places its own unique disruptive pressures on the teacher. But even this turns out to be nowhere nearly complicated enough; we have tried to show how, as the classroom develops over time, the teacher and the clusters of students are changing the basis and quality of their relationship in rather dramatic ways. These variations in the stage of group development are associated with different concerns, different crises, and different affective impediments to the task at hand.

In attempting this summary we shall review, one at a time, the six components of the task relationship between the teacher and the class, although by arranging things this way we cannot do justice to the all-important issue of how these task functions are balanced against one another. We shall need to make frequent references to the interplay between these six aspects of the task, but we hope, by separating out these functions, to show some of the major obstacles to establishing an effective task relationship. Effectiveness here means simply that in the pusuit of the particular task function, the larger goal of work is advanced. This is in contrast to outcomes in which disruptive affect gradually strangles and destroys both the task itself and the hope of creating a well-integrated work group.

The Issue of Expertise. If we turn first to the teacher as expert and look back over our data, what seems to be standing in the way of a satisfactory resolution of the teacher-student relationship in this area? The issue focuses primarily around competence. It would seem quite straightforward, really; the teacher has some knowledge to impart, the students something to learn. What can go wrong?

One thing that happens, perhaps on the first day, perhaps only later, and perhaps all term long, can be described as the coming together of a scornful and disappointed teacher with a set of students whose reactions vary from anxiety to depression to bitter resentment over the negative evaluation being received from the teacher. Since the central focus of the teacher as expert is on the course content, it is not surprising that the teacher's concerns tend, often in the early sessions, to include evaluations of what the students bring with them to the class: their "ingelligence," their mastery of the content of previous courses, and their ability to engage in an interesting intellectual dialogue. On the other hand, neither is it surprising that some students arrive on the first day prepared to be terribly impressed by the competence of their instructor, while others arrive prepared not to concede a thing, and all students seem determined to resist as long as they can being defined as stupid, ignorant, or unsophisticated.

There is no reason why this alternative in the affective relationship in the expert area need come first, and in Mr. C's class this phase was, in fact, rather delayed, thanks in part to Mr. C's effusive, whirlwind style at the beginning of his class. The point is that it did emerge in each group, and the causes for this deserve a bit more discussion. There is considerable reason to believe that deciding that the students were not terribly bright served some important purposes of the teachers. It would be comforting to conclude that since the teachers in this study were young graduate students, their purpose in being scornful had something to do with their own anxieties and their need to see undergraduates in this class as less able than the students where they themselves had graduated. By this logic, older teachers would be less likely to be scornful, since their situation is fundamentally different. It would be comforting, but we doubt this is the case. Young graduate students are not the only teachers afflicted by what we might call the "pearls before swine" phenomenon. Many teachers simply have not decided, at least when they walk in the door on the first day, whether their students are worth the time and energy that it will take to convey to them even part of their accumulated expertise. Whether the issue is that the teacher is boosting his own ego or rationalizing his low investment, or some other issue entirely, it is not uncommon to detect in college classrooms the signs of scorn, arrogance, or intellectual superiority that are so bound up with this particular distortion of the expert relationship.

How do the students react when they are faced with what they perceive to be their knowledgeable, intelligent, and perhaps slightly superior teacher? Life would be simple if "students" connoted a set of individuals who reacted uniformly to this or any other press from the teacher. However, the facts are that the students interpret this initial manifestation of the teacher's expertise in fundamentally different ways. Even to talk of clusters is to obscure the uniqueness of the diverse individuals, but we wish to settle for some level of generalization intermediate between *all* students and *each* student. In terms, then, of the eight clusters of students (counting here the low participators as the eighth cluster), we can ask again about the students' reactions.

The most immediate and probably the most lastingly negative impact falls on the students in cluster 2. These anxious, intellectually self-deprecating students find in the teacher's early display of erudition ample grounds for their pessimistic estimate of their chances of survival. What they are feeling and what they are likely to say are not the same thing, however. Given their uneasiness over whether they will fail the course, since both the teacher and most of the other students are so much smarter than they are, it is not surprising that they tend to conceal their feelings of intellectual inadequacy behind a barrage of questions designed to clarify the teacher's demands and standards of evaluation. The message to the teacher as expert is clear: "Am I going to have to be capable of your level of performance in the exams, or can I get by with my usual pattern of memorizing the text and the high points of the lecture notes?" The cumulative effect of these questions on the teacher is also rather predictable. However he feels about the unspoken awe underlying these questions, the teacher may be confirmed in his suspicion that these students are uninteresting and unworthy "grade-grubbers," thus deepening his scorn and intensifying at least some students' feelings of being in dangerous territory.

Two other reactions to the teacher's initial presentation of himself as expert should be mentioned. For many students the teacher's expertise is precisely what they had expected, and their responses convey their already considerable talents at managing such situations. Whether we are talking of the cluster 2 students, with their compliant, eager style of saying the expected thing, the more independent and self-assured students in cluster 4, or the loquacious and attention-seeking students in cluster 7, the teacher can expect to find at least some students who are ready, able, and willing to discuss the readings or a previous lecture without a great deal of distress or affective disruption. However, when we turn to clusters 5 and 6, made up, in our study at least, largely of males, we encounter another outcome altogether. To the extent that the teacher's assertion of himself as expert has conveyed feelings of superiority or has been intertwined with his role as formal authority, the content material becomes the medium through which the messages of challenge and contention will flow. Each content assertion by the teacher becomes a gauntlet flung at the already rebellious students, and they react as if the unspoken message from the teacher had been, "Are you going to believe what I say just because I say so?" Thus begins the fight, carried on at times over the most trivial of assertions, and the content of the teacher's expertise becomes, at least for awhile, hopelessly confounded with his position and power.

These rebellious students, especially in Mr. B's class, help us to identify a second obstacle to the establishment of the teacher as an effective expert. Their goal seems quite simply to have been one of proving that the teacher's competence was definitely not something that could be taken for granted. It had to be proved. In all of the classes the first exam had a similar effect; the great struggle over the correct answers to questions could not help but challenge the teacher's position as expert. However, in Mr. B's class the crisis came earlier and, unfortunately for Mr. B, it came during a period when his own interest and ability in the particular content material was not very high.

The negative outcome in the expert area that we need to delineate here joins together a teacher who seems quite apprehensive, even a bit discouraged with himself and his ability, with a set of contentious, scornful students trying their best to prove the teacher wrong or self-contradictory whenever possible. In many ways this is simply the reverse of the scene painted first; now it is the teacher's self-esteem that is under pressure.

The case material, especially from Mr. A's and Mr. B's class, suggested that we are dealing in this instance less with a direct assault on the teacher's competence than with one of the many confusions we have noticed, a confusion of what is at issue, with the teacher defining the situation quite differently from the students. Most of the serious efforts to challenge the teacher over content matters derived at least part of their considerable intensity from the students' surplus anger over other issues, usually issues directed to the teacher as formal authority. The teacher's power to grade is inextricably entangled with his competence to grade, and the students, especially those in clusters 5 and 6, loaded up any available "content issues" with their more covert interest in challenging the authority of the teacher. It would seem that at least some of these students (especially those in cluster 6) were endeavoring to create an alternative to the evaluation situation where the only issue was one's competence. To the extent that the teacher could be pushed and goaded into an authoritarian panic, defending his answers by reference to his own or someone else's putative authority, then a good grade would simply mean how compliant one had been, thus submerging the more threatening implication that a grade measures competence. In this and other ways the counterpressures do build up, from some because they are angered by the teacher's arrogance and from others because the expertise-competence issue is a useful smoke screen behind which to test out matters of power and control. When to these counterpressures we add the more capable counterpressure of the independent cluster 4 students, whose contention often has a rather condescending tone as they try to enlighten the teachers from the vantage point of their own major field, it is not difficult to understand why some teachers are at this point a bit shaken in their intellectual self-esteem.

The third negative outcome in the expert area, negative in the sense that it led repeatedly to unhandled disruptive affect, was for all the teachers an integral part of the discouraged, unpleasant phase leading up to the midpoint in the term. In contrast to the teacher-scorning-students and the students-challenging-teacher outcomes, this might best be called teacher abdication. Some teachers start off their class this way, sometimes with disastrous consequences, but these four teachers came, via quite different paths, to a point where they felt impelled to pull back from the expert role. Their conscious goal seemed to usually have been one of "getting more discussion," but in each case there were clearly other goals involved. For Mr. D, whose retreat from the expert role stopped short of total abandonment, the goal was to relieve the pressure on the students, to lift the mood of anxiety and gloom, and to alter the students' sullen unresponsiveness. For Mr. B, on the other hand, the decision to move the chairs and to define himself as consultant rather than *the* expert was a retreat as well from the counterpressures on him as expert and formal authority.

Viewed in the light of the literature of teacher-centered versus student-centered teaching (McKeachie, 1967), these shifts might seem to offer some real hope for the classes. How democratic, how nice of the teacher to let the students have their chance to speak! And yet, as the group development chapter made clear, this was not by any means an ideal time in these classes. It may, as we have argued, have been necessary for future developments, but all four teachers recoiled emphatically from the reactive, colleague style associated with this phase. What was happening? What were the disruptive affects associated with this negative outcome?

Perhaps it would be fair to say that all the teachers made two rather crucial mistakes: (1) they underestimated the extent to which they needed to feel good about their own contributions to the class in their role as expert, and (2) they overestimated the extent to which they would find interesting and valuable the task contributions by students. Thus, as facilitators they had set loose a series of discussions which, in their capacity as experts, made them increasingly concerned about whether they were "teaching anything" and increasingly eager to recapture the floor. We have suggested that out of this rather unsatisfying period came some important developments, the main one being an increased sense of respect for the students' capacities—a respect which, while increased, was evidently still not at a level sufficient to permit the teachers to sit back and listen any longer.

If the period of teacher abdication had some negative consequences for the teacher's affective state, what about for the students? Again, one simply cannot generalize across students or clusters of students. The students whose previous contention and challenge had set in motion this retreat were probably the happiest about the whole thing. The independent and the rebellious students did much to keep things going, but to the extent that the teacher felt impelled to have the last (and presumably the correct) word, their pleasure was mixed with mistrust and anger. Other students whose main goal was to impress the teacher found it confusing to have other students as the major audience for their contributions. Undoubtedly the unhappiest students during this period were those in clusters 1 and 2. The cluster 1 students, accustomed as they were to external rewards from on high, became increasingly perturbed at the wandering, "irrelevant" conversations. Their response was to put increasing pressure on the teacher to "wrap things up" and to "tell the class when it is off the topic." Equally distressed, but for different reasons, were the grade-conscious members of cluster 2. They agonized at any sign that the teacher was becoming self-deprecating, hurrying to reassure him that he really did know more than anyone, but even more commonly they found themselves unable to join the student-dominated discussions. Given their preoccupations with grades, they found student comments concerning "stuff which obviously wasn't going to be on the exam" boring and wasteful of class time. The teacher as expert was quite obviously the man to say the things with which one fills up one's notebook. Their guilt-inducing remarks about how this just was not going to help anyone learn the course content hit the teacher in a weak spot, and the teacher's growing impatience with his own abdication can be directly traced not only to his own misgivings but to the anger and distress stirred up in a significant segment of the class.

Thus the particular kind of negative outcomes for students that accompanied the teacher's abdication of his role as expert varied considerably. In the class where the teacher's abdication was extreme (Mr. B's class) the students "carried on," some with increased involvement and some with increasing disgust for their fellow students and annoyance at their "do-nothing" teacher. To the extent that the new egalitarianism seemed "phony," with the teacher only *seeming* to let go of the tether, coming in from time to time to give the "right" answer, a certain frustration seemed to grow up, a feeling of playing games. To the extent that the first negative outcome described above, teacher scorn and student distress, had preceded and still accompanied this phase, there is evidence that the students directed toward each other the scornful and critical mode of being the expert that they had learned in that classroom. The males in Mr. D's class were particularly contemptuous of the females; various individual students bickered overtly and condemned their peers in the ratings and interviews. The import of these outcomes is that one would need to know a good bit about what had preceded any backing off by the teacher from the expert role in order to predict what form the disruptive affect would take. What seems more general is that premature gestures in the direction of student-centeredness are no magical panaceas. Simply to say to oneself and to the class that now is the time to have the class take over the expert function seems, prior to the accumulation of more genuine regard and self-confidence, to head into a *cul de sac*.

The way out of this impasse was, for all four teachers, a strikingly similar move toward the role of formal, proactive expert. Under propitious circumstances this move represented a way station en route to work in a fuller sense, a seemingly necessary step for these teachers as a result of which they were able to integrate their job as expert with the various other teaching functions. Before discussing this denouement, we would now like to discuss the fourth negative variant of the teacher as expert, the outcome that best fits the classes of Mr. A and Mr. D. In neither case was the move to formality and lecturing a temporary and useful step; it became the way to survive until the end of the term. The negative outcome we envision here pairs up a proactive, formal teacher with a class that has many members who have given up hope for much of anything else besides a decent grade and a chance to start over again in another class. Since this acutely negative outcome was an outgrowth of the move, common to all four teachers, to return to a lecture style following the abortive period of abdication, it may be well to look at the period of increased teacher formality and dominance. For all the teachers this move was accompanied by a sense of relief. New horizons opened up; there was the chance to lecture to a group with which one was now rather well acquainted. It was, as we shall discuss shortly, a chance to carry out the gratifying role of teacher as ego ideal. For the teacher to "come on strong" had the effect of clearing the air; it was a welcome change from the tortured and not very satisfying periods of discouragement and early enactment.

If this period was welcome to the teacher, how did the students feel about it? The picture across the four classes is somewhat uneven, but several things are clear. The cluster 1 and 2 students who had chafed under the student-centered regimen were more satisfied, more active, and it would seem, more effective when they did speak. The most negative effect seems to have fallen on the cluster 5 students. Although this effect was minimized in Mr. C's class by the vigor and mutual validation of the confrontation that preceded it, this phase of teacher formality and distance seemed to most cluster 5 students like a betrayal. That this was so can be understood only if one recalls the needs for fusion and identity with the teacher that these males concealed behind their rebellious styles. These students, with their delicately balanced needs for individuality and partnership with the teacher, experienced the sudden return to lecturing as a demeaning rejection of all they had done in the class thus far. After all, had they not carried the ball, defending the teacher from the clinging, dependent students who only wanted to know how to get a good grade? Had they not been the ones who were brave enough to be creative and interesting? The return to formality was not well received by this cluster. Other clusters reacted with less intensity: the passive aggressive students of cluster 6 seemed to be relieved to have returned to familiar territory; the impulsive, talkative members of cluster 7 seem to have tolerated this evidence of the teacher's narcissism as a reasonable move on his part; and the cluster 3 students were rather less pleased with this new development.

The crucial question, however, is not one of how the students reacted to this sudden move away from discussion but of how, or if, the teachers and students ever moved beyond this phase. Mr. D really did not ever alter course after this point, whereas Mr. B and Mr. C, with considerable help from the class, made their way toward a more balanced arrangement, one in which work was possible both because the teacher's expert functions were in and of themselves well handled and because pursuit of these functions did not lessen the effectiveness of the group's pursuit of the other aspects of teaching and learning. Much of this cannot be discussed fully until we have considered the five other aspects of the task, and thus we shall defer further comment until that point in our analysis. We are tempted to conclude from our data that when the proactive, formal phase means not simply a temporary increase in teacher as expert (and ego ideal) but means instead a collapse of the group's ability or willingness to pursue creatively the other aspects of the task, then the group will begin to hold its breath and wait for the end of the term. Particularly crucial here is the gradual elimination from active involvement of first the rebellious students, then the rather personalizing (even sexualizing) students, and then the more independent and competent students, until all the teacher has left to deal with in his capacity as expert are the "good students", who will also drop by the wayside if too much scorn for their not very original efforts is mixed in with his expert functions, and the anxious, grade-oriented students who will probably be taking notes at a furious rate, if they haven't already given up hope of passing the course. Instead of being only one of the tasks facing the class, the mastery of content, since it is so obviously legitimate and since time can be filled so routinely this way, can become the functional equivalent of the ticking of the clock, each fact bringing the class closer to its universally desired termination.

The Issue of Formal Authority. As we turn from the issues raised by the teacher as expert to the equally pressing problems raised by the teacher as formal authority, we are struck by one contrast in the early sessions. In each group studied, the students received a far more confusing and disturbing initial set of messages from the teacher over the question of authority than they did over the competence issue.

The reasons for their initial presentations of self differed from teacher to teacher, of course, but they shared an inclination to display their connectedness with the larger system: the university with its deadlines, grade sheets, and established ways. However, the teachers were evidently far more willing to present themselves as experts than to take full responsibility for the rules and requirements that they were passing along to the students. Thus the confusion began early over who really was to be held responsible. Who can be blamed if some students do poorly or if the methods of evaluation seem incongruent with the desires and abilities of the students? The first gestures of dominance and control seemed rather ambiguous. As the teacher attempted to pass the buck to "the system," often with a clear implication that he, too, was subject to (and chafing under) the vagaries of an insensitive bureaucracy, the student's sense of helplessness grew apace. Is there or is there not a person who will represent the system? Or is there something to be gained by playing the teacher off against the system, setting the teacher against his own authority structure? Many of the students' early maneuverings suggested that questions such as these were on their minds. Thus, one confusion in the establishment of the teacher as the authority derived from the teacher's ambiguous location of himself within the bureaucracy of the university, but other pressures were generated simply by the unambiguous efforts of the teacher to have his own way from the start. Armed with the grade sheet as the final weapon, the teacher unfolded, sometimes with exasperating casualness, the full array of "what-to-do's" and "how-to-do-it's." For some students, and those in cluster 6 especially, the net effect of all this was that they adopted a strategy of resistance, limit testing, and that marvelously subtle gambit of leading teachers into increasingly petty and self-contradictory demands in order to make them show just how asinine authority figures can be. For other students, particularly the compliant and insecure students in clusters 1 and 2, the early emergence of the teacher as formal authority set in motion far more genuine and even pathetic strategies which reflected both the anxiety and the dependency of these students in the face of authority.

But all of this was only one part of the pressure on the students, and it may be that, taken alone, most students could have managed quite well. Unfortunately, shuffled in among the messages that read, "I am the authority around here (or at least someone upstairs told me I could act as if I am)" were messages that greatly confused the scene. These other messages said, in effect, "Since this is college and not high school, and since I am an expert not a drill master, and since you should care about the intrinsic rewards of learning and not the silly grades, then kindly refrain from expressing any anxiety, dependence, or resentment because we have serious work to do." It would be impossible to tell whether this second message was largely in response to the students' concerns, which had been stimulated by the teacher's efforts to establish his position of authority, or whether, regardless of the students' reactions, some teachers would still have needed to send this second message. Be that as it may, the function of the message was certainly a complex one. There is ample evidence in our study that these teachers did not like to be on the receiving end of students' expressions of anxiety. When the teachers moved to emphasize the intrinsic rewards of learning or when they tried to brush aside as childish and annoying the students' efforts to clarify the formal authority issues raised usually by the teacher himself, they were, in effect, trying to disown their actual place in the power structure whose hold over the students was not that easily loosened.

We recognize that different teachers will strike a different balance on these matters, and presumably some teachers can negotiate their way through early authority crises without arousing much disruptive affect in any quarter. We are struck, however, in this study by how regularly the students were put into an extremely difficult bind by the teacher's initial presentations.

Buffeted from one side by clear, but somewhat disowned, pressures to comply with rather specific demands, the students fanned out into reactive strategies which they hoped would accommodate them to this new situation. No sooner had these accomodations begun, all of which defined the teacher as the authority, when they were buffeted from the other side, accused of being preoccupied with authority issues, as evidenced by their anxiety, their quibbling over grading policy, or their excessive acquiescence. If work has to do with a group's ability to confront reality and to develop effective ways of altering what needs to be altered, then this joint pressure on the students must be called a major obstacle to work. Born of the teacher's desire not to be (or not to be seen as) an authoritarian monster, his wish not to be surrounded by passive, uninteresting companions, and his equally compelling need to establish and keep control of the class, this complicated set of pressures generated a serious distortion of the fundamental reality of the classroom.

There were, of course, wide variations in the students' view of this reality. The students in cluster 1, most of whom were females, represented one reality: arriving at this class with a history of effective submission, they were prepared to express by their dependent gestures their full acceptance of the teacher's legitimacy as formal authority. Whatever their educational philosophy, all four teachers had occasion to be grateful for the support given them by these loyal members of the class, but in the early sessions one cannot always distinguish these students from the more irritating members of clusters 2 and 6. Cluster 2 contained students who were so afraid of failing or being proved stupid that they demanded more clarity about formal authority matters than these teachers cared to provide. In contrast, however, the cluster 6 students tended more to see the issues of papers and exams as a challenge to their ability to beat the system. Their consistently irksome efforts to challenge the teacher were not so much in the service of anxiety reduction as they were in the service of their indifference to the established order. But in order to have a system one can fight, short of defeating it altogether, one must have a system which is both clear in its goals and absurd, petty, or ridiculous in its execution of these goals. Thus, from one side the teacher was pressured by students who, for very different reasons, wanted more clarity and more guidelines, while from the other side he was pressured by the more rebellious and, to some extent, the more independent students. The teacher who in one ear hears, "What percent is each quiz going to count?" and in the other ear, "Hey, why don't we all grade ourselves?" is in a very difficult bind. In response to the latter, he may fear that the students will get "out of control," and, therefore, respond with coldness and still further assertions of his authority. To the former, who are pleading for control, he may become disdainful, as if such concerns over grading were clear evidence of a second-class mind and, in the process of expressing this disdain, he will probably end up insulting even more students than those who had provoked him. Another possibility is that, early on or after consistent attacks from the rebellious minority, he may be tempted to deny the reality of his formal position in the classroom.

One of the major distortions of reality to which the teacher can contribute is the outcome that we might call premature or insincere abdication of authority. As in the case when the teacher affects uselessness over matters of intellectual competence, the various gestures of turning over to the class control over grades or work assignments can have many meanings and many effects. The question is one of reality, not of how egalitarian this or that structural change might seem. The crucial issue is one of unilateral versus bilateral transfer of power. The unilateral transfer of power ("All right, class, now you have the right to determine your own grades.") may work, but it also may fail, for understandable reasons. For some students, especially those in clusters 1 and 2, the whole idea of the teacher not playing his "proper" role is distressing and even a little disgusting. But for many others, even those who fervently wish to have more of a say about assignment and grades, the unilateral transfer of power is connected with the not very reassuring thought, "The Lord giveth and the Lord taketh away." If the teacher is still some kind of lord or philanthropist doling out power when he feels like it, who knows what has really happened? "What if we give ourselves all A's?" they begin to wonder; "Will he step in and say that that isn't within our power?"

To return to the issues of competence and mutual respect for a moment, we asserted that the teacher can praise and flatter and turn the discussion over to the students all he wants, but if he does not really trust or esteem them, if he really is not ready to be quiet and listen, and if the students simply do not recognize themselves in all that flattery, then it will create more disruptive affect than it will reduce. Just as work flows out of activities in the expert area only when genuine respect for an increasing number of the participants has reduced the feelings of being stupid or scornful or hurt, so, too, work proceeds in the authority area when an increasing number of the participants feels that the current distribution of legitimacy and power to effect change has been arrived at bilaterally or, more properly, multilaterally.

How does a group come to create a stable authority? What does the evidence from the four groups have to say about this? Two processes seem to stand out: confrontation and the gradual "withering away" of authority issues. The function of the confrontation of these groups would seem to be more one of flushing out the power issues than of causing, in and of itself, a drastic change in the distribution of power. Much of what we have said about the negative or unsatisfactory solution to the issue of authority has revolved around the unreal quality of having the teacher say either, "Get off my back and stop bothering me with your dependency" or "Power? What power? We're all equal here" strategies. As the essential instability of these strategies became clear, usually around the time of the first exam, all of the groups moved into a period of direct challenge to the teacher's authority. In some classes the confrontation was fairly heated; in others the student's anger was stifled and resulted only in a prolonged, bickering fight over exam points.

Our data indicate that the more direct and productive confrontations were led by the rebellious cluster 5 and the independent cluster 4 students. Parenthetically, the very process of expressing any anger or resentment toward the teacher was rather disturbing to the intrapunitive students in cluster 3 and even more so to the tightly controlled and anxious members of cluster 2. The more petty and, in the end, self-defeating sorts of confrontations seem to have been led by the provocative but basically more passive and pessimistic members of cluster 6.

Especially when the challenge was reasonably open and direct, the confrontation provoked the teacher into taking more responsibility for the matters directly associated with his formal authority. "Yes," he seemed to begin saying, "I am indeed the man with the grade sheet, the man appointed by the department, the dean, and the regents to teach, to evaluate, and to send in the grades." If this was one outcome of the confrontation, it may seem surprising or paradoxical that, again especially when the challenge was direct, the confrontation led directly to what we might call the multilateral transfer of power.

Having established that his power and authority were quite real, the teacher then could begin to share it. At this point the sharing seemed less like a gift than a set of genuine concessions to the further realities of the situation as it had evolved. How did this happen? Through responses to a whole series of specific requests; not by a great pronouncement from on high. Examples come to mind: "Yes, that was a lousy question, and you five guys should add a point to your score." "No, you don't have to turn the paper in next Monday if you really can't do it. Get it in as soon as you can." "What shall we do today?" Not great student victories, but developments that contributed, in two classes especially, to the gradual erosion of concerns over power and control issues.

It so happened that the two classes that made real headway on the authority issue ended up with a far more democratic, egalitarian structure than they started with and, we have claimed, they arrived there only after the essentially authoritarian structure, with which every class began, had been revealed for all to see. Furthermore, one class, Mr. D's, which ended up with little progress toward any multilateral transferring of power, was also the class in which an unproductive student docility characterized the last third of the sessions. Does this mean that the move toward democracy is a "good thing?" We are not prepared to argue that it is—certainly not for all teachers. Not only are many of the early, unilateral efforts to create a democratic group by fiat doomed to prove unstable, but we are not even sure that Mr. D, for example, could have possibly been convinced that the students' views on what they needed and what grades they deserved should prevail over his views. What, then, could he contribute to a democratic group but the empty forms of democracy, a miniature of the make-believe democratic forms and pseudo-power which characterize student government councils on so many college scenes? To advocate that the goal of the classroom is work is to advocate that reality be served, not that reality be disguised in the trappings of democracy or any other structural form in which group members cannot be honest to their convictions. We shall return to this in the final chapter, but for now suffice it to say that having advocated that no teacher should create artificial democratic forms, we need to add a few more thoughts: (1) this is not to overlook the options neglected by some *but not all* autocratic teachers of reducing to the lowest possible level the distress and anger created by such structures, and (2) this is not to urge that the students whose blood boils at the sight of power unevenly distributed must sit back and accept this arrangement. Maybe the confrontation will produce genuine concessions.

The gradual withering away of the authority issue is accompanied, in those classes where it happened at all, by an increasing sense of involvement in other aspects of the teacher's total function. Important reductions in the tension and resentment over the teacher as formal authority followed from sessions in which the teacher's expertise provided the teacher with *earned* legitimacy in contrast to the *ascribed* legitimacy he possessed on the first day of class. Similar reductions in disruptive affect followed sessions in which the teacher as a peer, as a person, came into sharper focus. It would be a mistake to assume when we refer to the disruptive affect generated by the teacher as formal authority that we mean only such phenomena as cluster 5's rebelliousness or cluster 2's manifest anxiety. The uncritical identification of the cluster 1 students with the teacher's role and power, and the compliant style that their dependency has produced, are disruptive affects in the very important sense that they disrupt the other tasks facing the class. To the extent that the teacher as expert or socializing agent places a high value on critical thinking, or to the extent that the teacher as facilitator places a high value on originality and creativity, the placid conformity of the cluster 1 students and their adaptation to the teacher as formal authority is as disruptive for their learning as the more dramatic disruptions of any other cluster.

It turns out that the establishment of legitimate authority, as was the case for mutual intellectual respect, is not something one can rush. The natural process of its development seems to include some rather unlikely and often unpleasant way stations. The dependency, anxiety, and self-deprecation of some students cannot be waved away with a magic wand; neither can the anarchic or rebellious inclinations of other students. By the same token the teacher's annoyance at being seen as mean or arbitrary is real, as is his frustration at being constantly challenged by one segment of the class. What we have tried to show is how these potentially disruptive affects lead in two directions: one path leads to the whole array of strategies that either intensify whatever affect is being stirred up or create new and equally disruptive disturbances; the other path leads to work, to the ability to face the reality of the situation and the reality of the feelings stirred up by it and the ability then to develop creative solutions which reduce or bind in the disruptive affect and permit the group to move ahead on this and all other aspects of the task.

The Issue of Socialization. Although the activities of the teacher as socializing agent overlap considerably with those of the teacher as expert or formal authority, different issues are raised in this aspect of teaching, and our focus here will be on the uniqueness of this teaching function and its impact on the students. Given the fact that the teacher stands before his class as the representative and gatekeeper for a whole series of interlocking collectivities (his department and field, the community of gentlemen, scholars, radical intellectuals, or whatever), what kinds of affective disturbances develop over time?

It should be pointed out that not all the students are interested in this aspect of the teacher. The older and more independent members of cluster 4 are just visiting; they tend to have concentration and career lines already worked out. The quarrelsome cluster 6 students and the loquacious students in cluster 7 also seem relatively uninterested in using the teacher as a stepping-stone into some further occupational grouping. One of the most interesting pictures, however, comes from the anxious, grade-oriented members of cluster 2. Although, for many, the fear of failure blinds them to anything beyond or behind the particular course, for a significant portion the world of psychology in particular and of academic (as opposed to religious) views of man can be both liberating and exciting. The professor becomes the one who can and does challenge the teachings of his parents and his home culture; at the very least, the intellectual's value on being able to tolerate ambiguity represents a useful prop for those trying to break free of traditional subcultures.

For two clusters of students the teacher as socializing agent can be very important: the cluster 1 students, with their tendency to identify with the teacher's role and their sense of wanting to be teachers, helpers, or good parents themselves, and the small group of studious and rather depressed members of cluster 3. If the teacher can expect to encounter some who welcome his gate-keeping, and some who are indifferent to it, where do things begin to go awry?

Perhaps one answer will flow from an exaggeration, a parody of the teacher as socializing agent. Consider the parallels between the teacher who represents his field and his significant reference groups and the white racist schoolteacher or the missionary newly arrived among the heathens. The double pressure placed on those being socialized combines (a) the insensitive intrusion of an alien and purportedly superior culture on the "unwashed" and (b) the tendency to defend the "purity of the stock" by not allowing "just anyone" to be passed along to the next screening process. The missionary's optimism about spreading the Word to all men is confounded often by the disheartening, but also rather necessary, conclusion that some people are too stubborn or too hopeless to accept the Word. Whether the missionary in question be a white teacher in the ghetto or an intellectual holding out the allures of graduate school and the professional life, this smugness about the superiority of one's group tends thus to go hand in hand with the conviction that only a few converts have the personal qualities needed to become members of the inner circle.

To separate this double message for a moment, need we elaborate on how the rebellious members of cluster 5 or the needling and blasé members of cluster 6 would respond to the teacher's assertion that his culture is superior to that of the students? Even the independent students tend to be provoked by these assertions and to counterpose their culture, the perspective of their major, against that of the teacher. To the extent that the teacher insists that students must learn the jargon of his field, in this an introductory course, or to denounce publicly the absurdity of either their home culture or that of other fields in which they have taken courses, the contentious students begin to level against him the charge of brainwashing.

The mark of acceptance is subtle and complex, but in our study we found two important ways in which the teacher indicated his approval or disapproval of the student as neophyte. In one the teacher communicated, by his willingness to drift into esoteric or "in" topics with some students, his conviction that here was a student sufficiently sophisticated and interesting to be passed along to a higher level of socialization. But perhaps the clearest and most painful process involved the use of grades. The issue tended to resolve into the distinction between an A and a B.

To back off for a moment, we have the sense that one of the secret rewards for the teacher as socializing agent is his own sense that whatever the outcome of the various battles over content matters, and regardless of how well the students have mastered the material, there still remains a certain elusive quality which they as teachers, but only a few of the students, could be expected to possess. "No matter," says the master of Lowell House at Harvard, "how bright this young candidate for resident tutor may be; if he wears green socks, he's obviously not one of us." "No matter," says the new graduate student teaching freshmen for the first time, "whether I'm challenged over the accuracy of a couple of facts here and there; few if any of the students can master the style of thinking, the tolerance of ambiguity, or the underlying value position which marks one as an intellectual." Given this tendency to comfort themselves with what, given the students' low probability of achieving it, might as well be called their ascriptive status, the grade becomes a terribly important signal to the student: "Stop where you are; try another field or another college," or "Go on into the series of courses at the end of which you will be part of the in group, 'my group.'"

Thus, to give an A or to give special encouragement to a student whom the teacher either does not think will "make it" or whom the teacher does not wish to find at some later date within his inner circle is to "cheapen the currency," to use a phrase heard rather widely in academic circles. But how can he turn off the eager but unacceptable student? There seem to be two ways, at least. To the rebellious, self-assertive, and immodest student, the one who presumes too much that he is already in, one can administer an "objective" test which reveals for all to see that in his enthusiasm to gain acceptance through developing his own unique approach to the field, he has failed to play the part of the lowly neophyte and learn "the basics," the fundamentals of the field. The students in cluster 5, who are particularly poor at playing academic "Mother, may I?" games are thus driven into a position of attacking rote learning and memorization, while the basic issue all along had been the teacher's efforts to screen them out of the selection process. At the other extreme, the students who do master most of the factual material and who do accept their lowly status, how does one screen them out? An essay exam in which it is revealed that they cannot "think for themselves" might help (since obviously one cannot have mere conformists among the elect), but probably the most effective technique used by the four teachers in this study was to reject in class the fawning or overly identified students until they picked up the message that while they might get their B (or even A), they should not expect support from the teacher in "going on," perhaps in some less demanding subculture, like teaching grade school, but not in "the field."

We have talked with what we hope is forgiveable sarcasm about the teacher as a rather smug and rejecting sort of socializing agent. We are convinced that much of the students' anger or what is more serious, their depressed sense of being rejected, flows from this performance of the teacher. But we would be inaccurate to suggest that no work, no satisfactory outcome is connected with this aspect of teaching. As the term goes along, the students in a more successful class, such as Mr. B's or Mr. C's, become less "the masses" and more a set of distinct individuals. More of their talents become visible, and the meaning of taking more courses in the teacher's field becomes clearer. To that extent, then, the teacher may develop more regard for some students and a clearer sense of what they could derive from and contribute to subsequent classes. Furthermore, we would not want to imply that the teachers err only in the direction of overstressing their socializing function. Faced with real and legitimate needs on the parts of the students to find their way, some teachers, perhaps because their own identification with the field is unsteady, tend to conceal or deprecate the means to what students see as worthwhile ends. Perhaps the common elements behind the overstressing and the understressing of their socializing function tend to be that: (1) the teachers, for whom "the field" has had career implications, tend to blur the distinction between encouraging the student to explore more courses and telling him in effect that he should decide "yes" or "no" at this early stage on a career in the teacher's chosen field, and (2) the teachers, by overlooking the complex personal and intellectual histories that the students bring with them, tend to exaggerate the potency of their signal, thus implying that the student is not capable of integrating the teacher's judgment into his own reality. In contrast, the teachers who came to know the goals and skills of the individual students and who could place these in the context of the students' already developing values had less and less difficulty in offering what turned out to be useful information and encouragment for these students in their own private struggle to shape their careers and their lives.

The Issue of Facilitation. By this point in our review of the sources of disruptive affect we can begin to be somewhat economical in our presentation of each teaching function. The clusters that chafed most under excessive doses of the teacher as expert, formal authority, or socializing agent can be expected to react rather well to the teacher as facilitator. Conversely, the students who were perturbed by any departure from the structured, content-oriented mode of teaching can be understood if they resist the teacher's efforts to foster that vague and perhaps unreachable goal of student creativity. There are, however, some interesting and as yet not fully discussed issues buried in this aspect of the teacher-student relations, issues that bear not only on the encouragement of creativity but on the role of emotionality in the development of work.

To sketch the general situation briefly, it would not seem unfair to assert that while some teachers begin with what some students feel is too little emphasis on facilitation and other teachers are rather too permissive, the early sessions in our study were filled with the confusing and double-edged messages we have discussed above. In terms of the facilitator role this early development begins with the teacher sending signals that the students should feel free to mold the general pattern of the course to fit their interests, should not hesitate to express their uneasiness or irritation, and should recognize the teacher before them as a nonauthoritarian helper who is there only to make it easier for them to reach their goals. In actual practice, this injunction to be free is soon mixed with other signals: "Well, in this field we don't view causality quite that way," or "Why don't you bring that up next Wednesday," or "There are, after all, certain constraints on the way in which grades must be turned in," etc.

Why do teachers use (or misuse) the facilitator role this way? And what happens to the students in all this? Most teachers, certainly the ones we have studied here, seem to be only partially at ease with the fact that they have greater knowledge, power, and access to the inner sanctum of their various reference groups. Heaven forbid, they seem to be saying, that because of these differentials this course would encourage mere rote learning, mere conformity, and mere aping of the manners and vogues of the field. What, then, to do? The early facilitator messages, when they are indeed efforts to undo or prevent these dreaded consequences, fail to have the desired effect simply because the teachers are not saying what is true, but only what they wish were true. Given their rather understandable lack of intellectual respect for the students, or their lack of trust in the students' judgment over plans and evaluations, they act to withdraw or negate the very freedoms they have just held out to the students. The consequences, which vary across the different clusters, include the increases in mistrust, resentment, uncertainty, and limit-testing we have already discussed.

One contrast between the sincerely meant and well-grounded efforts to be the facilitator and the unstable, unsuccessful efforts found in the first half of the group's history revolves around the teachers' denials of reality in a vitally important area: the abilities of the students. The premature, unilateral efforts to "give" the students freedom tend to be accompanied by an overestimation of how able and how ready the students are to do interesting work. It is as if the teachers were saying that, in contrast to colleagues who disparage students' capacities, they just know there is in the students a vast reservoir of fascinating ideas waiting to spring forth. Combined with the teacher's apparent unwillingness to stifle these potentialities with an alien (and oppressive) structure, the net result is a message that sounds like, "I expect nothing in particular from you, just that this be a sensational class. And I'm sure you can pull it off."

If we shift from the first few sessions to the discouraged middle sessions, and even to the period of early enactment, we find a major disruptive affect which we have not yet discussed. Beyond the anxiety generated in the insecure and conformist students, beyond the anger generated in those who are sensitive to the insincerity of it all, we find the humiliated and depressed reaction of those who feel they simply cannot fill the bill. We refer here not only to the rather chronically depressed students of cluster 3; we refer as well to both the dependent and the counterdependent students. Cut off from the clear structure within which they operate so well, the more compliant students found in cluster 1 suffer from the awareness that they are indeed lost. But even the males of clusters 5 and 6 begin to flounder. For the "get by" students of cluster 6, freedom in the context of the rapidly rising expectations that accompany the teacher's flattery is not a comfortable situation at all. For the rebellious students in cluster 5 the teacher who provides a blanket assurance of freedom, rather than genuine concessions, and a blanket assurance of his high opinion of all the students, rather than genuine regard for each of them as unique individuals, drains the challenge out of the situation and deprives them of their treasured fantasies of a special partnership with him. Furthermore, as freshmen they are not totally able to believe in their own worth. All in all the early efforts at being the facilitator seem likely to place a heavy load on the students. Perhaps if the teacher did not need to reassure himself of the wisdom of his strategy by overpraising and overestimating the students it would all turn out better.

Here is one final observation on the teacher's excessive or premature efforts in the facilitator direction. For some students the teacher's permissiveness is experienced in quite another way from how the teacher has intended it. To them what it means is that the teacher just does not give a damn about the class, about them as individuals, and about whether they learn or do not learn anything. The students, perhaps especially those in clusters 1 and 7 who count on a diffusely positive and attentive teacher in order to function well, come to see that what the teacher is handing out is not freedom but rejection. Neither the normally acquiescent nor the normally self-demonstrative students of these two clusters are particularly likely to be offended by the teacher as expert and/or formal authority and thus they are particularly hurt by the seeming unavailability of the teacher who would be only the facilitator.

Not all early efforts to play the facilitator role fail and, in fact, an increasing number of these efforts, more and more responsive as they are to the students' rather different needs for freedom, have the desired effect of clearing the path for a student or of encouraging him to follow down an expressed interest. Freedom becomes a process instead of static virtue to be thrust on unwilling students. Perhaps always at the core of being helpful to another who is learning and growing there lies an awareness that goals which are meaningful are not easily formulated and easily reached. Far from being the result of a harsh and total weaning, freedom means a slowly developed capacity to overcome obstacles, and here the teacher's role can become important without diminishing the students' freedom. Toward the end of the classes, we observe that the teacher as facilitator can more easily validate the students' discouragement or frustration, as if to say that "yes, indeed, it is hard." Complaining that something is hard is not always a prelude to quitting, but without the teacher or someone in the class to validate both the importance of the goal and the inevitable difficulties in reaching it the student may be left at the mercy of shame and guilt that he is not progressing any faster. Complaining that something is hard is also not necessarily an accusation. The teacher as facilitator can, by listening, also validate the fundamental separateness of people in their separate pursuits if he can avoid becoming defensive or mistrustful in the face of the predictable signs that the students' tasks are indeed difficult.

If this separateness is validated by the respect of another's goals and another's struggle, it is also validated by the process of leaving room for the other's self-evaluations. It is no surprise that some of the most anxious students found their class memorable especially because of their efforts on an independent project. Given their tendency to feel oppressed by the presence of the teacher and their evidently superior classmates, these and other students profited from the permission to do something on their own. They often chose questions which would have seemed embarrassingly naive to the class, but they went ahead and in the process managed as well to control at least a major share of the right to judge the value of their efforts. By a somewhat different route some of the rebellious males reached what was for them the pleasurable state of feeling that they were working for themselves and not the grade. These students, with their tendency to pursue special interests at the expense of full coverage of the course material, were to a considerable extent free, free from being ordinary and free from the teacher's every demand. The fact that their grade was "below their ability" was probably not a new experience for them. Thus, all the way from the most anxious to the most heroic students, and at many points in between, facilitating relationships did develop as private strugglings somehow not irrelevant to the presence of a useful but fundamentally separate person, the teacher as facilitator.

The Issue of Modeling. The single most drastic effect of the teacher's distress is probably found in the disruptive effect it has on his ability to function as an ego ideal. Even granting the quite different characteristics that will cause students in different clusters to accept the teacher as an ego ideal, the dimension of self-assurance and enthusiasm versus dullness and low self-esteem seems to be important throughout the development of a class.

What stands in the way of the teacher feeling good about himself in the classroom? Even a preliminary answer would take us back to all the entanglements and missed connections already discussed. Each bit of evidence that he is not respected or that he is too respected, that the students are uninterested or distressed, in short, each bit of evidence that disconfirms the teacher's hopes and expectations serves to undercut his self-esteem. Thus, when Mr. A finds that his students are not that easily intrigued by the raging battle between tough-minded and tender-minded psychologists, his performance falters and his own ability to say anything interesting quickly drains away. Other teachers, having communicated in subtle ways that the material now being covered did not interest them very much, would then be thrown off guard by the sudden barrage of contentiousness, and their lectures would become more and more filled with errors and apologetic corrections.

Thus, especially in a small class the issue of the teacher's self-esteem arises early and seems, in our data at least, to be resolved only after a rather complex history. The teacher has some things on his side from the beginning, however. The students in cluster 7, for example, seem particularly prone to believe in their teacher. Why this should be is not entirely clear. Perhaps it helps that in their somewhat narcissistic way they fail to see the teacher or anyone else very clearly and tend, rather, to paint the world in rosy colors designed to reassure themselves that everything is all right. They, and the more depressive students in cluster 3, tend as well to deny the existence of any negative characteristics of the teacher. From both these clusters, then, the teacher receives, at least at first, the sense of being admired as strong and competent. From the compliant members of cluster 1 the teacher receives not only validation of his formal status but an extra portion of idealization; these students tend to identify with the teacher's role and thus he is potentially an important model for their future careers. There are ways to disappoint each of these clusters, of course, but at least the teacher starts off in the plus column with them.

The situation with the rebellious cluster 5 students is considerably more complex. The interview data combined with our impression of these students in class has yielded the following picture. These male students were perhaps more deeply involved in the hope that the teacher would serve as a useful ego ideal than any other students, but their approach toward this goal was stormy and at times alienating. Their seemingly endless processes of testing the teacher derived from their need, in Erikson's terms, to preserve their own integrity and identify while at the same time moving closer to someone worthy of their fidelity. Fidelity was not something the teacher could demand, nor could it survive in the face of the teacher's bland, unconditional acceptance of all students. The teacher was tested to determine both his competence and his ability to enter into a mutually respectful relationship in which more than the semblances of equality would prevail. Those few students in cluster 5 who managed to establish a satisfactory relationship with the teacher did so only after a prolonged period of defiance and mistrust, interspersed with brief periods of joining forces with the teacher.

After numerous false starts, the teachers all managed, although in varying degrees, to arrive at the point of being more self-assured and comfortable with the material. This development began usually with the point, midway in the term, when they took and held the floor for long periods of time. These more formal, lecture-dominated sessions had generally beneficial effects on both the teacher and most students. The rebellious cluster 5 students were somewhat prone to feel left in the lurch, and the intellectually insecure students in cluster 2 tended to feel even more weak and insignificant after a brilliant lecture, but these consequences were not insurmountable. As the lecture phase faded, especially in classes B and C, into a more mutual process of exchanging expertise and interests, the teacher as ego ideal became a more intermittent force in the classroom. The lectures became "lecturettes," and the admirable qualities of the teacher came to include not only what he knew but that he sometimes did not know everything. His estimable qualities came more to be the intensity with which he tried to figure things out. This more accessible ego ideal could join for a while with the cluster 5 males in exploring matters of rather special interest to only some students, but he also could portray, in concert with his role as socializing agent, some of the real pleasures of being a young psychologist.

The Issue of Persons. The last of the teacher's functions to be discussed is that of developing a set of personal relationships which create a climate of acceptance and/or liking in which to carry on the task at hand. Let us say at the outset that we are rather struck by the extent to which, contrary to many teachers' fears, the students do *not* arrive at the class eager for a close, personal relationship with the teacher. We emphasize this now because evidently some teachers have so undifferentiated a sense of the interpersonal options in a classroom that even to imply that the teacher as a person is part of the total process conjures up images of "fun, but no work," "Buddy-buddy," and other distortions of the classroom reality. On the basis of our data we could recount at least as many instances from the early sessions where the teacher made unreciprocated gestures of a personal sort as we could instances of student over-personalness.

If we back off for a moment we can take stock of which students need and expect what from the teacher in the personal realm. Probably no cluster is more involved in the teacher as person than cluster 7. They seem particularly eager to reveal themselves and to have the teacher get to know them. But this is seldom a mutual proposition; at least not for a long while. Despite their joking, friendly, and occasionally flirtatious style, their goal in class is not one of etablishing a friendship as much as it is to be liked and to be vivid in the eyes of the teacher. Thus they find prolonged exposure to a cold and impersonal teacher quite upsetting, but no more so than a premature effort by the teacher to be self-revealing about his own misgivings regarding his performance. All in all, however, this cluster's inclination to focus more on the interpersonal relationship than on the intellectual tasks facing the group constitutes its most characteristic disruptive affect. We would be as concerned about how to reduce their pleasure at attracting and amusing yet another authority figure as we would about how to reduce cluster 2's fear of failure. Both of these affects interfere with the full range of concerns confronting the group. These hand-waving, self-dramatizing students can be turned off, but, as most teachers found out, it takes effort, and it is a rather delicate operation. No matter how annoyed other, less talkative students may be at these cluster 7 students, and no matter how glad they would be to have them be quiet, evidently this cannot be done harshly or with insensitivity without a sudden rush of identification with the victim and a correlated resentment toward the teacher. Thus the teacher as person is constantly communicating to all the students just how trustworthy and decent he really is.

Several of the clusters, to add to the pressure already created by cluster 7, want the teacher to be scrupulously impersonal. The cluster 6 students, for whom the teacher is and should be the representative of the system they are trying to beat, can become particularly critical of the teacher when he becomes the least bit self-revealing. For them, and for the conformist and largely female members of cluster 1, the whole issue of partiality and intimacy seems only to disrupt their chosen strategy. From these and occasionally other students the pressure is clearly to keep things impersonal, objective, and distant. The situation for the cluster 2 students, however, is considerably more intricate. Despite the fact they are usually much too anxious to indicate any personal feelings themselves, their memories two years later of their teacher were particularly likely, if this was at all appropriate, to indicate how much they had gained from the fact that their teacher liked and was genuinely concerned about them. This reaction of being touched by personal attention was something that flowed usually out of events in the later sessions.

Lest we seem to imply that pressures on the teacher to be a person mean only pressures to be warm, we should mention how very important it was to the defiant cluster 5 students that the teacher take seriously their anger and their criticisms. Clearly one way for the teacher to vacate his role as person is to remain bland and unruffled when a student makes a personal attack. Far more than warmth or total acceptance, these and many other students seem to be seeking a quality of personal authenticity in their teacher. As this need goes unmet and they conclude angrily that their teacher is not "for real," their involvement gives way to mistrust and alienation.

Faced as he is with the now familiar cross pressures and conflicting messages, what does the teacher do? Some try too early, before the students are at all capable of handling it (or capable of recognizing the motives behind it), to express the various feelings of uneasiness, discouragement, or irritation that the new class has aroused in them. At least in the classes we have studied we would be hard pressed to locate many times when this move on the teacher's part met with a response that the teacher found satisfactory. However, in two of the classes especially (B and C) we noted in the final third or quarter of the term some dramatic shifts by the teacher in the direction of the teacher as person. We mean here not simply that he was more open but that the students also began to show signs of integrating their prior histories, their current feelings, and the intellectual tasks of the course. They were more able to come up with personal but relevant examples, more able to hear the teacher's needs which, while perhaps pressing them in ways they did not wish to go, still seemed understandable. Mutual concessions were made for the ordinary, human reason that people's feelings were involved.

The teacher as a person has before him the task, among other things, of conveying to the students his own version of the struggle which, as facilitator, he is validating in the students. The unique and even the accidental reasons for choosing his field or for preferring one theory over another are part of what really makes up a particular teacher. The teacher's fears that his students will enter the next course without the necessary training are not just part of his capacity as formal authority or socializing agent. Perhaps, he begins to suspect, his own feelings are a legitimate part of the group, at least for some students. The end result of this late development is easily distinguished from friendship, but the relationships do seem warmer, more honest perhaps, and clearly a source of pleasure to many of those involved. That these positive feelings are recalled so vividly two years later is another sign that the people behind or within the roles came to be touched by what was going on.

The Teacher and Work. We turn now from examining the impediments to work in each of the six aspects of the task area to discuss the nature of work in general. Our review of the process of learning to work can be focused on one question: "What can the teacher contribute to the work function of the classroom group?" This question leads to the central paradox of teaching effectiveness. A classroom in which work is maximized is not the product of any one person. It is not the teacher's class. It is a group that has evolved particular structures, norms, goals, and procedures. It has become a unique social institution, to everyone's credit. At the same time, the teacher as the initially designated and formal leader of this work group has a unique role to play, and the ways in which the teacher can contribute, positively or negatively, to the work group need to be better understood. Thus the teacher is alone in undertaking certain contractual obligations to both the students and his institution, but this does not mean he must operate as if the group's success depended only on him. Much of the disruptive affect in classrooms can be traced to the teacher's actions, but there need be no blame or censure involved in saying this. It is impossible to satisfy every student's needs and expectations, especially at first. The reduction of disruptive affect is gradual, and each student plays a vital role in this process. Work is a matter of mutual and multilateral efforts to find the creative solution to as many of the group's problems as possible. We need to extract from this complex and varied process the ways in which the teacher manages to be useful without seeming to throw the whole burden on him.

To recapitulate, we have argued that: (1) there are numerous teaching functions, of which we isolated six and created the teacher-as typology; (2) each teaching function can be the source of important teacher and student motivation, but it can also be the source of disruptive affect; (3) the disruptive affects aroused in any area of the six teaching functions can decrease the effectiveness of a teacher in other areas; and (4) different students, different teachers, different content, and different points along the development of a class will call for different emphases on the various aspects of teaching. From these thoughts we conclude that it is a serious mistake to confuse a particular kind of good teaching with "the good teacher." Good teaching takes very different forms, and what works well given one set of conditions may do nothing but arouse disruptive affects under other conditions. In short, we emerge from our study interested not in advocating one style of teaching but in advocating a style of thinking about teaching.

One distinction we found useful throughout this study we might now summarize by saying that good teaching involves both skills and problem-solving abilities. Too often, thinking about teaching leads only to thinking about skills, about the *a priori* talents one would hope to find or develop in a teacher. To be specific: obviously anyone would hope that a college teacher is "up on his field," that he is brilliant, eloquent, and well prepared. These are *a priori* characteristics to some extent. One might at least imagine that a teacher would remain brilliant, well read, and silver-tongued from term to term. Just as one could specify the *a priori* skills of the expert, one could also specify some of the requisite skills of each other aspect of teaching. The good formal authority would have a fair way of examining and would give clear instructions of how he grades. The good socializing agent would know the entry requirements of further study and what work will help one advance to the next plateau. The good facilitator would have viable options open for the interested students to do independent work. Et cetera. Each aspect of teaching is associated with things one can prepare to do or be before the class meets for the first time. These are the diverse skills of the good teacher, and our study clearly indicates that they are important. We may have expanded the list to include skills and abilities others might tend to overlook, but we are not discounting the importance of skill.

However, what the study shows, in addition, is that things do not always work out as one had expected. Disruptive affect may be aroused by a perfectly competent (but slightly punitive) lecture. Disruptive affect may be aroused by a perfectly honest (but slightly premature) gesture to let the students work more on their own. At that point good teaching may mean adjusting one's emphasis to include other skills, other aspects of the teacher's function. Or it may mean employing what we call problem-solving ability: the ability to pursue the cognitive or other goals, to take seriously as well the affective, interpersonal realities of the classroom at that point, and to find some creative response to the total situation. We emphasize this mainly because the "good teacher" is usually described in terms of talents and skills which fail to include the reactive, problem-solving skills that are needed precisely when things stop going perfectly.

We turn now to a matter that is derived not only from the data but from the general dialogue among college teachers in many settings. The question can be phrased in such a way as to connect it with our current concerns, to wit: "Is it suggested or desirable, given the evidence that both the teacher and the students are experiencing all these emotions, that the classroom should resemble in its goals and procedures group psychotherapy or T-groups?" We wish to present a series of answers to this question, but the overall answer is definitely not, especially not with respect to the goals.

The major differences between, for example, the introductory psychology classes we have studied and self-analytic and therapeutic groups lie in the relative importance and legitimacy of the didactic or content goals, the goals of self-expression, and the values of self-awareness. There is no doubt that people can "learn" things in therapy which they could also learn in a course, just as in an introductory course they can express and become aware of feelings that they could also work on in T-groups (see Argyris, 1965a, 1965b; Weir, 1968). The question is one of priorities, and to speak of priorities means inevitably to speak of that point when one abandons a lesser goal, however worthy in and of itself, in favor of a more important or legitimate goal. The role of self-expression and insight in the traditional content course must be judged in the light of their contribution, positive or negative, to the complex teaching tasks that range all the way from the teacher as expert to the teacher as person. What we have tried to show in this study is both the spectrum of teaching functions and the need to keep them in balance. One clear finding, for example, was that as the expert functions were abandoned what was created was not simply a breach of the educational contract but a whole series of affective consequences of major importance to the group. Thus the reason why we argue that the

goals of self-expression and self-awareness should not eclipse the intellectual goals of the course is that evidently neither the teacher
nor a goodly share of the students find that situation to their liking.

How, then, can the teacher play a role in the reduction of disruptive affect without "turning the class into a therapy group?" We
have already suggested that he would be ill-advised to make self-
expression and insight the major goals of the classroom, but that
does not imply that these are illegitimate activities and gains in any
classroom if they serve, rather than replace, the task. Why encourage
students to express their feelings? To know what is on their mind.
If the teacher does not know what he needs to know in order to
alter an unpleasant or an unproductive situation, it is not "doing
therapy" to find out. He may or he may not need to be explicit
about it. He may get the message without its being spelled out in
so many words. If a cluster 2 student is sinking further and further
into a sense of intellectual inferiority, does he have to write his feelings on the blackboard? Does he even have to experience these feelings in all their full intensity? We think not; in a therapy group,
perhaps, if the time were ripe, but certainly not in a classroom. The
question is whether the teacher knows what he is feeling, and it
is often useful to hear something from this student in order to sense
what underlies that look which seems to say that things are not going
too well at the moment.

Once the teacher has found out what the students are feeling,
by whatever means, the divergence of the classroom from the self-
analytic group becomes even clearer. The teacher's goals, unlike the
typical therapist's, may be far better served by trying to change
the disturbing reality, with the students' help, than in soaking in
it until everyone is fully aware of how disturbing it is. By stating,
and trying to make consensual, new goals and alternative procedures,
the teacher can often reduce the disruptive affect without having
ever made it public to the class. He is not alone in this task, and
in the end it is the group's capacity to innovate, to create ideas of
freedom and appropriate challenge, which characterizes the successful class and its problem-solving ability.

While we are on the point of how the teacher might go about
reducing the level of disruptive affect, it is important not to seem
to be suggesting that reduction of the level of affect *per se* is the
only goal. We are talking only of disruptive affect. Many skillful
teachers can arouse massive amounts of anxiety or set up competition
which channels the student's raging anger, and the consequence is

not less work but more. When all is said and done, the reduction of affect is perhaps a less important goal for students or teachers than the development of ways to bind in and utilize these affective states. Pride follows the discovery that one was not, contrary to previous experience, prevented from being effective by the fact that one was mistrustful, angry, or discouraged much of the time. To be able to bind in and tolerate previously overwhelming amounts of affect is a genuine human accomplishment, and without ever making this goal explicit, perhaps not even to themselves, many effective teachers manage to create whatever it takes to make this accomplishment possible. We suspect that one thing it takes is that the class be "worth it," and this implies that at least some and perhaps all teaching functions be handled with the skill of an effective professional.

Our research suggests that disruptive affect is simply one of the givens, and one had better adapt to this by developing problem-solving skills rather than hoping that everything will go beautifully, only to get angry and discouraged when the same old issues arise in yet another class. In this light, then, the good teacher is one who has certain qualities of personal maturity and toughness in the face of reality so that he can perform creative acts and avoid the petulant, moralistic, and destructive moves that characterize the poor problem solver.

It is so easy to see our position as "going to the other extreme" that we feel and need to say it one more time. *The goal of the classroom is work.* The teacher is, especially at first, the formal leader of the work group. The work group has a serious, important task, as defined by the course content, the nature of the students, the dictates of the larger instructional system—in fact, all the aspects of the task isolated in the teacher-as typology. However, the work group in a college classroom very soon has affective, interpersonal stresses which interfere with the task. The leader of the work group, therefore, is the man who can balance and synthesize the stresses from both the task and the affective demands on the group. Neither stresses can be ignored. Every gesture, every act tends to influence both the task and the affect of the group. For these reasons our analysis of the good teacher or the good performance leans more heavily than in most accounts on problem solving on emotions, and on the goal of synthesizing the task and affective goals of the classroom.

Before concluding this review of the process of learning to work we wish to draw out of the several discussions of the obstacles to work some of the other common factors that characterize effective teaching. We wish to discuss the teacher's sense of balance, the teacher's commitment to reality, his sense of the likely, his sense of timing, and the appropriateness of his strategy for the particular student at the particular moment.

One characteristic of the later sessions, especially in the more successful classes, was the extent to which the teacher and the class could move flexibly and easily from one to another of the various functions of the more educational relationships. Each brief segment seemed both to fuse far more effectively than earlier the diverse tasks and also to give way more gracefully to some other, needed function. This stood in striking contrast to the early sessions when the teacher seemed trapped by the dichotomies of his own creation. Convinced that one could not control the class as a formal authority and, at the same time, be a good facilitator, that one could not be a good expert and a good ego ideal, or whatever, each teacher resembled the child who despairs of ever playing the piano with both hands. Back and forth they would go, often fully convinced that their either/or was some kind of immutable condition of existence. Similarly, they acted as if to talk about the content were incompatible with the expression of affect. Of course, the students often acted as if they, too, shared their teacher's or, to put it more accurately, their culture's compartmentalizing inclinations. The "good-for-you" stuff before the dessert, serious work precludes fun, familiarity breeds contempt—all the cultural teachings about what-cannot-go-with-what are revealed in the early sessions. Gradually, however, the possibility of both, the possibility of interlacing and even fusing seemingly antithetical goals, seems almost real. Work, it would seem, involves a creative alternative to the either/or's which force the teacher and the class to resign themselves to periods of first this excess and that deficiency, interspersed by confusing shifts to the opposite, but not much happier, alternative. Perhaps more experienced teachers know this, and perhaps they can avoid these erratic, zig-zagging developments. And, then again, perhaps it needs to be learned over and over again with each new class.

The second theme we have suggested to be an integral part of work is commitment to reality. We suggested above that work does not necessarily mean that everyone pours out his most humiliating and poorly controlled feelings, but this is not in the least to say that the teacher's sense of reality is an insignificant part of his contribution to the group's development. The teacher who conveys to the class a picture of the students which departs drastically from their own view of themselves, or who seems to be deluding himself about his own motives and feelings, is a serious detriment to work. When the teacher overpraises the class in order to calm his own misgivings about granting them freedom, many of the students are more disturbed than reassured. When the teacher's commitment to reality extends only to his insistence that the students be tough and face the reality of the ubiquitous unconscious or the reality of America's disastrous foreign policy only to stop short of accepting the reality of the student's (or his own) feelings, what does the student learn about "facing reality?" We are struck with the almost invariably negative consequences of pretense in the classroom.

The teacher's pretense that he trusts, respects, or likes the students seems usually to yield to the counterpressures of reality. His actual feelings keep on coming through, and pretense cannot obliterate scorn, or indifference, or even the teacher's own distress. Fortunately, these states do not inevitably last forever. The point we are reemphasizing here is the relative ineffectiveness of rushing the class into structures and latitudes which are bolstered only by distortions of the current state of affairs. Not only is the teacher peddling denial as a preferable mode of handling feeling, instead of expression and semideliberate control; he is usually not very likely to succeed in his venture.

The importance of being attuned to reality is perhaps best understood by looking at a few instances where the opposite holds true. The ineffective teacher is often the teacher whose sense of timing, or whose contact with the complexity of his own or his students' responses, is shaky. He lives in a dream world. Not the obvious dream world of the "out of contact" and "sick" individual, but the dream world of the man who confuses intention with actuality. The teacher who overwhelms the students with his mastery of his field and fails to detect any sign that most students are getting confused and upset is a teacher out of touch with reality. The teacher who moralizes constantly about how his students really *should* be interested in this or capable of that, when they are not, and who then deals with them as if they conformed to his expectations, is living in a dream world. The teacher who can tell you exactly *why* he assigned what he did or how he rationalized blowing up at a "lazy" student, but who cannot tell you about the correspondence between the intended consequences and the actual consequences, is a man content with a minimum level of reality testing.

To generalize across teachers, students, content, etc., we can say that good teaching has to do with reality. Creativity in teaching, the mutual stimulation and reward that characterize any good relationship, the issues of energy, problem solving, and even skill—all of the elements we have discussed are, in the final analysis, intertwined with the teachers' and students' sense of reality. The moralistic and punitive response to students is a way of breaking a relationship, or contenting oneself with only one's own standards and values. A rigid, mechanical, and uncreative teaching performance is the result of turning away from the reality of the developing relationship in the classroom and remaining self-absorbed and inattentive to the effect one is having on others (and, in all probability, remaining inattentive as well even to the effect one's failure is having on oneself).

Reassurance ("Yes, I know this new procedure seems odd, but I'm confident it will seem okay in a little while") and the effective use of problem solving to address the realities of the situation are altogether different processes from denial. It is particularly important that the members of a class, including the teacher, have the sense of having solved the problem facing them not by a stroke of luck but by a process of fitting the solution to the realities as they existed. In the more successful groups the various innovations and compromises seemed to most of those involved like particularly appropriate decisions, and they could feel pride in both the process and the outcome of their deliberations.

The inexperienced or unskilled teacher is somewhat like the general whose fantasies about how easily his troops can capture a certain village lead him to hold no troops in reserve. Then, when complications and counterpressures arise, he is confused and panicky. So, too, with the teacher whose intention to cover x, y, and z in a given week is not joined with a sense of what is likely. Keeping behind no psychic reserves to deal with the residual resentment from the previous week's exam or the counterpressures from those who cannot stomach the hidden value position underlying x, y, and z, he is left with too little energy to deal creatively with the situation. If this fine-grained analysis of classroom interaction has convinced us of anything, it is that the teacher's intentions, whether they be to get across a certain chunk of material or to get a good discussion going, are only one part of the picture. The early sessions especially are so filled with distressing and unexpected messages, caused only partly by what the teacher has said and done, that we suspect quite a bit of the early role dissatisfaction and general malaise stems simply from how unprepared the teacher was for all this complexity. We are not knocking optimism, but there is a line between optimism and naïveté. One had better be prepared at least for one's content (or freedom, or whatever) goals to be shaped by the as yet unknown affective realities of the new class.

Finally, we would like to underscore again the fact that groups develop. The teacher's contribution to the process of work is inextricably bound up with his sense of timing, his sense of when which student or students can hear and respond to what. At least in these classrooms, and we strongly suspect in most others as well, the students in the early sessions are so preoccupied with their special concerns, their *sine qua non's* of the educational process, that many messages directed at them are either ignored or reinterpreted to fit into quite a different meaning system than the one used by the teacher. For most students the first and primary meaning system has to do with the authority issue, but this is hardly uniform. The teacher who in the first session attempts to impress the students with the fascinating issues in his field may, as we have seen, accomplish nothing more than to convince some students they will surely flunk the course and other students that evidently the teacher wants to start the power struggle as soon as possible.

We have described many of the teacher's early efforts to reduce tension or increase participation as premature. We meant not only that the students were not ready; perhaps just as often it was the teacher who was not ready. The teacher's feelings go through evolutionary changes, and what is right at a later time emerges as false or contrived at an earlier time.

We have tried to break through the notion that any teaching style, any goal or structure, is superior to all others, independent of the current and changing realities of the classroom. Fortunately for their participants, the two most successful classes found their way slowly and via some unlikely detours back to the very goals and functions that had seemed so premature earlier. Not that these earlier failures were without consequences. To name but a few, the directness of the confrontation in class C had a liberating effect on the teacher and the major antagonists, but this was not visible for several weeks. The premature enactment phase in all groups set the stage not only for the teacher to reassert his right to lecture but for both the teacher and the students to have some sense of the students' still developing competence and responsibility.

The evident inability of some teachers to establish a comfortable, effective lecture style early in the term is also a matter of timing. We are not suggesting that no teacher can ever avoid the apprehension and discouragement caused by the early student displays of contention, indifference, and anxiety over grades. If they can, they can. More power to them. The teachers in this study could not, at least did not, avoid these crises. For them the early phases reflected the swirl of conflicting goals and feelings we have tried to summarize.

We are not suggesting, however, some universal unfolding of "first this, then that" crisis or stage of development. These four classes are far from identical, and we have each taught other classes that turned out quite differently from the developmental patterns sketched here. What, then, would we conclude from these four classes?

We would assert that we have touched on some of the major ways in which, en route to a working and satisfying class, the teachers and students can talk past each other, arouse and disturb each other, and generally block each other and themselves from reaching their various task goals. We offer these analyses more as a model for how classes can develop than as a blueprint for how they invariably do develop. The crisis one teacher will provoke, another will stumble into later, and another hardly at all or never. We are prepared to hypothesize that the gradual development of the classroom group can be expected to touch at some of the nodal points we have discussed. The implication for effective teaching is less ambiguous, however, than the prediction of similar outcomes. Whatever the pattern of their development, there is a natural history to classrooms and only slowly, and usually with some pain, do human groups come to coordinate their goals, agree on procedures, and find ways to respond to the various affects and pressures generated by the process of moving toward their task goals. To learn how to adapt to these complexities is to learn how to work and, in our view, that may be the most important thing to learn in the college classroom.

CHAPTER 8

THE EFFECTIVE
TEACHING CULTURE

In analyzing the process of learning to work we found it useful to think of the teacher as the nominal leader of the work group. That is, his relationship to the students encompasses the educational tasks and the emergent interpersonal realities of the classroom. The challenge for each individual teacher lies in adapting his special needs and skills to the particular content goals and the particular students and setting. In this final chapter we would like to raise the question of how teachers can meet this challenge more successfully. What are the implications of this study for improving college teaching?

In order to answer this question, we must look beyond the single teacher to the set of teachers in one office, one course, or one department. We would not deny that individuals can improve their own teaching even in the most unhelpful of settings. However, we are convinced that for most teachers what can and does make the greatest difference is the nature of the teaching culture. By the teaching culture we mean both a collection of teachers and the social structure that links them together. In groups whose size varies from a set of officemates to the staff of a course to the faculty of a department, teachers assemble and create in the process a culture. On close examination it turns out that each culture nurtures some values more than others and rewards some activities more than others. What a particular teaching culture does to reward and sustain good teaching needs to be better understood. We need to examine the process of recruitment, the division of labor, and the basis of power within the teaching units. Only when we understand the interpersonal context of the individual teacher will we know how to make major improvements in college teaching.

To put it bluntly, our conviction is that much of the ineffective and unsatisfying teaching in American colleges today can be traced to the disorganized and often destructive qualities of the many teaching cultures. When teachers almost never talk to each other about their teaching, or when the only references to students are derogatory, the teaching culture is to blame if each teacher walks into class unmotivated to do well. When teaching fellows feel that if they were any good they would have research fellowships and not have to teach, the teaching culture is not likely to support and stimulate creative teaching. Obviously these unhelpful conditions in the teaching culture are the result of larger forces, but only partially so. Some things can be done by the teachers themselves to invigorate the depressed and lackadaisical teaching cultures of American colleges and universities. Other changes require the support and even the reorientation of higher levels of the college. Before we pursue this matter, let us first try to spell out the characteristics of an effective teaching culture.

If we return to the distinction made in the previous chapter between skill and problem-solving ability, we can see that the effective teaching culture needs to be concerned with both the *a priori* skills of the teacher and with his capacity to react to the developing classroom. The first assignment we might give the teaching culture is to maximize the skills of its teachers. The teacher-as typology suggests six dimensions along which the teacher's skill might vary. How could the teaching culture influence each of these dimensions?

How might a set of teachers become more skillful experts? One obvious answer is that the teachers should be knowledgeable, should have had a good preparation in their field, and should be staying abreast of new developments and publications. This sounds like an assignment one might make to individual teachers. However, without disparaging the role of individual competence and industry, we may still wonder why it is that in some courses or departments only a few teachers read beyond the assigned textbooks, if they even read that much. We may wonder why some teachers seem to be parroting information when they lecture while others appear to be deeply interested and knowledgeable in their field. We would suggest that part of the answer to this and similar questions is in the quality of the teaching culture of which the individual teacher is a member.

Many teachers are thoroughly bored with the content of the introductory or middle level course they are assigned to teach. Others find the course content so broad that they are forced to relearn material they have not touched for years. Faced with a conflict between the allure of their specialty and the demand of rereading forgotten material, they may ignore the latter. In courses where the teacher and students alike agree that the job is "get through the textbook," it may become taboo to even mention ancillary readings in or out of class. It is to these collective problems that the teaching culture can and should address itself if the individual teacher is to function more effectively as the expert.

Some staff-taught courses create a seminar for the purpose of discussing the current reading and lecture material. This tends to create and reinforce the expectation that the instructors are interested enough to read and think about what they are teaching. Many teaching cultures could profit from some clearer division of labor. Each teacher has areas where his background is stronger than others and areas where he is weaker than others. Some form of presentation, written or oral, by the one who is most interested and most expert can be very useful. The compilation and circulation of annotated bibliographies is another expression of this effort to pool resources. Paradoxically, the first step toward increasing the expertise of a set of teachers may necessitate breaking an unspoken rule against admitting ignorance. Only when one can admit without disgrace that one cannot remember (or has never read) a particular source will the capacity of a collectivity to be useful come into play. The particular devices employed by a teaching culture to assist the teachers as experts will vary. What is central to our assignment, however, is that the teaching culture can do much to eliminate the faking of competence, the unwillingness of teachers to discuss content issues, and all the other detriments to the development of genuine teacher expertise.

Precisely the same logic can be applied to each other aspect of the teacher's task role. We have suggested that the teacher as formal authority can fail in a variety of ways. Some arouse so much anxiety and contention that the term becomes one long struggle. Others abdicate power so quickly and unilaterally that the class spends too much energy testing and complaining about the new structure. What have these and other imaginable consequences in the formal authority area have to do with the teaching culture?

Our first answer to this question is that the way an individual teacher functions as a formal authority in his classrom is often closely bound up with how he and his fellow teachers are treated by their superiors: the course coordinator, the chairman, and the dean. How often do teachers who are treated with authoritarian insensitivity by their immediate superiors turn around and recreate in their class-room the same sort of authoritarian structure for their students? How often is a teacher's rigidity over deadlines or the choice of a paper topic a reflection of the rigidity of those above him?

It seems that teachers are often thrown off stride by both their peer culture and their superiors when it comes to how to play the authority role. Many of those who abdicate abruptly and with nega-tive consequences do so less from conviction than from a sense that being authoritarian in any way is negatively valued by one's peers or by one's supervisor. The effects of the teaching culture are varied, sometimes impelling the teacher to be more inflexible than he wants to be and sometimes to be more "democratic" than he wants to be.

If the teaching culture is not a place where one can talk about the ambiguities of the authority role, then the individual teacher is deprived of a crucial source of support and enlightenment. If the teacher must beware always to seem hard line enough or democratic enough when he describes his class, then he is less likely to learn how it really is for himself or for anyone else. Panaceas and fads replace creative thinking. One term it will seem that take-home exams are the perfect solution, but this will give way to daily quizzes if the pendulum swings the other way. The question we are raising is whether the teaching culture can help the individual teacher under-stand which techniques of control and evaluation will work for him and why. He can understand this better if the immensely complicated process of being an effective formal authority is not confused by fiats and group pressure. The need is for clear thinking about the realities of power and one's dual responsibilities to the students and the university.

We would argue that the way in which a teacher can best relate to his class as a formal authority varies widely from teacher to teacher. The teacher's most effective stance may change over time, even within one term. Therefore it is quite likely that the effective teaching culture is one in which different solutions are permitted. The teaching culture needs to provide the developing teacher with alternative models, with freedom to choose, and with a place where the realities of the classroom can be discussed.

The effectiveness of the teacher as socializing agent can also be traced, at least in part, to the teacher's peer culture and to the place of that cohort in the larger system. In our study we noted several times when the teacher pressed the students too hard to become little psychologists. This pressure expressed the teacher's misgivings about his own career choice. Seeking reassurances from student neophytes about the attractiveness and value of the inner circle is not a useful way to relate to students. And neither is the tendency to discourage students from "going on" at just the point when one is most discouraged or frustrated with one's field. If a teaching fellow feels scorned and judged by the senior faculty in his department, if success is defined for him as being "the cream of the crop," will this not affect the way he responds to students' questions about graduate schools? We suspect that the teacher's own struggle to get into the inner circle of his choice deeply influences his response to students. The question is how the teaching culture can take this impact and deal with it creatively.

Clearly it can help one to be a more effective socializing agent if one does, in fact, know about the departmental requirements or the criteria for admission to graduate school. However, many students find that the teacher can only tell them how to be just like him. If they discuss even minor variations or neighboring fields, the teacher draws a complete blank. The flow of information within the teaching culture concerning what an interested student might do next or as a career could be much improved. At a more fundamental level, though, we suspect that one problem facing the teaching culture is simply whether a teacher need care about the students' future. If the teaching culture believes that its function is simply to let the students in one door, carry on for a term, and get them through the exit, then the task of helping teachers respond more effectively to their students' concerns goes beyond that of getting better information. The teaching culture that tells students, "Either we will relate to you as future graduate students or we don't even want to see you" is a culture that is willing to perform its socializing role in only the most minimal fashion.

If we view the classroom as an instance of culture contact, as a point of articulation between the dominant academic culture and the student or youth culture, we may assign to the teaching culture a most difficult task. Part of its job becomes one of understanding the latent assumptions of its own culture, the hidden values and world view of the academic and the intellectual. This may vary from field to field, but each teaching culture must know itself if it is to understand how its efforts at socializing will affect others. It is equally important to understand where the youth culture differs from the academic culture and where it does not. Without a sympathetic reading on the evolving culture of the students, teachers cannot make sense out of much that happens in the classroom. When people suddenly act stupid or retentive, it may mean they are stupid, retentive people. Or it may mean that they do not trust the person to whom they are speaking. They may be unwilling to discuss their own latent values simply because they fear that they will be misunderstood or scorned.

Many of the recent changes in youth culture are away from a value on rationality and toward a sensate life style and a value on personal contact and honesty. These new developments are particularly hard for some academics to understand and to respect. Young teachers are especially prone to feel hurt by the sense that students see them as alien, as "one of them." And some of the changes have been so rapid that even teaching fellows cannot use their experience of three or four years before to figure out what is happening in the students' world. The teaching culture that can foster awareness of where the teacher's world and the students' world diverge and can respond to this divergence with insight and tact is bound to be helpful to the teacher as socializing agent. It is bound to produce teachers who are not immediately wounded or infuriated when they sense the considerable amount of polarization which now separates students and teachers. The capacity to recognize the existence of a gulf is one precondition for the building of bridges, and that recognition needs to be part of any effective teaching culture.

One way in which the teaching culture can impair the facilitative function is to give the teacher very few degrees of freedom within which to operate. If the teacher must cover so much by a certain common exam date, he will certainly be reluctant to move with the students into areas of evident interest and reward. Conversely, if the teacher is free to let the students come up with their own topics or even their own evaluation procedures, then he may use that freedom.

Perhaps the second major function of the teaching culture in this regard has to do with the teacher's capacity to recognize diversity among his students. We have discussed seven or eight distinct clusters of students. The teacher as facilitator would need to determine the appropriate way to relate to these different students. He would need, ideally, to understand how best to relate to each student as a distinct individual. Counterposed to this way of seeing oneself as a teacher, we often find a teaching culture with its primitive and unhelpful way of distinguishing among students. If talk among teachers manages only to differentiate between the bright ones and the dummies or between the attractive chicks and the rest, then the teacher as a facilitator can get little help from his culture. To the extent that more and more students, or even kinds and types of students, enter the teachers' discussions and receive respectful and sensitive treatment, more and more students will find a teacher who can be facilitative. As conversations among teachers become more differentiated both with respect to different students and with respect to different phases in a class's development, the teacher who wishes to be the effective facilitator has the necessary cognitive schema for knowing with whom and with what he is dealing in the classroom.

The job of helping a teacher function more often or more wisely as an ego ideal might seem at first glance to be difficult, if not impossible. It is here that we run into the maxim that the teachers are born, not made. Most teaching cultures appear to accept as given that either a man will be an inspiring and exciting teacher or he will not. Nothing much can be done about it.

We would take strong exception to the prevailing derivations of this half-truth. The implications usually drawn from this maxim are that the dull teacher probably can not be helped much. He was just born dull. If the students are bored or discontented with a teacher, it is better to change teachers next time around than to work to help the teacher. Our experience and our data in this study do not support these views. We have found times when a teacher changed dramatically even within one term from a discouraged, self-effacing, and generally ineffective teacher to periods of self-confident performance during which he was widely received by the students as a potential ego ideal. We have known too many young teachers, including the four teachers studied here, whose performance improved with each passing term to believe the maxim or its implications.

At times we find ourselves wondering what the latent function of this maxim might be. Perhaps those whose teaching is not going well invoke it to reassure themselves that the problem is their genetic endowment rather than the fact that they are not working very hard to do an effective job. Perhaps even more likely is the possibility that the maxim is used to distract those whose course is going badly from noticing why it is going badly. The students, so the maxim suggests, are bored because this man is not a born teacher. But maybe the reality also includes the fact that he is not teaching what he wants to teach. He may be covering material he himself is bored with or following someone else's way of handling authority issues. The problem of the teacher who fails to excite students and to convey his own deep investment in the field may be a problem which can only be solved by letting the teacher have greater latitude to work out his own way of teaching. Too much supervision, too much coordination of plans, and too much uneasiness about the perils of doing something new can seriously impair the effectiveness of a teaching culture.

The challenge to the teaching culture is to not let teachers give up on themselves and to help them to find the combination of content and method that will bring out their best performance. There are implications of this statement for the design of courses. The rotating lecture series in the mass introductory course where the lecturer covers only his area of special competence reflects an effort to let students see teachers at their most excited and exciting best. The "post-hole" model of abandoning complete coverage in favor of a few topics (which are presumably of special interest to the lecturers) is addressed to the same goal.

In actual operation most teachers find that their peer culture is decidedly hostile to any teacher who succeeds at becoming the teacher as ego ideal. The teacher whose lectures are jammed and whose sections are over-enrolled is assumed to be a showman, an easy grader, or both. The net effect is to isolate and embitter many of the most successful teachers. Clearly, many teaching cultures dissuade teachers from even trying to become more dramatic, interesting, or colorful by constantly belittling one or two of their colleagues as clowns and prostitutes. Perhaps, then, one of the simplest contributions to more effective teaching would involve rewarding rather than punishing the qualities of commitment, integrity, and passion that go into making the teacher a useful ego ideal.

As we turn to the final aspect of the teacher's task role, the teacher as person, we are reminded of the many obstacles to any kind of mutual and authentic relationship between teachers and students. If one seldom hears a teacher talk about learning something from a student and even more rarely about the teacher just enjoying the time spent with students, the teacher as authority and expert can come to dominate one's whole view of the classroom. In the office or over a cup of coffee the teacher-student relationship can broaden to include far more than the content-bound interchange of some classrooms. But there are pressures from other teachers not to spend too much time with students. Colleges may have no teacher's lounge to which the faculty can retreat, but there may be just as great a gulf between teachers and students as in the high schools. Much of this gulf is created by the students, but not a little of the responsibility can be assigned to the teaching culture.

In the arrangement of office space, in the definition of office hours, or in their whole manner, many teachers communicate very clearly that the student is supposed to make himself scarce. Any intrusion into the teacher's world had better be for a good (that is, course-related) reason. In contrast, other suites of teachers and especially teaching fellows convey the impression that students belong in this setting. The arrangements whereby some faculty live in the dormitories and houses can be a further extension of this model of the teacher-student relationship. It is not at all clear how a given teacher might deal more openly or humanly with students. Probably the less teaching is seen purely in terms of a mechanical transfer of information the more relevant will be the person of both the teacher and the learner. Further, the more the person of the teacher seems to matter to his own peers, superiors, and even his teachers in the case of teaching fellows, the more the teacher will be aware that he is more than simply the expert, the authority, or whatever.

One important moment for the teacher as person comes when he finds he can discuss the values and experiences that underlie his orientation to the course material. This moment, at best, can become a mutual process in which teachers and students come to learn that their diverse interpretations of common reading or data are traceable to their diverse histories and beliefs. To the extent that the teaching culture is aware that its diversity is also a product of different politics, life experiences, and aesthetic preferences, the teacher can enter the class ready to explore this important dimension of education. At its core an effective performance by the teacher as person is one which respects the privacy and dignity of the other participant. If the teacher cannot perceive and value human diversity, then persuasion and intrusiveness will replace the delicate process of mutual acquaintanceship.

From these several thoughts about the ways in which the teaching culture can influence the teacher's task skills, we may now move to the more ambiguous question of how the teaching culture can be relevant to the teacher's problem-solving response to the particular class. If the goal of the classroom is work, we may inquire whether any qualities of the teaching culture are particularly relevant to the teacher's ability to lead the work group.

It matters a great deal whether the teaching culture believes that work, or some process similar to this goal, is the proper business of the classroom. Perhaps one good indication of how the culture stands on this matter is whether teachers are able or likely to discuss the reality of their teaching. If it is only permissible to talk about why a particular reading was assigned or what else one would hope to cover during a certain week, then such a culture does not believe in work. To believe that it is sufficient to have good intentions is hardly the same as believing in the process of work in the changing world of the classroom. By the same token, if a teacher cannot discuss a poor class period without other teachers immediately rushing in to blame it all on the dumb, lazy students, then his culture believes more in preserving his image as a teacher than in the process of work.

It may be only in *ad hoc* groups of teachers within a larger course or department that one can nurture the value on work, or it may be an important value of a whole course or department. One finds where one can the people who will listen to the whole reality of one's experience as a teacher, not just the antistudent part or the expert part or the good intentions. A teaching culture in which teachers can talk honestly about the consequences of their efforts can help the teacher far better than one where the topic of teaching leads mainly to bragging, defensiveness, or silence. The whole process of learning how to work in a new setting is unbelievably complex, and one property of the effective teaching culture is, at least in our view, an emphasis on work, on reality, and on the gradual process of creating successful adaptations in the classroom.

One technique that might be useful would be to provide an easy means for teachers to tape-record their own classes. Most teachers have very selective memories for what went on, and even though the tape-recording loses much it also captures a great deal of useful information. Two or three teachers who know and trust each other could then listen to their own and each other's classes. This is often quite a painful experience for teachers. Self-deceptions are exposed, and this is seldom pleasant. However, many of the students' reactions make much more sense to the teacher when he can hear more fully the messages he was sending. In this way the teacher can become aware of more than his good intentions. He can sense some of the veiled and subtle realities of his performance. This realization may then lead the teacher to reappraise his goals, his techniques, and his feelings about the students. The process of work in the classroom is furthered by just such a sequence of perceptions and reappraisals, by the students as well as by the teacher. The contribution of the teacher as leader of the work group is therefore closely related to his ability to hear what is happening and then make the appropriate move. It is during this process of figuring out what is going on that the teacher can use all the help he can get. He can use a friend who listens well, a friend who can help him past his blind spots, and a friend who is supportive of the very effort to become a better teacher. It is out of relationships of this sort that the effective teaching culture is created.

We wish now to share our convictions about some of the properties of the effective teaching culture, looking first at some of the structures and norms that contribute to the capacity of teachers to work.

Our thoughts take shape around three qualities which seem to us to be vitally important: diversity, autonomy, and answerability. The importance of encouraging and protecting diversity among teachers stems from the obvious fact that teachers as well as students differ widely in the talents, goals, and liabilities that they bring to the college classroom. Not every teacher can manage an "unstructured class," nor should every teacher operate under the illusion that his or any other teaching style is invariably superior to any other. The results of years of research on forms of teaching, as reviewed by McKeachie (1966), say little more to us than that the critics of any given innovation are usually too gloomy in their predictions of inferior results. The results of these studies do not come out clearly in favor of any given style of teaching. The individual teacher should mold his teaching style to fit his own skills and values and to fit the reality of the students. In order for this to happen, however, it remains for the teaching culture to value not this or that teaching style above all others but to value diversity and openmindedness regarding how best to teach. One of the least helpful factors in both Mr. B's and Mr. D's classes was the general pressure from their peers and their supervisor to "get a lot of discussion." They responded, or one might almost say overresponded, to this pressure without knowing why it was such a good idea, and the results were far from ideal.

An integral part of our notion of diversity is that the teacher's task is to figure out for himself, as a result of his experiences, what works best for him. One implication for the teaching system as a whole is that fear of one's supervisor's displeasure is not a very helpful force in the total process of shaping one's optimal teaching style. To the extent that one must check out one's approach toward teaching with one's superior, not in a mood of collaboration but in order to get his approval, then to that extent the energy of the system is deflected into the often irrelevant process of accommodation to an official position on teaching. For some teachers, the official line may be consonant with their skills and inclinations, but for others it is a distraction, a drain on the energy needed to develop their own skills and to react effectively to the problems created within the classroom.

The importance of teacher autonomy cannot be overly stressed. Too many college teachers today, especially in the junior faculty and teaching assistant ranks, feel and act as if they were simply robots controlled by the mastermind of the teaching system. Instead of trying to fit into someone else's scheme of things, most of these teachers could do a far better job if they could turn their attention to their own and the students' needs, talents, and ideals. Many aspects of college teaching are in flux today: the role of grades, the proper balance between active mastery and passive absorption—the whole issue of the optimal use of the teacher. These and many other parameters of the college classroom should be open to new and searching questions which will be generated only in an atmosphere of freedom, including the freedom to make mistakes. It could even be claimed that it is more important to start making new mistakes than to repeat the same old ones over and over again. But this raises a very important question. How can one introduce into a teaching system checks and cautions against "going wild" if one is at the same time loosening the top-down control formerly exerted by the senior members of the unit?

One commonly proposed solution is to collect student ratings or evaluations of the teacher. However, the effect of using student ratings depends largely on whether they are used for the teacher's own benefit, for the information of a supervisor, or merely to put up the appearance of being interested in student opinion. If the student ratings are used mainly by course coordinators and departmental chairmen in order to ferret out the ineffective teachers, then the effect may be to reduce risk taking and to enforce a restriction of output within the peer culture. In the end few will dare to show how deeply they care about finding their own path. Instead, the teaching culture may devise ways of protecting the weakest member and punishing the "rate-busters." We are aware of the arguments in favor of student ratings, and we strongly favor the teacher's use of some form of feedback for his own enlightenment. But we have found that teachers who are excessively preoccupied with how their classes will seem to a distant (and presumably unsympathetic) judge are often less able to respond creatively to the demands of their students and the developing classroom.

The most basic need in any teaching system is for answerability to one's peers and superiors as well as to the students. Some mechanisms are needed whereby the effects of a teacher's decisions become as salient to him as his intentions or the seeming worthwhileness of the approach before it was tried. Our comments on the importance of teacher autonomy, especially autonomy from the restrictive form of top-down control, were appropriate mainly to the needs of junior faculty. For them we would argue that answerability to peers and to students is the most appropriate form of control and feedback. However, most senior faculty operate with virtually no feedback, with no need to answer to anyone for their teaching. Some teachers obtain and respond to feedback from students, but most do not, and very few see their peers and junior colleagues as having anything relevant to say about their approach to teaching. If any element of the system has gone wild, in the sense of being without challenge to explain and defend its operations, it is the senior faculty members in their sacred preserves, the classrooms and lecture halls of the university. Thus, to argue for answerability is to argue for different controls on some teachers and for new controls on others. Many faculty who must answer for their research interests and mode of scholarly operation, at least to journal editors and granting agencies, are not at present equally answerable to anyone in their own universities with regard to their teaching goals, abilities, or success.

One distinguishing feature about a peer culture at its best is that each participant can feel pride in the diversity of teaching styles and successes without feeling that another man's success necessarily defines the path that all must follow. No matter how gentle the control from above, it is difficult to remove the aura of officialdom from the supervisor's suggestions and examples. We would prefer, therefore, to construct a model of the teaching culture where each member is a full and equal collaborator in the mutual process of maximizing the total effectiveness of the system.

In our experience it has been useful to have a weekly seminar of teachers in the introductory course, but exciting as these meetings were, confrontations one might almost call some of them, it was probably not the meetings *per se* which were most crucial. More probably, it was the whole array of conversations, arguments, and mutual consultations that these large meetings triggered off that kept the teaching culture alive. Very few teaching units have even begun to test out ways of building a cohesive culture. Almost any structure created and owned by the members, the teachers themselves, would seem to be an improvement over the atomized, low energy arrangements so prevalent in college teaching today.

Before we leave the matter of what teachers can do for each other, we wish to discuss the special case of "teacher training." Everyone knows of the college teacher's traditional aversion to methods courses. What, then, can be done regarding the new or even the aspiring teacher? Some have proposed a model approximating that of the apprentice system. The new teacher would ease in gradually, perhaps under the benign guidance of the senior or master teacher. Our reaction to this is twofold. It seems to have definite advantages over the current practice of using neophytes in the teaching systems as flunkies, left only the menial jobs of grading, repeating, and explicating the lecturer's "key points," and absorbing or deflecting as much student hostility as possible. The current "training" procedures seem to impress on the trainee that teaching is an unlikely place to seek either intellectual satisfaction or personal growth, a conviction that all too often is reflected later in a senior faculty whose interest in teaching has simply never developed. Bad as these arrangements are for the future of college teaching, there is reason to think that the apprentice model is not the answer either.

The matching of neophytes with models is a problem that plagues all such training procedures. Some models may establish mutual trusting relationships of the sort we see as the elemental building block of an alive and growing teaching culture. Other would-be models might, we fear, serve more to stifle than to liberate, and we are convinced that whether the new teacher gets off to a good start in teaching is related more to whether his own long-established skills and values are engaged than to whether some new model is held up before him. We would not exclude the possibility of creative linkages across variations in experience, but we would propose a somewhat different model.

We would suggest that there are some, even quite a few, preparatory activities that can facilitate the process of becoming a good teacher. These activities will vary with the convictions and the uncertainties of the teacher-to-be. We would do nothing to disparage the crucial importance of the teacher being clear about his syllabus or reading list or whatever. The unprepared teacher is certainly responsible for his share of the unsuccessful moments in higher education. But so is the mechanical man, the teacher who has evidently thought a great deal about which pages of which books are due before which exam but very little about why he wants to teach this material, who he is likely to find in his class, and what for him would constitute success.

We have found that if the teacher-to-be spends even a few hours a week during the term prior to teaching carrying out several activities, some involving learning about the mechanics of the course and some involving discussions of its basic goals, more teachers can get off to a good start even if they are fully autonomous in the conduct of their course. For some reason graduate teaching fellows seem more open to the idea that it would help to think about what one intends to teach, and why, than their busy fellow teachers in the professorial ranks. Be that as it may, we are suggesting that the preteaching seminar can serve as a model for what will hopefully be a continuous process of review and self-scrutiny. What is particularly appropriate about beginning this process before one starts teaching is that teachers can think through potentially troublesome issues before the first wild and confusing term begins. Many teachers find that one or more terms have gone by before they have regained sufficient composure to ponder the basic issues that come up spontaneously in a preteaching seminar. To the extent that here, as in the ongoing teaching seminar, the predominant model is one of peers engaged in exploration for their mutual benefit, rather than a model of someone prescribing the correct means and goals for everyone else, then the effective teaching culture stands to gain tremendously be each new wave of teachers. We realize that many of these thoughts are applicable mainly to the large, sectioned course using teaching fellows or assistants. However, the point worth stressing in general is that the gradual processes of figuring things out for oneself and of finding others with whom one can collaborate are probably not susceptible to any grand, *a priori* scheme. The preteaching seminar, paired with a system of giving even the newest teacher complete control over his course, its content, and grading, is designed to further this process, but even this structure falls short of guaranteeing that the new teacher can move ahead without some very rough moments (or terms).

Thus far, most of our comments have been devoted to the internal structure and process of the teaching culture. We shall discuss now the capacity of the teaching culture to act as a whole to create new teaching forms and possibilities. We turn to the matter of innovation. The collective energies of an effective teaching culture are often best used in creating new ways of carrying out the course or departmental assignment.

Our purpose is not to pass judgment on such innovations as pass-fail grading, independent study, reading logs, TV lectures, teaching machines, and so forth. Our purpose is to suggest that each innovation can be viewed in terms of its contribution to work in the classroom. The utility and timeliness of each innovative proposal cannot be assessed without knowing what problems the teaching culture has been encountering. To take a simple example, we could imagine one course in which the teachers were struggling to handle the expert and especially the ego ideal aspects of the task. Perhaps the course content was too broad and no single teacher could afford the time to do much more than the assigned reading. Or perhaps the teachers had poor preparation for their course. In this setting a successful innovation might involve having one or two central, mass lectures per week. Each teacher would handle what he knew best; movies or guest lecturers might be used occasionally; and the course might benefit greatly from a rise in both expert and ego ideal functions. However, we could just as easily imagine eight teachers whose students were already going to a few lectures in common in addition to their hours of recitation or section meeting. We could imagine that the common lecture series served mainly to block each teacher's capacity to function as both expert and facilitator. For these teachers the most effective innovation might be to scrap the common lecture and use their new freedom to develop courses better suited to their own talents and to the students' interests.

An innovation that one teacher would find liberating might lead another teacher straight to disaster in the classroom. Thus it is important not to insist that everyone be part of some new teaching form. But it is equally important that the process of innovation go on. New ways of defining the course goals and structure, new roles for students and teachers, new techniques for conveying information—all of these ways and more are desparately in need of being tried out and perfected. The very process of trying something new is often just what is needed in a teaching system that has become jaded with the old, partially successful ways. Everyone's optimism rises. Teaching seems like a more worthwhile activity. The trick is not only to change things but to find the changes that best fit the talents, unrealized hopes, and interpersonal styles of the classroom participants.

Before concluding our thoughts about the effective teaching culture, it is important to place this culture in its larger context. It would be naïve indeed to assume that the American college or university of today is oriented only toward improving the quality of its teaching. The resources and attention of the colleges are split between teaching, research, scholarship, public relations activities, bureaucratic featherbedding, and so on. New faculty are hired with the promise that they will not have to do much teaching, and what little they do can be in their special area of interest.

It is not hard to imagine that in some settings the teaching culture finds things so inhospitable that it settles for the most perfunctory of teaching performances. An attitude of "Why bother?" sweeps over the culture, and few teachers are tempted to try something new. Teaching fellows and young faculty are jostled to get on with the business of publishing and to spend less time on their teaching. However, the picture is not totally bleak. Teaching is valued more by some departments typically than by others. In short, those students, teachers, and administrators who are trying hard to improve college teaching are in something of a battle.

If one is not to be ground into hopelessness and cynicism as a teacher, there are two options, although they are not mutually exclusive. One option entails joining the struggle for greater support, freedom, or manpower for teaching. The other entails building a countercommunity of teachers within the university even if this support is not forthcoming. That is, the teaching culture may battle as vigorously and effectively as it can manage and still lose out to other interests. But this need not lead to a collapse of the resolve and capacity of those who are teaching to do an effective job.

What if competent teaching were declared to be an extravagant and unnecessary part of college life? What if building up research units and capturing Academy-Nobel-Pulitzer men came to dominate the official policy or actions of the college? There would still be the students. There would still be some faculty and graduate students who wanted to teach because they found it actively satisfying, exciting, and integral to their conception of the good life. There would still be some administrators who were attached to the old conception of a place of higher learning. Together these students, teachers, and administrators would carry on even if the official rewards and resources were going elsewhere in the university. They could build a countercommunity, and if they did not make too much of a fuss about where the money was going they would probably be allowed to stay around.

If this extreme case has not been reached, it follows then that with some official rewards, some support, and some of the resources, the teaching cultures can all the more easily carry on. They can struggle and sometimes win. But win or lose, they are still in a position to carry on the business of teaching and learning. The complex linkages make for a complicated and often frustrating job. We have moved from looking at the student in the classroom to the teaching culture to the organizational context in which the teachers operate. Throughout we have tried to focus on the educational and interpersonal factors that can influence the outcome one way or the other. Hopefully this descriptive and analytic framework will enable the participants in the educational process to understand both their reality and their possibilities.

METHODOLOGICAL FOOTNOTES

Chapter 2. Varieties of Affective Experience

1. The procedure for pooling the data from the four different groups was to (1) calculate the percentage of all acts in each category for a given 20-20 segment; (2) convert the percentages into standard score form *for each group separately* with means of 50 and standard deviations of 10; (3) combine the pool of 20-20 segments from each group into one large pool of 582 segments. Since our interest here is determining the covariation among categories *within* these or any other such groups, it is essential in studies of this kind to eliminate extraneous covariation of two sorts: (1) covariation attributable to the different rates at which scorers would perceive, had they scored all four groups, each of the 16 categories and (2) covariation attributable to across-group variations; for example, if one teacher were extremely high relative to the other teachers on Showing Dominance, his percentages would tend to be lower on all the other categories even though for him (and for all the other teachers) Showing Dominance might be positively related to at least some of these categories. Only by standardizing within groups will these positive correlations be clearly revealed.

2. The factor extraction procedure used was the principle axes method, using an iterative refactoring technique for arriving at communality

estimates. Seven factors were then rotated using Kaiser's normalized Varimax technique. The rotated matrices are found in Tables 2-1 and 2-2.

3. The factor estimates for the teacher or for the students on their respective set of factors were created by: (1) calculating the standard score values within the array of segments for each group for each of the categories (plus %T for the teacher) for each segment; (2) the appropriate categories were then added together (with appropriate sign) and major loadings were given double weight; and (3) the resultant sums were then standardized for each factor (with means of 50.0 and standard deviations of 10.0) and within each group, with the result that each segment was assigned a standard score on each of the seven teacher factors and each of the seven student factors.

Chapter 4. Variations Among Students

1. The cluster analysis that produced the first seven clusters was done with a program developed by M. Clemens Johnson. This program takes data on a number of variables for each individual and then finds groups of individuals who are similar to each other. In this case, the input data were the seven factor estimates over the whole term for each of 86 students who had at least 20 total scorable acts. We thought that Factors 1 (Enactment versus Anxious Dependence) and 2 (Consent versus Contention) were the most important, both theoretically and in terms of the percent of the variance they accounted for. Therefore we gave them extra weight in the cluster analysis procedure by including the factor estimate for the first factor three times for each student, the one for the second factor twice, and the last five factors only once. Thus, each student had a total of ten scores in the input to the cluster program. The way the program works is to first compute a matrix of correlation coefficients of each individual with every other individual, across the scores for each. The clusters of individuals generated by the program are those whose correlation coefficients with each other are high. We can best explain exactly how this is done by quoting directly from the program write-up by M. Clemens Johnson.

"*Clustering Procedure:* The program first computes the correlation coefficients between all pairs of individuals using all available data.

"A correlation coefficient between a particular pair of individuals, say, individuals 1 and 7, represents the degree of linear association between the sets of scores corresponding to the two individuals. For purposes of this program, the correlation coefficient is employed as an index of similarity or a *similarity coefficient* between the two individuals. (The correlation coefficient involving an item by item comparison of the data may be assumed to represent a different index of similarity than, for instance, total score on a test. The latter does not reflect variation in the way in which two individuals respond to the individual items comprising the test.)

"'In the clustering procedure all similarity coefficients for individual 1 are first scanned by the computer. Two separate scans are made. In scan 1 the computer identifies the highest similarity coefficient for individual 1, that is, the individual in the total sample with whom individual 1 is most similar. In scan 2 for individual 1, the computer identifies all individuals with similarity coefficients within *one half of a standard error* of the highest coefficient. As a result of the two scans, a list is comprised for individual 1, the list containing the numbers of all individuals with whom individual 1 has higher similarity coefficients.

"Suppose that it is found that individual 1 is more similar to individuals 7, 20, 21 and 32 (say, in a total sample of 75 individuals). Individual 7 is then scanned to see with whom he is more similar. Assume that the higher similarity coefficients for individual 7 are with individuals 16, 21, and 31. There would be no *mutually high coefficients* for individuals 1 and 7, and no cluster would be formed.

"The computer next examines individual 20 (since individual 1 is also more similar to individual 20). Suppose that it is found that individual 20 is more similar to individuals 1, 13, and 64. Since individual 1 was more similar to 20, and individual 20 was more similar to 1, the computer would form a cluster of the two individuals. All similarity coefficients for individual 20 would then be averaged with the corresponding coefficients for individual 1.

"The analysis would continue in a similar fashion, individual 20 no longer being considered as a single candidate for a cluster. The computer would scan the coefficients for individual 2, again seeking mutually high similarity coefficients with another individual in the sample, and so on, through all individuals. In the first iteration through the sample the computer would form clusters of two individuals whenever the criterion for clustering (mutually high similarity coefficients) was satisfied.

"In the second iteration through the sample the computer again would begin with individual 1, this individual now representing a cluster of 1 and 20. The second iteration through the sample may build up clusters of various sizes ranging from 2 to 4. A cluster of size 2 would result if further analysis of the data indicated that two individuals (not previously clustered) now met the criterion for clustering. A cluster of size three would result if one individual and a cluster of 2 individuals were found to have mutually high coefficients. In combining similarity coefficients for the cluster of size 3, or clusters of unequal size, a *weighted average* of the coefficients would be computed for the new cluster. A cluster of size 4 would be formed when two clusters of 2 individuals were found to have mutually high coefficients.

"In the third iteration the size of the clusters formed by the computer would range between 2 and 8, and so on. The computer would continue the iterations until the criterion of mutually high similarity coefficients was no longer satisfied or *until the number of clusters reached a minimum of 3.*

We chose the iteration that had six clusters, the smallest having four members, the largest 22, with most around 10 or 11, because this seemed to be a workable number. Later, when we examined the attributes of the members, the difference between groups seemed to have good intuitive appeal. There was one change which we made before going on to look at significant differences among clusters. It looked as if all but one of the clusters was either very high or very low on our most important factor, Factor 1, Enactment. Because we thought this factor was crucial in thinking about the class and because this particular cluster was very large (22) we divided it at the median on Enactment, thus creating clusters 5 and 6, the first of which is quite high on Enactment and the second quite low. This meant that each of the clusters tended to be either high or low—1, 3, 4, and 5 high, and 2, 6, and 7 low.

The next step was to find out, on all of the measures that we had available, how different the clusters actually were from each other and in what ways. The technique we used for this was analysis of variance, though we did not use it in exactly the same way in each case. To find out differences on the seven student factors, the 16 categories and four levels of the member-to-leader scoring system, and on participation, we did an analysis of variance testing for significant differences between each cluster and all the other students on each variable. The significant differences that we found are listed at the beginning of the descriptions of each cluster in Chapter 4. For all the other variables at which we looked, we did an analysis of variance that looked for significance across all the clusters as groups on each variable. When we found a variable that had significant differences, we looked to see which clusters were highest and lowest on this variable, and used this information to try to figure out what the important distinguishing characteristics of each cluster were. These significant differences are listed in Table 4-1, shown here, along with the names of the students in each cluster (pseudonyms, of course) for reference purposes in reading other chapters. The instruments from which these variables came may be found in Appendix B. They were (1) The Interpersonal Outcome Inventory (IOI) scales, (2) the Final Course Evaluation (FE), (3) the Teacher-As scales of the Follow-Up Questionnaire (TAS), (4) The Tri-Weekly

Table 4-1

Cluster One

	Males	Females
Class: A	Kurt	Donna
B	Cary, Richard	Eve, Elaine, Doreen
C		Jean Burr, Pamela Smith
D	Barney, Walter	Judith

Significant Differences

The teacher did not assign a great deal of reading (FE).

Self—low on Distress (Tri-weekly).

Others—low on Distress (Tri-weekly).

High female.

Teacher too much of a Person (TAS).

IOI: Enactment Loyalty scale high for Father, Mother, Other teachers.

Like-past, Course-predict, Counterdependent flight low for Like-past.

Colleague high for Other teachers, course-predict and Course-actual.

Depression, Distress high for Mother, Other teachers, and Like-past.

Anxiety-neutrality low for Like-past.

Sexual Object high for Father and Like-past.

Competence high for Father, Other teacher's, Like-past, and Course predict.

Cluster Two

	Males	Females
Class: A	Stuart	Lorna, Rita, Wendy, Ellen
B	Tod, Perry, Brad	Evelyn, Katy, Nora, Beatrice
C	Stan Avins, Marvin Manley, Ray Motley, Paul Rutter, Thomas Wallace	Karen Blossom, Leslie Vander, Sarah Straus, Kathryn Vine
D	Steven, Joe, Herb	Ann, Sue, Shirley

Significant Differences

Students did not volunteer their own opinions (FE).

Low Creative Personality (OAIS).

Low verbal (SAT).

Teacher high on Activity-Potency (Tri-weekly).

IOI: Enactment-loyalty high for Father, Mother.

Dependent-complaining low for Father, Like-past and Course-predict.

Rebellion low for Father, Course-predict, and Course-actual.

Counterdependent flight-Resistant complaining, low for Father

Colleague high for Father.

Depression-Distress high for Father and Mother.

Anxiety-Neutrality low for Father and Mother.

Nurturance high for Father and Course-predict.

Sexual Object high for Father and Mother.
Sexual Rival high for Father, Mother, and Like-past.
Competence high for Father and Mother.

Cluster Three

	Males	Females
Class: A		
B	Thad	Libby
C	Dennis Benjamin	
D	Eugene	

High Halo effect (TAS).
Low on others Distressed (Tri-weekly).
Students were free to comment and criticize (FE).
IOI: Enactment Loyalty high for Father, Other teachers, Course-predict, and
    Course actual.
Dependent Complaining high for Father and Mother.
Counterdependent flight-Resistant complaining.
Complaining high for Father, Mother, and Like-past.
Depression—Distress high for Father, Like-past, and Course-actual.
Involvement high for Father and Other teachers.
Sexual Object low for Like-past.
Sexual Rival low for Father, Mother, Other teachers, Like-past, and Course-predict.

Cluster Four

	Males	Females
Class: A	Frank, Edward, Mike	
B	Dave	Hilda
C	Rod Alter, Richard James, Henry Reed	
D	Morton	Margaret

High year in school (age)
IOI: Enactment-loyalty low for Father, Mother, Other teachers, Like-past, and
    Course predict.
Dependent-complaining high for Father and Like-past.
Rebellion high for Father.
Counterdependent flight-Resistant complaining high for Father.
Colleague low for Father and Other teachers.
Depression-distress low for Father and Like-past.
Anxiety-neutrality high for Father and Like-past.
Nurturance low for Father and Course-predict.
Sexual Object low for Father, Mother, and Like-past.
Sexual Rival low for Like-past, high for Course-predict.
Competence Low for Father, Like-past, and Course-predict.

Cluster Five

	Males	Females
Class: A	Edgar	
B	Curt, Ned	
C	Bruce Battle, Ken Brewer, Roger Meadow, Peter Warren	
D	George, Harry, Floyd	

High male.
High Verbal (SAT).
High Math (SAT).
Teacher not enough of an expert (TAS).
Teacher a bad facilitator (TAS).
Teacher not enough of a person (TAS).
Low halo effect (TAS).
Students were not free to comment or criticize (FE).
Teacher was effective in stimulating interest (FE).
Students did volunteer their own opinions (FE).
High Creative Personality (OAIS).
Low on Teacher-activity-potency (Tri-weekly).
Low on Others-activity-potency (Tri-weekly).
High on Others-distress (Tri-weekly).
IOI: Enactment-loyalty low for Father, Other teachers, Course-predict.
Dependent-complaining low for Father, Mother, high for Like-past.
Rebellion high for Course-predict and Course-actual.
Counterdependent flight-Resistant Complaining low for Father, Mother.
Colleague high for Father.
Depression-Distress low for Father, Mother, Other teachers, Like-past, and Course-actual.
Nurturance high for Father and Mother.
Sexual Object high for Father.
Sexual Rival high for Mother and Like-past.
Competence high for Like-past.

Cluster Six

	Males	Females
Class: A	Dale	Frances, Anna
B	Doug, Gary, Ron, Lawrence	Peggy
C	Arthur Monk, Toby Wicker	
D		

Students volunteered their own opinions (FE).
The teacher was too much of a person (TAS).
Low structure (TAS).
Teacher was low on Activity-potency (Tri-weekly).

Teacher was high on Distress (Tri-weekly).
IOI: Enactment-loyalty high for Other teachers and Like-past.
Dependent-complaining high for Like-past and Course-predict.
Rebellion high for Father.
Counterdependent Flight-Resistant Complaining high for Father and Like-past.
Colleague high for Other teachers and Course-actual.
Depression-Distress high for Other teachers and Like-past.
Anxiety-neutrality high for Father and Like-past.
Nurturance low for Father, Mother, and Course-predict.
Sexual Object low for Father.
Sexual Rival low for Like-past.
Competence low for Father, Mother, Like-past, and Course-predict.

Cluster Seven

	Males	Females
Class: A		Cindy
B	Lou, Roger	Lois, Mary
C	Alfred Alkin	Pat Jewel
D	Robert, Gus	Gloria, Lisa

Significant Differences
The teacher assigned a great deal of reading (FE).
The teacher was too much of an expert (TAS).
The teacher was not enough of a person (TAS).
High structure (TAS).
IOI: Enactment-Loyalty low for Father, Mother, Other teachers, and Like-past.
Dependent complaining high for Father, Mother, and low for Course-predict.
Rebellion low for Like-past.
Counterdependent flight-Resistant Complaining low for Like-past.
Anxiety-neutrality high for Father and Mother.
Involvement low for other teachers.
Sexual Rival high for Father, Mother, Other teachers, and Like-past.
Competence low for Father and Other teachers.

Cluster Eight

	Males	Females
Class: A	Don, Howard, Mel, Brian	Ruth, Sharon, Grace, Diane
B		Candy
C	Tim Stall,	Helen Farmer, Audrey Dabbs, Dorothy Fields, Louise Tuft, Eileen Weeks
D	Fred, Barney, Leonard	Carey, Bertha

Significant Differences

   The teacher was not effective in stimulating interest (FE).

   The students were not free to comment and criticize (FE).

   The students did not volunteer their own opinions (FE).

   Self-high on Distress (Tri-weekly).

   IOI: Enactment-loyalty high for Mother and Course-predict.

   Dependent-complaining high for Father.

   Rebellion high for Like-past.

   Colleague low for Other teachers, Course-predict and Course-Actual.

   Depression-distress high for Mother.

   Anxiety-neutrality high for Like-past.

   Involvement low for Father.

   Sexual Object low for Mother and Like-past.

Questionnaire factors (Activity-potency, Evaluation and Distress for object Teacher, Self- and Other) (Tri-weekly), (5) Fricke's Opinion Attitude and Interest Survey (OAIS) scales, (6) The Metaphor Check List of the Final Evaluation (MCL), (7) The Student's Scholastic Aptitude Test scores in both the Math and Verbal parts (SAT), (8) sex, male or female.

   There were data available that had no coding by number and therefore no way to test for significant differences, but that were none-theless terribly important in getting a feel for the kinds of people in each cluster. The interviews conducted with each student by the observers were the most helpful in this respect, and the open-ended questions on the Final Evaluation and the Follow-Up Questionnaires were also crucial. Also, we interviewed the observers once about their impressions of the classes. We would have liked to have had even more of the impressionistic kind of data, perhaps more information about students' backgrounds, or some projective material.

Chapter 5. The Teacher—As Typology: A Conceptualization of Task Strategies

1. The teacher-as (TAS) typology is the basic conceptual framework from which two distinct, yet related, research and assessment techniques have been developed. The TAS scoring system, which is described in some detail below, is a procedure for scoring ongoing teacher-student interaction, on an act-to-act basis, in terms of all the six strategies. The TAS evaluation questionnaire, a paper-and-pencil instrument that can be completed by students, is available upon request from the authors.

2. The reader will require some familiarity with the teacher-as scoring system, its rationale, assumptions, conventions and the meanings of the

different categories or codes, in order to work his way through this scorers' transcript. Our purpose in presenting the actual act-to-act codes is to illustrate their usefulness in understanding the ongoing process rather than as a quick means for the reader learning to score. The transcript, plus the earlier discussion of the six strategies and the outline of the scoring system which follows, form a package which could all be used in the training of scorers.

THE TEACHER—AS SCORING SYSTEM

We have maintained that every act on the part of a student or teacher, whether it is proactive or reactive, has implications for the teacher-student task relationships and for the kind and quality of work that is undertaken. Each act in turn may be relevant to a single teaching function and task strategy or, as is more common, the intent of the act may require an array of scores in order to capture the complex shadings and subtlety of the message. These considerations have led us to devise an act-to-act scoring system which enables one to code the different pressures and counterpressures that characterize the continuous, yet changing, flow of interaction between teachers and students. We had two purposes in mind in constructing this scoring system: to make available an observational technique specifically designed to fit our conception of the task demands of the classroom, and to provide teachers with a practical diagnostic procedure for assessing, evaluating, and understanding their own teaching styles.

The teacher-as scoring system may be used in the specific act-to-act coding of transcripts or tape-recordings of class sessions, or it may be employed in arriving at a more global assessment of actual on-the-spot interaction. It is possible for a well-trained and experienced observer to code directly ongoing interaction, but we have not as yet attempted this.

Consistent with our assumption that the teacher-as typology has practical implications for teacher training, evaluation, and development is our belief that a teacher who is somewhat familiar with the scoring system should be in a better position to arrive at a more global feeling for the intentions behind some of the complicated messages sent by students, to assess generally what was going on taskwise, to think hard about his goals and his attempts to implement them, and finally to gain some understanding of how he is being viewed and responded to by his students. Implicit in all of this is the notion that the acquisition of this kind of feedback may be useful in pointing to directions for constructive change and development. Finally, a certain degree of familiarity with the scoring system should be helpful to those who wish to acquire at least an intuitive understanding of the rationale and purpose of the teacher-as evaluation questionnaire described in Chapter 9.

Scoring Decisions. Operating as a scorer involves a continuous confrontation with a series of interrelated decisions. First, one must identify the act to be coded. An act must include a reference to the unit or sequence of interaction to be scored, and to the participants, that is, the message sender and the target. Next, the scorer must decide which teaching strategy or strategies are embedded in the act. Finally, the impact of the message within each strategy must be pinpointed. Let us deal briefly with each of these decisions.

1. *Definition of an act.* Generally speaking, an act is identified here similarily to the way it is defined in the Member-to-Leader scoring system in Chapter 1. An act is defined as any interaction (a grunt, silence, a single sentence, a burst of sentences, or a single speech) where the participants, strategy, and intention or impact of the message remain uniform. A change in acts is indicated by any major change in scoring, that is, the subsequent act is scored differently from the previous act. Thus the end of one act and the beginning of another is signalled by a change in the message sender, the receiver, the array or combination of categories or strategies involved, or the qualitative nature of the message across the categories. Since most acts are multiple scored for all six strategies, a major change in any one of the categories gives the act a slightly different shading and leads to a new act.

One inevitably encounters certain interactions where unitizing is exceedingly difficult and where arbitrary decisions become necessary. We have standardized these in the form of a series of conventions. Thus, natural pauses or even an arbitrary break in a speech may be made as long as there is a significant change in scoring. For a long, drawn out, unilateral speech, such as a lecture, it is suggested that the main opening thematic sentence be treated as one act. If a series of separate but related facts, data, or experiences follow this main sentence, each set of those facts or experiences can be treated as a single act. In general, when in doubt one may arbitrarily score short sentences or bits of information as a single unit. Our intention in the case of the latter two conventions is to capture a teacher's heavy reliance on a particular strategy without weighing it excessively or inadequately. Thus we do intend that a teacher who lectures for a whole session end up with a greater expert score than someone whose interaction covers a broader range of strategies.

2. *Identification of participants.* The problem of the level of inference one makes in identifying the initiator and target of messages is not as pronounced here as it is in the Member-to-Leader scoring system. Our concern is with the more direct rather than symbolic connections between the participants, although an attempt should be made to use the particular situational context in making inferences and in arriving at decisions. Basically, we are primarily interested in acts where there is a fairly clear and direct statement from a student to the teacher or from the

teacher to one or more students. In addition, acts may be scored where the object remains unspecified, but where the context enables one to make a pretty good guess about the identity of the target. An example might involve a student's complaint that he would like to know more about what it is like to function as a psychologist, or a statement that multiple choice exams are unfair. Here the call is for more socializing agent and a better formal authority on the part of the teacher. Basically, we are suggesting that an adequate job of scoring can be carried out by focusing on levels one and two of the Member-Leader scoring system. In the case of teacher to student acts it is also unnecessary to be able to identify the specific student targets. Thus, a teacher would receive a score as a facilitator if he asked why a particular student was feeling anxious or if he asked why the females in the whole class were anxious.

3. *Scoring student-to-teacher acts.* The scoring of a student's act once the unit has been identified involves a two-stage process. We have assumed that every student act, whether it is in response to the teacher's initiative, to a peer, or whether it originated with the student, contains some explicit or implicit reference to one or more of the six teaching strategies. The first step, therefore, involves a judgment as to which of the strategies are the most salient and which are essentially irrelevant for this act. Having decided on the relevant strategies, the scorer's task it to then determine the particular qualitative intention or thrust behind each strategy and code it. To illustrate the codes we shall use the teacher as expert abbreviated as X. The reader should keep in mind that the remaining five strategies are similarly coded by simply substituting the abbreviations FA, SA, F, EI, and P for X.

4. *TAS codes: student-to-teacher acts*

x: The strategy is not relevant or salient at the moment; the student communicates little or no concern about the strategy and seems to have little or no energy invested in the strategy at that moment.

X: The student validates the strategy: he seems to view it as quite legitimate and acceptable, he manifests neither great discomfort nor satisfaction with it, and there is no pressure for change implied.

+X: The student expresses considerable satisfaction with the strategy and how the teacher has been handling it.

—X: The student expresses generalized disappointment or dissatisfaction with the strategy or the way in which the teacher is functioning within the strategy; implied is the message that the teacher should somehow be doing a better job, but there is no clear indication of whether he should be doing more or less of the strategy or whether he should cease altogether and try another strategy, and there is no clear direction for change specified.

—↓X: The student reports, manifests, or seems to be experiencing considerable discomfort, tension, or frustration because the teacher is providing too much of a particular strategy; there is a fairly clear change message being sent and the teacher is being pressured to manifest less of, play down, or disengage himself from that particular strategy; frequently he is being asked to simultaneously manifest more of another strategy.

—X↑: The student reports, manifests, or seems to be experiencing considerable discomfort, tension, or frustration because the teacher is not providing enough of a particular strategy; the teacher is under pressure to manifest more of, to invest more energy in, or to be more engaged in that particular strategy; frequently he is also being pressured to provide less of another strategy.

Since these are six strategies each of which can be coded in any one of six ways, there are 36 scoring possibilities for each student act. These are summarized in the following 6×6 matrix.

Student-to-Teacher Codes	Strategies					
	X	FA	SA	F	EI	P
Not salient	x	fa	sa	f	ei	p
Validation, legitimacy	X	FA	SA	F	EI	P
Generalized satisfaction	+X	+FA	+SA	+F	+EI	+F
Generalized dissatisfaction, no clear direction for change	—X	—FA	—SA	—F	—EI	—F
Dissatisfaction because too much of strategy, pressure to be less	—X↓	—FA↓	—SA↓	—F↓	—EI↓	—P↓
Dissatisfaction because too little of strategy, pressure to be more	—X↑	—FA↑	—SA↑	—F↑	—EI↑	—P↑

A sample scoring for a student-to-teacher act might be as follows: —X↓, fa, —SA↓, EI, —F↑, —P↑, indicating the student's desire for less X and SA, more F and P, and his satisfaction with EI. FA is not relevant for this act.

5. *Scoring teacher-to-student acts.* Scoring a teacher's act similarly requires decisions concerning the strategies being invoked or rejected and the intent behind the act. The corresponding categories for teacher acts, again using X as a case in point, are as follows.

x: The strategy is not relevant or salient to the teacher, and he has little or no energy invested in that strategy at that moment in time.

X: Teacher is manifesting or being that strategy, he has a moderate amount of energy invested in it, and there is little or no evidence of the teacher's really asserting this particular strategy; it seems to form a continuous flow and is consistent with the previous and subsequent acts.

$X\downarrow$: The teacher actively ignores, rejects, deemphasizes, or plays down this particular strategy, possibly in response to student pressure; in the process the teacher may be shifting to another strategy on his own or he may be rejecting a student's bid that he may be more of or emphasize more the original strategy; there is a discontinuous quality to the teacher's transition.

$X\uparrow$: The teacher actively initiates or asserts this strategy; he spontaneously introduces it or does so as part of a simultaneous effort to reject a student's bid for more of another strategy.

The six strategies and four categories generate the following 6×4 matrix.

Teacher-to-Student Codes	Strategies					
	X	FA	SA	F	EI	P
Not salient	x	fa	sa	f	ei	P
Manifesting the strategy	X	FA	SA	F	EI	P
Rejecting the strategy	$X\downarrow$	$FA\downarrow$	$SA\downarrow$	$F\downarrow$	$EI\downarrow$	$P\downarrow$
Asserting the strategy	$X\uparrow$	$FA\uparrow$	$SA\uparrow$	$F\uparrow$	$EI\uparrow$	$P\uparrow$

A simple scoring for a teacher-to-student act might look like this: $X\downarrow$, fa, sa, ei, $F\uparrow$, P, indicating the teacher's efforts to play down his expertise and to use a more personal reference (P) to facilitate the group ($F\uparrow$).

6. *Some useful scoring conventions.* Experience with this scoring system suggests that certain arbitrary decisions are required frequently enough to justify the establishment of a set of conventions. A few of the ones we have evolved are listed below, and additional ones may become necessary if the system is applied to a markedly different set of data.

(a) When a teacher signals the beginning or end of a class, calls on a student to respond, or recognizes a student's desire to speak, code FA plus any other categories which may be appropriate.

(b) If a teacher makes a marked and assertive transition or shifts away from a student's request for a particular strategy, score on assertion ($\uparrow$) for the first and a rejection ($\downarrow$) for the second. Thus, when a student asks about a reference while the teacher is enthusiastically relating a story about his research, and he ignores the student's message, score $EI\uparrow$ and $X\downarrow$.

(c) At times teachers will use one strategy to build up or maintain another. We refer to this as one strategy being in the service of the other. For example, a teacher may be excitingly relating a series of studies in an area that really excites him. We would argue that X is being used in the service of EI and the act would be coded EI↑,X. Or consider the situation where a teacher shares his feelings of discomfort when he is being evaluated by the chairman of his department, in order to facilitate his students' showing how they feel about his evaluating them. Here the teacher's personal feelings are being used as part of a facilitator strategy and the act should be scored F↑,P.

(d) Multiple scoring in order to capture the rich nuances of an act is the rule, but a particular strategy-category combination may be used only once per act.

(e) Silences are a problem and should be scored only when the context is highly suggestive of what is going on. For example, a silence following a teacher's question about an assigned reading, and where it is fairly likely that some students know the answer, should be scored as —X↓.

7. *Reliability of the scoring system.* Experience suggests that certain people can be trained to be better scorers than others. Sensitivity to

The Member-To-Leader Scoring System Categories

Area	Subarea	Category	Abbreviation
Impulse	Hostility	1. Moving Against	MA
		2. Resisting	RS
		3. Withdrawing	WI
		4. Guilt Inducing	GI
	Affection	5. Making Reparation	RP
		6. Identifying	ID
		7. Accepting	AC
		8. Moving Toward	MT
Authority relations		9. Showing Dependency	DN[a]
		10. Showing Independence	IN
		11. Showing Counterdependence	CD[b]
Ego state	Anxiety	12. Expressing Anxiety	AE
		13. Denying Anxiety	AD
		14. Expressing Self-esteem	SE
	Depression	15. Expressing Depression	DE
		16. Denying Depression	DD

[a] For Leader-To-Member, score Showing Dominance, DM
[b] For Leader-to-Member, score Showing Counterdominance, CD

interpersonal relationships, especially the nuances and complexities of the teacher-student relationship, as well as some teaching experience are helpful assets. Relatively experienced people can be trained to achieve a respectable degree of reliability in about ten hours. Preliminary reliability data suggest that we are able to achieve agreement between independent experienced scorers close to the level of accuracy which we were able to achieve in the Member-to-Leader scoring system.

The inclusion of the Member-to-Leader scores adds a very rich dimension to the analysis in that we can begin to appreciate the kinds of interpersonal feelings which can be associated with particular ways of handling the task strategies, both for different students and the teacher. A brief explanation of the rationale and scoring categories is presented in Chapter 1. For the sake of convenience, we have not included on the transcript the codes for levels of inference for each act. Since the vast majority of acts were scored as Level I or Level II, it was decided that the confusion generated by yet another set of codes was not worth the limited gain. In order to facilitate the reader's being able to utilize the Member-Leader codes in arriving at his own analysis of the transcript, we have included above a brief summary of the meanings of the different abbreviations.

INSTRUMENTS

Appendix B-1. Rating Scales

The purpose of this study is to measure the *meaning* of certain things to various people by having them judge them against a series of descriptive scales. In taking this test, please make your judgments on the basis of what these things mean to *you*. On each page of this booklet you will find a different concept to be judged and beneath it a set of scales. You are to rate the concept on each of these scales in order.

Here is how you are to use these scales.

If you feel that the concept at the top of the page is *very closely related* to one end of the scale, you should place your check-mark as follows:

fair X : ____ : ____ : ____ : ____ : ____ : ____ unfair

or

fair ____ : ____ : ____ : ____ : ____ : ____ : X unfair

If you feel that the concept is *quite closely related* to one or the other end of the scale (but not extremely), you should place your check-mark as follows:

strong ____ : X : ____ : ____ : ____ : ____ : ____ weak

or

strong ____ : ____ : ____ : ____ : ____ : X : ____ weak

If the concept seems *only slightly related* to one side as opposed to the other side (but is not really neutral), then you should check as follows:

active ___ : ___ : _X_ : ___ : ___ : ___ : ___passive

or

active ___ : ___ : ___ : _X_ : ___ : ___passive

The direction toward you check, of course, depends on which of the two ends of the scale seem most characteristic of the thing you're judging.

If you consider the concept to be *neutral* on the scale, both sides of the scale *equally associated* with the concept, or if the scale is *completely irrelevant*, unrelated to the concept, then you should place your checkmark in the middle space:

safe ___ : ___ : ___ : _X_ : ___ : ___ : ___dangerous

IMPORTANT: (1) Place your check-marks *in the middle of the spaces*, not on the boundaries:

This   Not this

___ : ___ : ___ : _X_ : ___ : ___ X___ :

(2) Be sure you check every scale for every concept— *do not omit any*.

(3) Never put more than one check-mark on a single scale.

Do not look back and forth through the items. Do not try to remember how you checked similar items earlier in the test. Make each item a separate and independent judgment. Work at a fairly high speed through this test. Do not worry or puzzle over individual items. It is your first impression, the immediate "feelings" about the items, that we want. On the other hand, please do not be careless, because we want your true impressions.

> MY FATHER[1,2]
> MY MOTHER
> PERSONS IN AUTHORITY
> TEACHER I CAN LEARN FROM
> AVERAGE COLLEGE TEACHER
> THE IDEAL STUDENT
> MYSELF AS A STUDENT
> PSYCHOLOGY 101
> MYSELF IN A COURSE I
> REALLY ENJOY

[1] Each heading and the rating scales below were on a separate page.

[2] On the first administration at the beginning of the term, the eight headings above were used. During the term the headings used were Psychology 101, The Other Students, Yourself in the Course, and Your Instructor.

complaining	:	:	:	:	:	:	accepting
loyal	:	:	:	:	:	:	rebellious
trapped	:	:	:	:	:	:	free
feminine	:	:	:	:	:	:	masculine
weak	:	:	:	:	:	:	strong
hard	:	:	:	:	:	:	soft
distressed	:	:	:	:	:	:	secure
relaxed	:	:	:	:	:	:	fearful
anxious	:	:	:	:	:	:	calm
sad	:	:	:	:	:	:	happy
depressed	:	:	:	:	:	:	confident
distant	:	:	:	:	:	:	involved
active	:	:	:	:	:	:	passive
slow	:	:	:	:	:	:	fast
intense	:	:	:	:	:	:	casual
defensive	:	:	:	:	:	:	aggressive
heroic	:	:	:	:	:	:	cowardly
distracted	:	:	:	:	:	:	hard working
retreating	:	:	:	:	:	:	advancing
impersonal	:	:	:	:	:	:	personal
rewarding	:	:	:	:	:	:	unrewarding
taking	:	:	:	:	:	:	giving
open	:	:	:	:	:	:	closed
authoritarian	:	:	:	:	:	:	democratic
trustworthy	:	:	:	:	:	:	untrustworthy
insensitive	:	:	:	:	:	:	sensitive
kind	:	:	:	:	:	:	unkind
bad	:	:	:	:	:	:	good
competent	:	:	:	:	:	:	incompetent

Appendix B-2

INTERPERSONAL OUTCOME INVENTORY;
INSTRUCTIONS AND ANSWER SHEET: FIRST ADMINISTRATION

The Interpersonal Outcome Inventory Booklet presents a series of inter-
personal situations. Each one describes the relationship between a younger
Person and an Older Person, and the emphasis is on how the Younger
Person feels about the Older Person. After each situation there are five

questions, two asking how often such a situation arose with your parents and one which asks you to summarize the experience you have had with various teachers in the past five years. In all of these questions, try to remember that in any relationship lots of different things happen, and we are interested not in what you would have liked to happen, but what actually did happen. The important element, then, is your accuracy in recalling the various situations which may have arisen with various people. In the fourth question you are asked to indicate how much you liked or disliked each situation, or how much you would have liked it if it occurred. Finally, the fifth question asks you to estimate how often each situation will probably occur between you and your instructor of Psychology 101 this semester. You should base your guess on: (1) your past experience; (2) your present frame of mind; (3) what you have heard about Psychology 101 in general; and (4) the fact that your instructor will be a teaching fellow and will be male.

Read the description of each situation. Then answer each question by placing a number between 1 and 9 in the approximate box. *Questions A, B, and C* ask how often the particular situation occurred with your father (question A), your mother (question B), and your teachers in the past five years (question C). For example, if situation #1 occurred

KEY 9 = FREQUENTLY	9 = LIKE VERY MUCH	9 = FREQUENTLY
1 = NEVER	1 = DISLIKE VERY MUCH	1 = NEVER

Questions A–C	Question D	Question E
How often did such a situation occur when the Younger Person was you and the Older Person was:	How much did you like (or would you you have liked) such a situation?	How often do you think such a situation will occur with your Psych 101 instructor this semester?

	Your father	Your mother	Your teacher		
	A	B	C	D	E
Question 1					
2					
3 ↓ 60					

frequently with your father, put a 9 in the box under father (A) for situation 1. If the situation never happened, put a 1 in the box. If it occurred, but not frequently, put some number between 2 and 8 in the box. The more often the situation occurred, the higher the number in the box.

Question D asks how much you liked (or would have liked) such a situation. Enter your answer in the box under question D, where 9 means you *liked* it very much and 1 means you *disliked* it very much.

Question E asks you to guess how often you think the situation will occur with your instructor in Psychology 101 this semester. Use the same scale (9 = frequently, 1 = never) for this question as you used for questions A–C.

INTERPERSONAL OUTCOME INVENTORY ANSWER SHEET: END OF TERM

Read the descriptions of each situation. Then answer each question by placing a number between 1 and 9 in the appropriate box. Question A asks how often the particular situation occurred with your teacher in Psychology 101. For example, if situation #1 occurred frequently with your teacher, put a 9 in the box under (A). If the situation never

KEYS	(A)	9 = FREQUENTLY 1 = NEVER	(B)	9 = LIKE VERY MUCH 1 = DISLIKE VERY MUCH

	Question A How often did such a situation occur when the Younger Person was you and the Older Person was your teacher in Psych 101 this semester?	*Question B* How much did you like (or would you have liked) such a situation?
Situ-ation	A	B
1		
2		
3 ↓ 60		

Please do not write on this booklet. Use the answer sheet to indicate your responses.

happened, put a 1 in the box. If it occurred, but not frequently, put some number between 2 and 8 in the box. The more often the situation occurred, the higher the number in the box.

Question B asks how much you liked (or would have liked) such a situation. Enter your answer in the box under question B, where 9 means you *liked* it very much and 1 means you *disliked* it very much.

INTERPERSONAL OUTCOME INVENTORY BOOKLET

1. In this situation, the Younger Person works in close harmony with the Older Person, each one enjoying the sense of identity with the other one that develops in their relationship.
2. In this situation, the Younger Person feels disappointed in the Older Person for not providing enough direction and for being too weak and indecisive in matters affecting the Younger Person.
3. In this situation, the Younger Person feels affection and respect for the Older Person and desires to be noticed and liked in return.
4. In this situation, the Younger Person feels somewhat jealous and resentful of how many things the Older Person enjoys which are not permitted to the Younger Person.
5. In this situation, the Younger Person feels that the Older Person tries to make the process of learning too easy, and the Younger Person seeks out out more challenging tasks to master.
6. In this situation, the Younger Person feels disappointed in the Older Person for being cold, impersonal, or unsupportive.
7. In this situation, the Younger Person depends upon the Older Person for guidance and good judgment.
8. In this situation, the Younger Person feels angry at the Older Person, although the anger is somewhat rare in their usually warm and friendly relationship.
9. In this situation, the Younger Person cannot accept the advice or rules of the Older Person since the Older Person does not live up to them either, or at least did not when younger.
10. In this situation, the Younger Person feels that the Older Person intrudes too much into the Younger Person's efforts to learn something, and the Younger Person tries to keep all such efforts out of the Older Person's view.
11. In this situation, the Younger Person can trust the Older Person to be supportive and protective at the appropriate moment.
12. In this situation, the Younger Person rebels against the domination of the Older Person, insisting on the right to do things without interference and control.
13. In this situation, the Younger Person feels that the Older Person wants to be on friendlier terms than the Younger Person wishes

to be, and the Younger Person turns, instead, to people of the same age for friendship.

14. In this situation, the Younger Person feels that the Older Person is prying too much into matters that should be private, or at least they should be shared only when the Younger Person feels like sharing them.

15. In this situation, the Younger Person feels free to try out new ideas or skills, confident that the Older Person would respond as to the skills or ideas of a colleague.

16. In this situation, the Younger Person tries to argue the Older Person into giving the Younger Person assistance or special treatment, even though the Older Person seems unwilling to give them.

17. In this situation, the Younger Person feels that the Older Person if given half a chance, would be too dominating, and the Younger Person tries to avoid those times when the Older Person might expect some expression of dependency.

18. In this situation, the Younger Person does not like the fact that the initiative for being friendly and close is entirely in the hands of the Older Person.

19. In this situation, the Younger Person feels able to agree or disagree with the Older Person without the issue becoming a personal one.

20. In this situation, the Younger Person feels not quite able to complete a task without a few additional comments and "words of wisdom" from the Older Person.

21. In this situation, the Younger Person feels almost smothered by the Older Person's attention and efforts to help, and the Younger Person tries to break free of this close contact.

22. In this situation, the Younger Person feels critical of the Older Person for trying to control the Younger Person's thoughts and actions too much, and the Younger Person starts resisting all such efforts on the part of the Older Person.

23. In this situation, the Younger Person feels secure about the basic affection of the Older Person even without much visible display and the relationship between them is pleasant but not very personal.

24. In this situation, the Older Person provides a steadying influence in the Younger Person's life, especially at times when the Younger Person cannot resist being distracted from the important goals.

25. In this situation, the Younger Person feels that the Older could quickly and easily demolish the accomplishments of the Younger Person, showing up their flaws without caring about the Younger Person's wounded pride.

26. In this situation, the Younger Person feels critical of the Older Person for providing too much attention and support, and the Younger Person refuses to accept any further overtures along those lines.

27. In this situation, the Younger Person feels free enough and strong enough to be able to exercise self-control, which makes it possible

for the Younger Person to discuss goals with the Older Person without fearing any loss of autonomy.

28. In this situation, the Older Person seems to bring out the best in the Younger Person, and for that reason the Younger Person feels that being around the Older Person is like "having the batteries recharged."

29. In this situation, the Younger Person feels that the Older Person might be quite vindictive and mean if the Younger Person challenged the Older Person's authority and rights.

30. In this situation, the Younger Person feels incompetent and inexperienced in relation to the Older Person's skills and qualifications.

31. In this situation, the Younger Person feels secure and independent and able to relate to the Older Person without making any extreme demands for support or protection.

32. In this situation, the Younger Person feels uncertain and distressed at having to make the right decision in a matter and expresses these feelings to the Older Person.

33. In this situation, the Younger Person senses some personal dislike or rejection from the Older Person, and this results in a certain uneasiness around the Older Person.

34. In this situation, the Younger Person feels that the desirable qualities or charms of the Older Person set a very high standard for the Younger Person, a standard which can only be reached after a long time, if at all.

35. In this situation, the Younger Person feels that the process of learning from the Older Person involves a commitment to understanding the Older Person's whole way of looking at things.

36. In this situation, the Younger Person feels distressed at the difficulty of some new task and turns to the Older Person for encouragement and assistance in "braving the world."

37. In this situation, the Younger Person fears the judgments or criticisms of the Older Person.

38. In this situation, the Younger Person feels deficient in whatever personal qualities the Older Person finds appealing.

39. In this situation, the Younger Person spends a fair amount of time thinking about the Older Person, even though the relationship between them is just as often unpleasant as pleasant.

40. In this situation, the Younger Person tries to keep the relationship with the Older Person as impersonal as possible, limiting it mainly to technical matters where the Older Person is more experienced.

41. In this situation, the Younger Person feels mistrustful of the Older Person, and, as a result, the Younger Person feels tense in the presence of the Older Person.

42. In this situation, the Younger Person feels badly about how often the Older Person's suggestions and requests are neglected in favor of more selfish activities.

43. In this situation, the Younger Person feels able to see and to appreciate

the Older Person as a fellow human being, and the relationship between them is both warm and genuine.

44. In this situation, the Younger Person feels that the Older Person would take advantage of any personal information about the Younger Person, and so the Younger Person simply keeps all such thoughts away from the Older Person.

45. In this situation, the Younger Person admires the skills or talents of the Older Person so much that the Younger Person uses the Older Person as the model of what to become.

46. In this situation, the Younger Person feels rather lost and discouraged, but the Younger Person finds it hard to get much attention or support from the Older Person.

47. In this situation, the Younger Person tries hard to make sure that the relationshlp with the Older Person does not slip back from the current, friendly relationship into one where the Older Person has all the power, and where the Younger Person feels like a child.

48. In this situation, the Younger Person feels that the best way to handle the Older Person is not to get too involved and to keep everything as much on the surface as possible.

49. In this situation, the Younger Person feels a sense of rivalry with the Older Person and tries to excel in those areas where the Older Person seems superior to the Younger Person.

50. In this situation, the Younger Person feels disappointed because the Older Person tends to hold back on demonstrating the knowledge and skills which the Younger Person wants to acquire.

51. In this situation, the Younger Person takes great pleasure in being able to turn the tables on the Older Person and provide the Older Person with something of value which only the Younger Person can provide.

52. In this situation, the Younger Person finds it necessary to lead something of a double life, going along with the Older Person on the surface and keeping any hostile or rebellious thoughts completely private.

53. In this situation, the Younger Person feels so warmly toward the Older Person that it gives the Younger Person pleasure to do things the same way as the Older Person and to take the same position on things.

54. In this situation, the Younger Person feels that the Older Person has failed to insist upon a serious, or moral, attitude on the part of Younger People.

55. In this situation, the Younger Person expresses an eagerness to learn from the Older Person in areas where the Older Person is something of an expert.

56. In this situation, the Younger Person feels uninvolved and bored, as if the Older Person had nothing of value to offer to the Younger Person.

57. In this situation, the Younger Person learns the standards of the Older

Person so well that the Younger Person can adjust to meet those standards without specific directions or comments from the Older Person.

58. In this situation, the Younger Person finds it hard to feel any warmth toward the Older Person because the Older Person conceals those characteristics which might make the Younger Person feel some warmth or interest.

59. In this situation, the Younger Person is careful not to violate the Older Person's standards of mature and dignified behavior.

60. In this situation, the Younger Person feels irritated at all the senseless tasks assigned by the Older Person and feels sure that some other system of instruction would lead to a greater gain in knowledge and skill.

Appendix B-3. Course Evaluation Form

The following questions deal with your prior experience in college, your reasons for taking Psychology 101, and your expectations about the course. All information is confidential and will not be available to anyone evaluating your work in this course. Please answer all the questions.[3]

1. Why did you elect Psychology 101?
2. How is this course related to your overall goals in college? How would you describe these goals?
3. The best thing about this course was . . .
4. The worst thing about this course was . . .
5. The time I really felt we were learning something exciting was when . . .
6. The thing that bothered me most about my recitation instructor was . . .
7. The thing I liked best about my recitation instructor was . . .
8. After taking the course I feel that Psychology is . . .
9. If I had my way, the course would have . . .
10. One way in which the course has changed me is . . .

Answer each question below and give a specific example where possible.

11. When was your instructor most clear in communicating the course material? Give an example.
12. When wasn't he clear? Give an example.
    How often was he unclear?

[3] Here we have simply listed the questions.

(Circle appropriate number)   1   2   3   4   5

Always	Sometimes	Never

13. What do you think the goals of the class were? Give an example or two in which these were implemented.

14. To what extent did the instructor encourage independent thinking in the solution of a problem?   1   2   3   4   5

Always	Sometimes	Never

Give an example.

15. Did you feel free in class to ask questions, disagree, or express your own ideas?   1   2   3   4   5

Always	Sometimes	Never

If there were times when you did not feel free, give an example.

16. How effective was your instructor in stimulating your interest in the course material?   1   2   3   4   5

Very	Somewhat	Not at all

Give an example of a particularly stimulating class period.

Imagine that you are a poet and have just been commissioned to write a poem describing your instructor. Decide which of the metaphors in the list below apply to your instructor. If the metaphor *definitely describes* your instructor circle the *plus* sign (+). If the metaphor is *definitely unlike* the instructor circle the *minus* sign (−), and if it *does not apply* to him or her circle the 0.

Circle as many pulses as definitely apply to your instructor, and as many minuses as are definitely unlike him. Keep in mind that it is quite possible to use seemingly contradictory phrases if this is necessary for an adequate description. A descriptive metaphor does not imply anything about age, sex or status. E.g., "a compassionate mother" could apply as much to a male as a female, to a younger person as much as to an older person.

+0 −   1. a stranger in the night   +0 − 16. a meandering stream
+0 −   2. a treasured book   +0 − 17. a threatening father
+0 −   3. a powerful engine   +0 − 18. a door ajar
+0 −   4. a dissonant chord   +0 − 19. a just judge
+0 −   5. a driving rain   +0 − 20. a searing flame
+0 −   6. an intense rhythm   +0 − 21. a loving friend
+0 −   7. a tentative shrug   +0 − 22. a bouncing ball
+0 −   8. a probing searchlight   +0 − 23. an able seducer
+0 −   9. a compassionate mother   +0 − 24. a secret betrayer
+0 − 10. a scolding mother   +0 − 25. a lonely eminence
+0 − 11. cloudy weather   +0 − 26. a deep forest
+0 − 12. a catchy tune   +0 − 27. a comforting hand
+0 − 13. a secure fortress   +0 − 28. an unopened telegram
+0 − 14. a sharp scissors   +0 − 29. a gentle breeze
+0 − 15. a warm fire   +0 − 30. a nostalgic memory

In the spaces below write the numbers of the *two* metaphors which *best describe* your instructor, and the *two* which are *most unlike* him or her.

Most like him: _____ and _____
Why did you choose these two?

Most unlike him: _____ and _____

Why did you choose these two?

Below indicate any other metaphors that apply to your instructor.

For each question below circle the alternative that best fits your *recitation* instructor.

1. He put the material across in an interesting way.
    A. almost always
    B. often
    C. occasionally
    D. seldom
    E. almost never
2. He assigned a great amount of reading.[4]
    A. almost always
    B. often
    C. occasionally
    D. seldom
    E. almost never
3. He planned class activities in detail.
4. He invited criticism of his acts.
5. Students frequently volunteered their own opinions.
6. He maintained definite standards of student performance.
7. He seemed personally interested in the students.
8. He assigned very difficult reading.
9. He followed an outline closely.
10. He told the students when they had done a particularly good job.
11. He complimented students in front of others.
12. Students argued with one another or with the instructor, not necessarily with hostility.
13. He was permissive and flexible.
14. He was friendly.
15. How would you rate the recitation instructor in general (all-around) teaching ability?
    A. superior
    B. very good
    C. good
    D. fair
    E. poor

[4] The choices were the same for the first 14 statements.

16. How would you rate the overall value of the course?
    A. superior
    B. very good
    C. good
    D. fair
    E. poor

Have you any additional comments to make about the course, your instructor, or the field in general? Continue on the back of this sheet if necessary.

Classrooms differ in terms of the kind of behavior that is "acceptable." In some classes, for instance, the instructor does not encourage or want students' continued probing of a given issue. In others, personal anecdotes as examples of given principles are not allowed. What kinds of things were allowed or encouraged? How was this communicated to you by the instructor or the other students? How did this affect you? Would you have preferred broader or narrower limits? Etc.

Appendix B-4. Follow-Up Questionnaire:Two Years Later

Please answer the following questions in as much detail as possible. If additional space is needed, continue on back of page.

1. What was your initial impression of your Psychology 101 instructor?
2. What do you remember about the first few days of class?
3. How would you describe your involvement in the course?
    _____ very enthusiastic
    _____ generally enthusiastic
    _____ interested but not enthusiastic
    _____ often uninvolved
    _____ very uninvolved
4. How would you describe the involvement of other students in the class?
    _____ very enthusiastic
    _____ generally enthusiastic
    _____ interested but not enthusiastic
    _____ often uninvolved
    _____ very uninvolved
5. How would you describe the extent of student participation in the course?
    _____ students determined course content and really ran the course.
    _____ instructor determined course content and students took it from there.

———— sometimes instructor lectured and sometimes we had discussions.

———— sometimes we answered questions he asked.

———— instructor lectured and students took notes.

6. How would you describe the amount of your participation relative to other students in the class?

———— much more than most other students

———— usually more than other students

———— about average

———— usually less than other students

———— much less than other students

7. Describe any incidents or experiences in your 101 class that had a significant impact on you.

8. Was there any difference between the way male students and female students behaved in class? Why?

9. Please describe a typical Psychology 101 class session.

10. Did the course have any influence on your subsequent academic and/or vocational plans?

———— great influence

———— some influence

———— slight influence

———— no influence

Please explain.

11. How do you remember having evaluated your Psychology 101 course two years ago?

———— superior

———— very good

———— good

———— fair

———— poor

12. Looking back on your class, how would you rate the overall value of the course?

———— superior

———— very good

———— good

———— fair

———— poor

13. How would you rate your 101 instructor in general (all around) teaching ability?

———— superior

———— very good

———— good

———— fair

———— poor

14. How would you describe Psychology 101 relative to other courses you have taken at the University?

_____ best course I have taken
_____ better than most other courses I have taken
_____ about average
_____ not as good as most other courses I have taken
_____ worst course I have taken

15. How would rate your Psychology 101 instructor relative to other instructors (professors, etc.) you have had at the University?
_____ best instructor I have had
_____ better than most other instructors I have had
_____ about average
_____ not as good as most other instructors I have had
_____ worst instructor I have had

16. In what ways, if any, have your views of Psychology 101 and/or your instructor changed in the two years since you took the course?

Please complete the following so as to best express the way you feel.

1. The best thing about Psychology 101 was
2. The worst thing about Psychology 101 was
3. The most important thing I learned in the course was
4. The thing I liked most about my instructor was
5. The thing I liked least about my instructor was
6. After taking the course I felt that Psychology was
7. If I could have changed the course I would have
8. The part of the course most relevant to me was
9. The part of the course most irrelevant to me was
10. If my Psychology 101 instructor had been a female,
11. One way in which the course changed me was
12. My relationship with my instructor was
13. Ten years from now I think I'll be
14. Ten years from now I'd like to be

Please complete the following by the use of five adjectives or short phrases.[5]

1. I would like to be seen by peers of my sex as
2. I would like to be seen by peers of the opposite sex as
3. I would like to be seen by my instructors as
4. I would like to be (my ideal self)
5. I think peers of my sex would describe me as
6. I think peers of the opposite sex would describe me as
7. I think my instructors would describe me as
8. I would describe myself as

[5] Here we have indicated the statements only.

Appendix B-5. Standardized Questions Used in Interviewing Students

1. Can you make up a metaphor to describe Mr. X?
2. If you found yourself sitting next to him on a train what do you think would happen?
3. What would his wife be like?
4. What would he be like as the father of a child?
5. What would he be like as the father of a teenage son?
6. What is your own father like?
7. What is your own mother like?
8. Who in the class stood out most in your mind?
9. What struck you that went on in the class?

REFERENCES

Adelson, J. The teacher as a model. In N. Sanford (ed.), *The American college*. New York: Wiley, 1962, pp. 396–444.

Argyris, C. Explorations in interpersonal competence—I. *J. appl. Behav. Sci.*, 1965, **1** (1), 58–83.

Argyris, C. Explorations in interpersonal competence—II. *J. appl. Behav. Sci.*, 1965b, **1** (3), 255–269.

Bales, R. F. *Interaction process analysis: A method for the study of small groups*. Cambridge, Mass.: Addison-Wesley, 1950.

Bales, R. F. Task status and likeability as a function of talking and listening in decision-making groups. In L. D. White (ed.), *The state of the social science*. Chicago: The University of Chicago Press, 1956, pp. 148–161.

Barber, C. L. *More power to them: A report of faculty and student experience in the encouragement of student initiative*. Amherst, Mass.: Committee for a New College, 1962.

Baskin, S. Independent study: Methods, programs and for whom? In *Current issues in higher education*. Washington: Association for Higher Education, 1962, pp. 65–68.

Beach, L. R. Use of instructionless small groups in a social psychology course. *Psychological Reports*, 1962, **10**, 209–210.

Bennis, W. G., and H. A. Shepard. A theory of group development. *Human Relations*, **9**, 415–437, 1956.

Bennis, W. G, et al. (eds.) *Interpersonal dynamics*. Homewood, Ill.: Dorsey Press, 1964.

Biber, B. A learning-teaching paradigm integrating intellectual and affective processes. In E. M. Bower and W. G. Hollister (eds.), *Behavioral science frontiers in education*. New York: Wiley, 1967, pp. 112–155.

Bibring, E. The mechanism of depression. In P. Greenacre (ed.), *Affective disorders*. New York: International U. Press, 1953, pp. 18–48.

Bion, W. R. *Experiences in groups*. New York: Basic Books, 1961.

Bloom, B. S., and H. Webster. The outcomes of college. *Review of Educational Research*, 1960, **30** (4), pp. 321–333.

Bower, E. M. The confluence of the three rivers: Ego processes. In E. M. Bower and W. G. Hollister (eds.), *Behavioral science frontiers in education*. New York: Wiley, 1967, pp. 48–71.

Brown, H. S., and L. B. Mayhew, *American higher education*. New York: Center for Applied Research in Education, 1965.

Bugenthal, J. F. T. *Challenges of humanistic psychology*. New York: McGraw-Hill, 1967.

Caplow, T., and R. J. McGee, *The academic marketplace*. Anchor paperback, 1965.

Cattell, Raymond B. *Description and measurement of personality*. Yonkers-on-Hudson: World Book, 1946.

Couch, A. S. Psychological determinants of interpersonal behavior. Unpublished doctoral dissertation, Harvard University, 1960.

Cytrynbaum, S., and Mann, R. D. The community as campus: Project Outreach. In P. Runkel, R. Hanson, and M. Runkel (eds.), *The changing college classroom*. Jossey-Bass, 1969, pp. 266–289.

Della Piana, D. M., and N. L. Gage, Pupils' values and the validity of the Minnesota Teacher Attitude Inventory. *J. Educ. Psychol.*, **45**, 1951, 100–110.

Dixon, W. R., and W. C. Morse, The prediction of teaching performance: Empathic potential, *J. Teacher Educat.* **12** (3), 1961, 322–29.

Dubin, R., and T. C. Taueggia, *The teaching-learning paradox: A comparative analysis of college teaching methods*. The Center for the Advanced Study of Educational Administration, University of Oregon, Eugene, Oregon, 1969.

Fenichel, O. *The psychoanalytic theory of neurosis*. New York: Norton, 1945.

Frankel, Charles (ed.) *Issues in university education*. New York: Harper and Bros., 1959.

Getzels, J. W., and P. W. Jackson, The teacher's personality and characteristics. In N. L. Gage (ed.), *Handbook of research on teaching*. Chicago: Rand McNally, 1963, pp. 506–582.

Gibb, J. Climate for trust-formation. In L. Bradford *et al.* (eds.), *T-group theory and laboratory method*. New York: Wiley, 1964, pp. 279–309.

Grimes, J. W., and W. Allinsmith, Compulsivity, anxiety and school achievement. *Merrill-Palmer Quarterly*, 1961, **7**, 247–271.

Harrison, R., and R. L. Hopkins, The design of cross-cultural training: An alternative to the university model. *J. appl. Behav. Sci.*, 1967, **3** (4), pp. 431–460.

Jackson, P. W. The conceptualization of teaching. Paper presented at the American Psychological Association, Philadelphia, August 29, 1963.

Jencks, C, and D. Riesman, *The academic revolution*. New York: Doubleday, 1968.

Katz, J. Personality and interpersonal relations in the college classroom. In N. Sanford (ed.), *The American college*. New York: Wiley, 1962, pp. 365–395.

Keniston, K. *The uncommitted*. New York: Delta, 1967.

Klein, M. *Envy and gratitude*. New York: Basic Books, 1967.

Klein, M., and J. Riviere, *Love, hate, and reparation*. London: Hogarth, 1937.

Knapp, R. Changing functions of the college professor. In N. Sanford (ed.), *The American college*. New York: Wiley, 1962, pp. 290–311.

Kubie, L. S. Unsolved problems of scientific education. *Daedalus*, **94**, (3), 1965, 564–87.

Leary, T. *Interpersonal diagnosis of personality*. New York: Ronald, 1957.

Leonard, G. B. *Education and ecstacy*. New York: Delacorte Press, 1968.

Lewin, B. D. *The psychoanalysis of elation*. New York: W. W. Norton, 1950.

Lorr, M. C., J. Klett, and D. M. McNair, *Syndromes of psychosis*. New York: MacMillan, 1963.

Manion, J. P. Recent developments. In E. H. Hopkins (ed.), *Innovation in higher education, New dimensions in higher education*. Washington: U.S. Dept. of H. E. W., #19, 1967, pp. 10–37.

Mann, R. D., et al. *Interpersonal styles and group development*. New York: Wiley, 1967.

Mannheim, K. *Ideology and utopia*. New York: Harcourt and Brace, 1946.

Mayhew, L. B. The new colleges. In Baskin, (ed.), *Higher education: Some newer developments*. New York: McGraw-Hill, 1965, Chapter 1, pp. 1–26.

McKeachie, W. J. Research on teaching at the college and university level. In N. L. Gage (ed.), *Handbook of research on teaching*. Chicago: Rand McNally, 1963, pp. 1118–1172.

McKeachie, W. J. *Teaching tips: A guide-book for the beginning college teacher*. Ann Arbor, Michigan: George Wahr, 5th edition, 1965.

McKeachie, W. J. New developments in teaching. *New dimensions in higher education*, Number 16. U.S. Department of Health, Education and Welfare, 1967.

McKeachie, W. J. Student power motives, discussion teaching, and academic achievement. In *Research on the characteristics of effective teaching*. Washington: U.S. Department of H. E. W., Office of Education Report #05950, 1968.

Neill, A. S. *Summerhill*. New York: Hart Publishing, 1960.

Paivio, A. Personality and audience influence. In B. Maher (ed.), *Progress in experimental personality research*, V. 2. New York: Academic Press, 1965.

Parsons, T., and E. A. Shils, Categories of the orientation and the organization of action. In T. Parsons, and E. A. Shils (eds.), *Toward a general theory of action*. Cambridge, Mass.: Harvard University Press, 1952, pp. 53–109.

Peterson, R. E. The student left in American higher education. *Daedalus,* **97** (1), 1968, 293–317.

Rank, O. *Will therapy and truth and reality.* Alfred A. Knopf, 1945.

Rogers, C. R. Personal thoughts on learning and teaching. In C. R. Rogers, *On becoming a person.* Boston: Houghton Mifflin, 1961a, pp. 273–278.

Rogers, C. R. Significant learning: In therapy and in education. In C. R. Rogers, *On becoming a person.* Boston: Houghton Mifflin, 1961b, p. 279–296.

Rogers, C. R. The facilitation of significant learning. In L. Siegel (ed.), *Contemporary theories of instruction.* San Francisco: Chandler, 1966.

Roszak, T. *The dissenting academy.* Vintage Paperback, 1967.

Sanford, N. The development of cognitive-affective processes through education. In E. M. Bower and W. G. Hollister (eds.), *Behavioral science frontiers in education.* New York: Wiley, 1967, pp. 76–87.

Sanford, N. *Where colleges fail.* San Francisco: Jossey-Bass, 1967b.

Schutz, W. C. *FIRO: A three-dimensional theory of interpersonal behavior.* New York: Holt, Rinehart, and Winston, 1958.

Schutz, W. C. *Joy: Expanding human awareness.* New York: Grove Press, 1967.

Slater, P. E. *Microcosm: Structural, psychological and religious evaluation in groups.* New York: Wiley, 1966.

Slater, P. E. On social regression. *Amer. sociol. Rev.,* 1963, **23,** 339–364.

Stroup, Herbert *Bureaucracy in higher education.* New York: Free Press of Glencoe, 1966.

Sunderland, S. Changing universities: A cross cultural approach. *J. appl. Behav. Sci.,* 1967, **3** (4), 461–88.

Thelen, H. A. Methods for studying work and emotionality in group operation. Unpublished manuscript, Human Dynamics Laboratory, University of Chicago, 1954.

Thelen, H. A. Group interactional factors in learning. In E. W. Bower and W. G. Hollister (eds.), *Behavioral science frontiers in education.* New York: Wiley, 1967, pp. 261–287.

Trow, W. C. Group processes. In C. W. Harris (ed.), *Encyclopedia of educational research* (3rd ed.). New York: McMillan, 1960a, pp. 602–612.

Trow, W. C. Role functions of the teacher in the instructional group. In N. B. Henry (ed.), *NSSE Yearbook.* Chicago: U. of Chicago Press, 1960b, pp. 30–50.

Weir, J. R. Sensitivity training in the classroom. *Human Relations Training News,* **12** (1), 1968, pp. 5–6.

Wispe, L. G. Evaluating section teaching methods in the introductory course. *J. Educ. Research,* 1951, **45,** 161–186.

INDEX